T5-CWT-450

THE STUDENT'S
GUIDE
THROUGH
THE TALMUD

THE STUDENT'S GUIDE THROUGH THE TALMUD

BY THE EMINENT TEACHER
Z. H. CHAJES

TRANSLATED FROM THE HEBREW
EDITED AND CRITICALLY ANNOTATED
BY JACOB SHACHTER, M.A.
RABBI OF THE JEWISH COMMUNITY
OF NORTHERN IRELAND · BELFAST

NEW YORK
PHILIPP FELDHEIM, INC.

Second, Revised Edition

© 1960 PHILIPP FELDHEIM, INC.

The original edition of Chajes's work
appeared in Hebrew under the title
Mebo Ha-Talmud

The first edition was published
by EAST AND WEST Library, London, 1952

DEDICATED TO THE MEMORY
OF MY PARENTS

אדוני אבי מורי הרב ר״ אברהם שכטר זצ׳ל נפ״ כ״ח כסליו
תרעֿט

אמי מורתי טשארנא רעכיל ז״ל נפ״ ב״ טבת תשֿא

AND OF MY WIFE

העניא פרידה ז״ל נפ״ כ״ד כסליו תשֿיֿב

CONTENTS

PREFACE TO THE SECOND EDITION

I T is striking evidence of the popularity of "The Student's Guide Through the Talmud" that the need for a second edition has arisen. Indeed, the last decade has witnessed a revival of interest in the study of Talmudic subjects, students seeking to acquaint themselves with the researches of the labourers in this field.

I have reason to be thankful for the cordial reception the work has received. My hopes that information about Talmudic learning as an aspect of human culture would continue to excite the interest of those who are unacquainted with the riches of our heritage, seems to have been well founded.

This edition is a newly corrected (printing errors, spelling, etc.) offset reproduction of the original edition. I hope at some future date to investigate more profoundly some of the author's conclusions and to arrive at a still fuller appraisal of his contribution to Talmudic methodology.

Jacob Shachter

Jerusalem
Nissan 5720; April 1960

PREFACE TO THE FIRST EDITION

THIS volume is an English version, with introductory essays and notes, of the Mebo Ha-Talmud, a work of Zevi Hirsch Chajes. It is much to be regretted that the Author left behind him no introductory chapter or prefatory note in which he might have presented his scheme of the exposition of the Oral Law. I have endeavoured to supply this deficiency by my essay 'Introductions to the Talmud down to the time of Chajes', in which the aim and design of the work are set out. The output of Rabbinical literature in English is by no means extensive or commensurate with the scope, importance, and complexity of the subject, particularly in view of the distinct interest witnessed during the last decades in rabbinical studies. No apology is, therefore, necessary for the appearance of an addition to that library.

For myself, the translation of this work into the vernacular is the fulfilment of a lifelong desire to render accessible to students of the Talmud, both Jewish and non-Jewish, a work of one of our great luminaries of the first half of the nineteenth century. I have always cherished the idea that both the value of the subject matter, which for some time now has been brought to the attention of the English reader, and the importance of the author as one of the pioneers of the systematic study of the Oral Law, called for such a publication in order to assist two classes of students, those to whom the text itself presents difficulties, and those who need further interpretation of its meaning.

In order to make a work of this character serviceable to all, numerous explanatory notes were needed in order to illuminate the many Talmudic references, such elucidation being particularly called for in view of the author's brevity in quoting them. I have also given the authoritative sources, omitted by the author, for the host of quotations cited in the work, and I have taken all possible care to correct any errors which I observed in the sources given by him, errors which must have crept in, either because the sources were written from memory, and so subject to lapses, or as simple printing errors. Such corrections were indeed very frequently needed, and although the work went through a second edition, the publishers had not taken the trouble to rectify the sources as given incorrectly in the first edition. I have also called attention to such of the author's conclusions as appear to be at variance with later authorities, and have offered short biographical details of rabbis and scholars quoted in the work.

In order to spare the reader the need to consult a special glossary, I have included in the footnotes explanations of all the recurrent technical terms in halachic literature, and, to avoid confusion, several Hebrew and Talmudical terms are quoted in the original script. Scriptural quotations are given according to the version of the Jewish Publication Society, and, in the method of transliterating Talmudic terms, I have followed the Soncino edition of the Talmud which I have often consulted. I have also provided chapters with titles in order to indicate their contents.

As regards my task in translating the work, I recognize that no translation can ever take the place of the original, and that it can only aim at being as close as possible. The Italian proverb 'Traduttore Traditore' (a translator is a traitor), however, is certainly not as near to the truth as the rabbinic maxim that, when pouring balm from one flask into another, the oil easily passes, but the perfume evaporates.[1] The unprejudiced student who happens to be familiar with the nature of halachic and aggadic treatises will, I hope, acknowledge that, whilst I have conscientiously and faithfully adhered to the wording of the text, I have at the same time rendered it more comprehensible to the general reader. In some passages a paraphrase, or even a digest of the original, was inevitable because a more or less literal translation would, in these cases, have been entirely unreadable. But even in such cases, there has been no deviation from the text. In general, the rendering of such works into a non-Hebraic language is a responsibility greater than is usually believed. It requires one to be both thoroughly acquainted with the spirit of the author and soaked in the true spirit of the subject. Even a correct translation of a halachic or aggadic passage, if not properly elucidated, may result in a monstrous misunderstanding.

It remains, therefore, for the reader to judge to what degree I have succeeded in my task. I am painfully conscious of the unfavourable conditions under which I have laboured, in the absence of a well-stocked relevant library in the neighbourhood and the necessary books of reference, and with the many cares and burdens resting on me at my time of life. Indeed, the only leisure I could command was during the early and late hours of the day, when my time was less likely to be claimed by my professional duties. Taking these things into consideration, some excuse, I trust, may be found for such shortcomings as informed readers may detect here and there.

I should like to take this opportunity of expressing my deep gratitude to a small number of friends through whose wise-hearted support I was enabled to undertake the publication of this work.

Finally, I wish to tender my heartfelt thanks to my friend, Principal the Rev. Professor J. Ernest Davey, M.A., D.D., of Belfast, who painstakingly read through the manuscript, and from whose suggestions the work has greatly benefited; to my son Chaim, of Jerusalem, who has spent much of his valuable time in preparing the work for the Press; to Mr. Maurice Simon, M.A., for his careful reading of the proofs; and to Mr. Zalman Greenbaum, B.A., for his work in compiling the indices.

With my fervent prayer that this humble effort of mine may meet with kindly acceptance as a contribution to the study of rabbinic literature I commit it to the providence of God.

[1] Midrash Rabbah, Canticles 1, 3.

J. S.

SHORT BIOGRAPHICAL SKETCH OF THE AUTHOR

IN the year 1805 (28th Marcheshvan 5566), at the beginning of the century which witnessed the renaissance of Jewish scholarship, and ten years after the French Revolution, when Judaism was challenged by the platitudes of the so-called disciples of the Mendelssohnian School, Zevi Hirsch Chajes was born in Brody, a commercial frontier town in the north-east of Galicia, known in those days as a עיר מלאה חכמים וסופרים. He was a descendant of a family celebrated for centuries for the learning and piety of its members. Except for a few scattered notes, in various Hebrew annuals, on his life and works, we lack a detailed biography to facilitate a thorough estimate of his personality and activity.[1]

Some of our author's ancestors, originally exiles from Portugal in the fifteenth century, settled in Poland; others went to Italy and others, again, settled in the Provence. His father, Meier Chajes, a Florentine banker, who later came to settle in Brody, was a man of considerable wealth,[2] and he gave his son the best possible education which, besides the Talmud and other rabbinic studies, included modern and classical languages and literature. The secular subjects which the young Chajes particularly enjoyed were geography, history, and philosophy. Besides his native tongue, Polish, he mastered French, German, and Italian. He was gifted with a phenomenal memory from early youth, and was accounted a prodigy. He sat at the feet of the great savants of his time, Rabbis E. Z. Margulies of Brody, and Zevi Hirsch Heller, also called Reb Herschele Harif, of Bonihad, Hungary. His associates as disciples of the latter were S. J. Rappaport, Chief Rabbi of Prague, and the famous Gaon, Rabbi Aaron Moushe Taubes, Rabbi of Sniatyn and Jassy.

He mastered the two Talmudim and Commentaries when he was still very young, and at the same time absorbed our medieval philosophic literature. Generally, whatever he read became photographed in his mind, word by word, never to be lost, and, in this respect he was truly, as the Rabbis put it, 'a cemented cistern which loses not a drop.' No wonder that his fame

---

[1] We are, however, considerably indebted to Dr. N. M. Gelber, who, in the course of his essay on the late Professor Peretz Zevi Chajes, Chief Rabbi of the Juedische Kultur-Gemeinde of Vienna, gives us a short and most authoritative sketch of Z. H. Chajes's career, for in it he has made a chronological study of the stock from which the Chajes family sprang. See Ha-Olam, 7th March, 1928. Mention ought to be made that the main source from which Dr. Gelber has drawn his facts regarding the 'stock' was the 'Family tree', put on record by the later Professor Chajes, and published later by M. Rosenfeld (1933). It traces the descent of Rabbi Z. H. Chajes to R. Abraham Chajes, a descendant of the Provence scholars, who lived in the sixteenth century.

[2] In a letter from Chajes to the Hungarian Jewish scholar, Solomon Rosenthal (1764–1845), dated Marcheshvan 5595 (Oct., 1835), in which he submits privately his candidature for the rabbinate of Buda (part of Budapest), he writes, amongst other things, 'I assure you that I am not out for worldly gain or honour, G' has granted my father both wealth and honour, and he provides me with what I need (S. Bichler's collection of letters in Shai L'moreh, Budapest, 1895).

spread rapidly as of one who combined harmoniously the old and the new. At the age of twenty-two (in the year 1827) he was called to occupy an important rabbinic position as Kreis-rabbiner or District Rabbi of the district of Zolkiev, Galicia.

The period in which he lived was one of serious concern to Galician Jewry. It was just then that the Emperor Francis Joseph II began his campaign to Germanize the people under his rule, and one of the measures in this drive which affected his Jewish subjects was a decree by which District Rabbis were required to produce some proof of their knowledge of certain secular subjects, before being able to aspire to the rabbinic position. Chajes, with his powerful mind and intellect, had no difficulty in satisfying his examiners in the Lemberg University, where he gained a Doctor's degree in Philosophy. In Zolkiev he met the renowned Nachman Krochmal,[1] termed by Zunz the father of Jewish Science, as well as the eminent scholar, Samson Bloch.

It is not easy accurately to define the relationship between Chajes and Krochmal, or to say who benefited more from whom. It is believed that in addition to the several explicit references to Krochmal in his works, wherever Chajes quotes a scholarly observation as having been made by 'a certain scholar', he means Krochmal. He also refers to him as 'My friend, the renowned Rabbi and scholar, Rabbi Nachman Hacohen Krochmal'.[2] Zunz, in his Introduction to Krochmal's classical work *More Nebuche ha-Zeman*, which he edited and published, states that these two (Chajes and Krochmal) spent several years together in intimate association in the study of both Talmudim, although Krochmal's biographers, in referring to the Zolkiev period, which, after all, occupied an important place in his life, seem to have by-passed this fact intentionally or otherwise. Similarly, writers on the science of Judaism and its Galician builders pay most attention to Krochmal and Rappaport, omitting their contemporary, Chajes, though they indeed formed a triad of the school of historical research in Jewish learning.

True, Chajes was possibly more the old-type of Gaon than the modern scholar, but though he had lacked modern critical schooling, he outstripped his contemporaries in profound Jewish learning. Besides this, Chajes's historical and critical perception, displayed throughout his masterly works, could not be overlooked, as it was, with impunity. It is indeed difficult to establish the real reason for this omission, except perhaps by ascribing it to the fact that Chajes kept the orthodox views intact, and that his treatment of the subject of Oral Law was more traditional than critical. Yet, later scholars came to value his learned works as having enriched Jewish learning, and their author as a pathfinder amongst the Orthodox Rabbis of his

---

[1] Who was twenty years his senior and who was then the head of the Zolkiev Community. It is assumed that Krochmal, aided by his Office, brought about Chajes's appointment to the position.

[2] See Introduction to his Imre Binah. The regard was mutual and, according to Klausner (*History of Modern Hebrew Literature*, vol. ii, pp. 150–162), Krochmal's reference made anonymously to a beloved friend among the greatest of contemporary rabbis, in his 'Guide to the perplexed of this age', meant Chajes, whom he greatly revered.

generation, pointing the way along which a more or less critical study of the Talmud, in both the Halacha and Aggada, should be directed. Far from being a lesser light amongst the moving spirits of his time in the field of Jewish science, he was the greatest authority on Talmudic learning in Galicia.

In his activity as a spiritual leader we see signs of the age. Whilst Hasidism was the strongest dominating factor in Galicia in his time, the intellectual emancipation which the Revolution had brought in its wake to Germany at the end of the eighteenth century also gained a foothold in Galicia, at least in the larger Jewish centres. Being confronted with a new intellectual movement containing opposing tendencies within itself, one in which the scientific spirit of the century did not spare old-established doctrines, he chose a course which was a remarkable blending of the old and the new, a harmonious synthesis of historic method and strict adherence to tradition.

Though not strictly scientific as understood by his opponents, he answered the challengers of the truth of the Torah on their own ground. While he was one of the most valiant antagonists of the Reformers,[1] and while he remained the uncompromising champion and defender of the traditional formulation of Oral Law, he did not, at the same time, lose sight of the defects in the system of the religious education of the age, and so assailed the conservative fanaticism of the times, almost as vigorously as he did the Reform movement. In a Memorandum to the Government, he made practical suggestions regarding the training of rabbis and the responsibilities of their offices in the Community. He actively participated in the movement to encourage the Jews to take up agriculture as an occupation and means of livelihood; and he also strongly intervened in all matters tending to elevate the moral and social status of the Jews in Galicia, such as the abrogation of the medieval form of the Jewish oath in Court, even favouring some changes in the traditional Galician Jewish dress.

All these points show him as a leader with a keen, sober, and far-sighted view of the demands of the age in which he lived. It was only natural that by this attitude he incurred the displeasure of many of the contemporary rabbis, who, besides, could not tolerate his method of Talmudic learning, based as it was on critical investigation, a novel feature amongst the Rabbis of his generation. In view, however, of his mastery of the entire Talmudic and rabbinic literature and his extraordinarily deep knowledge of the medieval philosophic works, as well as his staunch stand against the attackers of tradition, he won the confidence of such orthodox savants as Rabbis Moshe Sofer, Jacob Ornstein, and J. S. Nathanson, and generally enjoyed the respect and admiration of his contemporaries, with the exception, perhaps of the extreme wing.

In the year 1852 he was appointed to the Rabbinate of Kalish,[2] Poland,

---

[1] In his work *Minchath Kenaoth*, Zolkiev, 1849.

[2] A letter from him recommending a book, *Ugath Eliyahu* on Aboth by R. Eliyahu Sarahsohn of Paiser (Poland) dated 5613 (1853), is signed Z. H. Chajes *Ab Beth Din* of Kalish.

which, however, he occupied for but a short time because of an illness which overtook him. He went to Lemberg for medical consultation, and died there at the age of 50 in the year 1855.

The fifty years of his life were years of storm and stress in Western Europe, following the epoch-making revolutionary years 1700–1848. They were also years in which new rays of the light of liberation appeared on the horizon and in which new chapters in Jewish history were written. They brought in their wake the agitations of religious controversy. Our author's place in the battle for tradition, which he fought and won with courage, skill, and energy, is one of lasting honour. Further, he succeeded in crowding into his very short life much that will remain of permanent value. The famous critic and scholar, Solomon Buber, described him as 'one of the rare Geonim of his age, versed in all the chambers of the Torah and unequalled as a research worker'.

His son, Rabbi Isaac Chajes, occupied the seat of the Rabbinate in Brody from 1894–1901, and his grandson, Peretz Zevi Chajes,[1] succeeded Dr. N. Guedemann as Chief Rabbi of Vienna until 1927. Their lifework, like that of their forbears, also lay in the field of the Torah and in the service of Judaism and Jewry.

---

[1] The Son of Solomon, one of the five sons of Rabbi Z. H. Chajes; the others were Leon, Haim, Isaac, and Wolf.

TALMUDICAL INTRODUCTIONS
DOWN TO THE TIME OF CHAJES

THE Talmud, our national religious creation which embodies the mental labours of our ancient teachers over a period of some eight hundred years, and which has since become not only the pivot of the whole religious literature of our people, but the main source from which Jewish law springs, is so vast in extent and in depth that if the student is to make himself familiar with the intricacies of this gigantic work of antiquity he needs the help of expert guides, not only in the methods and terminology employed by its authors, or in the grammar of its language, but also in the traditional and historical development of the Talmudic law, which has virtually the same authoritative character as the written Torah. Indeed, this body of laws, defined though it is as Oral Law, is not to be taken as one entity; it is divided and subdivided into several far-reaching categories under the main headings 'Pentateuchal' or 'Non-Pentateuchal Law'.

The Pentateuchal Law embraces (a) laws expressly laid down in the Torah, as well as (b) laws which, even if not explicitly stated in the Torah, were handed down by Sinaitic tradition, as presenting the meaning of the Torah by the application of certain canons of interpretation and deduction, known as Middoth (measures), or hermeneutical rules,[1] knowledge of which is essential to the understanding of Tradition. The Non-Pentateuchal Laws are similarly subdivided into (a) laws for which no Pentateuchal support can be found, either in the natural sense of the text, or through the application of any of the hermeneutical rules, and which cannot be traced to any Sinaitic tradition, and (b) laws which are described simply as 'Miderabanan', 'laws enjoined by the rabbis', as distinct from 'Mideoraitha', laws having their origin in the Torah. They include laws to be traced to the Prophets as committed to writing in the Post-Mosaic books.[2] The latter include a considerable body of those laws which are technically described as Takkanoth.[3] These were enacted in times as early as those of Moses, Joshua, the Prophets, or Ezra, and so down to the great Sanhedrin or Supreme Council, whose seat was within the Temple Area.[4]

Furthermore, besides the peculiar terminology employed by the authors of the Talmud, and the intricate fundamental rules upon which the deduction of their decisions was based, regarding which the student requires guidance, there is one other scientific aspect of the Talmud, which the student will need to explore before he can embark on a study of that vast region. That is its historical background and the chronological order of its material. Surely,

---

[1] According to Maimonides (*Yad Ishoth*, 1) such laws are singled out as דברי סופרים (words of the Scribes). In his view, all laws that are not explicitly stated in the Torah belong to the category of דברי סופרים although they enjoy Pentateuchal status. This view was not generally adopted. (See Yad Malachi Kelalei ha-Rambam.)

[2] Yet, although they are technically non-Pentateuchal, they have nevertheless equal authority with those of the Torah (see *Mebo*, ch. 5).

[3] Literally, repairs, improvements.

[4] The Beth-Din ha-Gadol of the Lishkath ha-Gazith.

the understanding of a structure that has taken hundreds of builders eight hundred years[1] to erect, requires a clear and critical comprehension of the ages during which the gigantic work was built up, as well as an insight into the various schools from which its scholars were drawn. Only when so defined and understood can Talmudical science in its several departments reach its highest level.

A bird's eye view of the chronological order of the schools and their scholars may serve as an illustration for the purpose in view. We begin with the Scribes, headed by Ezra and running down to Simon the Just, a contemporary of Alexander the Great. They were followed by the Early Elders, known as Zekenim, ha-Rishonim, who in turn were succeeded by the Tannaim (10–220 C.E.) beginning with the disciples of Hillel and Shammai. These latter were followed by the Amoraim and they again by the Saboraim, whose age terminated in the sixth century of the Common Era, the year being generally fixed at 589 C.E.

These architects who planned and accomplished this enormous work lived and worked not only in different countries, but also in centres of learning distant one from the other. No wonder that writers and historians have applied to the Talmud all sorts of high-sounding and unusual names, with a view to stirring the curiosity of the student. 'The Sea of the Talmud' was the stock phrase used by many, not merely because of its vastness, nor because, like a mighty ocean, it intermingles the various streams of Jewish thought, but also because of the surging waves, the rocks and the reefs by which the serious student is met when attempting to navigate it. Others were fond of calling it 'The Great Labyrinth', as it was made up of so many chambers and intricate entrances and passages. Others speak of the 'Sphinx-like' nature of the Talmud, in view of its enormous size and colossal architecture. Others again speak of the 'Body' of the Talmud, because it is not a book, it is a literature without a parallel in the literatures of the world. Furthermore, this vast edifice accommodates not only the religious, civil, criminal, and ethical laws which are usually embraced by the term 'Halacha'[2]; it embodies also legendary lore, moral maxims, and a rich material of historical and ethnographical value, together with witty sayings, personal reminiscences, and some references to science as it existed in those days.

In order to help the student to find his way in this uncharted expanse, many erudite and eminent scholars have written valuable works, and this phase of Talmudic learning, viz. the phase of methodology, has come to occupy a prominent place in Talmudic study, so much so that works on this aspect alone form a library which would fill many shelves, for the attempts at research in that realm of Talmudic learning began in the very early ages.

---

[1] Representing roughly the period of uninterrupted work from the Sopherim and the Great Assembly in the second half of the third century B.C.E. until the time of the closing of the Talmud in the sixth century of the Common Era. This is only an approximation, since the question of dates is a very complex one and the literature on the subject is quite extensive.

[2] Lit. 'The trodden path.'

Indeed, the seven rules[1] formulated by Hillel,[2] and later amplified by R. Ishmael[3] into thirteen, and still later expanded by R. Eliezer b Jose ha-Galili[4] into thirty-two, were the earliest beginnings in this realm, these rules having laid the foundations of Talmudic methodology.

These sages were the first to systematize the logical reasoning underlying the deductions of the legal decisions of the Oral Law, and to give a methodical background to the exegetical interpretations of the Midrashic homilies. From them down to Malbim[5] in our own time we have a vast array of great scholars who have offered their guidance to the student venturing into this vast area of Talmudical study. Each of them treated the subject matter in his own way, but each touched only upon certain aspects of the subject, without covering all its ramifications. Some dealt only with the terms, phrases, and style of the Talmud; others expounded and crystallized the rules by which the logical deductions of the halachoth are governed, i.e. the principles which have brought into unity both the Written and the Oral Law. Others, again, enlarged on the chronological order of the authors and builders of the Talmud, clarifying the different ages in which each lived, and the schools and teachers under whom they worked.

True, some scholars have already dealt with the subject I propose to discuss, but inadequately as regards chronology, authors, or contents. For thus while A. Jellinek in his *Kuntras Hakelalim* (Vienna, 1878) compiled a list of works on methodology, he did not go into the contents of the works in question. I. H. Weiss, the Talmudical historian of the latter half of the nineteenth century, next attempted a more or less detailed survey of such works in his *Beth-Talmud*, 1885–86.

Professor Hermann Strack and Dr. M. Mielziener, at the end of the last century, compiled a catalogue of works on Talmudic methodology, but did not give details of their character or of the particular aspect of the subject which they treated.

Dr. M. Waxman, our contemporary, in his monumental history of Jewish literature, did more or less enlarge on this activity in Talmudic research, but in view of the nature and form of this great work, a wide dispersal of the relevant material was inevitable.

[1] See Tos. Sanhedrin 7 and Aboth of R. Nathan 37.

[2] Hillel ha-Zaken, the Elder, a title given to the head of the Beth-Din (court). He lived during the time of Herod (73-4 B.C.). He and his colleague, Shammai, gave shape to the Oral Law, which was greatly developed by their disciples, who ranged themselves into the two schools known as Beth Hillel and Beth Shammai.

[3] Tanna of the first and second centuries. The school founded by him and continued by his disciples was known by the name of Be R. Ishmael.

[4] Tanna of the fourth generation (second century), disciple of R. Akiba. His hermeneutic rules are based on syntactical and phraseological or similar peculiarities of the Biblical texts, and are formulated in a Baraitha called after him, which is prefixed to the Midrash on Leviticus, the Sifra.

[5] Meir Lebush Malbim, one of the leading rabbinic scholars of the last century (1809–1880). The name 'Malbim' is derived from the initials of מאיר ליבוש בן יחיאל מיכל. His great work is his Commentary on the Bible, in which he displays a mastery of the science of the Hebrew language.

A humble attempt, therefore, to give some account of this phase of Talmudical study in chronological order, touching, at the same time, briefly on its many ramifications, may not be unhelpful to the student.

The output in this branch of Talmudical literature throughout the ages may conveniently be divided into three periods:—

(a) The ninth–twelfth centuries.
(b) The thirteenth–eighteenth centuries.
(c) The nineteenth century.

The earliest methodological work can be traced to the ninth century, when the Seder Tannaim V'Amoraim appeared. The authors, presumed to be R. Nachshon Gaon and R. Zemach b Paltoi Gaon, classify the Tannaim and Amoraim into generations and try to determine the dates in which they lived and the schools in which they were active. In addition, they explain certain Talmudical terms and set out the rules by which the decisions emerging from the discussions noted were determined. Another methodology of the Talmud, under the title *Kelalei Ha-Talmud*, is ascribed to Saadia Gaon (882–942).[1] At the end of the tenth century the famous letter of Sherira Gaon appeared. Of great historical and methodological value, it takes the form of answers to a number of questions affecting the authenticity of the Talmud and the chronological sequence of its schools.

The work of methodology, however, did not assume a scientific aspect until the early part of the eleventh century, when the Talmudical scholar, Samuel Ibn Nagrela, known as ha-Nagid, produced his *Mebo ha-Talmud*, a work more systematically arranged, and generally devoted to terminology and methodology. Mention might also be made of the *Sepher ha-Maphteach* (The Key), written by Hanagid's contemporary, R. Nisim b Jacob. Its very name is sufficiently indicative of the author's purpose.

Maimonides, who wrote in the twelfth century, contributed considerably to Talmudic methodology, by his Introduction to the Mishnah, which, though primarily historical, contains substantial portions in which the student is guided to a systematic study of the Talmud. Solomon Nisim Algazi of Smyrna, the distinguished methodologist of the seventeenth century, quotes in his *Gufei Halachoth* (the Principles of Halacha) from a work written by Maimonides on Talmudical Methodology under the title *Kelalei ha-Talmud*. According to Azulai, the work was in the possession of Bezalel Ashkenazi, author of *Shittah Mekubezeth*. The first era of books on the subject concludes with the extensive *Mebo ha-Talmud* written by R. Joseph b. Judah Kinin, a contemporary of Maimonides. The work was accepted in his time as being of great value. Generally the books mentioned are comparatively short treatises, limited for the most part to the setting out in chronological order of the successive bearers of tradition, and supplying, at the

[1] The work is mentioned by Azulai, the renowned bibliographer of the middle of the eighteenth century, in his *Shem ha-Gedolim*, ii, 23, and has been catalogued by Bacher in his Genizah 'Catalogue'.

same time, a number of rules for the deduction of the halachic decisions, as well as explaining some of the Talmudical terms and the style of the Talmud.

The works of the second period, produced by Franco-German scholars of the thirteenth to eighteenth centuries, made up for the many deficiencies from which the earlier works suffered. These begin with the introduction to *Aboth* by Menahem b. Solomon ha-Meiri of Perpignan, Provence (1249–1306), a fine essay in which he sets out in a logical and orderly manner the names of the leading men of the various generations, and in which he also gives an adequate account of the Tannaim, Amoraim, and Saboraim. In a lucid style, and with a fine historical and critical sense, he develops his study in accordance with his views on the nature, growth, and development of the Oral Law. He does not, however, offer any treatment of the hermeneutic rules, or of the terms and style of the Talmud.

This latter aspect of the study was taken up at a later date by R. Samson of Chinin, France, in his *Sepher Kerithoth*, covering the field more or less comprehensively. This work, which is divided into five parts, is an extensive study of almost all the aspects of the subject of Talmudical methodology, and has served as a foundation for several succeeding works on the subject.

The *Halichot Olam*[1] which was subsequently written by the scholar, Joshua b Joseph Halevi of Talmison, N. Africa, is a more comprehensive work than the *Kerithoth*. The clearness and simplicity of style of the *Halichoth Olam* which make it more accessible to students render it a great improvement on the earlier work; nevertheless, the Kerithoth was of great service to the author, and he utilized it considerably in his treatment of the subject.

The *Darkhei ha-Gemara*, another valuable contribution to the science of methodology, was written about the same time by their contemporary in Spain, R. Isaac Kamponton. In a very small pamphlet of about twelve pages, the author, who was recognized as a leading scholar, succeeded in explaining the terminology and style of the Talmud in a precise and lucid manner and on a scientific basis. Two of his disciples, Samuel b Serillo and Samuel Velencia, later amplified their master's work by writing special treatises on the subject.

The succeeding three centuries (sixteenth to eighteenth) witnessed the appearance, apart from smaller treatises, of such works as the *Kelalei ha-Gemara* by the famous Joseph Karo (1488–1535) and the *Sheyare Keneseth ha-Gedolah* by R. Hayim Benvenisti (1603–1673), and an essay on the principles of the Oral Law, included in his *Shelah II*[2] by R. Isaiah Horowitz (1555–1630), famous Talmudic scholar and ethical teacher and rabbi in many communities in Germany, and author of some striking and comprehensive works on the subject. Solomon Nisim Algazi, already mentioned, was a prolific writer on Talmudic hermeneutics and methodology. His *Yavin Shemuah* (He will elucidate the message), as well as a commentary on

---

[1] Translated into Latin in the year 1634 by the famous Christian scholar, Constantin L'Empereur of Holland (*History of Jewish Literature*, Waxman, ii, 193).

[2] An abbreviation of שני לוחות הברית.

Joshua Halevi's *Halichot Olam*, and both his treatises, the *Halichot Eli* and the *Gufe Halachoth* (The Principles of Halachoth), were valuable contributions to methodology.

R. Malachi ha-Cohen, in the middle of the eighteenth century, wrote his *Yad Malachi*, a detailed rather than a scientific work on every technical rule or expression of the Talmud.

R. Isaac b Samuel Lampronti (1679–1756) of Italy produced a unique work, פחד יצחק that may be described as a first attempt at a rabbinic encyclopædia, covering all subjects discussed in Talmudic and rabbinic literatures. It is methodically arranged in alphabetical order, and though primarily a halachic work, touches on almost every subject relating to terminology, and explains the hermeneutic rules in articles of considerable value for purposes of reference.

In making this survey of the literary output on the subject under discussion over a period of nine centuries, it must be remarked that although not all the works were necessarily written in the form of introductions, they were, nevertheless, all designed to serve the purpose of introducing the student to the vast expanses of the Talmud, and of helping him to attain clarity regarding every aspect of that many-sided work. However prolific such activity was during the ages we have already covered, it was only at the beginning of the nineteenth century that the study as a whole entered its modern phase, as a result of the general changes of the age which had their inevitable influence on rabbinic scholarship of the time. Before, however, dealing with the works of the nineteenth century a brief account of the influences of the age and their effects on our authors would not be amiss.

Jewish historians call the nineteenth century the 'Modern Period' or a 'New Chapter' in our history, in view of the great transformations that took place, not only in the external conditions of our people, but also in their mental outlook, as a result of Europe's experiences following the year 1789. The new intellectual currents of thought and the movements of opposing tendencies in Western Europe brought about by the French Revolution produced also in the minds of Jewish scholars a ferment of ideas, and the inclination to believe that all opinions which had been unchallenged in the past had now to be tested. In short, the old was to be reshaped, and so tradition, which had hitherto been unquestionably accepted, came to be sharply challenged by a controversial agitation as regards religion. And so a new horizon of Jewish scholarship came into view. A movement came into being not unlike that of the Sadducees in the days of John Hyrkanus or that of the Karaites in the time of Saadia, whose leaders concentrated their attacks mainly upon the authority of Rabbinical Judaism. Asserting that the Rabbis had built up a new system of laws grafted upon the old by means of casuistic devices, they threatened to undermine the very pivot on which the whole of our religious structure revolves, viz. the Mishna and the Talmud.

All this might not have seemed entirely new, for the authority of Jewish tradition had been questioned as far back as during the early years of the second Temple by the Samaritans, and continued to be questioned later by the Sadducees, and was challenged during the eighth and ninth centuries by the Karaites, yet the method and the extent of the opposition had never been so extensive and menacing.

During the early part of the nineteenth century the leaders of Jewish thought divided themselves into two, three, or even four different groups. The leading spirits of the great majority such as Rabbis Landau,[1] Banett,[2] Eiger[3] and Sofer,[4] were permeated with the belief in the basic dogma of תורה מן השמים, i.e. that both the Written and the Oral Law were divinely revealed. As far as they were concerned this belief was based on such an abundance of convincing evidence as to be no mere opinion, and no efforts of faith, therefore, were needed for its acceptance. The trend of thought diametrically opposed to the above was led by Geiger,[5] Holdheim,[6] Einhorn,[7] and Mannheimer,[8] who initiated a campaign which tended utterly to deny the binding authority of the Oral Law, and consequently to discard several of its vital precepts. Besides those two groups, however, another movement arose whose protagonists, such as Zunz,[9] Krochmal,[10] Rappaport,[11] and

[1] Ezekiel Landau (1713–1793) of Prague, combined vast erudition with great beauty of character. He was one of the first rabbis of his time to trace in the invasion of the Mendelssohnian Haskalah a danger to Judaism. Though he did not oppose secular knowledge, he differentiated between secular knowledge and that propounded by the Mendelssohnian school.

[2] Mordecai Banett, Hungarian Rabbi (1773–1854) of Neutra, of great reputation beyond the limits of his own country for his scrupulous conscientiousness, self-effacement, and piety.

[3] Akiba Eger (1761–1837) of Posen, universally known for his great Talmudic learning, noble and self-sacrificing character, and idealistic nature. An uncompromising opponent of reform, and a champion of extreme orthodoxy.

[4] Moses Sofer (1763–1839) of Pressburg, a disciple of Nathan Adler of Frankfurt-on-Main, famous for his Talmudic scholarship, combined with some knowledge of secular sciences, and for his fierce and unremitting warfare against the Reform movement.

[5] Abraham Geiger (1810–1874) theologian and Reform Rabbi of Frankfurt-on-Main and Berlin, advocate of radical reform of Judaism. In his principal work, *Urschrift und Uebersetzungen der Bibel in Ihrer Abhaengigkeit von der Innern Entwickelung des Judentums* (1857), he claimed to have discovered traces of alterations in the Hebrew text of the Bible, due to changing conceptions in various ages.

[6] Samuel Holdheim (1806–1860) of Berlin, opponent of Talmudic Judaism and leader of the extreme reform movement in Germany, held extremist views which even the reform rabbis of his day disclaimed, as constituting a negation of Judaism.

[7] David Einhorn (b. Bavaria 1809, d. New York 1879) Reform Rabbi and author.

[8] Isaac Noah Mannheimer (1795–1865), an outstanding preacher and orator in Vienna, wrote on religious reform and political emancipation.

[9] Leopold Zunz, Jewish German scholar (1794–1886) regarded as the founder of the modern science of Judaism. His *Gottesdienstliche Vorträge des Judentums* was among the most important Jewish works published in the nineteenth century.

[10] Nachman Krochmal (1785–1840), Galician Jewish philosopher and historian, who paved the way for the critical study of Jewish history. His only work *Moreh Nebukhe ha-Zeman*, the result of careful study, touches upon the profoundest problems of Jewish science.

[11] Solomon Judah Leib Rappaport (1790–1867) of Prague, Rabbi and scholar, renowned for his critical investigations. He excelled all his contemporaries in the establishment of historical dates.

Frankel,[1] aimed at steering a middle course. Whilst they were determined on the one hand to resist the negation of historic Judaism, they advocated, on the other, freedom of thought and the expression of critical opinions, declaring the Halacha in general to be the product of a long process of development, in the course of which elements from a variety of sources had been absorbed into the body of Judaism, and so tacitly admitted the desirability of changes in traditional Judaism. Thus, whilst the leaders of the first two groups each in his own way adopted rigorous attitudes of negation, the one by denying divine authority to all laws incorporated in the Talmud, and the other by negating that negation, and opposing the legitimacy of freedom for critical analysis of such laws as were claimed to have been handed down by Moses along with the written law, the third group adopted a view which was intended to secure an adjustment of tradition with the views of the new science and learning. How far, however, they were prepared to go in that adjustment, they did not determine. Suffice it to say that they regarded the greater part of the Halacha, including those 'halachoth' termed Sinaitic, as having developed merely in response to the demands of life. In his introduction to the Mishna, for example, Frankel never expressed himself clearly on the question of the origin of Halacha; he took the phrase הלכה למשה מסיני to indicate normally mere antiquity.[2] He branded as uncritical all those who, like the medieval authorities headed by Maimonides, claimed the same Mosaic authorship and high antiquity for the Halacha as for תורה שבכתב.

One may, therefore, very conveniently classify these three groups as follows: Extreme right wingers, who jealously guarded every custom and observance handed down to them by their ancestors, lest the complete structure of Judaism tumble; extreme left wingers who tended to undermine the very fundamentals upon which that structure rested; and a central group that believed in the freedom of research and in historical and critical analysis, in consequence of which belief they propounded many advanced views on the origin of the Halacha or at least of portions of it.

It would, however, be incorrect for the student to stop there. For it was just at that time that certain Rabbinic scholars of extraordinary distinction produced a viewpoint somewhat different from the above-mentioned. While their orthodoxy was beyond question, it possessed a peculiar flavour, and so they could be identified neither with the ordinary older type nor with the neo-orthodoxy of the scientific school. They were a remarkable blending of old and new. They remained throughout valiant champions and uncompromising adherents of tradition, but they also regarded it as their inescapable duty to initiate investigation into all the sources of Halacha which

---

[1] Zacharia Frankel (1801–1875) President of the Breslau Seminary, Germany, an eminent exponent of the rationalistic view of history and a great advocate of freedom of research. His attitude regarding Sinaitic laws was that they are not of Mosaic origin. Generally, however, he was vague on the subject.

[2] In this connection, see L. Ginzberg's Essay on Frankel in his *Students, Scholars, and Saints*, page 207.

might bear on the authority of the oral laws which were held to be binding for all time. These men were the eminent rabbinic scholars Malbim,[1] Meklenburg,[2] and Zevi Hirsch Chajes, who occupied a special place among their rabbinic contemporaries. While their contemporaries, mentioned above, had a remarkable knowledge of the entire field of Halachic and Aggadic literature, and were also possessed of penetrating minds which delved into many a complicated problem, they nevertheless made no attempt to elucidate the close relationship between the Written and the Oral Law, or to formulate, by analysis and classification, the various categories of Halacha belonging to תורה שבעל פה an activity which was to prove so essential at that crucial period in the last century. Malbim's *Ha-Torah v'ha-Mitzvah*[3] though not scientifically critical, was a distinct addition to the understanding of the methods of interpretation, as used by the rabbinic promulgators of the Oral Law, and so, too, Meklenburg, whose *Ha-Ketav Veha-Kabbalah* shows how the interpretations of the teachers of the Oral Law can be harmonized with the text proper, and proves the agreement of the text with the Oral, if properly explained. Chajes, however, rendered even greater service in that domain.

Chajes devoted himself to the systematic study of the specific subjects leading to the defence of Talmudic law, as being a natural and integral part of the divinely revealed written law, and in his prolific works in this field he reasserted the beliefs (*a*) that the Written, and especially parts of the Oral Law, were not the result of historical processes, but of a single Divine revelation ; (*b*) the belief that the two 'Laws' are organically interrelated; (*c*) the belief that the progressive and historical development of Jewish law is limited exclusively to laws of non-Pentateuchal statutes ; (*d*) the belief that the Talmudic savants claimed for their own teachings the finality which later authorities ascribe to them; (*e*) the belief that the Torah gave to the Rabbis of the Talmudic era Divine sanction for their legislation, and that such legislation could not be abrogated at will. In doing this he was using weapons of logic and scientific inquiry, similar to those employed by his opponents for their purpose.

The first fruit of his labour, composed when he was barely thirty-one, was the *Torath Nevi'im*, published in 1836, and which, notwithstanding many later scholarly productions in the same field, has not yet lost its worth as a classic in Talmudical research. In it he discusses the conditions under which Mosaic and Rabbinic Law could be adjusted or over-ruled, in the chapter of הוראת שעה. The question whether revelation was progressive in the Chapters בן נח, אבות, סיני נביאים. The Divine sanction for Rabbinic enactments in בל תוסיף and לא תסור, such as the character of הלכה משה מסיני and its limitations, and many other similar

---

[1] V. supra, p. xviii, note 5.

[2] Jacob Zevi Meklenburg, Rabbi of Königsberg (died 1865).

[3] On Leviticus, introduced by the treatise *Ayelet ha-Shahar*, setting out 613 principles (as compared with the 613 precepts) which had guided him in his work on the Bible in general, and on the Sifra on Leviticus in particular.

fundamental points, he treats elaborately and with great versatility. Regarding the latter in particular he presents a criterion which makes it possible to distinguish those Halachoth which really rest on ancient tradition from such as are merely so-called 'Sinaitic laws'. By his competent analysis, he was able successfully to combat an attack made by Bachrach[1] on Maimonides in his Introduction to the *Yad Hachazakah*, a statement also quoted by him in his Yad, Mamrim, on this vital subject.

With few exceptions[2] Chajes is, on the whole, a staunch defender of Maimonides, his defence of him not confining itself to the field of Oral Law, but extending to the wider field of Maimonides' works, both Halachic and philosophic. In his דרכי משה and תפארת למשה published in 1840, he contends vigorously with Reggio and Luzzato, Maimonides's critics of the last century, and presents irrefutable support from Talmudical and Midrashic sources for Maimonides's method of arriving at his Halachic decisions, and also for his views on doctrine.

Continuing his activity in the field of the Oral Law, he published in the same year his אגרת בקורת, an introduction to the Targumim and Midrashim[3] wherein he discusses the origin and dates of the Targum Onkelos and the principal Midrashim, deals with the nature of the Targum and discusses the methods employed by Onkelos to harmonize the Written with the Oral Laws. Notwithstanding Rappaport's severe strictures on it[4] and Zunz's complaint that Chajes had quoted in it from his *Gottesdienstliche Vorträge* without giving him the credit,[5] the book was nevertheless warmly received in the scholarly circles of the time. Dr. Julius Fürst[6] translated it into German (in *Orient Lit.* Nos. 44 et. seq.) and Jacob Brill[7] published (in 1852) a special edition of it with emendations and notes of his own.

Further, in the later years of his short life he presented the world with one other important work in which he attempted to formulate the nature, extent, and authority of tradition, viz. the Mebo Ha-Talmud.[8] Like the

[1] R. Jair Hayyim b Moses Samson, German Rabbinic scholar (1639–1702). His responsa Hawwot Jair were published in 1699.
[2] See *Mebo*, chap. XXXI, page 233.
[3] The impression which this work made upon contemporary scholars can be seen in a letter written to Solomon Rosenthal by the Galician Hebraist, J. Bodek, dated Iyar 5600 (April, 1840), in which he says, 'Our renowned friend and scholar, Rabbi Z. H. Chajes, has now published an invaluable essay entitled *Iggereth Bikoreth*. It contains new and useful material on the Targumim and Midrashim, etc.'
[4] Vide *Kerem Hemed*, vi, 204–259.
[5] Chajes in his Introduction to his אמרי בינה admitted this and apologized.
[6] German Hebraist and Orientalist (1805–1873).
[7] Rabbi and author of Moravia (1812–1889).
[8] The work was actually intended to serve as an introduction to his learned glosses on the Talmud; see his Preface to the *Tractate Berachot*. Chajes published several other treatises on vital Talmudic subjects, such as the מטבע הברכות and דרכי הוראה (1849), Responsa on practical religious questions, and מנחת קנאות (1849) directed against the Reform movement, as well as Annotations on practically the whole Talmud, including those on Aboth, quoted in Shaare Homath Jerushalaim, Introduction to the Wilno ed. of the Jer. Talmud. With these, however, we cannot deal here.

Talmud itself it bears a two-fold character. It deals with both the Halacha and the Haggada. In the part devoted to halacha he classifies the legal contents of the labyrinth of the Talmud, and divides all halachoth into six categories:—

(1) Interpretations traceable to Sinai and supported by Biblical text.

(2) Halachoth of Sinaitic origin which have no basis in Scripture.

(3) Rulings which the Rabbis inferred through the ordinarily adopted methods of exegesis.

(4) Halachoth that are based on ordinary human reasoning.

(5) Legal rulings derived from post-Mosaic sources.

(6) Halachoth that bear no relationship to the aforementioned. These come under the category of גזרות and תקנות.

To verify his analysis and to justify the above classification he brings forward a mass of halachic material, arranged methodically in well-defined chapters, illustrating precisely each category in turn. In particular he introduces chronological order into the last item on the list. Thus he gives a general survey of the Gezeroth and Takkanoth, describing how they were promulgated from generation to generation, and enumerating them chronologically from Moses down to the Amoraim. In this latter aspect of rabbinical study his critical and historical sense has been questioned by modern scholars, since he took Talmudic evidence as to the dates and authorship of such enactments to be authoritative, and saw no need to test its accuracy in a strictly scientific manner. In fact he did not always regard the method adopted by his contemporaries for testing the historical authenticity of rabbinic law as satisfactory. Hence whilst Krochmal and Frankel championed the view that even the halachoth termed Sinaitic were the result of development in response to the demands of life, and the term 'Sinaitic' normally indicated antiquity, Chajes considered all[1] halachot described by the Rabbis as 'a law of Moses from Sinai' to be actually of Mosaic origin and so held views in common with the medieval authorities headed by Maimonides. Thus, in the introductory chapter of the *Mebo* he writes 'Allegiance to the authority of the said rabbinic tradition is binding upon all sons of Israel, since these explanations and interpretations have come down to us by word of mouth from generation to generation, right from the time of Moses. They have been transmitted to us, precise, correct, and unadulterated; and he who does not give his adherence to the unwritten law and the rabbinic tradition has no right to share the heritage of Israel; he belongs to the Sadducees or the Karaites who severed connection with us long ago'. This same view is expounded by Maimonides in his *Commentary on the Mishnah*, Sanhedrin, chap. 10, 1, article 8, and in chap. ii, 3, and in his Code the *Yad* in chap. 3 of *Teshubah*, paragraph 6. 'My main business, however, in this book is not to deal with theological opinions. Nor is my object to teach the

---

[1] With such exceptions as were admitted by the early rabbinic authorities. See his treatise תורת נביאים.

philosophy of religion or to collect proofs in support of tradition. I have dealt with that subject adequately elsewhere.' His uncompromising adherence to tradition regarding Sinaitic laws is here clearly expressed. Similarly on several other vital issues in the study of rabbinic law, he did not allow himself to be swayed one way or the other by contemporary critics, but as Tcherno-witz summed him up, 'steered a middle course,'[1] and followed loyally the guidance of the Jerusalemite teacher who said,'The Torah may be compared to two paths, the one burning with fire, the other covered with snow. If a man enters on the former path, he will be burnt to death; if he walks on the latter path, he will be frozen by the snow. What then must he do? He must walk in the middle.'[2] Notwithstanding his attitude, however, both his con-temporaries and present-day scholars have appreciated his works as giving the serious student a deep insight into the labyrinth of the Talmud, and furnishing him with sound material for a foundation upon which to build his further critical investigations.

The second and greater part of the work he devotes to the Aggada,[3] the character of which he endeavours to elucidate. He classified the Aggadoth into norms and standards, into those that are, like the Halacha, governed by rules of exposition, and others in which the Biblical text was used by the Rabbis only as a peg upon which to hang their homilies in order to give them some semblance of authority.

The Aggadists, he maintained, were motivated by great ideas even when expounding their Aggadic deductions in an astonishingly far-fetched manner. Such expositions were intended either for the glorification of the deeds of the righteous, or the villification of the misdeeds of the wicked, or merely to describe Israel's sufferings in the past or to build up their glorious future. To the many curious passages of this kind which, by their exaggerations and gross anthropomorphism, arouse amusement, he has assigned a particular place and value. Like Maimonides, he warns the reader not to take them literally but as symbols or as things seen in a vision or a dream. He classifies all those elements in comprehensive divisions which comprise a vast collec-tion of the various phases of aggadoth from the phantasmagoria to the numerous miraculous events which are recorded as having taken place during the lives of the Tannaim and Amoraim. In the concluding chapters he brings under consideration such subjects as the additions of the Saboraim, the date of the completion of the Talmudim, and, finally, the committing to writing of the Mishna, and the question whether the Aggadoth were, or were not, under the same interdiction regarding commission to writing.

Over a hundred years have now elapsed since the Mebo was published. In these days when much later scholars have treated the subject under review more critically and more methodically, there are some who would depreciate the value of the work. They are both unfair and incorrect. It is true that

---

[1] See *Toledoth ha-Halacha*, i, p. 110.
[2] Jer. Chagiga II quoted by Chajes in the preface to his *Tifereth l'Moshe*.
[3] This part devoted to the Aggada is reprinted in the Vilno ed. of the יעקב

Chajes was often superseded by scholars of the second half of his own century, such as Weiss and others, as well as by some of the present century, such as Hoffmann, Halevi, Tchernowitz, Schechter, and Ginzberg, who did their research work more critically and more methodically and found much to rectify. Hoffmann for example, built up an elaborate system of defence for tradition, based on a careful scientific method of research. Isaac Halevi devoted the greater part of his life to combating point by point the arguments of Weiss, Frankel, and Graetz, that rabbinic law was only the result of a gradual development. Samson Raphel Hirsch in his commentary on the Torah tries to prove that tradition as transmitted by the Tannaim and Amoraim is the logical postulate of the divinely revealed Torah. Yavetz gives a historic basis to the traditional conceptions of the past. Nevertheless, the work of Chajes is not seriously impaired by such rectifications, since it was he who gave the impetus to later scholars who, it is to be regretted, have not accorded him the place he so fully deserves.

Professor Louis Ginzberg, in his appraisal of Chajes,[1] reckons him as a member of the triumvirate of the critical school of Galicia of the second third of the last century, the other two being Krochmal and Rappaport, and says that though he lacked the penetrating insight of Krochmal and the critical sense of Rappaport, he nevertheless excelled them both in acumen and range of knowledge. This was written nearly half a century ago. He has since been summed up by another scholar, more correctly, as the 'independent spirit of the trio' and as 'Krochmal's superior in Talmudic research'.[2]

Chajes's intellectual activity was of short duration, as he was only fifty when he died, but it was of lasting value. Not only was Chajes the moving spirit amongst his contemporaries, but we can speak of him as one of the great defenders of תורה שבעל פה. Like R. Akiba he made the Torah like to a chain of rings[3] by introducing the grouping of the Halachoth into definite divisions and sub-divisions, and, expert explorer of the vast sea of the Talmud that he was, he has greatly helped the student to become familiar with the intricate character of the rules, methods, and canons of interpretation upon which the deduction of these legal decisions rests.

[1] J.E., iii, p. 660.
[2] Shalom Spiegel, *Hebrew Reborn*, p. 448. Indeed, it was Rappaport himself who expressed his regard for Chajes in the highest terms. In a letter to a contemporary Hebrew scholar, S. Mohr, dated Teveth 5592 (December, 1838), he says, amongst other things, 'Despite his youth he has already established a wide reputation, in view of his thorough knowledge of both Talmudim, and commentaries which cannot be equalled. He is also extremely well versed in the works of both Jewish and non-Jewish philosophers, and has a gift of acquiring languages, with easy speed, and above all, there are few that have such an understanding of the spirit of the age.'
In another letter to Solomon Rosenthal, dated Adar 5592 (March, 1838) he has the following eulogistic words about him, 'He has attained a degree of learning that places him amongst the great scholars of the age. Moreover, coming from a distinguished family, he has the combined advantages of profound learning and noble birth. He is no respecter of persons and infinitely correct and just.' (S. Bichler's Collection of letters, Budapest, 1895).
[3] V. Aboth R.N. 18.

It is beyond the scope of my work to estimate the influence of his personality as a spiritual leader upon the life and thought of his generation. My aim here is to evaluate his greatness as a genius who stood in the forefront of Talmudic scholars of the last century; for he certainly stood out among the Rabbis of his generation, not only in the wide range of his knowledge, combined as it was with secular scholarship, but by reason of the strategic skill and sound methods he employed for the defence of the Oral Law.[1]

[1] Much of the latter part of this essay is contained in a paper which I read to the Conference of Anglo-Jewish Preachers in May, 1950.

CHAPTER I

THE ORAL LAW AND ITS RELATION TO THE WRITTEN LAW

THE Torah [1] is divided into two parts, the written and the un-written law. The former consists of the Pentateuch which was divinely revealed to Moses at Sinai. The latter comprises expositions and inter-pretations which were communicated to Moses orally as a supplement to the former. Without them the scriptural texts would often be unin-telligible since many of them seem to contradict others, and it is only by the aid of oral elucidation that their contradictions can be straightened out.

Many examples of such discrepant texts are quoted in the Introduc-tion to *Sefer Mitzvoth Gadol*.[2] The following is one of them: It is written 'The stay of the Children of Israel who abode in Egypt was four hundred and thirty years'.[3] Kehath the son of Levi was one of those who went down to Egypt (with Jacob).[4] If you add his age (133)[5] to that of his son Amram (137)[6] and combine this with the 80 years of Moses at the time when the word of God first came to him,[7] you will find no more than 350 years in all.[8] Again, 'Thy fathers went down into Egypt with three score and ten souls.'[9] Yet if you count each soul separately you will not find more than 69.[10] Again: 'All that were

---

[1] Literally 'instruction', applied in a wide sense to denote the whole body of the Jewish Teachings, including the Scripture and the Traditions connected with it.

[2] By Rabbi Moses of Coucy, near Soissons, French Tosafist (compiler of what is known as the 'Old Tosafot'), who lived in the first half of the thirteenth century. His great work *Sefer Mitzvoth Gadol* (usually known by the abbreviation SeMaG, and com-pleted in 1250), is a compilation of the expositions of each of the 613 divine precepts according to Talmudic traditions.

[3] Ex. XII, 40.   [4] Gen. XLVI, 11.

[5] Ex. VI, 18.   [6] Ex. VI, 20.   [7] Ex. VII, 7.

[8] Bearing in mind the deduction from the age of Kehath of the years before he went into Egypt, as well as the years of Amram and Moses, which were included in the ages of their fathers, the total will be still less. The explanation of this, however, is that the total of 430, as given in Scripture, covers the sojourning in other settle-ments, besides those of Egypt. In fact it goes back to the time when the decree 'Thy offspring shall be a stranger' was made at the covenant between the parts (Genesis XV, 13). The other settlements prior to Egypt come also under the term sojournings. Indeed, to be correct, the Israelites were in Egypt only 210 years (Gen. XXV, 6), and the remaining period of 220 years from 'the covenant of the parts' until they descended into Egypt are made up as follows: 30 years elapsed between 'the covenant of the parts', and the birth of Isaac (see Rashi Meg. 9a); at Jacob's birth Isaac was 60 (Gen. XXV, 26), while Jacob was 130 when he first appeared before Pharaoh.

[9] Deut. x, 22.

[10] The seventieth child which is not included in the enumeration was Jochebed, who was born 'between the walls' (i.e. immediately on arrival), and who is added to the number, but not mentioned by name (v. B.B. 123b and Rashi on Gen. XLVI, 26).

numbered of the Levites were twenty-two thousand'.[1] Yet on reviewing
the numbers in detail you will find that the total stated is exceeded by
three hundred.[2]

You will find a similar difficulty in connection with the payment of
the *beka*[3] which every Israelite was obliged to make, since in accordance with the number of *Shekalim* given,[4] the total should be two
hundred *kikkar* (and eleven *mana*).[5] In the detailed account, however,
as given in Scripture,[6] the total is stated to be only one hundred *kikkar*
and 1,009[7] shekels.[8] These and other difficulties were noted by the
Rabbis (v. Bech. 5*a*) and adequately explained by them. Take another
instance. Scripture says 'Seven days thou shalt eat unleavened bread'[9],
whilst elsewhere it says 'Six days thou shalt eat unleavened bread'[10];
again it says 'Seven days shall there be no leaven found in your
houses',[11] while another verse reads 'The first day ye shall put away
leaven out of your houses'.[12]

Furthermore Scriptural law is generally briefly worded and lacks
detailed directions, so that even the most versatile scholar is often left
in uncertainty and unable to arrive at definite decisions regarding
points which are left indefinite.

The first of the 613 Divine Precepts may be cited as an instance. 'And
God said unto them, Be fruitful and multiply.'[13] Here it does not explicitly state whether this is a distinct command, or merely God's
blessing. And even if it is a definite command, other difficulties are
bound to arise, such as whether the duty of reproduction is enjoined

---

[1] Num. iii, 39.

[2] The omission of the 300 appears even stranger for the simple reason that they
might have served to replace the 273 first-born Israelites who were in excess of the
sum total of the Levites (see Num. iii, 46). The reply to all this is that these 300
Levites in question were first-born themselves, and so, having had to redeem themselves, they could not act as exchanges for the Israelite first-born.

[3] Name given to the half shekel (from *baka* 'to split') (Ex. xxxviii, 26).

[4] Received from 603550 males, of 20 years of age and upwards (Ex. xxxviii, 26).

[5] Each *kikkar* consisting of 60 *mana* and each *mana* containing 25 shekels.

[6] See Ex. xxxviii, 27.   [7] In the Scriptural text 1775.

[8] The explanation of this is that the Biblical *kikkar* had twice the value of the
later one.   [9] Ex. xxxiv, 18.   [10] Deut. xvi, 8.

[11] Ex. xii, 19. The oral explanation of this contradiction is given in Men. 66*a*,
'Seven days ye may eat matzoth prepared from the old crop only, because the *Omer*
(Lev. xxiii, 10, 15) has not yet been offered,' for six days of the seven, however, ye
may eat matzoth prepared from the new crop, since the *Omer* is offered on the second
day of the feast (i.e. the 16th of Nisan).

[12] Ex. xii, 15. In that case the seven days are reduced by one, but 'The first day'
here refers to the eve of the festival. It is termed the 'first' because it comes immediately before the seven days. This view Rashi (on Pentateuch) bases on Job
xv, 7: 'Wast thou born ראשון—first—Adam,' i.e. 'Wast thou born before Adam?'
We see that the term ראשון means not actually first, but 'before'.

[13] Gen. i, 28.

upon both man and woman, or on the male alone. Again, what number of children is required (for the fulfilment of the command), or what happens if the children die. Or again, what happens if children (who have died) leave children, or if a son (who has died) leaves a daughter who gives birth to male children. Will they be regarded as his sons in connection with the fulfilment of the aforesaid command? Similar difficulties also arise in connection with the practice of other precepts which are worded in such general terms as to require further explanation and elucidation. The rabbis, in fact, have argued from what is clear in one case to other cases which are not so clear, by means of the exegetical rulings by which the Torah is expounded.

These exegetical renderings were in the mind of the rabbis when in connection with Lev. xxv, 1, they asked: 'What has the sabbatical year specially to do with Mount Sinai?'[1] (Quoted by Rashi on Lev. xxv, 1, and by Maimonides, Introduction to *Commentary on the Mishnah*.) It is to teach that just as in the case of the sabbatical laws the general rules together with the minute details were ordained by God at Sinai, so all the other commandments were given in the same manner.

Maimonides[2] in his introduction to the Code, the *Yad* makes the following statement. 'All the Sinaitic precepts were communicated to Moses with interpretations.' This is hinted at in Scripture.[3] 'I will give the tablets of stone, and the Law (*Vehatorah*) and the Commandments (*mitzvoth*).' By *Torah* (Law) is meant the written law, and by Mitzvah (commandment) is meant the oral law. This view is derived from the following statement (Ber. 5a): Resh Lakish said, 'What is meant by the passage—"And I will give these tablets of stone with the Law (*torah*) and the Commandments (*mitzvoth*) which I have written to teach them."[4] The tablets of stone refer to the Ten Commandments; the Torah refers to the Pentateuch; the Mitzvah (commandment) refers to the *Mishnah*; "which I have written," to the Prophets and Hagiographa; "to teach them," to the *Gemara*. This is to teach us that all were communicated to Moses at Sinai.'

A similar reference to the authority of the unwritten law is made by R. Johanan in his statement (Git. 60b) that 'The Holy One, blessed be

[1] i.e. Why is the phrase 'on Mount Sinai' (Lev. xxv, 1) found specially attached to this law and not to the others, seeing that the book of Leviticus which contains this law concludes with the words, 'These are the commandments which the Lord gave unto Moses for the children of Israel on Mount Sinai' (Lev. xxviii, 43)? The sabbatical laws were, therefore, included.
[2] Moses ben Maimon (Rambam 1135–1204), the famous author of the authoritative Code *Mishneh Torah*, also called *Yad Hahazakah*, in which he methodically codified, in a superb Mishnaic Hebrew, the whole *halachah* (rabbinic law).
[3] Ex. xxiv, 12.
[4] Ex. xxiv, 12.

He, concluded His covenant with Israel for the sake of the unwritten law alone.'

The authority attached to the oral law is also referred to in the following statement[1]: 'Words were given orally and words were given in writing, and we know not which of the two sets is the more valuable. However, from the verse, 'According to these words עַל פִּי הַדְּבָרִים הָאֵלֶה,[2] have I made a covenant with thee,'[3] we learn that those that were transmitted orally are the more valuable.

Allegiance to the authority of the said rabbinic tradition is binding upon all sons of Israel, since these explanations and interpretations have come down to us by word of mouth from generation to generation right from the time of Moses. They have been transmitted to us precise, correct, and unadulterated, and he who does not give his adherence to the unwritten law and the rabbinic tradition has no right to share the heritage of Israel; he belongs to the Sadducees[4] or the Karaites[5] who severed connection with us long ago.

This view is expounded by Maimonides in his *Commentary on the Mishnah*, San., chap. 10, 1, article 8, and in chap. 11, 3, and in his Code the *Yad*, chap. 3, *Teshubah*, par. 6. My main business in this book, however, is not to deal with the dogmas of faith. Nor is it my object to teach the philosophy of religion or to collect proofs in support of tradition. I have dealt with that subject adequately elsewhere.[6] The task I have set myself here is to analyse the essence of the unwritten law, and to indicate its basic principles as well as its many ramifications, for one must bear in mind that the term 'Torah She-beal-Peh' (oral law) is one embracing a number of subjects differing in character, as has been shown by Maimonides in the introduction to his commentary on the Mishna. My intention is to expound these subjects in even more detail.

According to Maimonides they are to be classified as follows:

The first category consists of interpretations of precepts which are worded vaguely in Scripture, such as would remain obscure without the traditional elucidation, as, for example, the taking of the four species at the feast of ingathering.[7] From the written text we should not

---

[1] Jer. Peah, ch. iii ; Hag. ch. 1; Meg. ch. 4.
[2] Indeed the Hebrew designation בְּעַל פֶּה is based on the two words in the verse quoted, i.e. the Torah transmitted orally, as indicated by the words כִּי עַל פִּי (Weiss).
[3] Ex. xxxiv, 27.
[4] Members of a party who maintained views and practices of the law opposed to those adopted by the Pharisees on the basis of tradition. Their existence dates back to the time of the Second Temple.
[5] A sect within Judaism which originated in 767 c.e. amongst the Babylonian Jews, and which rejected Talmudic authority.
[6] In his work *Darkhei Moshe* Chajes defended the dogmatic teaching of Maimonides.
[7] Lev. xx, 14.

know whether it was meant that they should be grasped by the hand or used to cover the *sukkah*, as, in fact, the verse is interpreted by some of the Karaites. Furthermore, how is one to know what precisely is meant by 'fruit of the tree *hadar*'? Might it not mean a fig, an apple, or some other fruit?

Again, as to the manner in which the death sentence by burning for the nine *arayoth* (forbidden relations) is to be executed.[1] It is not clear whether it was intended that the whole body should be consumed by a fire made of bundles of faggots, or whether it was intended to cause death simply by pouring molten lead down the throat, the body remaining intact.

Take again, as an illustration, the execution of the death sentence by fire upon a priest's adulterous daughter.[2] Does it apply to a married woman or to an unmarried one, or particularly to one betrothed? Again there is no definition of the manner in which the ritual slaughter of animals is to be carried out, whether by cutting the front or the back of the neck.

The *heleb* (fat) prohibition[3] leaves us in doubt whether it includes all sorts of fat substances, or only the fat which covers the kidneys, the flanks, and the first and second stomachs; also whether the fat on the tail or that of the *ben p'kuah*[4] is included in the prohibition.

The law prohibiting blood is also vaguely worded, and the question arises whether it refers only to the blood with which the life escapes, viz. that which spurts forth,[5] or whether the blood which remains in the meat also renders him who partakes thereof liable to the punishment of *kareth*.[6]

Again, in the text 'For I will appear in the cloud upon the covering,'[7] is the 'cloud' to be understood as the cloud of God's Pillar, or the cloud of incense which is to be prepared (by the priest) outside?[8]

Yet again, in the verse 'And they shall be for frontlets (לטוטפות)

[1] See M. San., chap. 7, 2, with reference to the manner of execution by burning. Also M. San., chap. 9, 1.
[2] Lev. xxi, 9.
[3] Lev. vii, 24.
[4] Animal ripped out of the slaughtered mother's womb (Hul. 69*a*).
[5] When the cut is made in the animal's throat, but excluding the blood which flows gently (Krithoth 21*b*, Tos. ibid., ch. ii).
[6] Literally 'being cut off', e.g. divine punishment. The Talmud discusses the exact nature of kareth, and the view is expressed that he who dies before attaining the age of 50 has received that punishment (M. K., 28).
[7] Lev. xvi, 2. With reference to the prohibition of the High Priest's entering the Holy of Holies, except on the Day of Atonement.
[8] The preparation of the cloud of incense outside prior to the High Priest's entry therewith into the Holy of Holies, which was advocated by the Sadducees, was sternly rejected by the Pharisees as being against tradition (v. Yoma, 53*a*).

between your eyes ',[1] the written law does not give us any elucidation thereof.

And in the text, 'And he shall serve him for ever' (לעולם) referring to the piercing of the servant's ear,[2] we should be in doubt whether 'for ever' is to have its usual meaning ' all his life', or whether it is limited to the Jubilee period. Explanations and interpretations answering all these doubts and questions have been transmitted to us orally as they came down from Moses at Sinai.

Several of the interpretations which have been handed down to us appear at first sight not to be in accordance with the literal meaning of Scripture. The following are some examples:—

'Even on the first day ye shall put away leaven out of your houses.'[3] According to the rabbinic interpretation this refers to the day preceding the first day.[4]

'Hand for hand, eye for eye'[5] in its literal sense would mean actual retaliation in kind, i.e. to cause the offender exactly the same physical injury. Tradition, however, maintains that it is a matter of monetary compensation. So also the command[6] 'Then they shall hew off her hand'[7] literally means the chopping off of the hand, whereas the oral interpretation requires only monetary compensation.[8]

'And his owner also shall be put to death,'[9] according to the letter means that he shall be killed, while the oral halachah interprets it again to mean monetary compensation; and even where this compensation is not forthcoming, the owner is not liable to capital punishment.

'Then she shall spit before his face;'[10] rabbinic interpretation requires her to spit upon the ground before him, and not, literally 'upon his face'.

'Thou shalt not seethe a kid in its mother's milk.'[11] By exegetical deduction oral law has included in the prohibition the mixing of all

---

[1] Ex. XIII, 1–10. Referring to the wearing of *Tefillin* (Phylacteries) by every adult male as required during the morning service.

[2] Ex. XXI, 6.

[3] Ex. XII, 15.

[4] See page 64, note 7.

[5] Ex. XXI, 24.

[6] Deut. XXV, 12.

[7] In the case of a woman who, intervening to help her husband in a fight, injures his opponent in a shameful manner.

[8] The payment of the equivalent of the injury caused to the man.

[9] Ex. XXI, 29.

[10] Deut. XXV, 9, in connection with the ceremony of the childless widow loosening the shoe of her brother-in-law, by which he is released from the requirement of marrying her.

[11] Ex. XXIII, 19. The command is repeated in Ex. XXXIV, 26, and in Deut. XIV, 21.

manner of meat and milk.[1] The phrase 'from the morrow after the Sabbath ',[2] mentioned in connection with the waving of the *Omer*, means literally the day after Sabbath (i.e. Sunday).[3] Tradition, however, has interpreted it as the day after the first day of the Passover, irrespective of which day in the week it may be.

'If he rise again and walk abroad upon his staff.'[4] This is interpreted figuratively by tradition as referring to the regaining of bodily strength and not literally to the stick which he uses for his support.[5]

'If the sun rise upon him.'[6] 'The rise of the sun' is taken metaphorically as denoting clarity—i.e. it is as clear as daylight that it was not his intention to murder.[7]

'And he shall spread the cloth.'[8] Here the 'spreading of the cloth' must be understood figuratively as clarifying the matter in dispute, rather than literally.

The Midrash Mechilta Mishpatim and Jer. San., ch. viii, quote from R. Ishmael, the following expositions of three Biblical texts which are relevant here.

(1) 'There shall no alien eat thereof.'[9] This refers to one who has, by his deeds, alienated himself from God or, as Onkelos[10] translates it, 'an Israelite who has chosen apostasy.'

(2) 'When thou comest into the vineyard of thy fellowman, then thou mayest eat grapes at thy will; when thou comest into the standing corn of thy fellowman, then thou mayest pluck the ears with thine hand.'[11] The text is taken to refer to a labourer (and not to a friend or visitor) engaged in the gathering in of the crop, and so agrees with the Targum of Onkelos 'when thou art hired for a vineyard . . . when thou art hired for a field of corn'.

[1] V. Hul. 115b and Rashi on Ex. XXIII, 19.
[2] Lev. XXIII, 15.
[3] Consequently Pentecost should always be celebrated on the first day of the week; so indeed the Sadducees have always contended. They insisted on a literal interpretation of the text, in opposition to the interpretation adopted by the Pharisees.
[4] Ex. XXI, 19, in reference to an invalid, as a result of injury caused by someone.
[5] See *Mechilta*, and Rashi ad loc.
[6] Ex. XXII, 2. In a case of a thief breaking in and being caught in the act, it was assumed that the burglar would, if resisted, not hesitate to take life.
[7] Hence the restitution of the theft alone is imposed upon him.
[8] Deut. XII, 17. In a case where the husband, immediately after marriage, charges his wife with unchastity.
[9] Ex. XII, 43, in connection with the partaking of the Paschal meal.
[10] Reputed author of the Aramaic version of the Pentateuch, known as *Targum Onkelos* (A.D. 40–120). See Meg. 3a. Modern critics, however, identify him with Aquila, the well-known translator of the Pentateuch into Greek, see Jer. Meg. i, 9 (cf. A. E. Silverstone, *Aquila and Onkelos* (1931).
[11] Deut. XXIII, 25, 26.

(3) 'Fathers shall not be put to death for children.'[1] This means that the father shall not be put to death on the evidence of his children. It is from this verse that the invalidity of testimony borne by relatives is deduced.[2] This also agrees with Onkelos's version, 'by the mouth (i.e. evidence) of children.' And there are many similar cases.[3]

Another category of oral interpretation of the Torah precepts have come down to us, which completely rescind the literal meaning of the text of Scripture, as is illustrated in the following expositions.

In the Torah we read, 'Forty stripes he may give him.'[4] Yet by tradition this was reduced to thirty-nine.[5] The Rabbis have referred to this fact as evidence of the standing of rabbinic authority, remarking, 'How stupid the people in Babylon are who arise[6] for a Scroll of the law but would not do so for Talmudic scholars. Actually in the Torah forty (stripes) are prescribed, and the Rabbis have reduced the number to thirty-nine.[7]

Ritba[8] in his *Novellae on Makkoth* maintains that the reduction of the number of stripes must have been based on one of the Sinaitic *halachoth*,[9] as the Rabbis could have had no power to depart from a definite written law except for the purpose of safeguarding some other principle which seemed at stake.[10]

In three instances the Rabbis say the approved practice rescinds the letter of the Biblical text (Sot. 16*a*; Jer. Kid., ch. i) :—

I. The Torah prohibits a razor.[11] The *halachah*, however, extends the prohibition to all other instruments as well.[12]

II. The Torah[13] used the word *sefer* for bill of divorcement,[14] while the traditional ruling allows all materials.[15]

---

[1] Deut. xxiv, 16.   [2] See San. 27*b*.

[3] i.e. many cases where the insufficiency of the written law can be illustrated, and which go to prove the authority of the oral law.

[4] Deut. xxv, 3, referring to the corporal punishment imposed by the Torah as a penalty for wrong-doing.

[5] V. Mak. 22*a*.

[6] As a mark of respect (cf. Lev. xix, 32).

[7] Their authority, therefore, must have been enormous as seen in the fact that they could thus override the written text.

[8] The initials of R. Yom Tob ben Abraham Ibn Ashbilli, a famous Talmudic commentator of the first half of the fourteenth century (d. 1360).

[9] *Halachoth* designated in the Mishna and the Talmudim as הלכה למשה מסיני, i.e. as traceable to the tradition deriving from Moses at Sinai.

[10] Cf. Chajes, Torath Nebiim, Chapter 'Hora'oth Sha'ah', in which he treats this subject extensively.

[11] Num. vi, 7, referring to one of the restrictions upon the Nazirite, not to cut his hair during his naziriteship.

[12] See Naz. 39*b*.   [13] Deut. xxiv, 3.

[14] *Sefer* literally 'book' implies that the bill must be written on paper only.

[15] See Sifre, Deut. xxiv, 3.

III. The Torah says 'cover it with dust',[1] whereas the approved practice is to cover it with anything available.[2]

Raba (Yeb. 24a) states that although it is generally accepted that we must not lose sight of the natural, i.e. literal, sense of a passage, yet we see in the following passage that the Rabbis have applied the method of the *Gezerah Shavah*,[3] thereby setting aside the literal meaning of the text. Notwithstanding the fact that the literal meaning of the passage in question,[4] 'And it shall be that the first born whom she beareth shall succeed in the name of his dead brother,'[5] is that the first-born son should actually bear the same name as the dead brother, i.e. if the latter's name was Joseph, the son should also be named Joseph, if Johanan, he should be called Johanan; yet by the application of a *Gezerah Shavah*, which notes that in the present passage we read 'in the name of his (dead) brother' and in another passage[6] we read 'shall be called after the name of their brethren', the rabbis have deduced that, as in the latter verse 'name' means right to inheritance, so in the former, 'name' means the second brother's right[7] to his dead brother's portion of their father's property.

Though we can see here an inconsistency with the ruling (Keth. 38b) that a *Gezerah Shavah* is not valid in a case where it sets aside the literal meaning of the text, yet the application here may be due to the rabbis having a specific *halachah* traceable to Sinai, by which they could cancel entirely the literal sense of the passage.

Another reference in support of such a suggestion is to be found in T. Suk. 6b. The word *bassukkoth*[8] occurs there three times, written once plene (in the plural, so counting as two references), and twice defectively, making in all four references. So, subtracting one as required for the command itself, there are three left to indicate the need of at least two walls of the prescribed dimensions and a third of a minimum width

---

[1] Lev. XVII, 13, referring to the covering of the blood of the slaughtered stag; other beasts are not brought under this law. (See Hul. 83b.)

[2] See Hul. 88b.

[3] One of the principal exegetical rules of interpretation, based mostly on the noting of identical words or parallel passages.

[4] Deut. xxv, 6.

[5] With reference to the law of Levirate marriage.

[6] Gen. XLVIII, 6, in connection with Jacob's recognition of Ephraim and Manasseh as two tribes.

[7] i.e. the right of the *Yabam* who undertakes the Levirate marriage.

[8] Lev. XXIII, 42–43, in connection with the command of the Festival of Booths. The author quotes the Talmudical argument very briefly, and for the sake of intelligibility the translator has had to expand it somewhat.

of a handbreadth. The reduction of the last to a handbreadth was made on the basis of a Sinaitic tradition.[1]

And so we see that (in some cases) the *halachah* overrides the literal meaning of the passage. In discussing the ruling of Maimonides in his *Yad*, (Hametz i, 7) that the prohibition of leaven during Passover applies to the very smallest amount, R. Elijah Mizrachi,[2] quoted in *Mishneh le-Melech*,[3] observes that the injunction[4] 'There shall no leavened bread be eaten' applies even to the smallest quantity. This literal meaning was, however, overthrown by an *halachah* derived from Sinai (regarding amounts) and consequently a ruling was established that the user was not to be liable to any penalty until a prescribed quantity ('*ke-zayit*')[5] had been consumed.

As for the class of interpretations mentioned above, although they were transmitted to us from Sinai, yet the Rabbis have endeavoured to give them Biblical support, thus demonstrating that these Sinaitic laws also rest on Scripture, in accordance with accepted exegetical rules. Thus for example the ruling that 'the fruit of goodly trees'[6] is the *ethrog* (the citron) is based on the dual meaning of the word *hadar*[7]— hence, a tree whose fruit dwells on it from one year to another—and also on other inferences (v. Suk. 35*b*). That the manner of execution by fire is by burning of the vitals, whilst the body remains intact, is based on a *Gezerah Shavah*: 'Burning' is decreed here[8] and burning was also the fate of the sons of Aaron[9] and the Assembly of Korah.[10] Just as the references there are to the burning of the souls (i.e. of the vitals), the bodies remaining intact, so here too (v. San. 52*a*). Similarly the manner of slaughtering animals (by cutting the throat) is inferred

---

[1] Specifically given with regard to the laws governing dimensions, divisions, etc., in connection with religious practices (see Erub. 4*a*).

[2] Talmudist of the fifteenth century (1455–1525), Chief Rabbi of Turkey, author of the Sefer ha-Mizrachi commentary on Rashi.

[3] By Rabbi Judah Rosanes, Chief Rabbi of Istanbul in the seventeenth century (d. 1727); author of several rabbinic works, best known of which is *Mishneh l'Melech*, glosses and comments on the *Yad* together with which it is usually printed.

[4] Ex. XII, 20.

[5] Equal in size to that of an olive.

[6] Lev. XXIII, 40.

[7] The one meaning 'adornment', and the other derived from the root דור, and so meaning that which dwells.

[8] Lev. XXI, 9. 'She shall be burnt with fire.' Although the punishment of death by fire was imposed upon a number of offenders according to the Torah, it is only mentioned in connection with the adulterous daughter of the Priest and with the adulterers and adulteresses mentioned in Lev. xx, 14, as a requirement of the Law.

[9] Lev. x, 6. 'Let your brethren bewail the burning which the Lord hath kindled.'

[10] Num. XVII, 5. 'And Eliezer the priest took the brazen censers wherewith they that were burnt had offered.'

etymologically from the word *shahat,* which in rabbinical speculation (Hul. 27*a*) condenses two terms in one—*shah-hat.*[1]

The distinction between the fat substances in connection with the prohibition of *heleb* and the differences in the punishment imposed for transgressing the prohibition of blood, based on the distinction between the blood in which the life spurts forth and that which remains in the meat—for all this they have found Scriptural basis (Kerit. 4*a* and *b*). Their interpretation of the words 'I will appear in the cloud upon the covering'[2] to mean that the cloud of the incense must be prepared inside the Holy of Holies, in opposition to the method advocated by the Sadducees, was inferred by the Rabbis from words in the passage concerned (*Torath Kohanim* on Lev. xv).[3]

In defining the precept of tefillin (phylacteries) R. Akiba inferred from the word לטוטפות (frontlets) that four are implied, since the word is composed of *tot* which means two in Kapti[4] and *fath* which means two in African[5] (San. 4*b*).

So, too, Biblical support was sought and found for the view regarding the indefinite law, 'He shall be a servant *le' olam* (for ever),'[6] that it means until the Jubilee (Kid. 15*a*).[7] That the first day (in reference to the clearing away of the leaven) means the eve of Pesach is also supported by various scriptural passages (Pes. 5*a*).[8]

The law of retaliation is similarly proved from scriptural passages to imply only money compensation (B. K. 83*b*).[9]

[1] שח from שחח (talking) and חת, meaning 'diminishing', i.e. a failing or missing (Jud. xx, 16), thus implying that it is the vocal organ that is to be injured.

[2] Lev. xv, 2.

[3] Their inference is based on these passages: 'And he shall take a censer full of burning coals of fire . . . and his hands full of aromatics and bring it within the partition wall and he shall (when in the Holy of Holies) put the incense on the fire.' He (the High Priest) shall not, the Rabbis say, prepare it (putting the incense on the fire) outside and bring it in as was the practice followed by the Sadducees.

[4] Coptic language v. Neubauer, *Geographie*, p. 418.

[5] The language of N. Africa or Phrygia in Asia Minor.

[6] In the passage relating to the servant whose ear is pierced. Ex. xxi, 6.

[7] This is corroborated by the passage (Lev. xxv, 10), 'and ye shall sanctify the fiftieth year and proclaim liberty throughout all the land unto the inhabitants thereof.'

[8] It is written (Ex. xxxiv, 25), 'Thou shalt not offer together with leaven the blood of sacrifice'—i.e. thou shalt not slaughter the Passover sacrifice whilst leavened bread is still present, and the Passover sacrifice was offered on the day preceding the first day of the Feast. Consequently leavened bread must have been cleared by then (*Mechilta*).

[9] They infer it from Lev. xxiv, 21, 'He that smiteth any man and he that smiteth a beast.' As in the case of smiting a beast compensation is to be paid, so also in the case of smiting a man. Also from Num. xxxv, 31, 'Moreover ye shall take no ransom for the life of a murderer.' The Talmud interprets this as meaning that ye may not take satisfaction for murder whereas you may take satisfaction for the injury of main limbs.

That 'thou shalt cut off her hand'[1] demands only a monetary fine
is again inferred from a *Gezerah Shavah* in Sifre. In the one case it is said
'thine eye shall not pity her'[2] and in the other,[3] concerning collusive
witnesses, it is said 'thou shalt not pity them'.[4]

So, too, 'and his owner shall also perish'[5] means that he shall pay
compensation; this is deduced in Sanhedrin from Scripture which
states,[6] 'He that smites him shall surely be put to death; he is a
murderer,' i.e. for a murder committed by himself you may put him
to death, but you may not put him to death for a murder committed
only by his ox.[7]

The prohibition of taking meat and milk foods together was deduced
by the Rabbis from the text 'Thou shalt not seethe a kid in its mother's
milk', as they found that wherever 'kid' is mentioned without further
description the term was used vaguely for any kind of beast (Hul. 113*b*).

The traditional view that 'from the day after the Sabbath'[8] means
the second day of the Passover Festival, i.e. the 16th Nisan, is established by the Rabbis on the basis of various passages (Men. 65*b*).[9]

That 'no alien shall eat thereof'[10] refers to an apostate Israelite,[11]
as Onkelos interprets it, is inferred by the Rabbis in the *Mechilta* ad loc.

The inference that the law regarding the plucking of fruit or grain
when one comes into the vineyard or the standing corn[12] concerned
the labourer engaged to do work there, and not a mere visitor, is based
on a *Gezerah Shavah* (B.M. 87*b*). In this passage we have the word *tabo*
('come'), and in a later passage[13] it is said 'the sun shall not go down'
(*lo tabo*). As in the latter case it refers to a labourer, so here, too.

The invalidation of testimony given by kinsmen which is derived
from the scriptural verse[14] 'and sons shall not be put to death for fathers,'
is similarly inferred exegetically from Scripture by the Rabbis (as in
San. 27*b*).

[1] Deut. XXV, 10.
[2] Deut. XXV, 12.
[3] Ibid., XIX, 21.
[4] In the latter case monetary compensation is the demand (since it falls under the
rabbinic interpretation of retaliation) so in the former case, too, monetary compensation must be intended.
[5] Ex. XXI, 29, in the case of his inflicting a fatal injury on another human being.
[6] Nu. XXXV, 31.
[7] Deduced from the words 'he is a murderer', which otherwise would be superfluous.
[8] Lev. XXIII, 15.
[9] The subject is fully treated in Hoffman, *Lev.* ii, pp. 159–215.
[10] Ex. XII, 43.
[11] Explained by Rashi as a man whose deeds have alienated him from God.
[12] Deut. XXIII, 25–26.
[13] Deut. XXIV, 15.
[14] Deut. XXIV, 16.

We are thus led to recognize that even without the above-mentioned methods of exegesis these precise interpretations were already known as ancient traditions transmitted orally from Sinai, for how otherwise could such a law as the taking of the 'fruit of a goodly tree' at the Feast of Ingathering have been given to Moses in general terms without instructing him in detail regarding the nature of the fruit and in what manner he should carry out the command, whether to take it to cover the Sukkah or to have it merely grasped by the hand. The same thing will apply in connection with the ordinance of the *tefillin* —surely, it could not be left in the bare form of Scripture, 'frontlets between your eyes,' without adding further elucidation in detail as to what they consist of as well as the method of carrying out the command. Such explanatory details, therefore, must have been given clearly to Moses in connection with every precept, and this in spite of the fact that the Rabbis endeavoured to deduce them from Scripture by means of the exegetical rules. Surely, if their only source had been the Biblical inferences quoted one might justly ask, How were these precepts practised before these exegetical rules were formulated? Was the precept of *tefillin*, for example, not properly practised before these methods of Biblical exposition were devised?

The fact is that neither Moses, Phinehas, Joshua, Samuel, nor the Elders had ever any doubt about the explanatory details of the written precepts, because they were all handed down from generation to generation by oral tradition as received at Sinai; the Rabbis merely sought to find Biblical support for them.[1]

An important principle was laid down by the Rabbis when they said:[2] 'One may apply *Gezerah Shavah* to support his teaching, but not to invalidate it.' This was meant to convey that they employed exegetical rules only for the purpose of giving a scriptural basis to the *halachoth* which were already expounded and accepted orally. On the other hand, none of the said rules would be of any avail if used to oppose those *halachoth* orally defined and transmitted. No device or method of study, whether the *Gezerah Shavah* or the *Kal Va'homer*[3] or any of the other exegetical rules would be of any use if its application had as its object the superseding of well-established *halachoth*, because we have it as an accepted principle[4] that one has no right to invalidate by a *Gezerah*

---

[1] Thus by their devices, such as comparisons of passages, logical analogy, and similar means of synthetic exegesis, they bring these Sinaitic Laws into strict relation with the written Law.

[2] Jer. Pes., ch. 5.

[3] Lit. light and heavy, or major and minor, the first of the hermeneutic rules of Hillel and R. Ishmael, very frequently used in the Talmudic system as an argument or proof of a contention or inference. [4] See Keth. 38*b*.

Shavah the literal meaning of the text, still less to nullify *halachoth* clearly known and expounded. One has, however, permission to apply exegetical rules to strengthen such *halachoth* as have already the sanction of tradition, by giving them Biblical support.

A statement of a similar character is found in the Jerusalem Talmud[1] (Ber. ii, Erub. ii). 'R. Johanan says, When a passage is not clear one should use other passages for its clarification.' Commentators, as quoted in the *Nimuke Yosef*[2] (B.K., chap. viii), interpret the above statement to mean that whenever a *halachah* is sanctioned by tradition but has no scriptural basis, it is permissible to apply scriptural support to it in any way that is in accord with the methods accepted by scholars.

It is true that as far as punishment is concerned, one is allowed to apply any of the exegetical methods of inference, as long as it is supported by the authority of oral tradition[3] (Tos. Suk. 11*b*, s.v. לְקוּחָה); but in cases where the laws are clear and need only some written evidence, one may use even a far-fetched analogy, so long as it is applied in a scholarly way, to gain for these laws a basis in the written Torah. The reason why, indeed, the Rabbis sought to establish methods by which they might give these accepted traditions a basis in the Pentateuch or in the other sacred writings was that in ancient times it was not permitted to reduce the oral law to writing.[4]

Since such *halachoth* were liable to be forgotten, the Rabbis employed even strained and far-fetched Biblical interpretations and supports to enable memory to retain them, as will be explained later at length.

It was with this in mind that the Rabbis stated[5] that one may apply *Gezerah Shavah* in order to substantiate his teaching, i.e. to give some scriptural basis to laws which have been transmitted by oral tradition, regardless of whether such a *Gezerah Shavah* had been handed down to him by his teachers, since, after all, he does not intend to form a new law thereby, but rather to strengthen the one which he already knows.

---

[1] Completed about 425 C.E., written in a Palestinian Aramaic dialect and comprising only 39 of the Mishnah Treatises.

[2] A commentary on the *halachoth* of R. Isaac Alfasi (Talmudist and Codifier of Spain 1013–1103) by Ibn Habib, a Spanish Talmudist of the fourteenth-fifteenth century.

[3] See Pes. 66*a*.

[4] Cf. Git. 60*b*. R. Judah b Nahmani: 'What has been said orally thou mayest not say in writing.' See also Tem. 14*b* for Resh Lakish's direct rebuke of the compilation of written *halachoth*. The question when this prohibition came into force and when it ended, or whether it was indeed ever properly enforced is a subject of extremely diverse views advanced by Talmudic scholars of all ages. Even from the Talmud and Midrashim themselves one can find support for all the diverse views on the matter. Chaim Tchernowitz in *Toledoth ha-Halachah*, i, pp. 1–10, presents a scholarly digest of the various opinions held by rabbinic authorities on this vital subject.

[5] Jer. Pes., ch. v, see *supra*.

In view of all this, one should not be astonished at some of the homiletic expositions employed in support of clear and definite *halachoth* even if the literal meaning of the passages used appear to be far removed from the *halachoth* of which they are intended to serve as proof, because their main purpose was only to assist the memory in preserving *halachoth* transmitted orally and already practised. The question may of course be asked: Since these *halachoth* were already known orally, why did they need Biblical support?—The answer is that since these texts are needed for their own subject matter, they are not used expressly for the purpose of teaching these *halachoth*, but only for lending them support. Why then is the question asked by the *Gemara* (Nid. 32a) as to the need of Biblical support for a rule already adopted in practice, where the answer as given above is obvious? This difficulty was noted by the author of *Yad Malachi*,[1] chap. i, para. 227, who also refers to Rashi on Nid. ad loc. He explains that the question in the Gemara was raised mainly because the *Vav* of the word *V'isha*[2] is definitely superfluous[3] and is not needed for another purpose. In such a case a question may reasonably be raised why the need of this redundancy (for the support of the *halachah*)? On the other hand where the passage stands for what its literal meaning implies and the rabbis have only used it as a support for *halachoth* already orally accepted, such a question will not arise.

The Tosaphists (M. K. 3b, s.v. ניסוך), referring to the assertion of the Talmud[4] that the libation of water at Tabernacles is a Sinaitic law whereas elsewhere in the Talmud[5] they find a Biblical origin for it in the additional letters *mem yod mem* in three passages which refer to the libations,[6] give a solution (for this discrepancy in treatment) by saying that this latter deduction is merely to give the *halachah* some Biblical support.

In identical terms Maimonides in his *Introduction to the Mishnah* refers to an objection raised in the Talmud (Ber. 7a, b), viz. why, if there was

---

[1] A methodological treatise by R. Malachi Hakkohen, prominent Italian Talmudist (middle of the eighteenth century).
[2] Lev. xv, xviii, from which they have inferred the age of three years and a day for the liability to the laws regulating sexual relations. This ruling was already adopted in practice as a Sinaitic law.
[3] It marks the beginning of a law and has no connection with the law contained in the preceding paragraph.
[4] V. Suk. 34a, 44a; Taan 3a.
[5] Shab. 103b.
[6] Num. xxix, 19, 31, and 33, which relate to the offerings during the Feast of Tabernacles. In connection with the second day we find נסכיהם (their libations) referring to the two daily offerings instead of נסכה (her libation) corresponding to מנחתה (her meal offering) which precedes it. On the sixth day similarly we read נסכיה 'her oblations', and on the seventh כמשפטם (after their manner) instead of כמשפטה (after her manner).

written proof[1] for the standard measures and sizes, did the Rabbis refer to them as oral laws traceable to Sinai (Erub. 4*a*, Suk. 5*a*), and he asserts that such *halachoth* except in so far as they are hinted at in the Torah are most suitably designated as halachoth transmitted from Sinai.

[1] According to the view of R. Hanan (Ber. 41*a*) that the whole verse (Deut. VIII, 8) 'A land of wheat and barley, etc.' is meant to give standard measures and sizes.

CHAPTER II

TRADITIONAL LAWS WITHOUT ANY EXEGETICAL BASIS IN THE TORAH

IN addition there is a class of orally transmitted and attested *halachoth* which provide detailed explanations of such scriptural precepts as require minute elucidation of the manner of their fulfilment, even though their main sense is set forth in Scripture.

The following may be given as illustrations of this class :—*Shehitah* (Ritual Slaughter) is derived from the verse[1]: 'And thou shalt kill (וזבחת) of thy herd, and of thy flock, as I have commanded thee.' That the *shehitah* is to be carried out by an incision in the throat is deduced etymologically from the term זבח,[2] but such details as to whether the severance of one or both pipes[3] is necessary and the like, were handed down by word of mouth. This is expressed by the Rabbis in the following statement (Hullin 28*a*): 'The text[4] goes to prove that Moses was instructed with regard to the mode of slaughter, i.e. the severance of the greater part of both pipes in the case of a beast and the greater part of one in that of a fowl, and also with regard to the five rules, non-observance of which invalidates *shehitah*.'[5]

Scripture states[6] 'Ye shall not eat any flesh that is torn by beasts in the field.' It was inferred from this that any ritually clean creature which, though still alive, suffers from a disease by reason of which its life cannot continue for long, is taref.[7] (*Yad*, M. Asuroth 6, 5.)

This ruling is followed by details which have been handed down by

---

[1] Deut. XII, 21.

[2] Lit. injure the place from which the blood runs, referring to the place at which, if cut, the blood is drained off. See Hul. 27*a*.

[3] The trachea (windpipe) and the œsophagus (foodpipe).

[4] i.e. the words 'as I have commanded thee'.

[5] The slaughterer must guard against the following five things: (*a*) *Shehia* from שההה akin to נשה to forget (Deut. XXXII, 18), pause, interrupt. An interruption, even of the shortest duration, during the *shehitah* is forbidden, Hul. 9*a*. (*b*) *Derasa* from דרס Talmudic term for treading, pressing, to avoid making the cut by pressing upon the knife. The cut is to be made by movement and not by pressure. Ib. 27*a*. (*c*) *Haloda*, from חלד Talmudical term for to hide, passing the knife under cover. The knife should not make the incision from behind the pipes outwardly, but in the reverse way. (*d*) *Hagrama*, from גרם to cut in a slanting direction, to let the knife slide beyond the space prescribed for cutting, e.g. higher than the point of the windpipe where the circumference is greatest. (*e*) *Ikkur*, from עקר to root out (Aram.) Dan.VII,8.The pipes must not be severed by tearing action. Their severance must be done by the cut of the knife.

[6] Ex. XXII, 30.

[7] Lit. torn, also abnormal, hence forbidden as food by Talmudic law. See Ha-Ketav V'hakabalah by Meklenburg.

Sinaitic tradition. The Talmud (Hul. 42*b*) gives a list of eighteen main signs, the appearance of any one of which in an animal renders its flesh taref.

Similarly the Scriptural Ordinances of the Sukkah,[1] Shofar,[2] and Lulab[3] are not accompanied by written details, such as the dimensions of each of these articles; but tradition has provided such information, as is indicated in the Rabbis' statement (Erub. 4*a*, Sukkah 5*b*) viz., that standard sizes, divisions and interpositions are matters of Sinaitic Halachoth in which there are embodied other ritual details, such as Gud,[4] Labud,[5] and the curved wall.[6] And so there are many other Biblical ordinances, such as the prohibition of certain articles of food, or the abstention from food on Yom Kippur, or the prohibition of work on Sabbath and festivals, in relation to which the Biblical text only states the prohibition in general terms, leaving us in ignorance of the extent of the prohibition of either the food or the work in question. The gap is thus filled in by tradition, by which we are informed of the correct measures and sizes of all relevant materials (liquid or solid) which render one a transgressor or not. Not only were such definitions required in connection with the imposing of punishment or in connection with ritual observances, and therefore handed down by tradition, but all other rabbinic laws which depended on fixed measures and weights and periods of time were included amongst these traditions received by Moses at Sinai, as is evidenced in the following Rabbinic statement (Jer. Peah; Jer. Hagiga): One silver[7] and two silver shekels are fixed as the minimum for the two offerings (Olah and Hagiga brought at the three festivals)[8]; similarly the beginning of the age of maturity for the male at thirteen years and a day and for the female at 12 years and a day are also found amongst the standards transmitted by tradition from Moses at Sinai. See the Responsa of the Rosh[9] and of R. Jacob Weil[10] as well as Rashi on

[1] Cf. Lev. xxiii, 43.
[2] Cf. Lev. xxiii, 24.
[3] Cf. Lev. xxiii, 40.
[4] A talmudical term which denotes the legal fiction of assuming the imaginary prolongation of partitions so as to reach the ceiling or descending of partitions so as to reach the bottom. V. Shab. 101*a*, Suk. 4*b*.
[5] Another such term which also denotes a legal fiction, viz., that whatever is separated by less than three handbreadths is deemed to be closed up. V. Shabb. 97*a*.
[6] A similar legal fiction by which part of the ceiling may be regarded as part of the curved wall.
[7] Refers in some cases to the Biblical shekel equal to the Tyrian sela, and in other cases to the Rabbinic sela the value of which varied from time to time.
[8] See Deut. xvii, 16–17.
[9] The abbreviation of Rabbenu Asher, eminent Talmudist of the fifteenth century, born in Western Germany and later settled in Spain. His fame rests on his digest of Talmudic laws and decisions.
[10] German rabbi and Talmudist of the fifteenth century.

Naz. 29*b* and on Aboth chap. 5. The latter on the *Mishnah* Shevuoth 14*b*[1] includes also in the category in question the point in time before which the unclean person who enters the precincts of the Temple becomes liable to *Kareth*.[2] Similarly Maimonides, *Yad, T. Zaraath* 13, 8 includes the size of a garis[3] as the diagnosis of leprosy, and in his view, the dimensions of the other items which are found in connection with the ritual of purification of the leper, such as the length of the cedar wood (one cubit) or that of the hyssop (one handbreadth), also belong to the above category. Only the primary objects of all these precepts were stated in general terms in the Torah, whilst the detailed instructions were transmitted by word of mouth, and no Biblical support even in the remotest way could be found for them.

There is, however, another category of *halachoth* which are universally accepted yet have no relation whatever to the written text. They consist of practices that were established independently and are not merely expansions of particular Torah precepts. For example the beating of the willow[4] is designated as a Sinaitic tradition (Suk. 44*a*); but actually this practice stands by itself and it has no relation whatever to the precept of the four species. Similarly, the 'libation of the water' at the Feast of Tabernacles, which is also designated as a Sinaitic tradition, is entirely a law standing by itself without any basis in the Torah. To this category will also belong the *halachah* that a father has the power to impose a Nazirite vow upon his (minor) son (*Mishnah* Nazir 4, 6). If this is really a Sinaitic *halachah*, its origin is certainly not traceable in the written text. The same is true also of the following *halachoth* (San. 81*b*):

(*a*) He who has twice been flogged[5] is to be placed (by the *Beth-Din*) in a cell and fed with barley bread until his stomach bursts.[6] (*b*) He who steals a *Kiswah*[7] exposes himself to attacks by zealots.[8] (*c*) A priest who ministers in the Temple while unclean is to have his skull split with clubs.[9] There is certainly no Biblical origin for these types of punishment—they are different from those ordinarily prescribed in the Torah,

[1] s.v. חייב.
[2] See Num. XIX, 13.
[3] Cilician bean. The spot to qualify for leprosy must be as large as a garis.
[4] The practice of taking a bunch of five willow-twigs during service on *Hoshana Rabba* and of beating it on the ground after chanting the refrain of *Hoshana*.
[5] For two transgressions, and has again offended.
[6] The offences committed were punishable by extinction (*Kareth*), but the warning was for a lesser penalty.
[7] One of the service vessels of the Temple (cf. San. 81*b*).
[8] i.e. pious men, zealous for the honour of Judaism, have the right to punish him if they catch him in the act.
[9] i.e. he is not charged with an offence before a *Beth-Din*, but the young priests lead him out of the precincts of the Temple and punish him themselves.

which as a rule consist of flogging and the four death penalties.[1] Rashi referring to the Rabbis' question 'Where is this penalty alluded to in Scripture?' and their reply that it is to be found in Ps. xxxvii, 22, 'Evil shall slay the wicked', observes that, though these penalties go back to Moses, nevertheless some allusion to them is sought in the Bible. This view is corroborated by the Ran[2] in his disquisitions on Sanhedrin.[3]

At all events the above-stated *halachoth* cannot be regarded as expanding any particular Biblical commands. They were adopted by the Rabbis on their own authority without any record in the Torah.

The following practice may also be included in the above category. Two burial places were set apart by the *Beth-Din*, one for those who were stoned or burned, and the other for those who were strangled or beheaded[4] (San. 6, 5). On this point, Maimonides, in his *Commentary on the Mishnah*, asserts that the enactment providing these two burial places has no basis in Scripture, and that the law was merely handed down by tradition, for though the obligation on the *Beth-Din* to bury those punished by death is stated in Scripture, no mention whatever is made of the duty to provide for them two different burial places.

[1] Stoning, burning, beheading, and strangling.
[2] The abbreviation for R. Nissim, Spanish physician, astronomer and halachist of the fourteenth century. In the last-named capacity he is known for his commentary on Alfasi's *halachoth* on several tractates and also by his commentaries on the Talmudic tractates themselves.
[3] Such punishments were presumably carried out very rarely. Their infliction as in the case of the ordinary death penalty must have been surrounded by such regulations as would ordinarily have made execution impossible. Cf. Makk. 7a, where the Rabbis tell us that one death sentence in seventy years would brand the Sanhedrin as a destructive Tribunal, and San. 71a where they say the death penalty on the disobedient son was never once carried out, and that the recording of the Law was meant to serve as a warning.
[4] The author, apparently quoting from memory, gives the clauses in the reverse order.

CHAPTER III

THE CATEGORIES OF ORAL LAW

W E are in possession of certain rules of interpretation which have come down to us from God through Moses at Sinai, and by which the Torah is expounded. It is through these logical principles that we are able to elucidate many points of detail in connection with the observance of the commands. R. Ishmael[1] has enumerated them as thirteen.[2] But besides these principles of R. Ishmael certain other rules have been devised for the interpretation of Biblical passages. For example: Hekesh[3]; Semuchin[4]; the Argument of Redundancy[5]; the Method of Lessening and Increasing and Expounding[6]; Extension and Limitation[7]; Extension following extension, limitation following limitation, and limitation preceded by extension and again succeeded by it,[8] or again

---

[1] A Tanna of the first and second centuries who helped to consolidate Judaism during the troublous period that followed the destruction of the Temple.

[2] On the basis of Hillel's seven rules of interpretation R. Ishmael developed thirteen which henceforth became the adopted instruments of the Midrashic method. They are enumerated in detail in Sifra I (Midrash on Leviticus). For an English version, see Singer's Prayer Book, pp. 13–14. See Frankel, *Darkhei ha-Mishnah*, p. 19, Weiss, *Dor.* II, p. 105, Graetz (S.P.R.) II, 192, Bacher (A.Z.R.) II, p. 1.

[3] To make a comparison between two subjects in two different passages.

[4] An analogy made from the juxtaposition of two laws in Scripture, so that the meaning of one is explained from the other.

[5] If the passage appears to be redundant in respect of its own subject-matter, purpose, or content, it may be applied to elucidate another passage (see San. 61a).

[6] For example, by taking a letter which appears servile in one word in the text, and adding it to another word for the purpose of interpreting the law. For examples of such application in the Talmud, see B.B. 111b; Yoma 48a; Zeb. 25a.

[7] By this law certain particles or conjunctions in the text are regarded as intended either to extend or to limit its provisions.

[8] This hermeneutic rule termed רבוי ומיעוט is distinct from that termed כלל ופרט (generalization and specification) included in Hillel's seven rules.

The differences between them are as follows: (a) Whilst in the case of כלל ופרט the particular restricts the general completely to its own content, in the case of רבוי ומיעוט the מיעוט merely limits the preceding רבוי. (b) In the case of פרט וכלל the general following the particular includes everything falling under the general, whereas in the case of מיעוט ורבוי the extension following the limitation includes only that which is similar to the מיעוט. (c) In the case of כלל ופרט וכלל we include only that which resembles the particular, whereas according to the principle of רבוי ומיעוט ורבוי the רבוי includes everything, even that which is not similar to the מיעוט, with the exception of that which has the least similarity to it.

There are many illustrations scattered in the Talmud of the application of those exegetical rules, quotation of which would require much space. The sources for such distinctions are in Rashi on Kidd. 21b, Sheb. 5a, B.K. 64b and Hul. 67a.

The principle of כלל ופרט was adopted by the school of R. Ishmael and that of רבוי ומיעוט, which was originated by R. Nahum of Gimzo, was later developed into a system by his disciple R. Akiba.

the theory that what illuminates another passage is itself illuminated thereby,[1] the rules concerning words written defectively and plene,[2] the rule of Mikra (reading) and Masora (tradition).[3]

All these rules were handed to us directly by Moses as the means whereby the written law was to be elucidated by throwing light on what appears to be ambiguous in one passage, from a similar and more clearly defined statement in another, and by resolving problems that arise in connection with the practice of the law. All the inferences which the Rabbis have derived or will yet derive by means of these exegetical methods have their root in the written text, like branches which grow out of the stem of the tree or like the fruit which develops from the seed.

The Rabbis (referring to Deut. ix, 10)[4] put forward a similar view, when they said (Megillah 19b):—'It goes to teach that God showed Moses in advance all the subtle details in the Biblical law and its scribal interpretation, and all those of the future rabbinical enactments such as the public reading of the Book of Esther.'

The same view is quoted on the authority of R. Joshua b Levi in Midrash Koheleth on the words 'That which hath been is the thing that shall be'.[5] Quoting Deut. ix, 10, 'And on them was written according to all the words'—'*The words*,' the Rabbis state, embody *Mikra* (Holy Writ), *Mishnah, Halachoth, Toseftoth,*[6] *Haggadoth,*[7] and all that a conscientious student may develop from them in the future, all this was given through Moses. (This view, by the way, is ascribed in the Babylonian Talmud to R. Johanan). The Rabbis intended thereby to convey that since Moses acquired in advance all the methods and necessary principles for the exegesis of the text, consequently all that the scholars of future generations will discover by means of these rules is to be viewed as the natural development of the text itself.

[1] See San. 73a for the case of a violated betrothed girl being compared to the case of a murdered man.
[2] See Kiddushin 30 on our competence in the use of these rules.
[3] Dealing with the difference between the spelling of the words and their pronunciation. There are two opposite opinions in this respect, one school advocating that the reading according to its natural vocalization is the main source of the law, and another maintaining that the spelling of the word as fixed by the Masora is of prime importance. (See San. 4a and Suc. 6b.)
[4] 'And on them (the two tablets) was written according to all the words God spoke with you in the Mount.'
[5] Eccl. i, 9.
[6] Lit. addition, supplement. In the numerous critical studies that have appeared on the Tosefta the problem of the relation between the two works is dealt with (see Tosefta, Zuckermandel, Jerusalem).
[7] Agada or Hagadah. lit. narration, discourse, is the name given to that part of the Talmud which does not deal with the exegesis of the Law.

Having accepted this theory we can now easily see and meet the serious difficulty raised and answered by Nahmanides[1] in his *Sefer Hamitzvoth*, Root 1. In the Babylonian Talmud, Tractate Megillah (19a), he says, the reading of Esther is regarded as one of the injunctions handed to Moses on Sinai. This view is corroborated by the Palestinian Talmud (Megillah, chap. i, 5) in the statement that the (public reading of the) Megillah is a Sinaitic law but that there is no chronological order kept in the events associated with the Torah.[2] In Shevuoth 39a, however, the Rabbis seem to state an absolutely different view by drawing a distinction between precepts received at Sinai and others issued later, such as, for example, the reading of Esther. Thus it follows that they regarded the reading of Esther as one of the observances which were to be adopted in the future. How, then, do they reconcile this view with the aforementioned statement made on the authority of R. Johanan and R. Joshua b Levi that the reading of Esther was amongst the observances transmitted to Moses on Sinai? According to our interpretation, however, both views are quite correct. It is undeniable that the details of the whole story, which followed as a result of the decree of Ahashverosh and Haman, as well as the deliverance and redemption brought about by God through the agency of Mordecai and Esther, really took place during the Babylonian exile nine centuries after the giving of the Torah on Sinai. The Rabbis thus correctly designated it as an observance which was to occur in the future; but to account for the permission to incorporate the Book amongst the Hagiographa, so that it should not be considered as an addition from outside, the Rabbis (Megillah 7a and Jer. Meg., chap. i) drew the required inference from the text: 'Write this for a memorial in the book.'[3] Similarly in Meg. 14a they said 'The Prophets added naught to what is written in the Torah save the reading of the Megillah. Whence did they derive it?' From the reasoning of a *Kal V'homer*. If the *Hallel*[4] was adopted merely to mark the deliverance from slavery to liberty, all the more should some other kind of literature (Esther) be introduced to mark the deliverance from death to life.' And these methods of interpretation, such as the inference from a superfluous letter or through a *Kal v'Homer*, are all of Sinaitic origin. And since the rules by which the adoption of the book of Esther and its incorporation in Scripture were

---

[1] Rabbi Moses b Nachman, known as Ramban, Spanish Rabbi and Kabbalist (b. 1194, d. 1270).
[2] This is the answer to the question, How it is that an account of later times was given earlier?
[3] Ex. XVII, 14.
[4] Lit. praise. Name given by the Rabbis to Pss. 113–118, which were written to be sung publicly. They are sung on full and semi-festival days.

proved to have come down by tradition from Sinai, it is correct to say
that they (i.e. the reading of the book of Esther and its incorporation in
Scripture) were amongst the things transmitted to Moses at Sinai in
advance, i.e. Moses was shown in advance these exegetical methods by
which the Torah was elucidated and which were applied by the Rabbis
to deduce from the Torah the practice of reading the book of Esther
publicly.

On the Talmudic statement (Taanith 28b) that the recital of *Hallel* on
Rosh Hodesh (New Moon days) is not a Scriptural command, Rashi
observes that this statement holds good actually as regards Hallel on
Rosh Hodesh, but not as to Hallel on Hanukka,[1] because since the
Prophets required its recital on all days on which deliverance from
tribulation is commemorated, Hallel on Hanukka ought to be regarded
as having Biblical sanction. He takes the view that there is a standing
Biblical command to recite *Hallel*[2] as words of praise to God for His
wonderful deeds to us at all times. This is found also in a homily quoted
by the Palestinian Talmud (last page of *Tr. Pesahim*) on the words
'Praise ye the Lord for the avenging of Israel, when the people willingly
offered themselves',[3] i.e. the leaders of the people offered to recite songs
to the Lord when He should show wonders to Israel. Thus the enactments which came down by tradition have the same authority as the
commands of Scripture, so that even if such a miraculous deed should
occur in our own days, we are, by Biblical command, required to recite
the *Hallel* publicly. Consequently, the recital of the *Hallel* on Hanukkah,
even though the events commemorated occurred eleven centuries after
the revelation at Sinai, is regarded as a Biblical command.

The above elucidation will help us to understand a controversy
mentioned in the Babylonian as well as in the Palestinian Talmud
(B. Gittin 60a and J. Peah, chap. ii, 4., and Hagigah, i, 8, respectively)
on the words 'I have written him the great things (rubei) of My law,
but they are counted as a strange thing.'[4] Some rabbis are of the opinion
that the exegetical deductions orally received are fuller than the laws
of the written text; others take the view that the latter are fuller than
the former.[5] The strangeness of this dispute was observed by the author

---

[1] The post-Biblical Festival of Lights celebrated on the 25th of Kislev for eight
days in memory of the successful rising of Judas Maccabaeus. Hanukkah is regarded
as a half festival only.

[2] Not necessarily the particular Psalms constituting the *Hallel*, but hymns of
thanksgiving and praise generally.

[3] Deborah's song of praise, Jud. v, 2.

[4] Hosea VIII, 12.

[5] Both groups of Tannaim based their views on the above-mentioned verse,
interpreting the word 'rubei' as meaning 'the greater part of'.

of the book *Beer Sheba*[1] on *Horayoth*. Surely, he says, there is no ground for dispute, for is it not obvious that the *Halachoth* contained in the *Mishnah*, *Tosefta*, the Babylonian and Palestinian Talmuds and the *Midrash*, which are commentaries on the written law, are definitely greater in amount than those contained in the written text of Scripture? This was also observed by the author of the *Yefeh Mareh*[2] on Jer. Peah, chap. ii, 4, but in the light of the elucidation given above there is no difficulty here. For he who takes the view that the quantity of *halachoth* in the written Torah is greater than that contained in the commentaries has in mind those deduced by the exegetical rules by which the written text itself is elucidated. On whatever basis the interpretation rests, whether on the redundancy of a letter, or on the particular way the passages are arranged, all such laws are regarded as the written Torah, irrespective of whether they are explicitly given therein or are only inferred as a result of the application of the various logical principles of interpretation, such as of redundancy, or the *Kal v'Homer*, the *Gezerah Shavah*, the *Hekesh*, etc. According to this view what is called rabbinic law comprises only those laws which, as explained in Chap. II, have not even a remote support in the written Torah, but are only accepted on the strength of tradition.

On the other hand he who takes the view that the oral laws are greater in quantity than those recorded in Scripture, holds that since the methods of exegesis are not provided in the Torah, these thirteen methods must, therefore, be regarded as Sinaitic tradition, and, consequently, all those laws which are deduced by the said methods, although they may have Scriptural support, must only be designated as the Oral Torah, because all the inferences involved were made possible by the application of methods which themselves were given us only by word of mouth.

Now that I have analysed the Oral law into three different categories I shall put before the reader an example of one precept, in which the three different types are found together. It will give him a clear conception of the above analysis, and also enable him to assign each case, as it arises, to the category to which it belongs. The precept is that of the *Tefillin*. We read in the Torah:—'And thou shalt bind them for a sign upon thy hand, and they shall be as frontlets between thine eyes.'[3] The

---

[1] R. Issachar Beer b Israel Leizer Eilenburg, born in Posen in 1570, Rabbi of Austerlitz, Moravia. Beer Sheba, one of his chief works, is a commentary on those treatises of the Talmud on which there are no *Tosafoth*. His commentary on *Horayoth*, referred to in the text, is known as *Ner-Mitzvah*.

[2] S. Jaffe, Rabbi at Constantinople during the sixteenth and seventeenth centuries. Author of many commentaries on the Midrash, and of responsa on *Halachah*.

[3] Deut. VI, 8.

Rabbis (San. 88*b*) designate the *Tefillin* as a command which is fundamentally Biblical in essence, whilst its interpretation[1] comes from the
Soferim.[2] This means that the primary duty of wearing *tefillin* on the arm
and on the forehead is explicitly found in the Torah, but that the
details, such as the actual meaning of the term *totafoth* (frontlets), or
what passages are to be selected (for placing in the phylacteries) or their
number, are not stated. The Rabbis, however, had received these
details by tradition, and have, in addition, found Biblical support for
them. For example, the number of Scriptural sections to be used was
deduced in a rather far-fetched way, as said before, from the word
totafoth, '*tot*', denoting two in Katpi, and '*foth*', two in Afriki (San. 4*b*).
These interpretations were classified by the Rabbis as interpretations of
the Scribes, i.e. as belonging to the first category which as aforementioned consists of interpretations traced back to Sinai, and associated (though in far-fetched ways) with the written text. They have also
designated them as 'words of the Scribes'. It will later be shown that, in
the view of Maimonides, the phrase 'words of the Scribes' is a collective
noun.[3]

There are, however, *halachoth* such as those concerning the passages
used, the type of script, or those concerning the straps attaching them
to the arm, which were universally accepted as coming from Sinai, and
for which there is no Scriptural basis. These are classified as *halachoth*
transmitted orally to us by Moses from Sinai. They do not come under
the category of interpretation of the written text, but consist merely of
isolated details necessary for the correct carrying out of the command.
There are ten such *halachoth.*[4]

    1. That ink shall be used in the writing of the Scriptural passages.
    2. They shall be written on parchment[5] and on the side which
faces the flesh.
    3. The boxes shall be square and their stitches be so made as not
to spoil their squareness.
    4. The box containing the head phylactery shall have on the
outside the letter שׁ both on the right and on the left.[6]

---

[1] Regarding the number of the compartments, the passages to be inscribed, and
deposited therein, the manner in which they are to be worn, etc.
[2] The designation *Sofer*, originally used of himself by Ezra, is applied to the interpreters of Law to the people in Biblical times. The Soferim were by later tradition
sometimes called also the Men of the Great Assembly, which, in fact, they were.
[3] i.e. a general term with a variety of usages.
[4] See Men. 35*a* and *b* and *Yad, Tefillin*, i, 3; for their sources.
[5] Made from the hide of a ritually clean animal.
[6] On the right with three strokes and on the left with four strokes. In the latter
case it was intended that the spaces between the strokes should form the letter שׁ.

5. The Scripture passages shall be enveloped with parchment lining.

6. They shall be twined with hair (of a clean animal).

7. The thread for the stitching shall be from the sinews (of clean animals).

8. The boxes shall be provided with loops for the fastening of the straps.

9. The straps shall be black.

10. The knot on the strap of the head-phylactery[1] is to be in the shape of the letter ד.[2]

All these *halachoth* are designated by the Rabbis in many passages[3] as Sinaitic laws. On the other hand, such *halachoth* as, for example, that the *Tefillin* ought to be worn on the left arm and that the passages enclosed ought not to be written on skins from unclean animals, were deduced by rabbinic exegesis from the written text. The former is inferred from the fact that since the word ידכה (Ex. xiii, 16) is written in the full form (not ידך) it is as though it read יד־כהה[4]; it means the hand that is weak (Men. 37a). The latter is inferred from the verse, 'that the law of the Eternal may be in thy mouth,' (Ex. xiii, 9) 'in thy mouth' is interpreted as meaning that which is permitted in the mouth[5] (Shab. 108a). There are yet other exegetical inferences, as for example the law requiring the removal of the head phylactery first, which is inferred from 'And they shall be as frontlets between your eyes',[6] i.e. that both phylacteries must be on you when the frontlets are on your forehead. These latter cases belong to the third category of *halachoth*, which were inferred by the application of the ordinary rabbinic methods of interpretation.

Thus the precept of the *Tefillin* which, as mentioned before, is fundamentally of Biblical origin, comprises the three different categories of *halachoth*, which go together under the name of *Torah she-b'al Peh*, viz.:

1. Interpretations traceable to Sinai and supported by Biblical texts.

---

[1] The text erroneously states 'arm-phylactery'.

[2] These two letters, the ש on the box of the head phylactery and the ד at the back as represented by the knot of the strap, with the י shaped by the knot near the box of the arm phylactery, make up the letters of שדי, one of the names of God.

[3] See Men. 35, 36a and b, Mak. 11a.

[4] The word כה, the latter half of יד־כה, may be taken as akin to the verb כהה (to grow feeble or dim, cf. Gen. xxvii, 1).

[5] i.e. the material to be used for the *Tefillin* should be taken from ritually clean animals.

[6] Deut. vi, 8.

2. *Halachoth* of Sinaitic origin which have not even the remotest basis in Scripture.

3. Rulings which the Rabbis have inferred through the ordinarily adopted methods of exegesis. Following this example one can analyse other precepts, and place them in the category to which they belong.

CHAPTER IV

AUTHORITY FOR RULINGS BASED ON LOGICAL INFERENCES

BUT there are still many cases in the unwritten law which belong to none of the three categories mentioned. Their basis is simply human reasoning. Yet such *halachoth* have the same authority as those which are supported by the written text, as the talmudical statement asserts: 'It is either a matter of reason, or based on Scripture.' (See the beginning of Tr. Zebahim and elsewhere.)[1] Thus you see that Biblical texts and logical reasoning are of equal weight, since things which originate in human reason by logical inference are as authoritative as those derived from a Biblical source by the exegetical methods of the Rabbis. This will be clear from the illustrations which follow. The question is asked in *Keth.* 22a, 'Whence do we learn that the mouth which has forbidden may also permit?'[2] From the verse: 'I gave my daughter unto this man to wife.'[3] But the objection is raised: 'Why do we need Scripture to tell us this? Is it not common sense, that if you rely upon him for the one matter you ought to trust him in the other?' See also B. Kamma 46b, where the question is asked: 'Whence do we learn that the burden of proof falls upon the claimant?' and the reply is: From the passage 'If any man has any matter to see to let him at once come unto them.'[4] But the objection is raised: Is it not common sense that if a man has a pain he visits the physician? Why then the need of Scripture to prove this?' Here then you have it explicitly stated that any ruling which is based upon ordinary human reasoning is as authoritative as if it were deduced from Scripture, for the Talmud would not have questioned the necessity of Scriptural evidence in the above cases if reasoning alone did not suffice.

You find this point put still more clearly in *Pesahim 25a* and San. *74a* where, in answer to the question 'How do we know that one should expose himself to death rather than commit murder?', the Rabbis

---

[1] See Ber. 4b for all the sources.
[2] Since if we rely on a witness as a source for the prohibition, it is only logical to accept his testimony in the reverse case as well.
[3] Deut. XXII, 16. By virtue of the father's statement—I gave my daughter (to wife) without specifying the particular person to whom he betrothed her, she becomes prohibited to the whole world, but with his concluding words 'unto this man' he grants her to a particular person.
[4] Ex. XXIV, 14.

answer: 'This is common sense: who knows that your blood is the redder; perhaps his blood is the redder.'[1]

And in connection with incest,[2] they have deduced the law by analogy from what is written of murder,[3] for just as 'when a man riseth against his neighbour and slayeth him, etc.' even so is it with incest. What is used to throw light is itself illuminated. For just as in the case of murder one must rather be willing to die than to commit murder, so also in the case of a betrothed maiden must he (the violator)[4] be killed rather than allow himself to violate her.

Thus we see that the Torah has proved a case by the method of analogy, deducing a ruling for the prevention of incest from a similar ruling in connection with murder, though the whole basis for that ruling is but common sense; for common sense was of such importance to the Rabbis that they adopted it as a sound foundation even for rulings on other cases. See also *B. Metzia 4a* with reference to the exemption (of a debtor) from taking an oath in the case of הֵילָךְ[5] on the ground that he (the debtor) regards the part of the claim which he offers on the spot as a loan in his possession, whereas the remaning sum he disavows entirely,[6] and although this is only common sense, yet the Rabbis found the argument sound enough to exempt from the taking of an oath which one would otherwise be obliged to take according to Biblical law. Indeed they have designated both monetary and ritual laws inferred from common reasoning as 'Biblical laws', as they are derived from Scripture.

The case of the monetary law is illustrated in the following Talmud statement.[7] According to D'var Torah (so-called Biblical law) it is the payment which effects the purchase,[8] yet this has no Biblical support.[9]

---

[1] i.e. His life is not less valuable than yours; and therefore if one is ordered by the authorities to take life, under the threat of being killed himself he should face that threat rather than commit the murder.

[2] i.e. That it may not be practised even to save one's life.

[3] Deut. XXII, 26.

[4] One who was forced to violate a betrothed maiden. See Tos. San. 74*b* s.v. אסתר.

[5] Lit. (here it is)—a legal term for the instantaneous delivery of the amount admitted. But in case of an admission of part only of the amount claimed, an oath is to be imposed upon the debtor.

[6] And in the case of a complete denial he is exempt from the taking of the legal oath (imposed by the Torah), only it is imposed upon him as an equitable oath. See Sheb. 40, b.

[7] See B.M. 46*b*.

[8] The medium accepted by the Rabbis for effecting purchase was the משיכה, i.e. the buyer's drawing of the purchased article into his possession.

[9] The author prefers the view of the *Nimuke Yosef* ad loc. and makes no reference to the view upheld by Rashi that there is Biblical support for this ruling; and although the former view is favoured by the Sema (the abbreviation of Sefer Meirath Einayim, a commentary to the *Hoshen Mishpat* by R. Joshua Falk, a great Polish rabbinic

It is only according to common sense that it is by the payment that the transfer of the article to the buyer is effected, so giving him the necessary ownership or title. The Rabbis have designated such rulings as 'Words of the Torah'. See *Nimuke Yosef* and *Shittah Mekubezeth*[1] ad loc.

And in the case of ritually prohibited articles they state[2] that the half of the legal minimum is prohibited by Biblical law. This view is advanced on the ground that each of the halves is capable of being joined to the other, thus making up the minimum. And there are further instances where, although the ruling has no scriptural basis and is only inferred from common sense, yet the prohibition is designated as derived from the Torah. Indeed the Tosaphists and the *Ran*[3] have, on this account, raised the question why there should be any necessity for seeking Biblical support from the passage 'Ye shall not eat[4] any *heleb*' (Lev. VII, 23) in the case of a law which is founded on common reason, in this case with reference to the possible joining of the halves.

At all events we can see definitely that a ruling derived from common sense is also designated by the Rabbis as 'Words of the Torah'.[5]

authority of the sixteenth century) (*H. Mishpat* 198, 1), it is refuted by other rabbinic authorities.

[1] Lit. 'Gathered interpretations', a collection of glosses on the greater part of the Talmud by one of the leading Talmudists of his day, R. Bezalel Ashkenazi of the fifteenth century, born in Palestine, but domiciled in Egypt.

[2] Yoma 14*a*.

[3] An abbreviation of R. Nissim Gerundi, commentator on Alfasi.

[4] Lev. VII, 23. 'Any' denotes any quantity, even the half of its legal limit.

[5] And accepted by them as being as authoritative as though it were based on the written text.

CHAPTER V

ENACTMENTS DEDUCED FROM POST-MOSAIC BOOKS

Legal rulings derived from the post-mosaic books, the Prophets and the Hagiographa, were also regarded by the Rabbis as being equally as authoritative as those actually derived from the Torah. I have elaborated this point at length in my treatise *Torath Nebi'im*.[1] These *halachoth* are introduced as Biblical laws founded on the Biblical text, as we can see from the query asked in regard to them (Yeb. 4*a*), 'Where are we taught in the Torah the method of exegesis founded on the proximity of two subjects?'[2] It is written 'They stand fast for ever.'[3] Here is a passage from the Hagiographa and it is quoted and regarded as though it were from the Torah. In Sanhedrin 37*a*, we read: A Min[4] said to R. Kahana, 'You maintain that a menstruant woman is permitted *yihud*[5] (privacy) with her husband. Can fire be near tow without singeing it?' He retorted that the Torah testifies this for us in the words 'Set about with lilies'.[6] See further in Mak. 24*a*: 'If concerning matters which are usually not performed in private[7] the Torah enjoins "and walk humbly",[8] how much more in those which are.'

See also Jer. Ab. Zara, chap. I, 1: The Torah says 'Did I not choose him (the Levite) out of all the tribes of Israel'[9], and the voice of the idolater retorts,[10] 'and he (Jeroboam) made priests of the lowest of the people.'

There is a still better illustration in Ber. 48*b*[11]: 'R. Nathan says there is no need to search for a source in the Torah for the benediction before the meal, for it is written[12] 'because he doth bless the sacrifice and

---

[1] A work in which the author attempts to show the close relation between the oral and the written law and the rabbinic authority to enact additional laws.

[2] Heb. *Semukhin* from סמך to join, hence deduction based on the exegetical principle of proximity.

[3] Ps. cxi, 8.

[4] A sectarian, probably from the Heb. מין (species, sect). Used variously of Samaritans, Sadducees, agnostics, Jewish-Christians, and other sectaries according to the epoch to which the passage belongs.

[5] Private meetings of the sexes.

[6] Cant. vii, 3. The exegetical deduction in the Talmud is as follows: 'even through a hedge of lilies they make no breach'.

[7] From the words 'and walk humbly' they infer the moral duty of providing dowry for poor maidens and burial expenses for the poor dead.

[8] Micah vi, 8.

[9] Sam. iii, 28. An interpretation of the words of the Man of God to Eli.

[10] I Kings xii, 31.

[11] Where the Biblical source for after-meal grace is sought and then a similar origin for the benediction immediately before the meal is discussed.

[12] I Sam. ix, 13.

afterwards they eat'.[1] We thus see that the Tanna preferred a deduction from a passage of the Prophets to one from a passage in the Torah[2] though the latter is traceable to pre-Sinaitic[3] revelation.

Again in Hullin 17b, in answer to the question whence the obligation to examine the knife before the *shehitah* is derived as a Biblical law, the answer is given: In the words 'and slay them בזה (here)'.[4]

Again, in Gittin 36a, following the words 'you call this a precaution for the general good',[5] the question is asked, Is this not inferred from the Torah where we read[6] 'and subscribe evidence and seal them and take witnesses'? See further Sanhedrin 52b, where 'burning'[7] is referred to as being of Sinaitic origin on the ground that[8] it is written 'as with the burnings of thy fathers so shall they burn for thee'. All these cases go to prove that the words of post-Mosaic books were regarded as having the same efficacy as those of Sinaitic origin. Furthermore, their words were accepted as a sufficient authority for the imposition of the punishment of flogging,[9] as is evidenced in the following ruling (*Yad, Biath Mikdash 6*). 'An uncircumcised priest who has served in the Temple is liable to flogging, just as a non-priest would be in a similar case; and the whole basis for the incompetence of an uncircumcised priest for Temple service is the passage in Ezekiel[10] (San. 22b, and also Taan. 17b). See Radbaz[11] in his Responsa on the versions of Maimonides, Part II, 86, and Gerondi[12] on Berachoth I. With reference to the question raised in the

---

[1] Referring to the indications given to Saul how to trace the Man of God (Samuel).

[2] Referring to the words (Deut. VIII, 10) 'When thou has eaten and art full then thou shalt bless'(which is enjoined by Moses in his reformulation of the law).

[3] More correctly Sinaitic revelation.

[4] I Sam. XIV, 34. The Hebrew word בזה may also be interpreted 'with this' instead of 'here'. Hence the inference that Saul had given them a knife already examined wherewith to slaughter.

[5] With reference to the ruling in the Mishnah (Git. 4, 3) that witnesses shall sign the bill of divorce as a precaution to prevent abuses. Although the view was that those who witness the delivery of the bill effectuate the divorce, yet since it might happen that these may either be far from the place of divorce or may have died, it was enacted as a precaution that the bill should be signed by the witnesses so that even in their absence the signatures could be vouched for by those who knew them.

[6] Jer. XXXII, 44.

[7] Referring to the funeral pyres which were lit in honour of deceased kings.

[8] In Jer. XXXIV, 5.

[9] With reference to a stranger—non-priest or non-eligible priest who entered and served in the Sanctuary.

[10] XLIV, 9: 'No uncircumcised in heart and uncircumcised in flesh shall enter unto My sanctuary to serve Me.'

[11] The abbreviation for David Ben Abi Zimra, Spanish Talmudist and Cabbalist of the fifteenth–sixteenth centuries. Author of many works.

[12] R. Yona, Spanish Rabbi and moralist of the thirteenth century, author of many works, one of which is the Novellae to Alfasi in Berakot written in his name by his pupils and known from its initials as תר"י Hebrew רבנו יונה תלמידי.

Talmud Ber. 8*a* as to whether the prohibition of leaving[1] the Synagogue
during the reading of the Law also applies to the period between the
portions read no answer was given, though, in such a case, they
uphold the stricter opinion by a rule that in the case of an unsolved
question on a Biblical Law, the stricter view is to be adopted, even
though the whole Scriptural basis for this prohibition is in the verse[2]
'and they that forsake[3] the Lord shall be consumed,' which is
only from a post-Mosaic book. In my Treatise referred to above,
I have quoted the Ramban[4] in his *Sefer Hamitzvoth*, Root II, where he
raises the following difficulty. Since we have it as a definite ruling that
no prophet has the authority to introduce any new law,[5] how were the
above-quoted halachoth derived from the words of the prophets?' But,
as he says, this was already dealt with by the Rabbis in their retort
(San. 22*b* and M.K. 5*a*) 'Before Ezekiel came and told us this, who had
stated it?[6] What they meant was that it was not the prophet who
initiated the ruling, because he indeed has no authority to do so, but he
must have been in possession of a traditional law to which he only gave
textual support. In other words, prophets only recorded *halachoth* which
had already been received orally as Sinaitic laws, and so revealed
nothing new, since those rulings had been in existence already as oral
law.

I have already dealt at length with this category of *halachoth* in my
Treatise, Torath Nebiim, quoted above. I would only refer to the
conclusions reached there, namely, that these rulings which may
appear, at first sight, to have been laid down by the Prophets, were none
other than *halachoth* transmitted orally from Sinai, for the writing down
of which they had received the necessary divine permission.

---

[1] Or doing anything else which interrupts his attention to the reading (See Orach
Haim 146, 2.)

[2] Is. I, 28.

[3] Hebrew וְעוֹזְבֵי from עזב which literally means 'leave, abandon'.

[4] The abbreviation for R. Moses b Nahman, also known as Nachmanides; See
p. 23, n. I.

[5] Shab. 104*a* and Tem. 16*a*; Yoma 80*a*.

[6] Surely if there was no other source except the words of the prophet, they could
not have imposed the punishment referred to upon the offender.

CHAPTER VI

TAKKANOTH (ENACTMENTS) AND GEZEROTH (DECREES)

ALL those legal decisions of the *Mishnah* or *Gemara* which come under the above-mentioned categories, whether they were inferred from the interpretation of unintelligible passages or as a result of the elucidation in detail of the implications of the precepts of the Torah and the manner of their observance; whether they were deduced by means of the exegetical rules which we received by way of tradition or whether they were suggested by common sense; or again, whether they were based on the words of the Prophets—they are all as authoritative as those derived from the clear statements of the Torah, and he who transgresses any of them is as liable to punishment as he who breaks any of the laws of the Torah.

There is still another category of observances, cited in the *Mishnah* and *Gemara* and in several *baraitoth*, that are of different character, and bear no relationship to those before-mentioned. They come under the category of '*takkanoth*' (enactments)[1] and '*gezeroth*' (decrees)[2] which were found necessary by the Rabbis as precautionary measures to safeguard the Torah.

Every Talmudic teacher in his own period, understanding the conditions of the people of his own days, felt the need of promulgating various enactments and decrees for the purpose of protecting the walls of the law against breaches. These *takkanoth* and *gezeroth* belong to the category of Rabbinic laws, and they carry no authority even for the infliction of the ordinary punishment of flogging upon the disobedient, let alone that of capital punishment. Transgressors of such Rabbinic decrees, however, were liable to *makkath marduth* (beating for rebellion).[3]

In doubtful cases connected with such enactments the decision should be in favour of the more lenient view. This is in accordance with a definite ruling that in a doubtful case, where the violation of a rabbinical enactment is under consideration, the decision favours the more lenient practice.

---

[1] Lit. improvement, from תקן. An ordinance instituted by recognized authorities throughout the ages to reinforce the moral teachings of the law and to promote religious observance.

[2] Lit. to cut, to decide, from גזר. Gezeroth are the antitheses of *takkanoth* in this respect, that the former are applied to positive ordinances, whilst the latter are applied to negative decrees, instituted as a preventive measure to guard a Biblical law.

[3] As distinct from the stripes prescribed by the Torah, the '*makkath marduth*' was a disciplinary measure for dealing with disobedience to demands of rabbinic laws.

Notwithstanding this, Maimonides in his *Yad Mamrim* I and *Sefer Hamitzvoth*, Root I, advances the view that even *takkanoth* and all rulings under the category of 'fences' are included in the positive command of the Torah[1] 'according to the word of the law which they shall teach thee'. 'We have it by tradition,' he claims, 'that it is this positive command which requires us to abide at all times by the decision of the *Beth Din ha-Gadol*.'[2] Thus all adherents of Moses and his Torah are bound to rely in their religious observance upon the Supreme Court and to trust in its judgments. He who disobeys them has transgressed, in addition to the positive command quoted, also the negative command[3], 'Thou shalt not depart from the word which they shall tell thee, to the right nor to the left.' According to his view *takkanoth* and *gezeroth* and rulings formulated by the Rabbis as precautionary measures may appear to be man-made innovations, decided upon by the Rabbis on the strength of their own logic, in order to fulfil thereby the task laid upon them to safeguard the fortress of Zion[4] and to watch continually over the safety of the structure of Israel's faith, but the Sages were invested with authority to promulgate such enactments when necessary in order to assure the continuity and permanence of their observance by the people. Hence the ruling that no court can annul the decisions of another court, unless it surpasses it both in wisdom and in numbers.[5] And where these decrees or prohibitions have already received universal acceptance they cannot be repealed even by a court which excels the former in wisdom and in numbers, as is explained by Maimonides in *Yad Mamrim* II. In my treatises *Mishpat-ha-Horaha*[6] and *Darkhei-ha-Horaha*[7] I have elaborated this subject in all its roots and branches. Yet although, as said before, Biblical law had bestowed the authority on the Rabbis to make enactments and decrees, where and whenever they thought appropriate, they still lacked the power to inflict upon the offender the *malkuth* (flogging) imposed by the Biblical law, because the offender in such a case would be guilty of the breach of a prohibitory law involving capital punishment (in which case there can be no flogging), since the rebellious elder was liable to death by strangulation for the transgression of the prohibition in question.

[1] Deut. XVII, 11.
[2] The Supreme Court of the Great Sanhedrin of 71 members, the final authority in *halachic* disputes. It is this court to which Deut. XVII, 8–13 refers.
[3] Deut. ibid.
[4] A Biblical idiom. Cf. Lam. II, 8, 18.
[5] Eduyoth, I, 5.
[6] A study of the procedure of the voting of the members of the High Court. (Zolkiew, 1840.)
[7] An examination of the different standards of the Talmudic rulings. (Zolkiew, 1842.)

Another difference between these rulings and Biblical law is that leniency was favoured in cases of doubt involving these *takkanoth* and *gezeroth* because they were originally formulated by the rabbis, so that they did not include cases of doubt or any other difficulties of a similar character. (V. *Lehem Mishneh, Mamrim* I.)[1]

I shall set before the reader in detail and in chronological order all such *takkanoth* and *gezeroth*, following the above classification of *halachoth*, specifying which belong to the class of Biblical laws as analysed and arranged in the previous chapters under three categories, and which were enacted by the authority of prophets and other teachers for the purpose of safeguarding the words of the law.

First, the *gezeroth* enacted by the Prophets.

---

[1] A commentary on the *Yad* by R. Abraham Arya de Boton, Rabbi at Salonica in the sixteenth century. *Lehem Mishneh*, his chief work, treats especially of those passages which appear to contradict the Talmud.

CHAPTER VII

GEZEROTH IN CHRONOLOGICAL ORDER

M OSES, the teacher of Israel, was the earliest to promulgate *takkanoth* and *gezeroth*. They were not the outcome of prophecy, but of his own judgment. Thus we read[1]: 'Moses our teacher promulgated many *gezeroth* and enacted many *takkanoth*'. Rashi ad loc. refers to *Meg.* 4*a* to the effect that Moses taught the duty (of the people) to inquire (and of the teacher) to expound the subject peculiar to the festival in question. *Maharsha*[2] in his novellae observes that in this reference *takkanoth* only are mentioned, not *gezeroth*. The fact is, however, that there are some *gezeroth* attributed to Moses. Thus *Yeb.* 79*a* says that it was he who issued the decree prohibiting the *Nethinim*[3] from intermarriage with Israelites.

The author of *Penei Yehoshua*[4] (R. H. beginning of chap. 4), quotes a question by the *SeMag*[5] as to the reason why the unclean[6] are relegated to a second Passover, when they had sufficient time to offer the Paschal Sacrifice on the evening of that (seventh) day,[7] on the basis of Sukkah 25*b* where, from the words 'they could not bring the Passover lamb on that day',[8] it is inferred that it was only on that day that they could not bring the offering, but that in the evening they could cleanse themselves (and so offer the Paschal Sacrifice).[9] Yet they are relegated to a second Passover as they have not received the necessary sprinkling because the eve of that Passover fell on the Sabbath,[10] and already in the days of Moses it was prohibited to sprinkle the unclean on the Sabbath day.

---

[1] Shab 30*a*.

[2] The abbreviation (from the initials) of מורנו הרב שמואל אליעזר איידלס R. Samuel Eliezer Edels, a Talmudist of the sixteenth century, author of elucidations of the *halachoth* and Aggadoth of the Talmud which became very popular.

[3] From נתן, lit. the given—descendants of the Canaanites in the days of Moses and of the Gideonites in the days of Joshua and Moses, whom afterwards Joshua made into Temple slaves (Deut. xxix, 10; Josh. ix, 21). Their status was low and they were forbidden marriage with Israelites (cf. *Kidd.* 69*a*).

[4] Novellae on the Talmud in four parts by R. Jacob Joshua b. Zevi Hirsh, Polish rabbi, chief rabbi of Frankfort-on-Main (1680–1764).

[5] See note 2, p. 1.

[6] Referred to in Numb. ix, 6.

[7] See Num. ix, 11–12, with reference to the purification of the unclean on the seventh day by immersion and the sprinkling of the water of purification. To the unclean in question, the eve of Passover was the seventh day.

[8] Num. ix, 6.

[9] Cf. note 7.

[10] v. Sab. 87*b* on the words 'in the first month, in the second year, in the first day of month that the *Mishkan* (dwelling) was set up'. 'That day was the first of the week,' hence the eve of Passover was on the Sabbath.

Thus the author of the *Penei Yehoshua* concludes that this restrictive measure was one of several *gezeroth* enacted by Moses, and was, in this case, adopted as a precaution against a possible transgression of the Sabbath law prohibiting the carrying of any object in a public thoroughfare farther than four cubits.[1] There is then obviously here an additional *gezerah* enacted by Moses. See also *Aboda Zara* 76a, where against the view that where forbidden food imparts a bad taste the vessel in question is permitted for use, the objection is raised 'How is it then that the Torah imposed cleansing[2] of the vessels of Midian?'[3] The answer given is that the rule applies only to vessels which were used on the same day.[4] But if so, why should vessels not used on the same day be forbidden without cleansing?[5] The gist of the objection rests on the fact that *gi'ul* (cleansing) could be avoided by leaving the vessels until the next day, and they would then, according to the view stated, need no cleansing at all. To this the Talmud replies that a *gezerah* had been enacted forbidding the use of vessels even not on the same day, in order to safeguard the observance of the Law in regard to vessels used on the same day. Here we find another *gezerah* traceable to the days of Moses. The latter suggestion is supported by Yavetz[6] in his *Mor u-Kezi'ah*, chapter *Seyag l'Torah*.

JOSHUA confirmed the *gezeroth* of Moses against intermarriage with the *Nethinim*[7] (Yeb. 79a). The Tosaphists in Kiddushin 38a s.v. ממחרת[8] with reference to the requirement to offer the Omer[9] when entering the land before they could eat of the new corn,[10] raise a problem by asking, 'Surely the new corn was needed for Matzoth,[11] and, in that case, the positive law of the Matzoth could have set aside[12] the

---

[1] A similar precautionary measure is found against sounding the Shofar or the taking of the four species on the Shabbat (v. Sukkah 43a).

[2] From the effects of the forbidden food which they contained.

[3] v. Num. XXXI, 22–23.

[4] So that the taste of the food they absorbed has not yet deteriorated.

[5] The prohibition actually applies מלכתחלה (at the outset) because the *halachah* permits their use בדיעבד (in cases where cooking had already taken place).

[6] The abbreviation of Jacob b. Zevi Ashkenazi, known as Jacob Israel Emden, German Talmudist, 1697–1777. Author of many works, the *Mor u-Kezi'ah* consisting of novellae on the *Orach Hayim*.

[7] See Jos. IX, 27.

[8] אקרוב and not ממחרת as stated by the author. From the words (Jos. v) 'On the morrow after the Passover they ate', the Gemara deduces that it means not before, i.e. they brought the Omer first and only then ate it.

[9] The wave-offering (Lev. XXIII, 10–11) which made permissible the eating of the newly harvested grain.

[10] See Jos. v, 11, 'and they did eat of the (new) corn of the land on the morrow,' i.e. after the Passover, 16th Nissan, when the Omer had been offered. Before that they could not eat of the new grain.

[11] Cakes of unleavened bread. Cf. Ex. XII, 39.

[12] v. Yeb. 3b where this ruling is given.

command prohibiting the eating the new produce before the Omer offering?' Their answer, however, is that since the command of Matzoth is fulfilled by the first *K'zayith*[1] alone, the first is forbidden[2] for the sake of the second.[3] Here then we have another *gezerah* traceable to the days of Joshua.

PHINEAS formulated a *gezerah* against wines of heathens of which it is not known whether they had been dedicated to their deities.[4] This *gezerah* he decreed in the Ineffable Name (of God) and in the writing used on the Tables of the Law (see Pirkei d'R. Eliezer xx quoted by *Ramban* in *Sefer Hamitzvoth*, Prohibiting Laws, p. 194).

DAVID confirmed the *gezerah* against the *Nethinim*.[5] His court also promulgated a *gezerah* against *Yihud* with an unmarried woman (A. Zara 36*b*).[6] R. Yomtov Lipman Heller[7] in his commentary on the *Mishnah* ascribes to the above court a *gezerah* against ploughing with two kinds of unclean beasts.[8] His argument is as follows. In *Jer. Kilaim* 8, 2, a difficulty is raised regarding the words used of David's sons that 'Every man took a mule and fled',[9] for was it not forbidden to ride on the mule in view of the prohibitory law of *Kilaim*?'[10] But he points out that there would be no difficulty if Maimonides in Yad Kilaim ix, 8, were correct in his view that the prohibition in question does not apply where both beasts are unclean, as is the case of the hybrid mule. Hence Heller concludes that a *gezerah* to this effect had been in existence already at the time of David, although there is no explicit reference to it in the Scriptures. He supports his deduction from the assumption made in Tosaphoth to Kiddushin referred to above, in connection with the other

---

[1] The size of an olive ritually applied as a standard to articles of food which ought, or which ought not, to be eaten. See Yoma 80*a*.

[2] As a precautionary measure.

[3] Which is no longer necessary for the fulfilment of the law.

[4] See Hul. 4*b* and San. 106*a* for the statement that at the time of Balaam and Phineas wine of heathens had not yet been forbidden. An anonymous reviewer of the Mebo in the A.Z. d. J. 1845, N. 30, points to the incongruity of this statement with the one quoted from Maimonides in his commentary on the Mishnah, Shab 1, that it is of a much later date than that of the Schools of Shammai and Hillel (see page 49). The author, however, in a later number justifies the consistency of both statements by the fact that Nachmanides in quoting the Pirke d'R. Eliezer adds as follows: 'Yet the decree of Phineas was not widely accepted until Daniel reconfirmed it and later Shammai and Hillel; only then did it find general acceptance.'

[5] Yeb. 79*a*.

[6] See also San. 21*a*, in regard to the incident of Amnon and Tamar (2 Sam. xiii).

[7] Rabbi and liturgical poet, best known for his commentary Tosefoth Yom-Tov on the Mishnah (1579–1654).

[8] Cf. Lev. xix, 19; Deut. xxii, 10.

[9] 2 Sam. xiii, 29.

[10] The forbidden copulation of heterogeneous animals (Lev. xix, 19).

gezerah enacted during Joshua's time,[1] although nothing about it is mentioned in the Book of Joshua.

SOLOMON instituted a *gezerah* by which the hands (in their ordinary condition) are assumed to be unclean.[2] He also promulgated a *gezerah* restricting the removal on the Sabbath of objects out of the house into the alley[3] or from one alley into another; yet in order to facilitate such transportation he enacted the law of *Erub*.[4] This is what the SeMaG says on this point: 'Biblically it is lawful to move a burden from the house into the courtyard or from the courtyard into the alley on the Sabbath day; but King Solomon and his Beth-Din detected an erroneous impression amongst the people who thought that since the house and the yard were different domains, and since there is no restriction against the removal of things from one to the other, the removal of objects need not be regarded as falling within the category of work, and so it was lawful to move things even from a private into a public domain. Hence the *gezerah* by which the removal of an object from the house into the alley or into the courtyard was forbidden except by an *Erub*.[5]

Thus we see that, in order to prevent the removal of things from a private into a public domain, Solomon prohibited it even from the house into the courtyard or from the courtyard into the alley.

This institution of *Erub* is regarded on the one hand as a *gezerah* (i.e. a restrictive measure) and on the other as a *Takkanah* (i.e a reform for public welfare). Solomon also formulated the *gezerah* against marriage with relatives in secondary grades (of the forbidden degrees).[6]

[1] See note 8, p. 39.
[2] Thus rendering invalid קדשים, lit. holy things, generally animal offerings. The קדשים are divided into three categories, holy, less holy, and most holy. Later authorities, such as the schools of Shammai and Hillel, extended this law also to *Terumah*, Heave-offering.
[3] The מבוי was a rectangular space with courtyards opening into it on three of its sides, the fourth side opening on to the public road. If there is a semblance of a doorway on its fourth side, the courtyards and the alley are regarded as a single private domain in so far as movements on the Sabbath are concerned.
[4] Lit. commingling, i.e. the fusion of the Sabbath limits. This is effected either by connecting the two parts by a single rod or wire placed across the open space or by a pole placed at one of its sides. There are another two categories of Eruvim: (1) *Eruvei hatzeroth*, where the inhabitants of various courtyards combine by each contributing towards a meal which is placed in a room accessible to all; (2) *Eruvei Techumin* made for people who intend proceeding on the Sabbath beyond the standard radius of 2,000 cubits from the city boundaries. This is effected by placing some food on the Friday at the end of that radius, by which act he marks the transfer of his abode to that point for the Sabbath day, thus gaining permission to walk another Sabbath day's journey from that point in any direction.
[5] See also Maimonides, Yad, Erubin.
[6] The Talmud Yeb. 21a gives 24 cases of these, such as father's mother, mother's mother, father's father's mother, etc.

JEHOSHAPHAT,[1] King of Judah, and the Sanhedrin during his reign prohibited the entrance of a Tebul Yom[2] into the camp of the Levites.[3] According to Tosaphot[4] the Rabbis had it by tradition that the aforesaid *gezerah* was enacted on the occasion when Jehoshaphat stood in the congregation of Judah and Jerusalem in the New Court.

HEZEKIAH,[5] King of Judah, and his Court declared all contact with idols as rendering unclean. Tosaphoth[6] with reference to the Talmudical statement 'Hezekiah declared a leap year because of uncleanness' make the suggestion that his uncleanness was due to contact with idols,[7] and although the law[8] was only of rabbinic origin, it had already come into force during the reign of Hezekiah. See Sab. 83a where it is stated that the uncleanness conveyed by idols is only a rabbinic ruling, notwithstanding its deduction from the verse[9] 'Thou shalt cast them away like a monstrous thing; thou shalt say unto it 'Get thee hence!', yet it must be assumed that it was known to the Rabbis by tradition that although according to the Torah idols do not convey uncleanness by being carried, the restriction was instituted in the time of Hezekiah and Isaiah.

The PROPHETS who went into the Babylonian captivity established the following fast days—the third of (the seventh month) Tishri and the tenth of (the tenth month) Tebeth, the seventeenth (of the fourth month) Tammuz, and the ninth of (the fifth month) Ab[10] in commemoration of the sad events that had befallen the nation on those days. When the Temple was restored these fasts ceased to be obligatory, but on its second destruction they were re-established.[11]

DANIEL prohibited oil of the heathen for food purposes.[12]

EZRA issued a *gezerah* concerning the Levites, depriving them of their right to tithes.[13]

---

[1] See 2 Chron XIX, 6–7.

[2] Lit. one immersed on the same day, i.e. an unclean person who has duly undergone Tevilah, immersion, but who is not deemed fully clean until after sunset.

[3] See Pes. 92a, Yeb. 7b. The camp of the Priests and Levites covered the area from the Temple mount to the Temple court. Prior to that *gezerah* the restriction was confined to the Temple court and to a further space called the *Camp of the Divine Majesty* (see sources ad. loc.).

[4] Zeb. 32b.

[5] 2 Kings XVIII.

[6] On San. 12a s.v. שעיבר.

[7] They refer to Rashi, ad loc, who explicitly states that the uncleanness was caused by the contact Hezekiah had with idols during the reign of Ahaz his father.

[8] i.e. that idols render unclean.

[9] Is. XXX, 22.

[10] See Zech. VIII, 19.

[11] R.H. 18b.

[12] Ab. Zarah 36a.

[13] There is no express statement in Scripture to this effect, but the Rabbis, according

NEHEMIAH the son of Hachaliah instituted the *gezerah* against the handling of utensils on the Sabbath day.[1] This Mishnah,[2] the Gemara states, was taught in the days of Nehemiah b Hachaliah: First they (the Rabbis) permitted their handling,[3] then forbade them, and then again permitted them.[4] Also from explicit statements in Scripture it would appear that it was Nehemiah who prohibited business transactions on the Sabbath day, for it is written: 'There dwelt men of Tyre also therein which brought fish and all manner of ware, and sold on the Sabbath unto the children of Judah and in Jerusalem. Then I contended with the nobles of Judah and said unto them 'What evil thing is this that ye do and profane the Sabbath day!'[5] Hence although the prohibition of commercial transactions on the Sabbath day is actually only rabbinic, made for fear that one might have to write something,[6] it appears that it had already been promulgated before that time, for he noticed a state of laxity with regard to the Scriptural Sabbath laws, and therefore found it necessary to forbid even such acts of work as sh'buth.[7] See *Sefer Hamitzvoth*, by Ramban, end of Root II. See also Rashi ad *Betza* 27b, s.v. אין פוסקין who states that commercial transactions are forbidden on the Sabbath day, as intimated in Nehemiah XIII, 15. Pick[8] in his glosses observes that Rashi elsewhere (Betza 37a s.v. ומשום), quotes as source for the said prohibition the verse 'and thou shalt honour him by

---

to Rashi ad Hul. 131b; Mak. 23b; Yeb. 86b found it hinted at, in the passage: (Neh. x, 39), 'And the priest, the son of Aaron, shall be with the Levites when they (the Levites) take the tithes,' i.e. the priests assumed the right to the tithes, as well as in the passage following that 'For the children of Levi shall bring, etc., unto the chambers where are the priests that minister'. According to Tosaphoth (Yeb. 36b, s.v. מפני) the source is to be traced to Malachi III, 10, 'Bring ye all the tithes into the storehouse' identified with the chambers referred to above into which Ezra ordered all the tithes to be gathered. Indeed Malachi himself is identified with Ezra by R. Joshua b. Korha (Meg. 15a). The reason that prompted Ezra to formulate such a drastic measure against the Levites was that they did not answer the summons to return from Babylon to Palestine, as is stated in Ezra VIII, 15, 'and I viewed the people and priests and found there none of the sons of Levi.'

[1] Shab. 123b.

[2] Forbidding the handling of all utensils except those mentioned in the Mishnah Shab. XVII, 4.

[3] In cases where the object itself is needed.

[4] In cases where the space they occupy is needed. Nehemiah, however, had prohibited them, as in his statement (Neh. XIII, 15): 'In these days saw I in Judah some treading wine presses on the Sabbath.'

[5] Neh. XIII, 16.

[6] Which is a Scriptural transgression, and included in the thirty-nine Acts of Work (Shab. 7, 2).

[7] An act of work not mentioned in the Torah nor even in Tradition, but forbidden by enactment of the Rabbis, as being out of harmony with the sanctity of the day.

[8] Rabbi Isaiah Pick, eminent Talmudical critic and authority (1729–1799). He is credited with having laid the foundation for a critical study of the text of the Talmud by suggesting numerous textual corrections.

the Sabbath, etc., not finding thine own pleasure nor speaking thine own words.'[1]

Again the prohibition of intermarriage with all gentiles, besides those of the seven nations of the land of Canaan, is, according to the view advanced by R. Jacob Asheri in his Tur, and by other Rabbis following him, of Rabbinic origin only (see Tur Eben ha-Ezer 16). Here Nehemiah's arbitrary measures against intermarriage need elucidation, for it is stated[2]:— 'I saw Jews that had married wives of Ashdod, of Ammon, and of Moab, and I contended with them and cursed them and smote certain of them, and plucked off their hair.' At first sight it is difficult to see why he regarded their conduct as rebellious, as they were not of the seven nations of the land of Canaan and, consequently, had not transgressed a Scriptural law by intermarrying with them. It must, therefore, be assumed that the extension of the *gezerah* to all Gentiles was already in force[3] in his time. Or again it may be that since he (Nehemiah) concludes his words of rebuke with 'did not Solomon, King of Israel, sin by these things?'[4] this was the main offence of Solomon even if he had proselytized these women, since during his and his father's reign the admission of proselytes was prohibited. See Yad, *Issure Biah* 13, 16, in which Maimonides advances the view that the *gezerah* against admitting proselytes was in force during the days of Solomon and even as far back as the days of Samson, lest they (the proselytes) should abandon their idolatry merely to join the more favourably situated people of Israel.

HAGGAI, ZECHARIAH, MALACHI, ZERUBBABEL, and JEHOSHUA the HIGH PRIEST, convened an assembly of the people by the blowing of three hundred shofars by three hundred priests and banned to the Israelites the eating of Cuthean[5] bread (Tanhuma Vayeshev, quoted in Tosafoth, Hullin 4*a*).[6]

---

[1] Is. LVIII, 13, which shows that the *Gezerah* did not emanate from Ezra. Weiss, *Dor.* I, p. 53, suggests for the purpose of reconciling Rashi's contradictory views, that in the former statement he refers to *Yom-tov*, to which the allusion is made in Ezra; while in the latter he refers to *Sabbath*, to which Isaiah alludes. The fact, however, remains, that Rashi in his former statement refers to both *Sabbath* and *Yom-tov*, and so the suggestion is unfounded.

[2] Neh. XIII, 2, 3.

[3] Weiss, *Dor.* I, 52, in rejecting this suggestion is more than unfair to our author, since he omitted the most relevant point of the suggestion, viz. that this view is advanced only on the strength of the opinion held by the *Tur* and others.

[4] Neh. XIII, 26.

[5] The Cutheans or Samaritans were a sect which originated with the settlers brought by the King of Assyria from Cutha after he had captured Samaria. At first they were more or less heathen, but by stages they adopted certain forms of Judaism. See J. E. IX, 507.

[6] s.v. מצת; it is quoted from Pirke d. Rabbi Eliezer and not from Midrash Tanhuma.

The Rabbis also testified on the authority of Haggai (Yeb. 16a) that no proselytes may be accepted from the Tadmorites.[1] We also find that in the days of Haggai the Rabbinic authorities imposed the laws of uncleanness[2] upon liquids. See Rashi (Pes. 17a, s.v. אישתבוש) who states: 'We may also infer that Haggai had tested the knowledge of the priests in the Rabbinic law of uncleanness (as well as the Scriptural) since the law of uncleanness upon liquids was already in force in his time, and he lived in the time of the Great Assembly.' See also Rashi, ibid., 14a, s.v. מקרא to the effect that the conveyance of uncleanness from food to food is not inferred from Scripture, and that the question of Haggai (Haggai 11, 12) 'If one bear holy flesh in the skirt of his garment, etc.'[3] is based on Rabbinic law only.

[1] Tadmor, identified with Palmyra in the Syrian desert. 1 Kings IX, 18, 2 Chron. VIII, 4. Opinions on this point differ, see Tos. (l.c.) s.v. רבי יוחנן. The original testimony however on behalf of Haggai was that proselytes from Tadmorites may be accepted.

[2] The question whether the law that liquids convey and contract uncleanness is Scriptural or Rabbinic is a subject of discussion in Talmud. Pes. 14, 17, 18. See also Yad, Aboth Hatumah, 81. The author, however, does not enter into this divergence of opinion, he quotes only Rashi as an authoritative source for this purpose.

[3] The passage continues 'and with his skirt do touch bread or pottage or wine or oil or any meat, shall it be holy?' Hence we assume that he was testing the priests on the Rabbinic law of uncleanness imposed upon liquids.

CHAPTER VIII

ENACTMENTS PROMULGATED BY
POST-BIBLICAL AUTHORITIES

SOME institutions which are well-established with us to-day originate with the Princes, the heads of the Sanhedrin and chiefs of the *Batei-Din*[1] in whom the Torah had vested the authority to introduce any enactment which has the object of furthering the welfare of the people and of erecting fences round the law as well as to mend breaches. These originate either with the Princes and Chiefs of Courts of the days of the Second Temple, or with those who functioned after the destruction of the Temple by Titus, all of whom aimed at protecting the Torah from infringement. The men of the Great Assembly after their return from the Babylonian exile, when they began to rebuild the House of God, put forth great efforts to erect a steadfast house in the midst of the people by preserving the commandments of the Torah, in order that the precious gift might never again be forgotten from our mouths and those of our children, and they fitly expressed that endeavour in their saying 'make a fence about the Torah'.[2] One can see how through their safeguarding measures they strove to implant in our hearts a fervent love both for the Torah and for the people, and how they succeeded in preserving the Torah by means of those 'fences', as I have already pointed out in my brief introduction to the *Mishpat Hahoraha*.[3]

Indeed, if we cast a penetrating glance at our history, we find that while the generation of the first Commonwealth, when those fences and safeguards had not yet been instituted, forgot the Torah and its precepts, so much so that they became oblivious even of the laws of the Festivals, as it is mentioned in Ezra,[4] the teachers of the second Commonwealth remained faithful to the Torah by virtue of their adherence to the above-mentioned instruction from the Great Assembly to build a fence about the law; thus although we have been subject to constant persecutions and wandering for almost 1,800 years, we have, thank God, only increased our knowledge of His Torah, so that it adorns us like a crown. And the thousands of works written by Israel's great scholars show that the efforts which those sages made on our behalf have not been in vain. Indeed, that is all due to the fences and

---

[1] The plural of Beth-Din.
[2] *Aboth* 1, 1, i.e. enact measures by which the Torah will be safeguarded.
[3] See page 36, note 6.
[4] See Neh. VIII, 13–14. The rabbis attributed the books of Nehemiah and Ezra to one author. See Sanhedrin 93b, 'The book of Ezra was composed by Nehemiah.'

safeguards which were instituted by the men of the Great Assembly whose work was continued by the Princes throughout the years of the Second Temple. And even after the destruction of the Temple our teachers did not cease in their endeavours to achieve their precious goal—of setting up a reliable Torah structure, to serve as some compensation for the great afflictions which had befallen them as a result of the loss of their independence, land, and heritage. For they knew that the bonds of the Torah would be able to keep them together.

JOHANAN, the High Priest,[1] who followed Simon the Just (Yad, Ma'aser 9, 1) decreed that not all are trustworthy in regard to tithes, only reliable people,[2] and that produce purchased from the *Am-Haaretz*[3] is generally assumed not to have been tithed[4] (Sot. 48a).

Johanan furthermore decreed that no hammer should strike in Jerusalem on *Hol ha-moed*.[5] Although work was permissible in cases where loss was involved, still, where the work was too conspicuous or noisy, he thought it proper to forbid it. (Sot. 48a.)

YOSE B. YOEZER of Zeredah and YOSE B. JOHANAN of Jerusalem[6] both

---

[1] Traditions concerning his identity vary. Frequently quoted in the Mishnah under this name (*Sot.* 9, 10; M. Sh. 5, 15; *Par.* 3, 5; *Yad.* 4, 6), one source identifies him as the father of Matthatias the Hasmonean (Halpern, *Seder Hadoroth*); while other sources identify him with the latter's grandson, the son of Simon Maccabeus, known as John Hyrcanus (136 B.C.). Whether, however, he is to be identified with Jannaeus who after ministering as High Priest for eighty years, became a Sadducee (Ber 29a), and openly declared his opposition to the Pharisees (Kid. 66a), is again a subject of divergent opinion among Talmudical teachers (cf. Ber 29a). See also *Kesef Mishneh* on *Yad*, Maa'ser 9, 1. According to the latter, Maimonides purposely treats Simon the Just as the predecessor of Johanan, thus indicating that he is not Jannaeus the Sadducee. Hence, Simon the Just (concerning whom there is no definite tradition) might be identified with Simon Maccabeus (see J. E. XI, p. 352), Johanan's father, and Jannaeus the Sadducee with Johanan's son (see *Otzar Israel* IV, p. 130).
[2] Scrupulous observers of the Torah are trusted to have observed the laws concerning tithes.
[3] Lit. people of the land, i.e. uninstructed and careless about religious duties.
[4] Their produce is styled *demai*, open to doubt as regard tithes. His ruling, however, applied only to the Terumah (heave offering) of the tithe, because of the associated penalty of Kareth (lit. cutting off—i.e. death by divine agency), and not to the first tithe which belongs to the Levite, or the poor man's tithe, since in such cases the onus rests upon those who buy the produce to prove that the dealer has not already tithed the produce which they have sold. The basis for this attitude towards the Levites must have been identical with that of *Ezra* (see page 42, note 13) who punished them for not returning with him to Jerusalem from Babylon.
[5] Intermediate days of the feast. Only such work as served the needs of the festival and which, if postponed until after the feast, would involve loss or damage, was permissible during these semi-festival days.
[6] Both were the successors of Antigonus of Soko of the last Tannaitic generation. They began a period known in Jewish history as that of the '*Zugoth*' (duumvirates). The first-mentioned, it is said, occupied the office of Nasi, the President of the Sanhedrin, and the other, that of *Ab Beth-Din*, Father (Chief) of the Court of Law. See Peah 2, 6, Hag, 2, 2. The rise of these types of appointment is a subject of study

of the pre-Hasmonean period declared all heathen countries and all glass utensils unclean.[1] (Shab. 14b.)

The BETH-DIN of the Hasmoneans[2] prohibited 'Yihud'[3] (privacy) with a female heathen (A. Zarah 36b). They also forbade the teaching to one's son of the Greek wisdom[4] and the rearing of swine[5] (Sot. 49b) v. Tos. B. K. 82b.[6]

SIMON B. SHETAH[7] issued a ruling that metal vessels[8] are susceptible to uncleanness[9] (Sab. 14b).

HILLEL and SHAMAI[10] defined the hands[11] as contracting uncleanness[12] of the second grade such as to render also the Terumah (Heave offering)

amongst the historians. Cf. Frankel *Darkhei ha-Mishnah*, p. 32; Weiss, *Dor*, i, 103, and the Introduction to *Sanhedrin*, Soncino edition 1935, page 12; see 2 Chronicles, XIX, 11, tor the early practice of appointing a dual authority.

[1] The former *gezerah* was prompted by the fear of undetected graves being scattered there; while the latter aimed at preventing Jews from settling outside the Holy Land, and endeavoured to restrict the use of glass utensils manufactured abroad. For the value of this assumption, see Weiss, *Dor* i, 105. A more likely reason is the fact that glassware is akin to earthenware.

[2] The 'religious council' during their rule.

[3] A similar *gezerah* against privacy with a Jewess had been enacted by the Court of David (see page 40, note 6).

[4] The phrase does not refer to the Greek language, but rather to the sophistry of the ancient Greeks. This *gezerah* is believed to have originated in the days of Hyrkanus II and Aristobulus, both members of the Hasmonean dynasty, who contended with each other, and a betrayal is said to have occurred which was facilitated by a knowledge of the said art. See B.K. 82b.

[5] This *gezerah* probably followed the incident recorded in B.K. 82b, that during a siege of the city arising out of civil strife an arrangement had nevertheless been made for a regular supply of cattle for the regular daily *tamid* sacrifice (cf. Numb. XXVIII, 2–4), but one day a swine had been sent up instead.

[6] s.v. ואסור where it is contended that the *gezerah* regarding the teaching of Greek wisdom had been made during the time of the war against Titus, and so is of a much later period.

[7] President of the Sanhedrin during the reigns of Alexander Janneaus and of his successor Queen Alexandra whose brother he was (b. 139 B.C.). He enjoyed great influence, and succeeded in making the Pharisee party dominant in Israel.

[8] The text erroneously states 'glass vessels'.

[9] Actually, his *gezerah* pertained not to original vessels, which are susceptible to uncleanness according to Biblical law, but to broken vessels put into shape again, for according to Biblical law metal vessels once broken are no longer susceptible to uncleanness.

[10] Founders of schools, called after them, in the time of King Herod.

[11] In their ordinary condition, i.e. unless they are washed with the intention of rendering them clean, they are assumed to contract second-grade uncleanness, which makes the Terumah unfit.

[12] Uncleanness is classified into degrees. The highest and first origin of uncleanness is the human corpse designated אבי אבות הטומאה (father of fathers of uncleanness). By the conveyance of the uncleanness from one article to another, the uncleanness in the second case is a stage below the degree of that by which it was defined. There are no more than four degrees, beginning with one who has had contact with a 'father of uncleanness'. See *Yad, Aboth Hatumoth*.

invalid.[1] Similarly they decreed that repaired metal vessels should return to their former state of uncleanness (see Shab. 15*a* and *b*, and *Yad*, Kelim 1, 5).[2]

The elders of the schools of Hillel and Shamai decreed *gezeroth* on thirty-six matters. On eighteen of these they were in agreement, and on the other eighteen they differed, the Shamaites out-voting the Hillelites, hence the total of thirty-six *gezeroth*. And so we read in Jer. Sab. 1, 4: 'These[3] are among the halachoth which the sages formulated in the upper room of Hananiah b Hezekiah b Gurion.[4] We were taught that they issued eighteen *gezeroth* in agreement, that over another eighteen *gezeroth* they had indeed differed, but that the Shamaites had out-voted the Hillelites, while over another eighteen matters they remained at variance.' The *halachoth* to which both agreed are enumerated by Maimonides in his Commentary on the Mishnah, Sab. 1, 4, as follows: 'Eight of the Halachoth (says Maimonides) are made up of the four halachoth with reference to the poor man who stands outside, and the other four halachoth with reference to the householder who is inside.'[5]

(9) The *halacha* that one shall not seat oneself before the barber close to the time of the Mincha prayer[6] (on Friday afternoons).

(10) That one may not enter the baths during the said time;

(11) Nor a tannery;

(12) Nor engage in a law suit;

---

[1] The *gezerah* to impose second grade uncleanness upon the hands was originally decreed by King Solomon upon 'hallowed things' which are susceptible even to a higher degree of uncleanness than is *Terumah*. Hillel and Shamai, however, imposed it upon Terumah as well (see Sab. 15*a*).

[2] In the text the author ascribes Simon b Shetah's *gezerah* on metal vessels also to Hillel and Shamai. I can however find no source for it.

[3] i.e. the rulings contained in the *Mishnah*, with reference to searching clothes and reading on Friday evenings.

[4] Other authorities read Garon, the head of the School of Shamai, also mentioned in connection with the restoration of the Book of Ezekiel to its place in the Canon (see Sab. 13*b*). According to Graetz the upper room belonged to Eliezer b Hanania b Hezekiah, see Heb. ed. ii, p. 95.

[5] The poor man and the householder are used by the Mishnah in illustration of the case where two persons are involved in the act of removing a burden from one domain to another on the Shabbat. Wherever the act is not completed by one person alone, one is culpable only according to Rabbinic injunction. S. P. Rabinowitz, in his footnote on Graetz Heb. ed. ii, pp. 90–95, enlarges at great length on the identity of Eliezer and on the details of the last eighteen gezeroth. They are enumerated by R. Simeon b. Yohai in the Jerushalmi Sab. ad loc. as a rigorous political measure to intensify the separateness between the Jewish people and their neighbours. In this connection he assumes R. Eliezer to be a political leader.

[6] The afternoon prayer may begin shortly after mid-day and continue until late in the afternoon.

(13) Nor begin to eat a meal.[1]

(14) That a tailor shall not go out with his needle on Friday near nightfall.[2]

(15) Nor shall the scribe go out with his pen (at that time).

(16) That a man should not search his clothes (for fleas, etc.).

(17) Nor shall he read by lamplight.[3]

(18) That a man and his wife both suffering from fluxes[4] may not dine together.[5] On these eighteen *halachoth* they had agreed when meeting in the upper room mentioned, whilst over another eighteen *halachoth* they had differed, but as the Shamaites had a majority on their side they were accepted in perpetuity in accordance with the Biblical law to incline after the many.[6]

They are as follows:—

(1) He that eats food which has contracted first-grade uncleanness[7] (is unclean).

(2) He who eats food which has contracted second-grade uncleanness.

(3) He that drinks liquids that are unclean.

(4) He that immerses his head and the greater part of his body in drawn water.[8]

(5) A clean person on whose head and greater part of the body had fallen three logs of drawn water.

(6) That *Terumah* (heave-offering) which has come into contact with Scrolls of Scripture[9] (renders unclean).

---

[1] These injunctions apply also to weekdays, lest one should forget about the Mincha service. They are set forth in the second Mishnah of Shab. chap. i in view of their similarity to those of the third Mishnah.

[2] Lest he forget and carry it with him on the Sabbath day from one domain to another. The verse Ex. xvi, 29 (lit. let no man *go out*), is interpreted by the rabbis as 'let no man carry' (see Tos. Erub. 17b, s.v. לאו cit. Rashi, s.v. לוקין.

[3] Both these injunctions apply to Friday night, lest through forgetfulness one should trim the lamp to make it give a brighter light, of course, is forbidden on the Sabbath.

[4] See Lev. xv, 1–15, 25–30.

[5] Lest it lead to intimacy.

[6] Ex. xxiii, 2.

[7] All these, according to rabbinic ruling, render the heave-offering unfit, but not unclean, i.e. the *Terumah* does not defile other *Terumah* by contact. For the source of these rules, see Zeb. 5, 12; Shab. 13b.

[8] i.e. water that has been standing in any kind of receptacle. This measure was taken as a precaution against the misunderstanding which had found place in the minds of the people. Having taken their ritual ablutions by immersion in pools of filthy water the necessity arose for washing with clean standing water from vessels, and so the idea became current that it was not the pool which rendered the person clean, but the drawn water with which one washed subsequently. Hence for the decree that immersion in three *logs* of such water over the head and body convey uncleanness of the second grade, see ibid.

[9] This rabbinical rule was prompted by the custom of storing *Terumah* together

(7) As do the hands.[1]

Similarly (8) He who has contact with (unclean) food, and (9) he that puts vessels under the waterspout.[2]

(10) That all movable objects convey uncleanness if they are as thick as an ox-goad.[3]

Similarly (11) he who cuts grapes for the wine-press.[4]

(12) That which grows from *Terumah* is to be considered *Terumah*.[5]

(13) If darkness overtakes a man while on a journey (on the eve of Sabbath) he should give his purse in the keeping of a Gentile.[6]

(14) That Cuthean bread[7] is forbidden

and likewise (15) the oil of the heathens

and (16) the wine of the heathens are unclean.

(17) That *Yihud* (privacy) with the daughters of the heathens be prohibited.

(18) That even day-old infants of heathens are susceptible to uncleanness by reason of a flux.

Here we have thirty-six *gezeroth* enacted by the elders of the Schools of Shamai and Hillel. (So far Maimonides.)

Besides these *gezeroth* there are others which belong here, such as the permissibility, or otherwise, of laying on hands on the heads of the sacrifices on feast-days,[8] over which controversy had gone on between our ancestral teachers for a period of two hundred years,[9] without an approved decision (Hag. 7*b*). Ultimately, however, the matter was

with the scrolls, with the result that the latter were destroyed by the mice attracted by the cereals, hence the rule that scrolls render *Terumah* invalid by contact having contracted second-grade uncleanness thereby.

[1] In their ordinary condition, see p. 48, n. 11.

[2] That feeds the immersion pool. The water gathered in the vessels is regarded as drawn water.

[3] If they have overshadowed something unclean, they transfer the uncleanness to a man or a vessel simultaneously overshadowed (see Ohol. 16, 1).

[4] The juice pressed out from them during handling renders them susceptible to uncleanness.

[5] Even in the case of the seed disintegrating after the inception of growth.

[6] Even though the Gentile, in this case, is his messenger. In consideration, however, of the fact that his perturbation over the safety of his money might induce him to carry it himself, the said adjustment was made. Where there is no Gentile companion the purse is to be hidden on the ass.

[7] See p. 44, nn. 5, 6.

[8] The laying on of hands on the head of the offerings is a Biblical law (Lev. III, 2). It was done with pressure and, according to the Shamaite school, was a transgression against the rabbinically ordained rule of *Shebuth* (see note 2, p. 59). The Hillelites, however, maintained that *Shebuth* did not apply to the sacrificial service in the Temple (see Betza 2, 4; Hag. 2, 2, for the difference between peace-offering, freewill offering, and whole-burnt offering in connection with this ruling).

[9] This controversy had arisen between the President of the Sanhedrin and the *Ab Beth-Din* (Chief of the Court), Jose b Yoezer and Jose b Johanan, and continued down to Shamai and Hillel (Hag.16*a*; Tosefta Hag. ii, 8; Jer. Hag. ii, 7).

decided in the time of the School of Shamai and Hillel, when the majority voted to permit it, the vote having been secured by the efforts of Baba b Buti[1] (see Betza 20b) but the long controversy over this *gezerah* remains an historical fact.

The Shamaites and the Hillelites also issued a *gezerah* against the ploughing of a field planted with trees in the sixth year (the eve of the Sabbatical year), but from two different dates, according to the one party (Shamaite) from the Passover and, according to the other, from Pentecost (see M. Katan 3b).

According to R. Meir, the Shamaites outnumbered the Hillelites over the *halachah* that water gathered in vessels placed under the waterspout invalidates the *mikvah*.[2] (See *Mikvaoth* 4, 1, and Shab. 16b.) Similarly they decreed that daughters of the Cutheans are menstruant from birth (ib.)

They also enacted that scrolls of scripture render the hands unclean just as they had enacted that they render the *Terumah* unclean. On this, Maimonides on Yadaim 3, 2, advances the view that it was with the object of buttressing the latter *gezerah*, which was one of the eighteen *gezeroth*, that they added the former to them. According to this view the *gezerah* that scrolls of scripture also render the hands unclean belonged also to the eighteen *gezeroth* above mentioned. See also a reference to this in Tos. Yom Tob., Yadaim 3, 2.

In this connection enumeration must also be made of the four *halachoth*, quoted in Eduyoth 5, 6, as coming from Akabia b Mahalalel.[3] The rabbis put his ruling to the vote and, as those in their favour were outnumbered, they consequently annulled them, for had he enforced them in practice, they would have declared him a *Zaken Mamre*[4] (see San. 88a).

One of these four *halachoth*[5] deals with hair which had fallen out of

---

[1] Though himself a disciple of Shamai (cf. Betza 20a), he endeavoured to prevent his teacher's opinion from becoming a rule, because he was convinced of the correctness of Hillel's opposing opinion.

[2] As does any other drawn water.

[3] Talmudic teacher of the second Tannaitic generation (1–2 C.). He is portrayed as a fearless and persistent upholder of some *halachoth* which were handed to him by his learned predecessors. (Ed. v, 6.)

[4] Rebellious elder, a teacher who rebels against the decisions of the recognized court.

[5] The following are the remaining three:—(a) in connection with leprosy, where a bright spot has appeared in which the hair turned white (a symptom of uncleanness, Lev. XIII, 3), and afterwards the spot has disappeared, the hair remaining, and consequently a second spot has appeared, Akabia declared the leper unclean despite the fact that the hair had not turned white in the second spot, and that the first spot had disappeared; (b) that yellowish fluid issuing from a menstruant woman renders her unclean, just as fluid of a red colour (Lev. XV, 19); (c) that the water of bitterness (Numb. V, 12, 31) is not to be administered to a proselyte or a freed bondwoman.

a blemished firstling while still alive, and had been preserved until after the beast was slaughtered. In Akabia's opinion, just as its flesh becomes permissible (as food) after slaughter, so also the hair (which had fallen out previously). The rabbis, however, prohibited it by a majority vote, as a precautionary measure against those who might, on that account, purposely retain the firstling indefinitely to allow its hair to grow.[1]

The Rabbis of the eighty years,[2] namely, R. Gamaliel Ha-Zaken[3] and his son, R. Simeon b Gamaliel,[4] the father of R. Gamaliel of Jabneh,[5] issued a *gezerah* (to put *Terumah* which has had contact with the air of the heathen countries into the suspended category[6] (Sab. 15b).

R. Johanan b. Zakkai,[7] the Nasi of Israel after R. Simeon b. Gamaliel had been martyred, decreed that a court should not be set up to declare a family of doubtful stock[8] clean,[9] or a widow who has married into such a family[10] (Keth. 14a). He also decreed that the eating of new produce is prohibited throughout the whole day of waving[11] (R.H. 30b), and, although in the Gemara (ibid.) this is included amongst his nine *takkanoth* yet, since a prohibition resulted from it, it is to be included amongst the *gezeroth*.

During the war of Vespasian[12] a *gezerah* was enacted against the wearing of crowns by bridegrooms and the use of a wedding drum (Sot. 49a and b), and as Ben Zakkai was the nasi during that time, it was he who besought the Emperor Vespasian to restore the Gamaliel

---

[1] And thus lead to another breach of the law, namely by shearing it off whilst alive (Deut. IV, 19).

[2] i.e. who lived during the eighty years before the destruction of Jerusalem by Titus.

[3] The grandson of Hillel.

[4] One of the ten martyrs who suffered martyrdom at the hands of Romans for defying his edict not to instruct their pupils in the Law. (See Aboth. d. R. N. Ch. 38.) Weiss (Dor I, p. 191) questions this.

[5] Who followed Ben Zakkai in his great work of the restoration of Judaism.

[6] The *gezerah* mentioned before as issued by the Joses concerned the soil itself as rendering the *Terumah* which it touched liable to burning, whilst according to this *gezerah*, since it puts the *Terumah* under suspicion of uncleanness, the latter is neither liable to be burned, not may it be eaten.

[7] The most important Tanna in the last decade of the second Temple, founder and President of the Academy of Jabneh.

[8] Lit. 'dough', used here in the sense of an admixture, e.g. a family suspected of being mixed with doubtful stock (see Kidd. 4, 1).

[9] i.e. legitimate.

[10] In order to render other members of such a family eligible for marriage with a priest.

[11] i.e. the day in which the Omer is offered, namely the second day of Passover. Prior to this *gezerah* the fresh produce was permitted soon after the Omer offering had taken place.

[12] Titus Flavius Vespasianus (A.D. 69–79); while he was in Judaea engaged as general in the war against the Jews, tidings reached him of his proclamation as emperor. He was the father of Titus, the destroyer of Jerusalem.

family to its former position (Git. 56b), and we might therefore ascribe the said two *gezeroth* to him. See Tos. to B.K. 82b, s.v. ואסור (with reference to the *gezeroth* on the teaching of Greek wisdom)[1] where it is observed that while in Sot. 49 that *gezerah* is attributed to the time of Titus, in B.K. it is ascribed to the Hasmonean Courts (which were much earlier).

After the destruction of the second Temple, the rabbis of that generation, namely Ben Zakkai and Eliezer b Hyrkanus, Joshua b. Hanania, Eleazar b Azariah and R. Gamaliel of Jabneh issued the following enactments (as a mark of mourning), namely that buildings should not be built and painted like royal palaces and that they should leave a square ell by the entrance bare of dressing. At the same time they enacted that in setting the table for meals some part of the table should be left empty of dishes. Also that women, when applying cosmetics, should leave some minor part of the body, such as part of temple, untouched; again, the bridegroom was to place cinders on his head during the marriage ceremony. (B.B. 60b; *Yad, Taanith* 5, 13.)

Several other *gezeroth* are enumerated in the Gemara which were enacted at that time (Taan. 26b), namely that when Ab[2] comes round, festivities are to be reduced, or that it is forbidden to cut the hair, wash the clothes, or to put on an ironed garment in the week in which the 9th of Ab falls. Again, that no wine may be drunk or meat eaten at the last meal before the beginning of the fast.[3] Other restrictions to be observed on the 9th of Ab, additional to those applying to the ordinary fast days, were that the fast must begin on the preceding evening, and the prohibition of the use of cosmetics and of the wearing of (leather) shoes, and of the study of the Torah. All such *gezeroth* were undoubtedly issued after the destruction of the second Temple, with the concurrence of R. Johanan b Zakkai, R. Eleazer b Azariah, R. Eliezer b Hyrkanos, and R. Joshua.

On the very day that R. Eleazar b Azariah was appointed Nasi and head of the College, in succession to R. Gamaliel of Jabneh,[4] the Rabbis of the time, namely R. Gamaliel, R. Joshua, R. Eleazar b Azariah and R. Akiba, decided by vote that (the Scrolls of) Ecclesiastes and the Song of Songs should render the hands unclean[5] (*Yadaim* 3, 5).

---

[1] See note 4, p. 48.

[2] The fifth month of the Biblical calendar. The Temple was destroyed by fire on the ninth day of this month.

[3] Although in the Mishnah text the prohibition applies to the eve of the fast, i.e. the 8th of Ab, it is understood to refer only to the last meal.

[4] See Ber. 28. R. Gamaliel was temporarily deposed from the Patriarchate, and R.Eleazar, though still very young, was elevated to the office by the choice of his colleagues mentioned in the text.

[5] See p. 52 for the background of such *gezeroth*.

On that day, too, they decided by vote that a footbath is susceptible of *medras*[1] uncleanness. The enactment quoted in the context to the effect that the (Scrolls of the) Aramaic portions of Ezra and Daniel[2] render the hands unclean was probably also issued on that day after a vote taken by the same authorities.

R. *Gamaliel of Jabneh* and his court invalidated the *Shechitah* carried out by a Cuthean (Samaritan)—(Hulin 5*b*).

Rabbenu ha-Kadosh[3] and his court decreed that a disciple must not give decisions unless he has received authority from his teacher to do so. (Sanhedrin 5*b*.)

---

[1] Lit. 'place of pressure of treading', i.e. it puts it amongst the objects fit to sit or lie upon without affecting its proper function (see Lev. xii, 2; xv, 2–25). Thus a footbath of from a half *kab* (two *logs*) to nine *kabs* capacity which becomes cracked is susceptible to uncleanness on account of Medras, i.e. it can be sat in and none can interfere and say 'Go away and let the object be put to its proper use!' (see Kelim 20, 3).

[2] i.e. Ezra iv, 8, to vii, 18; Dan. ii, 4, to vi, 28.

[3] 'Our holy rabbi,' referring to R. Judah ha Nasi (the prince) the redactor of the Mishnah (135–220 C.E.). He is generally called 'Rabbi', the master *par excellence*, but occasionally 'Rabbenu' (Yeb. 75*a*; Men. 32*b*). The epithet 'ha-Kadosh' (holy), is sometimes given him on account of his singularly pure moral life (cf. Sab. 118*b*).

CHAPTER IX

ENACTMENTS HANDED DOWN FROM ANONYMOUS AUTHORITIES

T HE Mishnah cites several *gezeroth* the authorship of which is undefined, and which apparently did not encounter any opposition, nor can the time be ascertained when the vote and decision on them were taken. Undoubtedly, however, they must all have come down directly from the *Great Beth-Din*[1] and have been unanimously approved. The Rabbis had probably found them necessary as precautions whereby to safeguard the laws of the Torah themselves against easy transgression, consequently they adopted them by unanimous vote so that they became established for all time. Especially in later generations there could have arisen no opposition, as no *Beth-Din* has power to oppose decisions of preceding authorities, unless it excels them in wisdom and in numbers.[2] I intend dealing with some of those *gezeroth* in their Mishnaic order, but I shall have to do so briefly, merely touching upon the principal *gezeroth* and not upon those which grew out of them like branches from a tree, because these latter are too numerous to be dealt with in detail.

The Rabbis, as a precautionary measure against transgression, limited to midnight the end of the time for the reading of the *Shema*[3] and the consumption of the offerings,[4] even though the duty extends over the whole night; and this ruling was not opposed by anyone. The Mishnah in question (Ber. 1, 1) reads as follows: 'Why did the sages say "until midnight"?' In order to keep people far from transgression'. It appears that this 'fence' was set up by a court before the time of R. Gamaliel,[5] for he (R. Gamaliel) explains that the reason for the time limitation of the Rabbis (before him) had been to establish a preventive measure.

---

[1] Of the Hall of Hewn Stones. The Central body representing the highest civil and religious authority of the Jews. The Talmudical teachers speak of such a body as existing ever since the time of Moses (R.H. 29).

[2] See Ed. 1, 5.

[3] Lit. 'Hear, O Israel', the first word of a group of three passages from Scripture (Deut. vi, 4–9; xi, 13–21; Num. xv, 37–41) which is to be recited daily.

[4] Such as are to be consumed the same day and the following night (Lev. vii, 15). For the observance of Sabbath and Festivals, the Scriptural reckoning of the time begins with the preceding evening (see Lev. xxiii, 32, also Gen. i, 5); however, in reckoning the time limit for the consumption of offerings, the evening follows the day (see Hul. 83a; Tem. 14a).

[5] Since this is quoted in the Mishnah on the authority of R. Gamaliel.

Peah[1] should not be less than a sixtieth part of the harvest, although the Torah prescribed no quantity for it. The Rabbis, however, issued the said ruling fixing it at a sixtieth as a minimum, and there is no evidence that it was opposed by any authority (Peah 1, 2).

The rabbis also enacted that the law of *Kilaim*[2] should also apply even in the case of ten mattresses laid one on the other, lest a single thread should adhere to one's body.[3]

It appears to have been a generally accepted ruling, meeting with no opposition, and is anonymously quoted (in Yoma 69a) by R. Joshua b Levi in the words 'but the rabbis have forbidden one to do so' (see Betza 16a).

Similarly they enacted the other additional restrictions in connection with *Kilaim*, such as those upon cloth which was not spun or woven as, for example, felted stuff of diverse kinds, or an edging of wool on a linen garment. In accordance with the Torah, these do not come under the law of *Kilaim*, and are only rabbinically ordained *gezeroth*. Indeed, the Rabbis (Niddah 61b) definitely stated that, in the Torah, *Kilaim* is defined by the word *Shaatnez*,[4] and thus the above additional restrictions come under a rabbinic law, yet these *gezeroth* have been accepted without opposition.

The prohibition of traffic in ritually forbidden things is rabbinic only, having been inspired by the fear that through possessing them one might involuntarily eat them (Shebiith 7, 3).

Benefit from *Kilaim* in the vineyard is forbidden outside the land of Israel[5] by the words of the Soferim.[6] Since they are strictly forbidden in the land, the prohibition was extended to apply also abroad (Orlah 3, 9). To these preventive rulings we find no opposition.

---

[1] Lit. 'corner of the field'. According to Biblical law (Lev. xix, 9, 23; xxii, 22) the owner is to leave part of his crop unreaped for the benefit of the poor.

[2] Lit. 'two kinds'. The Torah (Lev. xix, 19; Deut. xxii, 9–11) forbids various types of 'diverse kinds' to be put together. In our case Kilaim refers to two kinds of woven material, woollen and linen, mingled together.

[3] The Scriptural law forbids the weaving of any cloth made of Kilaim. As a preventive measure, however, the rabbis ruled that one may not lie on a mattress of Kilaim, or even on a heap of mattresses of which one is made of Kilaim.

[4] The word Sha'atnez (Lev. xix, 19) is taken to be an abbreviation of three words: שׁוֹעַ (pressed), טוּי (woven), נוּז (twisted together). This is one example of the Midrashic way of making play with the consonants of such unusual words as שַׁעַטְנֵז.

[5] This ruling applies only to Kilaim of the vineyard, because benefit from it in the land of Israel is Biblically forbidden, and not to Kilaim of seeds, benefit from which even in the land of Israel is permissible. (See Bartenura ad. loc).

[6] Scribes, lit. 'people who know to write'. The Rabbis explain the term as from מִסְפָּר (number) to count, i.e. those who count the letters of the Torah or count and classify its laws. In the time of Ezra the designation was applied to the body of teachers who interpreted the Law, who began with Ezra and ended with Simon the Just.

All the *gezeroth* which the rabbis issued in connection with restrictions of work on Sabbath, for the safeguarding of the Torah laws, are referred to anonymously and as without opposition. They have come down to us from former generations, undoubtedly from the men of the Great Assembly which originated in the time of Nehemiah b Hachaliah. I shall refer to them briefly.

There is the prohibition of setting cooked food[1] on a double stove heated with wood or peat, lest the owner might be tempted to stir up the coals under the ashes (Sab. 3, 1). There is a similar prohibition of covering up hot food with something which might generate fresh heat (ibid. 4, 1).

Again, there is the prohibition for a woman to go out with certain ornaments on the Sabbath day lest she might forget and take them off to show them to her friend[2] (ibid. 6, 1, 59b). There is the prohibition of removing bread from the oven on the Sabbath[3] lest it might induce one to leave the bread in the oven until its baking is finished (Sab. 4a).

One must not use in the Sabbath lamp oil which is not drawn up by the wick, because the owner might be tempted to bend the wick towards the oil. Wicks of bad material must not be used for a similar reason, or because the wick might go out and so disturb the peace of the house (Shabb. 25b).

There is again the restriction against carrying an object from a private or public domain into a Karm'lith.[4]

Again, there is the prohibition of making or untying a knot which does not remain fast, but the making of which requires skilled hands,

---

[1] i.e. before the beginning of the Sabbath so that it remains there throughout the Sabbath.

[2] Becoming thus guilty of the transgression of carrying things on the Sabbath from one domain to another, or of carrying it on the public highway a distance of more than four cubits.

[3] The ruling here concerns a case where one has involuntarily stuck a loaf to the wall of an oven on the Sabbath. It was forbidden to detach it on the Sabbath day, *before it was baked*, as a preventive measure, as mentioned in the text (Sab. 4a).

[4] An area which can be classified neither as private nor public ground. It is a marked-off plot in a public thoroughfare (Shabb. 6b, Orach Haim 345, 14). Of the word כרמלית there are different interpretations, see Yer. Shabb. 5b from כרמל Lev. II, 14, a compound word denoting something which is רך soft, soothing (Ps. LV, 22), and yet מל, from מלילה dry ear of corn (Deut. XXIII, 26), see Tos. Men. 64b, s.v. משום The transposition of כר into רך is not uncommon in Hebrew. It is the same as that of שמלה into שלמה. Rashi, Lev. II, 14, does not accept the said transposition. He holds that כרמל is compounded of כר and מל viz., the husk is yet full. Kohut, in his *Aruch Completum*, therefore is inclined towards the interpretation of Maimonides, *Commentary on the Mishnah*, Shab 1, 1, that the word כרמלית is a shorter form of כארמלית a place undefined, like the status of a woman who is neither married nor a virgin, e.g. a widow.

or even of one the making of which does not need skill but is one that remains fast.[1]

Things medicinal are forbidden to be taken or applied on Sabbath lest the person concerned might be tempted to grind up drugs.[2]

Again, to prevent Sabbath observance being taken lightly, the Rabbis forbade on the grounds of *Shebuth* (Sabbath rest) the procuring by a Jew of a non-Jew to do work for him.[3]

They forbade the administration of justice, the concluding of a betrothal or the performance of *Halitza*[4] or the contracting of levirate marriage (on the Sabbath), lest one might be led to write some document.[5]

Similarly the transaction of a loan on the Sabbath is forbidden lest it should involve writing.[6]

Again, it is not permitted to clap the hands or dance (on the Sabbath) lest it should lead to the repair of musical instruments.[7]

One may not swim in water (on the Sabbath), lest it should involve the repair of the swimmer's vessel.[8]

Again, it is not permissible to replace a plaster on a wound (on the Sabbath) since it may lead the man in question to rub its ingredients with his hand.[9]

Again, one may not cut off a wart from his finger even with the hand, lest he should use a surgical instrument to do so.[10]

One may not dedicate anything[11] or make a vow of valuation[12] or

---

[1] Biblically, knotting or unknotting is forbidden only where it fulfils both conditions, viz., has durability and also involves the work of skilled hands (Sab. 112a).

[2] This law applies to a case when one is suffering some pain but otherwise is in good health (*Yad*, Sabbath 21, 20; *Orah Haim*, 328, 1).

[3] This rabbinically ordained restriction to ensure the complete observance of the Sabbath is quoted in several places in Talmud (Sab. 110a, *Yad*, Sab. 6, 1).

[4] The ritual prescribed for the man who refuses to carry out the levirate marriage (see Deut. xxv).

[5] Mishna Betza 5, 2. Orah Haim 339, 4.

[6] Sab. 23a. The basis of this restrictive measure was that the usual period for payment given in the case of a loan without any specific term for payment is 30 days (Makk. 3b). It was, therefore, anticipated that he might be led to note the date in his diary.

[7] Nor is one permitted any other movement which accompanies music, lest it should involve the offence referred to in the text (Betza 5, 2).

[8] Used for practice (ibid.).

[9] So involving a Biblical violation of the Sabbath law (*Erub.* 120b; *Yad.* Sab. 10, 6).

[10] Which would then make him guilty of a Biblically forbidden violation of the day (*Erub.* 103a, *Yad.* Sab. 9, 8; *Orach Haim*, 340, 2).

[11] For the sanctuary.

[12] Dedicating to the sanctuary a man's valuation, according to his age, as described in Lev. xxvii, 1–7. The details of these *halachoth* are dealt with in Tractate Arakhin.

devote[1] anything (on the Sabbath) since in doing so one appears to be doing business.[2]

Numerous acts again were forbidden on the Sabbath where there appears to be an endeavour to make some improvement.[3] The following are examples:—One may not set apart *Terumah* or *Tithes*.[4]

One may not immerse (unclean) vessels[5] on the Sabbath and Festivals, nor sprinkle the blood of sacrifices[6] on the Sabbath. One is not to cut a reed pipe[7] nor is one to rinse dishes or stew pots.[8] Similarly, the Rabbis prohibited a Sabbath journey exceeding 2,000 ells (paces) in any direction on Sabbaths and Festivals[9] lest it should lead the traveller to extend his journey beyond 12 miles, which was the tehum (limit) fixed by the Torah.[10]

Again, there is a *gezerah* that one may not examine accounts[11] on the Sabbath lest he should be led to make notes. Nor is the reading of a secular document permissible on that day lest he should be led to erase[12] part of it.

And there are several other such restrictions which come under the category of '*Shebuth*', and which, since they were seemingly opposed by no one, were issued by the great Beth-Din by common consent, except that regarding some of them doubts were raised as to whether they come under the category of *gezeroth* or not.

[1] Lit. doom—i.e. to declare things doomed or set apart to the Sanctuary as described in Lev. xxvii, 28.

[2] As in the case of a commercial transaction, one causes an object to be transferred from his possession into that of the sanctuary. Transactions in themselves are only rabbinically forbidden. v. *Yad*, Sab. 23, 12.

[3] And thus substantially change the status of the object in question.

[4] See Deut. xiv, 22.

[5] In a *Mikvah* made up of forty seahs (approximately 60 gallons) (see *A.Z.* 75b on Num. xxxi, 23).

[6] Sacrifices are not permitted to be offered on the Sabbath with the exception of the additional and continual daily Sabbath offerings and the Pascal offering (see Numb. xxviii, 2, 10, and Pes. 66a, 77a).

[7] I cannot trace the source of this *halachah*.

[8] Except when they are still needed on the same day (Shab. 118a, Orah Haim 328, 6).

[9] 2,000 cubits (of six handbreadths), the rabbinically ordained Sabbath day's journey (Erub 51a).

[10] Since the instruction by Moses (Ex. xvi, 29) 'let no man go out of his place on the Sabbath day' from which the law of Tehum is actually derived (Erub.51a) applies to the whole length and breadth of the Camp whose distance in all directions was 12 miles. It ought, however, to be added that the question whether that journey limit is enjoined by Biblical or rabbinical law is still a matter of dispute between the rabbinical authorities (see *Magid Mishnah* on *Yad* Shab. 27, 1). (Alfasi Erub. end of chap. i, and Tur Orach Haim 397.)

[11] Except where by so doing a religious cause benefits (Sab. 150a, Orach Haim 306, 6).

[12] See Sab. 116b, 149a; *Yad.* Sab. 24, 19.

Again one may not bake or stew on a festival[1] day (which falls on the eve of Sabbath) for the Sabbath day that follows, except by the use of an *Erub-Tavshillin*.[2]

Work which [is permissible on the Festival but] could quite well have been done on the eve of the Festival, such as reaping, grinding, threshing, etc., is not allowed to be done on the Festival day, lest this should lead to postponing all such work till the Festival day and, consequently, the whole day would be taken up with such kinds of work, denying one the time even to eat, and so mar the proper celebration of the feast.[3]

Again there is the prohibition of all manner of work[4] on the second day of the New Year.[5] It is not permissible to bake in a new baking oven because its first trial may possibly mar the festival joy.[6] One may not heat tiles white-hot to roast upon them nor may one oil them.[7]

One may not produce fire from wood, stone,[8] or water[9] (on festivals).

Here too belong the prohibitions of certain kinds of work on the days

---

[1] Cooking or baking on a Festival day which fell on the eve of the Sabbath is permitted only if it is intended solely for that day, and not if, from the outset, it is intended for the Sabbath. If, however, any food is left over, it is then the ruling that it is left over for the Sabbath (see Betza 2, 1).

[2] Lit. 'mixture of cooking', a dish which is prepared on the eve of the Festival day. By the formal beginning of the preparation of this dish before sunset of the Festival day, the cooking for the Sabbath may be continued after sunset, i.e. on the Festival day itself (see ibid.).

[3] See Tur Orach Hayim 495.

[4] Even such as is permissible on the second days of the other Festivals (see note below).

[5] Before the fixation of the calendar by calculation, the authorities of Jerusalem, when fixing it on the basis of the appearance of the new moon as testified to by witnesses, found it necessary, as a precaution, to add a second day to the Festivals for the outlying communities. And on the ground of the *Minhag* (tradition) of the fathers as one to be scrupulously observed, they extended its observance by the communities of the Diaspora even after the calendar was determined by calculation, and made its sanctity equal to that of the first day, except that, in some cases, such as the burial of the dead, it has the status of an ordinary working day. The second day of the New Year, however, even in such cases, is not excepted, as its two days were legally regarded as forming one (Betza 4*b*; R.H. 4, 4).

[6] See Betza 34*a*.

[7] To polish them, since by doing so, one appears to be working for the increase of their usefulness.

[8] By rubbing the wood or the stone together.

[9] This is possible in the tropical countries if a glass vessel filled with water is placed in a hot sun. The glass, it is stated, could kindle a wick brought into contact with it. The reasons for these restrictions were that, in such cases, one might bring into being something which was not already in existence, which is ruled to be forbidden on a festival day.

of *Hol ha-moed*[1] according to the view that those prohibitions are only rabbinically ordained.[2]

A man should not induce[3] others to mourn over his dead[4] nor make lamentation over him within the thirty days before a Feast.[5]

Before the eating of unconsecrated food or the second tithe[6] or the *Terumah*, only the ablution of the hands is necessary[7]; for hallowed things[8] immersion is required.[9] As regards the sin-offering water,[10] if a man's hands are unclean his whole body will suffer from uncleanness, an immersion will then be required and ablution will not suffice. For the various grades of uncleanness in relation to hallowed things, *Terumah* and the sin-offering water, see Hagiga, end of Chap. II.

Here, again, belong the ruling that, if a man immerses himself without the intention of purification, it is as though he had not immersed himself at all, and if he had the immersion with the intention of handling *Terumah*, he is forbidden to handle hallowed things, and that a mourner,[11] and he whose atonement is still incomplete,[12] need immersion for hallowed things. Utensils that have been completed in a state of cleanness[13] require immersion before being used for hallowed things.[14]

On the case of the flesh of *Tarefah*[15] that has been ritually slaughtered, even though, according to the Torah, the slaughtering renders the beast

[1] See n. 2, p. 47, for the status of these days.

[2] The rabbinic authorities are at variance, with regard to the origin of these restrictions. See Karo on *Tur Orach Haim* 530 and *Magen Abraham* on the *Shulchan Aruch* ad loc.

[3] Lit. stir up by hired mourners, i.e. people who, by their eloquence, stir up the family of the deceased to mourning (see M.K. 1, 5).

[4] i.e. for one who has been dead for some time.

[5] The expenses incurred for these professional mourners deprive one of the means necessary for the proper celebration of the Feast.

[6] The tithe of the first, second, fourth and fifth years of the seven-year cycle. The owner must either bring it to Jerusalem and consume it there, or redeem it (Deut. XIV, 22).

[7] By pouring a quarter-log or more of water over them (see Yadaim 1).

[8] Things devoted to the Altar, which are consumed only within the Temple Court.

[9] In a pool containing 40 seahs.

[10] This water requires conditions of cleanness a grade higher even than is required for hallowed things (see Num. XIX, 17–18). See Rashi Hagigah 18*b* s.v. ולחטאה.

[11] For his near-of-kin, e.g. father, mother, brother, sister, son, daughter, or wife, until after the burial, even if he has not contracted uncleanness.

[12] Those who suffered from uncleanness but have passed the prescribed time and have duly had the immersion, and have passed the sunset yet have not so far brought the prescribed offerings.

[13] Kept free by the maker (a חבר, associate) (the opposite of Am ha-Aretz) from uncleanness.

[14] For they were still exposed to the risk of becoming unclean at the time of completion from an issue of an Am ha-Aretz such as spittle or flux (Hagigah 3, 2).

[15] See n. 7, p. 17.

clean yet, according to the *Soferim*[1], if the flesh touches hallowed things, it renders them unclean.[2]

Regulations of a higher degree of strictness were applied to the Priest who was appointed to burn the heifer.[3]

The *Great Beth-Din* enacted that the water or the ashes of the sin-offering[4] should not be carried over a river in a ship.[5]

They enacted that the barber's scissors and the carpenter's plane are to be treated as wholes[6] with regard to their susceptibility of uncleanness, but not with regard to sprinkling[7] even while in use.

And they enacted regulations of a higher grade of stringency in connection with the cleanness required for those engaged upon the heifer. One who, so far as hallowed things are concerned, is clean, even if actually (at the time) serving at the Altar, is nevertheless regarded as unclean in relation to the heifer. He is sprinkled, too, all the seven days[8] owing to this great stringency, and the vessels used in connection with this expiation offering were to be of stone,[9] the sprinkling during these seven days was to be done by one who had never contracted uncleanness[10] from a dead body, and there were several other such regulations of a higher degree of strictness prescribed in connection with the heifer proceedings.

There are eleven cases in all where greater stringency is applied to hallowed things, and all of them cases of *gezeroth*.[11] There are five such cases in connection with clothes[12] and numerous others in connection

[1] Mishnah Hullin 4, 4; *Yad*, Aboth-ha-Tumah 2, 6.

[2] Because they assigned a higher grade to hallowed things, Hullin 73*a*, 123*b*; *Yad*, ibid. 2, 8.

[3] Referring to the red heifer whose ashes mingled with those of cedarwood, hyssop and scarlet were to be sprinkled on those who had been defiled through contact with the dead. For a full description of the heifer itself and of the several other meticulous proceedings, see Num. xix, 1, and Parah 3.

[4] After having been consecrated.

[5] As a precautionary measure against a recorded incident of part of a corpse being found attached to the bottom of the transporting vessel (Parah 9, 6).

[6] i.e. one of their parts (when they are fastened together) suffering from uncleanness renders the other unclean.

[7] The sprinkling of one part does not exempt the other (Sab. 48*b*, 58*b*). Tosefta Kelim B.M. 3, 2.

[8] The seven days during which he was kept away from his home (Parah 3, 1), i.e. as required for hallowed things.

[9] Which is not susceptible of uncleanness. This law refers to the seven days during which he was away from his home. See Rashi, Sukkah 37*a*, s.v. נפסל and *Yad*, Parah, 2, 1–7.

[10] See Mishnah Parah, 3, 2, and *Yad*, Parah, 2, 7, for illustrations how this is possible, i.e. how one can avoid uncleanness.

[11] As enumerated in Mishnah Hagigah 3, 1, and according to the view of Rabba b Abahu, Hagigah 22*a*.

[12] Where, in some cases, greater stringency is applied with regard to their susceptibility to uncleanness (see Mishnah Hagigah 2, 7).

with the laws of immersion,[1] all of them *gezeroth*, and there is the
enactment that all utensils found in market-places, or the streets, require
immersion and sprinkling.[2] A similar *gezerah* was issued regarding all
spittle[3] found in such places.

There was no opposition to any of these *gezeroth*, which is clear proof
that they all emanated from the *Great Beth-Din*, whether by unanimous
approval or by a majority vote leading to the decision.

Again, there is the prohibition of eating *hametz*[4] on the eve of Passover
from a certain time[5] prescribed by the Rabbis,[6] lest one should be led
into the error of eating it during hours when it is Biblically forbidden.[7]

There is, again, the rabbinically ordained duty to search for *hametz*[8]
though, according to the Torah, its nullification alone would suffice.[9]
Again, abstention from work from mid-day on the eve of Passover[10] and
from the eating of *matzah* on the eve of Passover from mid-day until the
evening.[11]

Yet, again, there is the abstention from food altogether on the eve
of the Passover, from about the time of the afternoon offering[12] until
nightfall.[13]

Again, the requirement that the kneading of the *matzah* must be
done with water that has stood overnight,[14] and that it must not be done

[1] Ibid.

[2] Lest they should be unclean, see Tohoroth 4, 5. This did not apply to the ruling
in the Jerushalmi Shekalim 8, 2, with reference to the city of Jerusalem which was
treated differently in this respect.

[3] Which might possibly have originated from a man who had a flux, see Kel. 1, 3.

[4] Anything made from or containing leaven.

[5] Lit. hours, yet not actually hours but portions of time, varying according to the
season. The rabbis, for ritual purposes, divided each day into twelve portions (see
Maimonides'commentary on Mishnah Ber. 1, 1, Glosses of Rema 233, 1).

[6] According to R. Meir, five hours, and on the sixth it is to be burned; according
to R. Judah, four hours and on the fifth it is to be left in suspense, neither being eaten
or burnt. The point of difference is over the question as to how long one is subject to
error (Mishnah Pes. 1, 4, *Yad*, Hametz u-Matzah 1, 9).

[7] That *hametz* from the sixth hour onwards is Biblically forbidden is inferred from
scriptural passages already quoted (see page 6, note 5).

[8] Mishnah, Pes. 1, 1. *Yad*, Hametz u-Matzah 2, 3. Rashi Pes. 4*b*, s.v. בביטול.

[9] Deduced from the fact that in the passage Ex. XIII, 15, the word תשביתו
(cessation) is used and not תאכלו (consumption).

[10] Lest it should absorb one's mind to the extent of diverting attention from the
many other duties of the day, such as the removal of the *hametz*, the offering of the
Pascal lamb, and preparation for the evening ceremonial (see Rashi, Mishnah Pes.
4, 1).

[11] In order that one might with more relish eat the Biblically ordained *matzah* in the
evening. R. Levi in Jer. Pes. 10, 1, severely censures the offender.

[12] Numb. XXVIII, 1–8.

[13] The reason is somewhat similar to that mentioned in note 11.

[14] One of the conditions for preventing the leavening of the dough is the use of
cold water, and by the keeping of the water in a cool place overnight its temperature
will be lower than if it were drawn in the morning from the well. See Pes. 42*a*.

with water heated either by fire or even by the sun, lest it should hasten the leavening of the dough.

The prohibition of a common priest marrying a woman who has performed *halitzah*[1] was not by a Scriptural law, but ordained by the *Soferim*, to indicate the higher degree of the priestly stock.[2]

In accordance with the ordinance of the Torah, the daughter of an Israelite, even when only betrothed to a priest, is permitted to eat *Terumah*[3]; the Rabbis, however, declared it forbidden by a *gezerah*, lest she should offer her brothers and sisters some of *Terumah* wine. The second *Mishnah*[4] on the subject made the restriction still more stringent, so that even where the time[5] has fully passed and she has not married, she may still not eat *Terumah* until after she has entered the bridal chamber, lest the husband should find some blemish in her.[6]

A woman who has noticed a bloodstain (on her body) is menstrually unclean to her husband, by virtue of an ordinance of the *Soferim* only, though, in accordance with the Torah she is regarded as clean, since the woman is liable to menstrual impurity, unless she has been conscious of the discharge.[7]

By an ordinance of the *Soferim*, again, the levir[8] must not consummate the levirate union[9] before declaring his sister-in-law betrothed to him.[10]

Again, the betrothed is to continue to be forbidden to her husband until she has entered the bridal chamber.[11]

If a woman whose husband has gone oversea marries again after receiving information of her husband's death, and then the former husband returns to her, a child from the first husband (conceived after his return, but born) before the second husband has divorced her, is

[1] See note 10, p. 6.
[2] Yeb. 24a; Kidd, 78a, *Yad*, Issure Biah 17, 7.
[3] Such is the view of Ula in Keth. 57b who derives it from the verse (Lev. XXII, 11) 'If the priest obtain any soul as property with his money' on the ground that the betrothed woman, too, is an acquisition obtained by this money (Mishnah Kidd 1, 1).
[4] That of R. Judah the Prince. An earlier Mishnah is mentioned several times, Sanh. 3, 4, Eduy. 7, 2. Either there was a complete set of the Mishnayoth or the משנה ראשונה refers only to another ruling on the point referred to above. See Danby, *The Mishnah*, pp. 21 and 24, note 4, and *Sanh.*, Soncino edition, p. 163, note 7.
[5] Usually granted for preparation for marriage—twelve months for a virgin, and thirty days for a widow. (Keth. 5, 2.)
[6] And reconsider his marriage.
[7] See Mishnah Niddah 8, 3, the Midrashic deduction from Lev. xv, 19, 'And if a woman have an issue, and her issue in her flesh be blood,' i.e. not a stain but blood. *Yad*, Issure Biah 9, 1, 2.
[8] Brother-in-law.
[9] As required by Deut. xxv, 5.
[10] See Yeb. 52a; *Yad*, Yibum 2, 1.
[11] Keth 4, 5; *Yad*, Ishuth 10, 1.

also regarded as illegitimate, by virtue of an ordinance of the *Soferim*.[1]

A suspected bastard[2] is also forbidden to enter the congregation, to maintain the higher standard of purity in the stocks. There is again the prohibition of *Yihud* (privacy) with an unmarried woman,[3] the ruling not to leave cattle in the precincts (of the inns) of the heathen,[4] and that of expounding the forbidden degrees of relationship before three persons.[5]

There is, again, the prohibition of the cheese of the heathen because they make it with rennet from the stomach of a *nevelah*.[6]

The vessels of fat and blood[7] are forbidden by an ordinance of the *Soferim* only,[8] lest from them one might be led to the eating of the actual fat and blood itself.

Similarly the milk of a beast after it has been slaughtered is forbidden along with meat only by an ordinance of the *Soferim*, and not by Scripture.[9]

Several forbidden things in the way of food cannot be neutralized by mixture with larger quantities, either in view of their importance[10] or of their being things which might in other ways or times become permissible,[11] or as pieces given as marks of distinction[12]; also living creatures.[13] In connection with these *halachoth* we do not find any opposition recorded, yet, in accordance with the *Torah*, these things

[1] See Mishnah Yeb. 10, 1, and *Yad*, Gerushin 10, 7.

[2] Biblically only one ascertained to be a bastard is under the restriction of entering the congregation, but not one merely under suspicion (see Kid. 73*a* on Deut. XIII, 1–3).

[3] See above where it is referred to as one of the *gezeroth* of David.

[4] Since they were suspected of bestiality (Mishnah A. Zarah 2, 1).

[5] Lest two of these three should be lax in their attention, and so there should be some wrong impressions regarding some of the relations not specifically mentioned in the Torah. This restrictive measure was particularly found necessary in connection with sexual relationship. Mishnah Hagigah 2, 1, and Gemara Hagigah 11*b*.

[6] A beast not ritually slaughtered (cf. A. Zarah 2, 5).

[7] See Hul. 93*a*. There are five such strings or veins, three are of fat and two of blood.

[8] Cf. Hul. 92*b* for the *halachah* of R. Shesheth on behalf of R. Asi. I can, however, find no source for the reason advanced by the author. See also Yad, M. Asuroth 7, 16.

[9] Once slaughtered, the beast no longer qualifies for the appellation mother. Thus it does not correspond with the Biblical restriction of Ex. XXIII, 19, 'in its mother's milk'. Rashi Hul. 113*b*, s.v. ולא בחלב.

[10] See Orlah 3, 7, Y.D. 110, Par I.

[11] See Betza 3*b*.

[12] See Hul. 100*a*. That forbidden articles of food when mixed with larger quantities can be neutralized and again made permissible is a Talmudic law definitely laid down in Hul. 99 and 100, Zeb. 72, Betza 7, 1. Y.D. 109, 1. The exceptions however to this ruling are these referred above in the text.

[13] See Y.D. 110, 2, where this ruling is subject to a difference of opinion.

should become neutralized by mixture with larger quantities. They have been placed under this stringent law only by rabbis.

An unmarried man is restricted by them from teaching children, because the mothers may bring their children to the school,[1] nor may a woman be a teacher of children because of the fear that women may attract the fathers to come there.

By an ordinance of the *Soferim* the cancellation of loans in the sabbatical year[2] is in force at all times and in all lands (outside the land of Israel).[3]

Although all beasts from the eighth day onwards become fit for the altar[4] yet according to the *Soferim* they are not to be used until after the 30th day.[5]

Again (according to the *Soferim*), seven days before the Day of Atonement, the High Priest was to be separated from his family lest his wife should suffer from menstrual impurity,[6] and (the sin-offering water) was to be sprinkled upon him on the third and seventh day,[7] owing to his elevated position, lest he might have contracted a corpse uncleanness (unwittingly).[8] On the night (preceding) the Day of Atonement he was to be kept awake, lest he should get nocturnal pollution.[9]

Again, the stone that seals a grave, and also its buttressing stone, convey uncleanness, the one by its contact, and the other by its overshadowing, by the ordinance of the *Soferim* alone.[10]

Again, by their ordinance, uncleanness is conveyed by any contact with a person suffering from seven-day uncleanness.[11]

---

[1] And possibly be the cause of indecent conduct.

[2] Deut. xv, 1 ff.

[3] See Kiddushin 38*b*. According to the Torah, the law should be in force only during the time when the law of Jubilee is observed. The rabbis, however, connected it with the land sabbatical laws. See *Yad*, Shemita V'Yovel 9, 2, 3.

[4] Lev. xxii, 27. See *Yad*, Issure Mizbeah 3, 8.

[5] The details of this provision are given in M. Parah 1, 4. *Yad*, M. ha-Korbanoth 1, 12. See Tos. Yom-Tov, ad loc., which says that it is based on common sense reasoning only. This rule does not apply to free-will offerings.

[6] And convey the uncleanness to him (see Maimonides, *Commentary on Mishnah*, Yoma 1, 1.

[7] The author here mistakenly says 'on all seven days'. The translation follows the Mishnah text. The procedure of sprinkling on all seven days was applied to the Priest who carried out the burning of the red heifer (see Yoma 8*a*).

[8] Yoma 8*a*; *Yad*, Yom ha-Kippurim 1, 4.

[9] Yoma 1, 4, 7; *Yad*, ibid., 1, 7.

[10] See Nazir 7, 3, Ohol. 2, 4. The author in maintaining that it is only a rabbinically ordained *halachah* follows evidently the decision of Maimonides, *Yad*, Tumath Meth 2, 15, whose ruling, however, is contested by RabaD (Abraham ḥ David of Posquières, 1125–1198, French Talmudic commentator), in his glosses, who bases his view on the Midrashic deduction quoted in Hul. 72*a*.

[11] See Bekhoroth 45*a*.

On the strength of a *gezerah*, the three additional members in a woman's body[1] convey uncleanness by contact and carrying, but not by overshadowing.

The uncleanness attaching to a grave area[2] rests on rabbinical ordinance only.[3]

Men or utensils, by touching or carrying or overshadowing land belonging to heathen,[4] or a grave area,[5] or mingled blood,[6] or the stone that seals a grave and its buttressing stone,[7] become Aboth ha-Tumah[8] according to the injunction of the *Soferim*.

The dwellings of the heathen are unclean even if the man has had no woman with him. This was a measure to guard one against entering a heathen dwelling when there is a woman in it, because the heathen bury abortions in their houses.[9]

A *gezerah* was also issued concerning all coffins with a space of one cubic handbreadth[10] that one should not jump over them, lest that liberty be taken over such that have not a space of a cubic handbreadth.[11]

A projecting wall which projects over the door of the house, whatever its depth[12], gives passage into the house to any uncleanness that it overshadows, by an injunction of the Soferim.[13]

If a man or a woman that have had a flux, or a menstruant, or a woman after childbirth, or a leper, have died, such convey uncleanness by carrying until the flesh has decayed away. This was a rabbinic measure, lest such should have only appeared to die.[14]

---

[1] Connected with her sexual organs.

[2] A piece of land wherein there is either an undiscoverable grave (Ohol. 17, 5) or a grave that has been ploughed up (ibid. 17, 1).

[3] *Yad*, Tumath Meth 10, 1; also Maimonides, *Commentary on Mishnah*, Ohol. 17, 3; Ber. 19*b*.

[4] See Shab 14*b*, where it is mentioned as a *gezerah* of the Joses.

[5] See note 2 above.

[6] Ohol. 3, 5. Blood from a corpse from which an eighth part of a *log* had issued before death and an eighth part after death.

[7] See note above.

[8] See note 12, p. 48.

[9] Ohol. 18, 7.

[10] Space of a cubic handbreadth between the corpse and lid acts as a screen over the uncleanness (see Ohol. 3, 7). Without such a space the uncleanness passes through upwards (see Ohol. 7, 1.)

[11] See Ber. 19*b*.

[12] Even where it is less than a handbreadth.

[13] *Yad*, Tumath Meth 17, 1.

[14] The point of difference between a corpse and one of these cases is that the corpse lying on a heavy stone would not convey its uncleanness to the things beneath it, whereas the other would. The rabbinically ordained measure was that the ruling applied in their case when alive should also be applied after their death. Nid. 10, 4, 69*b*; *Yad*, Mishkav u'Moshav 6, 4.

The rule not to have intercourse with a woman on the day of her period is a rabbinically ordained law.[1] Similarly it is the man's duty to keep apart from her for one '*onah*'[2] before her period.

If in the course of travail the unborn child has stretched forth a limb outside, and then withdrawn it, the mother becomes, by rabbinical law, unclean, just as she would as a result of childbirth.[3]

What is slaughtered by a heathen is carrion,[4] and it conveys uncleanness by carrying, according to rabbinic ordinance.[5]

Libation wine[6] conveys uncleanness like any other thing which is offered on a heathen altar[7]; but that the latter conveys uncleanness is only a rabbinical law as explained before.[8]

Other heathen wine[9] conveys uncleanness of a lesser degree to food and liquids, whilst libation wine definitely conveys uncleanness of a more stringent nature to man and utensils, even by such a quantity as a *ke-zait*.[10]

The law that liquids convey uncleanness to other objects is also rabbinical.[11] It was ordained as a safeguard against liquids that have had contact with a man or a woman with a flux.[12]

According to the written law, immersion is not invalidated by interposition[13] in a case where the greater part of one's body is involved[14] and the person is not particular, nor where the smaller part of one's body is involved, and the person is particular,[15] but it is only the Rabbis who have deemed it 'interposition' in the case of a small part of the body of one who is particular; and similarly in the case of the greater

[1] Nidda 15a; *Yad*, Mishkav u'Moshav 3, 9. Since the rule requiring a woman to examine herself on the day of her period is only a rabbinically ordained law.

[2] A Talmudic term for period, usually one half of the full day and night, i.e. twelve hours (Nid. 63b).

[3] According to the written law childbirth uncleanness comes as soon as the greater part of the child has emerged. According to this rabbinical ordinance, the days of her purification (Lev. XII, 4) do not begin until after the birth is completed (Nid. 28a).

[4] Like the flesh of a beast that has died of itself.

[5] Hul. 1, 1; *Yad*, Aboth ha-Tumoth 2, 10.

[6] Which a heathen has dedicated to his god to be poured out as a libation.

[7] A. Zar. 30b; *Yad*, Aboth ha-Tumoth 6, 8.

[8] In connection with what is slaughtered by a heathen.

[9] i.e. wine belonging to a heathen concerning which it is unknown whether it was dedicated to a deity or not. See p. 40 re *gezerah* of Phineas.

[10] A. Zar. ibid. and *Yad*, ibid.

[11] In accordance with the written law, liquids cannot convey uncleanness to other food. See Pes. 15b.

[12] In which case it becomes a 'father of uncleanness'. See Sab. 14b; *Yad*, Aboth ha-Tumoth 7, 2.

[13] If immersion is to be valid, no part of the body's surface may be left untouched by the water. Erub. 4b.

[14] By reason of clay or dirt having been stuck to it.

[15] About having even a particle of such clay or dirt stuck to his or her body.

part of the body of one who is not particular, they deemed it inter-position, thus guarding against the same case where one is particular.[1]

Again, the sages enacted that three *logs* of drawn water[2] falling into the immersion pool[3] renders it invalid; that the water of an immersion pool whose colour has changed[4] is unfit, both for immersion and for the washing of the hands (before meals), and water in which any work has been done is also rendered unfit for the washing of the hands.[5]

Because of six doubtful cases of uncleanness, *Terumah* must be burnt,[6] i.e. the *gezerah* was enacted because there may have been a grave area involved, or earth which may have come from a heathen land, or again, because of garments which may have belonged to an *Am-Haaretz*, or because of vessels which have been found (and which may not be clean), or by reason of spittle encountered by chance, or by reason of urine of an unclean man mingled with that of a beast, half and half.[7]

There are many things which the Rabbis have restricted on grounds of robbery, even where there was not real robbery involved, for example, they have forbidden the breeding of small cattle in the land of Israel, because it is the habit of such to stray into the fields of other owners (causing damage).[8] They have forbidden gambling with dice[9] and pigeon flying[10] and have prohibited the catching of doves in inhabited places, and the spreading of bird nets within a perimeter of four miles round an inhabited settlement.[11]

One who appropriates what has been caught in traps set for wild animals and birds is guilty of robbery, according to rabbinic ordinance. Similarly when a poor man beats the top of an olive tree, and another poor man takes the olives that have fallen beneath it, he is guilty of robbery, according to rabbinic injunction.[12]

---

[1] Erub. 4*b* and several other places in the Gemara.

[2] Water that has been standing in a vessel or in any kind of receptacle.

[3] Which is filled with genuine rain water, or water from a well (Mik. 2, 7).

[4] Either through its situation or by reason of something having fallen therein.

[5] Mik. 7, 3.

[6] The cases in question are, in themselves, of a doubtful nature. In reference to cases where there is a secondary doubt as to whether they even arise there is a dispute between the Rabbis and R. Jose (M. Tohor. 4, 5).

[7] i.e. even in a case of an equal intermingling where doubts are even more pronounced. (Shab. 15*b*, Ned. 33*b*).

[8] B.K. 7, 7.

[9] Dice-playing, a popular game of antiquity. The term dice, קוּבְיָא in Aramaic, is applied by the Rabbis indiscriminately to any form of gambling.

[10] Or pigeon training, also for gambling purposes. Although it cannot be considered as actual robbery, since the gambler does not obtain his gain by violence, the Rabbis nevertheless took the more serious view. See San. 25*b*.

[11] Since privately owned pigeons might be snared into the nets. B. Kamma 7, 7.

[12] Git. 5, 8.

Similarly one who draws off to his own property a swarm of bees, even if he merely prevents them from swarming towards their owner, is guilty of robbery.[1] The Rabbis, again, have forbidden Israelites to lend money to a heathen on usury[2] lest the Israelite should (by contact with him) come to copy his way of life.[3]

A shadow of usury (i.e. indirect usury) such as that paid prospectively or retrospectively is forbidden by rabbinical ordinance,[4] lest it should lead one on to lend on fixed or direct usury.

Ante-dated bonds[5] are invalidated to the extent that the creditor may not collect his debt from the debtor's pledged property, even from the later date (the time of transaction), lest he should be tempted to seize under that bond property which the debtor had transferred prior to the loan transaction.[6]

The duty of mourning for one's wife (married not betrothed) rests only upon rabbinical ordinance.[7]

A proselyte is forbidden to marry his mother or his sister by rabbinic law (that no proselyte might be able to assert that he had abandoned a higher grade of holiness for a lower one).[8]

Maimonides (Yad, Issure Biah 21), has compiled several safeguards and *gezeroth* enjoined by the Rabbis, concerning forbidden relations between the sexes, in order to prevent anything which might seem indecent.

All these *gezeroth* already mentioned, and others like them, were prompted by the obligation which rested on the Rabbis to guard the words of the Torah. They understood the ways of men, and so knew that, by reason of the stress of life, it was easy for people to forget and transgress the prohibition of the Torah. For example, commercial

---

[1] B.K. 10, 2.

[2] Biblically this was permissible, Deut. xxiii, 21.

[3] B.M. 71*a*.

[4] Illustrations of these are given in Mishnah B.M. 5, 10. If a man intends to borrow from another and he makes him a present, saying 'This may induce you to lend me money', this is prospective usury. If a man has borrowed from another and repaid it, and then sent him a present, saying 'This is to compensate you for the money which you could not use while I had it', this is retrospective usury.

[5] i.e. where the date given in the bond is before the date of transaction.

[6] See Shebiith 10, 5.

[7] This is according to the view of Maimonides, *Yad*, Abel 2, 1. It is, however, questioned by *Kesef Mishneh*, ad loc.

[8] On the basis of what was established by the Rabbis, viz., that after the proselytization he is like a newly born child, having severed thereby all his former ties, he would be permitted to have a marital relationship even with his mother or sister. In order, however, not to give an impression that there is some looseness in our laws in this respect, where even the heathen observed restrictions of that nature, the said *Gezerah* was enacted.

transactions such as buying and selling should be permissible on the Sabbath day,[1] according to the Torah, but were prohibited by them because one cannot avoid writing or making notes of accounts in such transactions, and it was almost a certainty to them that men would fall into transgression inadvertently. Similarly the prohibition of riding on a beast on the Sabbath was enjoined, because they were practically certain that it would result in the cutting of twigs.[2] And so many other *gezeroth* and *takkanoth* instituted by the Rabbis, where the apprehension involved, at first sight, appears to be remote and strange, were issued only after the rabbis had come into possession of the necessary facts, as is evidenced by the *takkanah* cited in Gittin 17a. They enjoined that the date be embodied in the divorce bill[3] lest he (the husband) might be induced to cover up (the unchastity of) his sister's daughter who might have committed adultery and save her from capital punishment, viz. by divorcing her and thus disclaiming her guilt on the ground that she had already been divorced[4] at the time. The Jerusalem Talmud Gittin[5] actually mentions such an occurrence, stating that it was from that time on that they began dating bills of divorce.

Again there is the *takkanah* ordained by Ezra that a woman must wear a *sinnar*[6] following upon an incident, quoted in Jer. Meg. 4, 1, where an ape had bestially assaulted a woman, so that from that time, the rabbis ordained that a woman must wear a *sinnar*, both front and back.

Similarly, the ruling that a man may not go out on the Sabbath with hob-nailed sandals (Sab. 6, 2) was ordained, as a result of a calamity brought about by such hob-nailed sandals in which many were killed (Sab. 60a).[7]

Likewise the prohibition to take the sin-offering water over a river in a boat was ordained because of what had once happened when a *ke-*

---

[1] See *Yad*, Sab. 23, 12.

[2] For the purpose of goading on the animal. Betza 36b.

[3] In bills of loan, the date was deemed necessary in order to mark the time from which the creditor is legally entitled to distrain for his debt on the debtor's pledged property, whereas in a divorce bill that provision seemed, at the outset, unnecessary.

[4] And in view of the fact that the bill is undated, it will be difficult to disprove it.

[5] Chap. iv, *hal.* 3.

[6] Sort of protective breech-cloth or petticoat. See B. Kama 82a.

[7] The tragedy occurred at a time of religious persecution, when a number of Jews faithful to their religious tenets hid themselves in caves to escape destruction, and decided that none should be allowed to leave, lest their hiding place be uncovered. One of them, wearing such sandals, left footprints which suggested that someone had left the cave. Fearing that they might be detected by the enemy, they became panic-stricken and surging towards the exit, killed one another in even greater numbers than the enemy might have done. Because the disaster occurred on a Sabbath day, the Rabbis prohibited the wearing of hob-nailed sandals on that day.

zait[1] of a corpse was found stuck in the bottom of the boat on which
sin-offering water was being carried (Hagigah 23*a*).

Again, the decision by Rab[2] to forbid meat which had not been
under observation was also due to an incident. A man had been
cleaning the head of a slaughtered beast in a river. On the head falling
into the water, he searched for it and brought up two. Rab. forbade
them both and issued the above *gezerah*. Similarly he forbade the udder
as food, when he once visited Tatlapus[3] and found that the inhabitants
were unaware of the law concerning meat and milk. To make it more
stringent for them, he forbade them even the eating of the udders[4] (Hul.
110*a*).

When R. Ishmael[5] heard of one of the *gezeroth* enjoined by the elders
of the school of Hillel and Shamai in the upper room of Hananiah ben
Gurion[6] to the effect that one should not read by lamplight (on the
Sabbath), lest one should turn the wick up or down inadvertently, he
thought that the possibility was very remote, and said that he would
prove it by reading himself and not turning the wick, but, on doing so,
he was himself nearly involved in the transgression,[7] so that he was
moved to admit that the sages were right (lit. great) in their *gezeroth*. On
two other occasions,[8] after finding out the profoundness of their ideas,
R. Ishmael enthusiastically praised the rabbinic ordinances, expressing
himself in similar terms, 'How great are the words of the Rabbis (who
had laid down the ruling).' If one keeps an object in mind to guard it

---

[1] See note 1, p. 40.
[2] Celebrated Babylonian Amora and founder of the Academy of Sura in the third
century. His real name was Aba Arika.
[3] טטלפוש identified by Kohut, *Aruch Completum*, with Thiluta-Olabus, in the
south of Mesopotamia.
[4] After being emptied of the milk the udder might be used in any way. See Hull. 8,
3; *Yad*, M. Asuroth 9, 12.
[5] b. Elisha, Tanna of the first and second centuries (third Tannaitic generation).
[6] See p. 49.
[7] Others (R. Nathan) maintain that he had actually turned the wick inadvertently
and vowed that, when the Temple was rebuilt, he would offer an expiatory sacrifice
(Sab. 12*b*).
[8] The Talmud Hag. 20*a* records the following two incidents: A woman once called
on him with the question: 'Rabbi,' she inquired, 'this cloth I have to my knowledge
woven in a state of cleanness, but I did not have it in mind to guard it against
uncleanness.' On further investigation she confessed that a menstruant woman had
joined her and had pulled a string connected with the loom. On another occasion a
woman called and asked him about a bandage which she had woven in similar
conditions and, on investigation, it was revealed that, before she managed to weave
the prescribed size which makes it susceptible to uncleanness (three finger's breadth
by three finger's breadth) she had joined a severed thread in her mouth. She was a
menstruant before immersion at the time. Thus, even after the required size was
completed, her spittle was still capable of conveying uncleanness. R. Ishmael,
following on these discoveries, made the exclamation quoted above.

(against uncleanness) it is clean, if he does not keep it in mind to guard against uncleanness, it is unclean (see Hag. 20a).

In particular, as the number of the violators of the law grew, and they did things in forbidden ways, claiming to have done them in permissible ways, the Rabbis forbade them even the permissible way, so they should no longer have an opportunity of justifying their actions. Here are some examples. The transgressors of the law who seek to improve their lands in the Sabbatical year,[1] claiming that they are merely picking up wood and grass, have been forbidden to remove anything from their fields[2] (during such year) (Shebiith 4, 1).

The same is true of the prohibition of cooking on the Sabbath. At first the ruling was that if one had cooked inadvertently on the Sabbath day the food might be eaten[3]; similarly where food had been forgotten on the stove. Since, however, the number of those who deliberately left the food on the stove and then pleaded forgetfulness grew, they changed their policy to one of penalizing also those who pleaded forgetfulness (Sab. 38a).

Again, originally, bathing (on the Sabbath) in water heated on the previous day was ruled to be permissible, but when the bath-attendants began heating up the water on the Sabbath, and then excused themselves by saying that it had been heated the day before, the Rabbi forbade hot baths altogether on the Sabbath (Sab. 40a).

So also they forbade all Sabbatical aftergrowth[4] because of the transgressors, to prevent one from sowing cereals or beans secretly and from eating them when they grow up, on the plea that they were only aftergrowth. *Yad*, Shemita 4, 2. This reason for the prohibition is derived from the Mishnah ad loc.[5]

Numerous *gezeroth* were promulgated to prevent suspicion, i.e. where the deed in itself is lawful, but might lead to a suspicion that it had been done unlawfully. For example (*vide* Shekalim 3, 2) one who enters the Shekel-chamber to take up the *Terumah* (offering) must wear neither

[1] By removing stones or twigs from their fields. See Shebiith 3, 1, for several restrictive measures against doing things in the field which indirectly lead to its improvement.
[2] Including such things as big stones, the removal of which does not, at the outset, lead to the improvement anticipated above.
[3] Cf. Ket. 34a on 'Ye shall keep the Sabbath therefore, for it is holiness unto you' (Ex. xxxi, 14).—Anything done by an intentional violation of the Sabbath is prohibited, just as hallowed things are.
[4] i.e. produce not sown, but growing out of seed that had fallen into the ground during the previous harvest. After declaring it free for everyone, the owner of the field may also consume it (Lev. xxv, 5).
[5] Shebiith 9, 1. From what R. Judah says, that aftergrowth of mustard is permitted because transgressors here are not suspected, it follows that as regards other aftergrowths transgressors are under suspicion.

shoes nor a bordered cloak, lest he becomes rich, and it is said that he got his riches from the *Terumah* of the Shekel-chambers. A man must satisfy men according to the word of Scripture 'and be ye guiltless towards the Lord and towards Israel'.[1]

Two Hanukkah lamps must be lit in the courtyard (of a house) with two separate entrances, because of suspicion.[2] Whence can it be proved that we are apprehensive of suspicions? From the teaching of the following baraitha : R. Simeon[3] said that for four reasons the Torah had ordained that *Peah*[4] should be left at the extreme[5] end of one's field[6] (Sab. 23*a*).

So, again, the Rabbis enacted a decree against the bringing out of dung to the manure-heaps in the Sabbatical year, in order to avoid the impression being given that the owner is about to manure his field.[7]

Charity collectors, again, may change (the money collected) for

---

[1] Numb. XXXII, 22.

[2] Strangers thinking the house divided into two dwellings might suspect one of the occupants of not having kindled his lamps.

[3] R. Simeon bar Yohai, Tanna of the second century and pupil of R. Akiba, in asking this question manifests his particular characteristic of interpreting Biblical law on the basis of its reasonablenes. See B.M. 115 in connection with the prohibition against taking a widow's raiment in pledge (Deut. XIV, 17) where he differentiates between rich and poor widows. See also San. 20*a*, with reference to the Biblical ordinance '(The King should) not multiply wives to himself', (Deut. XVII, 17) where he argued that he may not marry many, but a small number is permissible; also San. 112*a* which quotes the reason he gives for the destruction of the property of the righteous in the seduced city (Deut. XIII, 17).

The author, in a sub-note, observes that there is more direct proof from the Mishnah Shekalim 3, 2, quoted above, since it deals with a case which, though lawful in itself, might create suspicion amongst outsiders, whilst in the case of *Peah* the reasons include a protection against deceitful men; besides, the proof from a Mishnah is more weighty.

[4] The corner of the field, a portion which according to the Torah (Lev. XIX, 9) must be left uncut to be gleaned by the poor.

[5] And not at the beginning or in the middle of it. Besides, the underlying reason is deduced from the Hebrew 'Thou shalt not *wholly*'.

[6] (*a*) To protect the poor against loss of *Peah*. The owner, on seeing that the poor are not present, might hurry up one of his own poor relations to collect it, to the detriment of others, whereas, in the case of *Peah* being left at the end, everyone can see whether the end of the field has been reached.

(*b*) Against loss of time. Had it been permissible to leave *Peah* in the first part of the field to be cut, the poor would have to spend much time in watching it, whilst now they can come at a time when the reaping is nearing the end.

(*c*) To prevent suspicion, since if it is not left at the end of the field, people might suspect that no *Peah* had been left.

(*d*) Because of the meaning of 'Thou shalt not wholly reap it', as explained in note 5. This latter is amplified by Raba's interpretation that the text implies a protection against deceitful men who would evade the *Peah* if it had not to be left at the end.

[7] See Shebiith 3, 1, where this restriction was limited to such time as the transgressors ceased to tend their fields.

others but not for themselves.[1] They are not to count the coins in twos, but in ones only. These restrictions were introduced with a view to preventing suspicion.[2]

Again, we find a type of suspicion which was imposed as obligatory, because some people acted in forbidden ways, and it was an unlawful act to assist them. The following examples are given—None may buy wool or milk or kids from herdsmen, or wood or fruit from those who watch over fruit trees.[3] Similarly none may buy wine or oil or fine flour from servants or from children and women,[4] for fear that they might have acquired these things illegally.

Maimonides in *Yad*, Shemita 8 cites many such cases where transgressors are not to be assisted and where the line of conduct adopted is to be determined by suspicion.

Several undisputed *Mishnas* (laws) are incorporated in A. Zarah, chap. i, with reference to restrictions against selling to a heathen armour, weapons, horses, bears, or lions, or anything with which harm to the public might be done, since the heathen were suspected of behaving improperly, and it was forbidden to an Israelite to help them.

Many *gezeroth* were decreed for the sake of appearance, that is, the Rabbis sought to prevent suspicion of the kind referred to above, viz., where the persons concerned actually did the thing in question lawfully, but where people might suspect them to have done it unlawfully. Most of the laws concerning *Kilaim*[5] were based on this reason alone since, according to Biblical law, *Kilaim* are forbidden only where they have been sown intentionally[6]; the Rabbis, however, prohibited them even in unintentional cases for the sake of appearance[7] (Kilaim 2, 1).

We find a similar restriction concerning garments of diverse kinds of materials as, for example, fine silk and coarse silk[8] which do not come under the actual law of *kilaim*,[9] but are forbidden for appearance sake (ibid.9, 2).

---

[1] They may lay themselves open to suspicion that, where they themselves were involved, the exchange fee which goes to the benefit of the fund was smaller than that which they might otherwise have obtained.

[2] In the latter case people might be led to suspect that he had thrown in two coins and counted them as one.

[3] Mishnah B.K. x, 9.   [4] Gemara ibid. 119a.   [5] See note 10, p. 40.

[6] See *Tos. Yom-tob* on Kilaim 2, 1.

[7] One of the illustrations given in the Talmud is that where as much as a twenty-fourth part of one kind of seed is found mixed with another, it must be reduced before sowing, although by Biblical law it is neutralized by the larger quantity (Hul. 99a). In this case the reduction is required by the Rabbis for appearance sake. See Jer. Kilaim 2, hal 3, 11, and *Yad*, Kilaim 2, 6, 7.

[8] The first resembles flax, and the latter wool.

[9] In the Bible only wool and linen are mentioned, but since these kinds of silks have a close resemblance to both wool and linen, confusion may result.

So also a ruling was promulgated neither to sink vine-shoots nor to plant nor graft trees on the eve of the seventh year, except where there is enough time for them to strike root and for thirty days subsequently to elapse (Shebiith 2, 6). The reason for this is also for appearance sake, as given by Maimonides, *Yad*, Shemita 3, 11.[1]

Again, the ruling that a non-Jew may not work on contract[2] for a Jew on the Sabbath or on *Hol Hamoed*[3] is for the sake of appearance[4] (see A. Zarah 21a).

Again, they have forbidden slaughter (to be performed in such a way that the blood flows) into the sea, or into rivers or into a hole,[5] because people might suspect the slaughtering to have been done for idolatrous purposes (*v.* Hul. 2a). In continuation of this ruling, they said that the slaughterer may not make a hole (for the blood) in the open street, lest he should appear to have imitated the ways of the heretics.[6] Similar reasons were given in connection with several other matters, such as the following—the lamb (for the daily offering) was not wholly tied up, to avoid imitating the idolatrous way[7] (Tamid 4, 1). Again, they (the elders of the Priesthood) adjured the High Priest on the eve of Yom Kippur to change nothing,[8] because they suspected him of following the Sadducees[9] (Yoma 1, 5).

The heifer was handled by a *Tevul Yom*[10] in order to counteract the view of the Sadducees who said it must be handled only by those on whom the sun has set[11] (Yoma 2a).

Another reason which prompted the promulgation of some *gezeroth* was the apprehension of danger, as in the following cases. The Rabbis prohibited the drinking of liquids left uncovered, lest a serpent might have drunk of them (Terumoth 8, 4, 5).

---

[1] Namely that people should not be given grounds to suspect that the work had been done in the seventh year.

[2] Although one who works on contract does so for his own advantage.

[3] See note 5, p. 47.

[4] To prevent the suspicion that they had been given the work on the Sabbath. See M. Kat. 12a; *Yad*, Sab. 6, 14.

[5] In contradistinction to his courtyard where he is permitted to do it because, to outsiders, it appears that he does it merely to save the place from becoming dirty.

[6] Lit. Sadducees, who adopted this method of slaughter.

[7] Who used to bind all the four legs of the animal when on the altar.

[8] In the prescribed ceremonial. See Tamid 31b.

[9] Who maintained that the incense should be prepared outside and then brought in into the Holy of Holies (see p. 5, note 8).

[10] See note 2, p. 42.

[11] In the text our author quotes the passage 'And the heifer was performed by those on whom the sun has set, in order to take it out from the hearts of the Sadducees'. That there is here an omission is obvious (see Parah 111, 7, Yad Parah 1, 17).

One should not put his mouth under a tap and drink, nor should he drink at night lest he should swallow a leech (A. Zara 12a; Pes. 112a).

Similarly one should not eat the flesh of a beast, or animal, or fowl which had either been bitten by a serpent or had swallowed a deadly poison, because it is a danger to life (Hullin 2, 5). Maimonides, *Yad*, Rotzeach 11, 12, cites all the restrictive measures decreed by the Rabbis on the grounds of danger. In addition we find that they prohibited the remarriage of a pregnant woman, or the mother of an unweaned child, because it would be injurious to the child[1] (Yeb. 42a, Keth.60b). Even where pregnancy is not noticeable, she may not remarry[2] because of the necessity to differentiate,[3] and this was on the basis of the Biblical law that the son is legally identified with his father (Yeb. ibid.).[4]

They also apprehended dangers which could not generally be foreseen, as in the following cases:—They decreed that a woman twice widowed[5] might not marry a third time on the ground of her ill-luck in being the cause of the death of successive husbands.

Again, they prohibited the eating or drinking of two portions of food or liquid,[6] and so many other things which were intended to support the restrictions which they had introduced on the grounds of danger (Pes. 109b).

I have so far quoted a number of *gezeroth* and the reasons by which their formulation was prompted and which are cited in the Mishnah without opposition. Most of them have come down to us from the period of those Tannaim who lived during the Temple epoch. But, although I have mentioned that some of these *gezeroth* are given only in the Gemara and not in the Mishnah, yet it was not the Amoraim[7] who initiated them. They had been preserved among them by tradition from former generations, for had they (the Amoraim) originated them there would have been no logical grounds for advancing arguments

---

[1] In the case of pregnancy, even after the birth she is required to wait until the child is twenty-four months old. During pregnancy an injury might be caused to the embryo in the mother's womb; and before the expiration of the said period, the child might suffer from inferior feeding as a result of the early birth of another child.

[2] Before the expiration of ninety days from her husband's death, or from the day the bill of divorce was handed to her.

[3] Between the first and the second husband as possible fathers in order to establish the paternity of the child.

[4] B.B. 109b,

[5] Whose two husbands died natural deaths (Yeb. 64b).

[6] Even numbers were thought in Talmudic times to be unlucky. Maimonides, by excluding these restrictions from his code, signified his non-acceptance of such beliefs.

[7] The interpreters or expounders of the Mishnah which was drawn up very briefly and concisely. They investigated reasons and sources, thus often reconciling seeming contradictions. Their epoch, which is usually divided into generations, extended over a period of some 300 years from the death of R. Judah the Prince to the completion of the Babylonian Talmud.

against them from a Mishnah or Baraitha, since the *gezerah* might not have been in existence at that time. There might, indeed, have been opposition amongst the authorities of the time when they were about to be formulated; yet since these *gezeroth* have remained in force to our day they must surely have been enacted by a majority vote, in view of the written ordinance to 'incline after the many',[1] and so we cannot invalidate their rulings.

There are many subjects on which no decision could be obtained by vote at the time of their discussion and which consequently were left to the *Great Beth-Din* of R. Judah the Prince for decision.

In all the *halachoth* which are mentioned in the *Baraithoth* as subjects of disagreement between the Tannaim, and where Rabbi Judah subsequently decided in the Mishnah in favour of the opinion of one (against many)—a fact which suggests that he followed a minority opinion—it is nevertheless certain that he had not arrived at such a decision without the support of his *Beth-Din*, and it is on that assumption that these *halachoth* were recorded later as definite rulings. A similar assumption applies also to all the rulings which the Babylonian authorities decreed subsequently to the conclusions of the Mishnah, and which yet the Amoraim disputed throughout their period, until R. Ashi[2] and his *Beth-Din* gave their decision in favour of one of the conflicting opinions, following the rules which they had set up for their own and later guidance.

From none of these can one depart, since the *Beth-Din* of R. Ashi was the most authoritative of his time, and no other similar institution since has enjoyed equal standing. R. Ashi's rulings and conclusions, therefore, are of perpetual authority. These definite rulings have been enumerated above, and now we shall proceed to enumerate the cases that come under the section of '*Takkanoth*', which I shall here set out in chronological order.

---

[1] Ex. XXIII, 2.
[2] The celebrated Babylonian Amora, the editor of the Babylonian Talmud (352–427 C.E.). His commanding personality, scholarly standing, and wealth are indicated by the saying that 'from the days of Judah I learning and social standing were never found so fully united in one person as they were in Ashi' (San. 36a).

CHAPTER X

THE TAKKANOTH IN CHRONOLOGICAL ORDER

THE following *Takkanoth* are ascribed to MOSES: the seven days of marriage festivities (for a virgin); the seven days of mourning for the dead (Jer. Keth. 1, 1)[1]; the first benediction in the grace after meals (Ber. 48b)[2]; that the *halachoth* referring to the major festivals be studied on the festivals, i.e. the laws of Pentecost on Pentecost, etc. (Megillah 32a); the institution of eight *mishmaroth* (Patrols) of Priests for duty[3] (Taanith 27a); the reading aloud from the Torah (publicly) on the Sabbaths and on Mondays and Thursdays (B.K. 82a, *Yad, T'fillah* 12, 1[4]).

JOSHUA instituted the second blessing in the grace after meals (Ber. 48b).[5] He and his *Beth-Din*, in dividing the land (to Israel) laid down ten provisions. Maimonides in *Yad*, Nizke Mamon 5, brings them under the category of *takkanoth*.

Likewise in Erub. 17a, they are designated as *takkanoth*. They are as follows:—(1) that (cattle be permitted to) pasture in woods[6]; (2) that firewood[7] and grass may be gathered in any place; (3) that shoots[8] may

[1] There are much earlier Biblical proof-texts adduced in both Talmudim for these days, v. Jer. M.K. I, hal. 7; III, hal. 5, and M.K. 20a; Pirke de R. Eliezer 16, 36. It is noteworthy that the commentators on Jer. Keth., from which the author has quoted, attribute the *takkanoth* to Moses, but merely as a personification of the Torah, in which proof-texts are found for the observance of those seven days. Maimonides, *Yad*, Abel 1, 1, seemingly had this in mind when he says that, notwithstanding the earlier Biblical texts for these observances at the time the Torah was given, the observances were later renewed. Hence it was Moses who enacted them, but yet they are treated only as rabbinical ordinances.

[2] The saying of grace after meals is a Biblical ordinance derived from Deut. VIII, 10. To Moses, however, is ascribed the framing of the first of the four benedictions.

[3] Four by Eliezer and four by Ithamar. These Mishmaroth were changed every week. They were later increased by Samuel to sixteen and by David to twenty-four (see inf., p. 82). References to these mishmaroth are found in Neh. XIII, 30, and in 2 Ch. i, xxxiv, 2.

[4] In B.K. loc. cit., there is no reference to Moses as the author of this *takkanah*. The reference is to "the Prophets amongst them". Maimonides, however, states definitely that it is to be ascribed to Moses, the greatest of all prophets, whose consent had to be obtained prior to the enactment (cf. *Kesef Mishneh*, ad loc., v. also Jer. Meg. IV, 1).

[5] Contains words of thanks for the inheritance of the Holy Land, for the deliverance from Egypt, and for the Covenant and the Law.

[6] And the landlord is unable to raise an objection. This applied only to small cattle and big woods. Where small groves or large cattle are concerned it would not be permitted on account of the damage resulting to the trees (see Gemara, ad loc.).

[7] This applies only to prickly shrubs, even where they are still attached to the ground (ibid.).

[8] With the exception of the stumps of the olive trees.

be cut off in any place; (4) that a spring which emerges even for the first time may be used by all the townspeople[1]; (5) that anyone may fish with a hook in Lake Tiberias[2]; (6) that one may ease one's self behind a fence[3]; (7) that paths across private property may be used by the public until the time of the second rain[4]; (8) that one may turn aside to (private) sidewalks[5]; (9) that one who has lost his way in a vineyard may cut his way out to the road[6]; and (10) that a dead body that is discovered acquires the right of burial on the spot where it was found.

Besides these, there are other *takkanoth* ascribed in the Gemara to Joshua, namely that anyone may remove dung belonging to him to the public ground, and heap it up there for a period of thirty days,[7] or, again, the concession granted by a Court of Law that a man (viz., a beekeeper) may enter his neighbor's field and cut off a branch[8] but must pay him the value. Similarly the regulation that the owner of a flask of wine should pour out its contents in order to use it for saving his neighbour's honey.[9] It was again a stipulation that one should remove the wood loaded upon his ass and load upon it his neighbour's flax[10] and then recover the value of his wood, for it was on such terms that Joshua divided the land among the Israelites. Alfasi quotes these *takkanoth* as definite *halachoth*. *Vide Lehem Mishneh* on *Yad*, Nizkei Mamon 8, 1.

BOAZ initiated the use of the Divine Name in greeting one's fellow men, i.e. one is to greet the other with 'Shalom', which is also one of the names of the Holy One, Blessed be He.[11] (Ber. 54a, 63a; Makkoth 23b).

---

[1] The landlord having no right to object.

[2] Though it was situated wholly in the portion of the Tribe of Naphtali.

[3] Regardless of whatever objections the owner of the property may raise.

[4] Because from that time, the 17th of Marcheshvan, the seed begins to sprout, and so the crops may be damaged by pedestrians (see Ta'an. 6b; Ned. 8, 5).

[5] To avoid an uneven road.

[6] Though damage to the vineyard may result.

[7] So that it may be trodden upon by the feet of men and animals, and thus become fitted for manuring the fields.

[8] Upon which his bees have settled and so save his swarm.

[9] This refers to a case of two people carrying, the one a flask of wine, the other a jug of honey. The jug broke and the honey, which was much more valuable than the wine, was in danger of being lost, so the honey was put into the wine flask. The owner of the wine was entitled to the value of his wine for thus saving his neighbour's honey.

[10] Where a flax-laden ass had fallen dead, and its burden was in danger of being wasted if not saved in time.

[11] By this observation the author seems to favour the second of Rashi's interpretations (Mak. 23b, s.v. שאילת) whereas the *takkanah* as elucidated in the Mishnah, Ber. 9, 5, is applied to the word 'Adonai'. The text reads 'and behold Boaz came, etc., and said "The Lord be with you", and they answered "The Lord bless thee"' (Ruth II, 4). It is in the Midrash on Ruth IV, 7 that the *takkanah* is attributed explicitly to Boaz and his Beth-Din. In the Talmud the *takkanah* is attributed anonymously to the rabbis.

SAMUEL the Ramathite[1] increased the number of the divisions of the priests for duty to sixteen (Ta'an. 27a).

DAVID increased them to twenty-four for both service and cantillation (ibid.). Abraham Ibn Ezra[2] in his Commentary on the Pentateuch, speaking of the verse 'This month shall be unto you, etc.' (Ex. XII, 2), states that the prophets enacted nothing new, subsequent to the giving of the Torah, except in matters of emergency, as in the cases of Gideon[3] and Elijah.[4] We may also assume that the introduction of the cantillation in the Temple by David was a *Takkanah*, originated by David and Solomon, according to the text, as it is written[5] 'whom David and Samuel did ordain for their fidelity'; obviously it was for fidelity[6] and not on the basis of prophecy. Again the benediction (in grace after meals), calling for God's mercy on Israel and Jerusalem, is ascribed to David (Ber. 48b). According to Natronai Gaon,[7] as quoted in Tur Orach Hayim 48, it was David who instituted the hundred daily benedictions.[8]

SOLOMON introduced the words 'upon the great and holy house' in the aforesaid blessing (Ber. 48b); also the permission for wayfarers to walk along the paths in the fields of others (after the harvest)[9] (B.K. 81b; *Yad*, Nizkei Mamon 5, 4). He also instituted the practice regarding the Erub mentioned earlier.[10]

DANIEL instituted the recital of the prayers three times daily.[11] He

[1] He was born in Ramah in the hill country of Ephraim.
[2] Hebrew poet and Biblical commentator, b. Toledo 1093–d. 1167. He also wrote on mathematics, astronomy, and astrology.
[3] Who offered a sacrifice to God in a way that involved many forbidden things, see Jud. VI, 25, and Temura 28b. This was at a time of emergency.
[4] Who built an altar on Mt. Carmel to demonstrate the impotence of Baal (1 Kings XVIII), at the time when the *bamoth* were under a ban. It was similarly a time of emergency (see Yeb. 90b).
[5] 1 Chron. IX, 22.
[6] i.e. the appointment of the Levites to their offices as singers was a matter left to their discretion, and not prompted by prophecy.
[7] Ben Mar R. Hillai Gaon, b Mar R. Mari of Sura, of the ninth century.
[8] Cited by R. Meir, see Men. 43b. Their number is shown by Abudraham (Spanish commentator on the Liturgy of the fourteenth century) in *Birkath ha-Mitzvah* 3, to correspond with the benedictions found in the daily prayers.
[9] This is derived by inference from what Solomon wrote 'withhold not good from him to whom it is due when it is in the power of thy hand to do it' (Prov. III, 27). If a man's produce has already been removed, and yet he does not allow people to enter, he may regard himself as a mean man (see B.K. 81b).
[10] Relating to courtyards. It is by the means of an Erub that the courtyard inhabited by several householders becomes a single domain (see Shabb. 14b, Erub. 21b).
[11] That Daniel was the original author of this enactment has been questioned by later research. The Psalmist speaks of prayer, evening and morning and at noon (Ps. LV, 18). The Rabbis (Ber. 26b) refer to the institution of the daily services anonymously, and merely discuss the question of the fixing of the times of the day, whether they are to be ascribed to the Patriarchs or follow those of the daily offerings.

also enjoined that the prayers be said in a house with windows.[1] (Coucy, Sefer Mitzvoth Gadol, Introduction.)

The MEN OF THE GREAT SYNAGOGUE,[2] headed by Mordecai and Esther, ordained that the 14th and 15th of Adar should be days of feasting and joy and holiday for the distribution of gifts to the poor, and for the sending of portions to one another. They also enjoined the public reading of the *Megillah* (Scroll of the Book of Esther) on the 14th of Adar in the unwalled cities and on the following day in the large cities.[3] For those who live in villages[4] they ordained that it should be read (earlier) on the day of Assembly[5] preceding the day of Purim, namely on the 11th, 12th, or 13th of Adar.[6] (Meg. 2a). For the reading of the *Megillah*[7] they obtained the consent of the divine authority (ibid. 7b). This is inferred from the words 'they (the Jews) established and agreed',[8] i.e. that which they agreed upon below had been ordained above. They also enacted that the 13th of Adar should be a fast day (*Yad*, Ta'an.).[9]

EZRA enacted the following *takkanoth*:—

(1) The public reading of the Torah in the Sabbath *Minhah*[10] Service.

[1] See Ber. 31a.
[2] The highest legislative institution, consisting of Prophets, Scribes, Sages, and Teachers, of the second Commonwealth during pre-Hasmonean times, who continued the spiritual regeneration of Israel begun by Ezra. Many of the legal principles upon which Judaism is based are to be traced back to it. They also laid the foundations for the Liturgy and edited several of the books of the Scriptures. Their activity is summed up in the words: 'They restored the glory of the Torah to its pristine splendour' (Yoma 69b). As to the number of its membership, opinions differ in the Jerusalem and the Babylonian Talmuds. According to the former it consisted of 85; according to the latter of 120. See Jer. Meg. 1, 5; and Bab. Meg. 17b. Although we are not in possession of details as to the exact nature and character of this Assembly, there is no reason whatever to doubt its extensive and fruitful activity, to which constant allusion is made in Talmudic literature.
[3] Cities surrounded by a wall in the days of Joshua. This was enacted after the precedent of the first celebration in Shushan, the fortress (Est. IX, 19).
[4] And who might not have amongst them anyone sufficiently educated to read the Scroll of Esther.
[5] i.e. a Monday or Thursday when the Courts of Law were in session (Keth. 1, 1), and many people were gathered together on that account. They would then certainly find some educated person to read it for them.
[6] It depended on what day the 14th (Purim day) fell, whether on Tuesday or Wednesday, or on the day after the Sabbath.
[7] The Scroll of Esther.
[8] Est. IX, 27.
[9] Chap. v, 5.
[10] See note 11, p. 82. For those who by reason of their occupation, were prevented from attending the public readings on Mondays and Thursdays (see Rashi B.K. 82a, s.v. משום).

(2) The public reading of ten verses of the Torah (by three men on Mondays and Thursdays).[1]

(3) That Courts be held on Mondays and Thursdays.[2]

(4) That the washing of clothes be done on Thursdays.[3]

(5) The eating of garlic on Fridays.[4]

(6) The early rising of women on Fridays for the purpose of baking bread.[5]

(7) That a woman must wear a *sinnar*.[6]

(8) The combing of the hair and cleansing of the body of a woman before taking the ritual bath.[7]

(9) The travelling about of pedlars in the town.[8]

(10) The requirement of immersion for those who have become unclean by pollution.[9]

The above Babylonian version of these *takkanoth* of Ezra is given also in Jer. Meg. 4, 1, with some variations, for instance, in the *takkanah* that a woman must wear a *sinnar*, there is added 'both front and back'; again Mondays and Thursdays only are mentioned there for the public reading of the Law, whereas the Babylonian Talmud has, in addition, the *Minhah* Service on the Sabbath.[10] See *Magen Abraham*[11] 131 and his reference to Alfasi's quotation of the said passage from the Jerusalem Talmud.[12]

---

[1] By this enactment he regulated only the number of verses to be read and the number of men to be employed in reading them, viz., ten verses divided among three men. The actual duty of reading on those days had already been enacted but the rule had been to have either one man reading three verses or three men each reading one verse.

[2] Because on those days the people gathered for the said public reading.

[3] So that the Sabbath may be duly honoured by the wearing of clean clothes.

[4] Since the carrying out of the conjugal duty fell on that night and it was believed that the eating of that legume helped to increase love.

[5] So that there might be bread ready for the poor in good time.

[6] See note 6, p. 72.

[7] For the sake of an absolute certainty that there should be no interposition between the body and the water of the immersion pool, either by the knotting of the hair or by any dirt on the body.

[8] Even against the wishes of the townspeople, in order to make it easier for the women to obtain their toilet articles.

[9] Actually this immersion was enjoined by Biblical law, Lev. xv, 16, but, according to the Torah, this was required for eating *Terumah* and hallowed things alone, while, by this enactment, it is required even for the study of the Torah.

[10] In our present version of the Jer. Talmud there is no such variant.

[11] A commentary on the Shulhan Aruch Orach Hayim by R. Abraham Abele Gombinn, Rabbi in Kalisz, Poland, in the seventeenth century.

[12] Printers' errors in the text of the Jerusalem Talmud and the Alfasi have been cause for the raising of unnecessary difficulties and consequent observations by the commentators on this subject.

My attention has been called, by a scholar,[1] to the fact that, amongst these *takkanoth* enumerated in the Jerusalem Talmud, there is an additional one not found in our (usual) list, viz., that women while in the closet should talk to one another; and this *takkanah* is quoted (in the Bab. San. 19*a*) as from R. Jose of Sepphoris[2]; and again I have found that the *takkanah* of immersion for those unclean by pollution, which is included in both the Babylonian and the Palestinian Talmuds amongst Ezra's enactments, is also included in the Jer. Sab. 1, among the eighteen rulings decreed by the Shamaites and Hillelites.[3]

There are several other *takkanoth* ascribed to Ezra, though not included in the ten enactments, cited in B.K. 82*a* as, for example, the use of the words 'min ha-olam we ad ha-olam'[4] (Ber. 63*a*). Again, he instituted the reading of the chapter of the curses in Leviticus before Pentecost and that in Deuteronomy before the New Year (Megilla 31*a*).[5] Ezra also enacted the appointing of one teacher beside another[6] according to B.B. 21*b*. In Tosaphoth, ad loc. the attribution of this *takkanah* to Ezra is denied, on the ground that it is not included amongst his *takkanoth* (enumerated above). Indeed I do not know why they did not raise a similar objection to the *takkanah* quoted above from Megillah, which also is not included among the said *takkanoth*.

Again, the appointment of a *Methurgeman*[7] is traced back to the days of Ezra (*Yad*, Tefillah 12, 10). The men of the Great Synagogue, con-

---

[1] It is believed that in his not infrequent references to 'a scholar' Chayes was alluding to N. Krochmal, who spent years in the author's company in Zolkiev (cf. introduction to this work.)

[2] Rammi bar Abba quotes it from R. Jose, and adds further that the reason for the *takkanah* was 'privacy'. It may be noted that the Bab. B.K. 82, in omitting this, refers to the public reading on Mondays and Thursdays and at the Sabbath Minhah Service as two *takkanoth*, whereas in the Jerusalem they are counted as one.

[3] See p. 49.

[4] 'From everlasting to everlasting' at the conclusion of each blessing of the morning prayer in the Temple. Earlier they used to say 'for everlasting', but after the Sadducees had imparted the corrupt idea that there is only one world, it was ordained that 'from everlasting to everlasting' should be used. The Hebrew word 'olam' means both 'world' and 'eternity'. See Ta'an. 16*b* for the wording of this phrase.

[5] The reason given in the Gemara is that the year should end with its curses. Pentecost was also regarded as a New Year for the fruit of the trees.

[6] And the earlier teacher had no right to argue that the newcomer would interfere with his livelihood because, in the case of teaching, we have the principle that 'the jealousy of scribes (teachers) increaseth wisdom'.

[7] Also known as Targeman or Torgemon, interpreter or translator (see Meg. IV, 4). He was a communal official set up to translate the weekly Pentateuchal portion for those of the congregation to whom the Hebrew language, on the return from Babylon, was less intelligible than the vernacular Aramaic. He exercised his function in accordance with several rules (see M. Meg. IV and the Talmud, ad loc. 25*b*). That such an appointment originated with Ezra is hinted at, according to Rab in Megillah 3*a*, in the word 'meforash' of the verse Neh. VIII, 8, which is taken to refer to the Targemon.

sisting of one hundred and twenty elders, including many prophets,[1] are credited with the authorship of the compilation of the 'Shemoneh Esrei',[2] in their present order (see Megillah 17b, also Ber. 33a). The men of the Great Assembly also instituted for Israel the berachoth (benedictions), *tefilloth* (prayers), *kedushoth*[3] (sanctifications), and *habdaloth* (distinctions).[4]

Maimonides, *Yad*, Tefilla 14, credits Ezra and his court with the institution of the prayers and distinctions,[5] as Ezra was the head of the Assembly from whom these *takkanoth* originated.

The identification of the men of the Great Assembly with Ezra and his court is corroborated by Rashi (Ber. 33b)[6] dealing with the statement of the Gemara that, had it not been for the men of the Assembly who introduced into the prayers the Divine epithets 'great, mighty, and awful', we should not have dared to use them.[7] He (Rashi) gives the source for this statement as the prayer of Ezra (Neh. ix) hence the Assembly's identification with Ezra and his court.

Some *takkanoth* are ascribed to the prophets without giving their names as authors. See Jer. Erub. III, 9. The institution of the two days[8] of the New Year is a *takkanah* of the earlier prophets. That Israelites living in Ammon or Moab in the Sabbatical year[9] had to pay the poor

---

[1] This is the Babylonian version; the Palestinian, Ber. 2, 4, has the number 80 for the prophets.

[2] The eighteen benedictions, in addition to the one later known as ולמלשינים against the Sectaries (*Minim*). This is the most important part of the daily service, known as Tefillah, 'The prayer,' and afterwards called Amidah, in view of the fact that it is recited whilst standing. Various explanations are advanced for the number eighteen (Jer. Ber. IV, 3).

[3] In which the congregation (of not less than ten men) sanctifies the name of God proclaiming by the threefold repetition 'Holy, holy, holy', His ineffable holiness.

[4] In which the everlasting distinctions between light and darkness, holy and profane, are stressed. This prayer is introduced on Saturday nights, so marking the distinction between the Sabbath and the working days.

[5] But the text of the Yad has 'benedictions'.

[6] s.v. ותקנינהו

[7] They strongly opposed the use of many attributive names. One of his disciples was heaping up epithets in the presence of R. Chanina, saying 'O God who art great, mighty, formidable, magnificent, strong, terrible, valiant, powerful, etc.' When he had finished, R. Chanina asked him, 'Hast thou really completed the praises of thy Master?'

[8] To be legally considered as forming one day (Betza 4b, R.H. IV, 4), so that the second day is not excepted even in the matter of the burial of the dead, as is usual with the second days of the Festivals.

[9] In the land of Israel, during the Sabbatical year, when what grows is ownerless property, the inhabitants are exempt from tithes, but not so those living abroad. As they are not subject to the rules of the Sabbatical year, they are required to pay tithes.

man's tithe[1] is again an enactment of the prophets[2] (Yadaim 4, 3). Similarly the beating of the willow-branch (on the floor)[3] is ascribed to the prophets.[4]

Also the form of the *Kedushah de-Sidra*[5] is traced to the prophets and the early elders (Tur Orach Hayim 132).

[1] The tithe given in the third and the sixth year of the seven-year cycle, in the absence of the second tithe.

[2] Our author includes this as a *takkanah* of the prophets, though its authorship is not specified, but in Yeb. 16a it is quoted as from Haggai.

[3] See note 4, p. 19.

[4] In Suk. 44b, it is designated as a Minhag or custom of the prophets and not as a *takkanah* instituted by them. The difference is obvious, see Tos. ad loc., s.v. כאן.

[5] The *Kedushah* of the Biblical lesson (see Rashi, Sota 49a s.v. אקדושתא), with which the morning service actually ends. Early commentators explain that its recitation was introduced to enable the latecomers to repeat individually the *Kedushah* which they had missed in its congregational form. It was introduced, however, later as an integral part of congregational service for all, and it is preferable to adopt the alternative explanation that its daily reading takes the place of the prophetical lesson in the Sabbath morning service.

CHAPTER XI

ENACTMENTS PROMULGATED BY THE NESIYYIM (PRINCES) AND THE SANHEDRIN (SUPREME COURT)

I SHALL put before the reader the *takkanoth* of the Princes and the heads of the Sanhedrin[1] in chronological order.

JOHANAN THE HIGH PRIEST[2] did away with the awakeners[3] and the stunners,[4] and introduced the use of rings in the shambles to force the animal which was to be sacrificed to stand still (Sota 48*a*).

THE COURT OF THE HASMONEANS instituted the kindling of the Hanukkah lights for eight days (Sab. 21*b*), and also the repetition on these days of Hallel and songs of praise (ibid.). They also introduced the semi-feast days[5] set out in the Meg. Ta'anith[6] as a mark of their opposition to the Sadducees.[7]

SIMEON B. SHETAH[8] instituted the giving of the *Kethubah*[9] to the wife[10] (Sab. 14*b*).

[1] The Supreme Court of Justice which, in the latter part of the period of the Second Temple, administered the law. There were two kinds of Sanhedrin, the great Sanhedrin with seventy-one members, and the lesser with twenty-three. The great Sanhedrin met in the Lishkath Hagazith (Chamber of Hewn Stone) in the Temple at Jerusalem, and the lesser one met sometimes in Jerusalem and sometimes at other places (*Yad*, Sanhedrin I, 3).   [2] See note 1, p. 47.

[3] i.e. he did away with the daily singing by the Levites of the verse (Ps. XLIV, 23) 'Awake! Why sleepest Thou, O Lord?' because of apparent unseemliness in thus addressing God.

[4] Of animals, before slaughtering them, since the stunning might cause a forbidden blemish in the beast.

[5] On which abstention from mourning and from fasting is enjoined.

[6] A chronicle which enumerates eventful days of glorious deeds. The authorship is traced in Sab. 13*b* to Hananiah b. Hezekiah of the Garon family. The days referred to by our author are given in the first chapter of the Meg. Ta'an.

[7] As, for example, over the daily offering, *vide* Meg. Ta'an. 1.

[8] See note 7, p. 48.

[9] i.e. the written marriage contract containing, *inter alia*, undertakings to pay (*a*) a statutory sum of 200 zuz (a zuz = 7*d*.) for virgins and 100 zuz for non-virgins; (*b*) an additional sum consisting of any amount the husband wishes to add.

[10] The actual requirement of the undertaking by the husband of a financial obligation towards his wife in case of her being divorced, or after his death, is of ancient origin. See Rashi on *Mohar* (dowry), Gen. XXXIV, 12, and the *Mechilta*, Ex. XXII, 16, quoted on the authority of R. Ishmael in Jer. Keth. III, 5. In Talmudic times, some regulations were instituted with the object of checking hasty divorces which, seemingly, occurred too frequently. The making of such a check effective depended greatly on how far the said obligation could be enforced on behalf of the wife. Many attempts made towards that end proved unsatisfactory (see Keth. 82*b*), until Simeon b. Shetah ordained the rule requiring a written undertaking that the husband's fortune is pledged for the *kethubah*. It also appears that prior to this it was not a definite rule to have the *kethubah* put down in writing (see Keth. 89*a* and *Yad*, Ishuth 16, 22).

HILLEL THE ELDER enacted the rule of Prosbul[1] (Sheb. x, 3; Git. 36*b*) to avoid the cancellation of debts by the Sabbatical year and so as not to bolt the door against borrowers. In the Mishnah (Shebiith) this rule concludes with the words 'this is one of the *takkanoth* that Hillel the Elder enacted'. Yet we find no other *takkanah* ascribed to Hillel, except the one referred to by the Rabbis[2] (Gittin 74*b*): 'Earlier (the buyer)[3] would hide himself on the last day of the twelve months' term so that the house might become his in perpetuity. Hillel the Elder enacted that he (the seller) should throw the money (received into the Temple chamber) and then break down the door (of his house) and enter.'

But, apart from the above, I know of no other *takkanah* actually ascribed to him, except perhaps the two terminal periods of restriction[4] in ploughing prior to the Sabbatical year. Although in Talmudical language it falls under the category of *takkanoth* (M.K. 3*b*), yet, in view of its being of a restrictive character, and of the fact that the authors of the measure are the Beth Hillel (Hillelites), and not Hillel himself, it should be classed among the *Gezeroth*, as was pointed out above, in the discussion of the *Gezeroth*.

The following may also be included amongst the *takkanoth* ascribed to Hillel, viz., a woman may not lend a loaf to her neighbour without first ascertaining its value (B.M. 75*a*). Since this was a measure designed to prevent transgression of the prohibition of usury,[5] it too belongs to the category of the *takkanoth*. These *takkanoth* were probably in the mind of the author of the aforesaid Mishnah at the end of Tractate *Shebiith*.

Rabban Gamliel the Elder, Hillel's grandson,[6] was the originator of

---

[1] A legal instrument executed and attested in Court at the time of lending money whereby the cancellation of the debt by the Sabbatical laws (Deut. xv, 2) is avoided. Although the regulations of the Sabbatical year include also the annulment of all monetary obligations, Hillel instituted the said enactment, lest this annulment should lead to a serious upsetting of commercial and social intercourse.

[2] See Arakhin 9, 4, with regard to the redemption of a house sold in a walled city within a twelve-months' period (Lev. xxv, 29–30).

[3] The buyer of a house in a walled city.

[4] With reference to the time in the pre-sabbatical year at which tillage must be stopped, although the Sabbatical year begins only with the New Year. According to R. Simeon, a white field (i.e. sown with grain and not planted with trees) may be ploughed until Passover, and a tree-planted field may be cultivated until the Feast of Weeks. The School of Hillel, however, hold that the former may be cultivated until Pentecost and the latter until Passover. However, these restrictive enactments were afterwards abrogated by the Court of R. Gamliel, so that the cultivation of both fields was extended to the end of the year.

[5] i.e. as pointed out in the Mishnah, lest wheat should advance in price and the returned loaf consequently cost more.

[6] Known as Gamliel I, son of Simon, lived during the second third of the first century. He received the cogname *Ha-Zaken* (the Elder) in view of his leading position in the highest religious council of the time.

four *takkanoth*—(1) that the witnesses who (come to Jerusalem to) give evidence regarding the appearance of the new moon are allowed to travel a distance of 2,000 cubits in any direction[1] (R.H. 23*b*); (2) that the husband's annulment of a *Get*[2] sent through a messenger shall be valid only if it has been drawn up in the presence of the bearer, for the general good[3] (Gittin 32*b*); (3) that the scribe shall enter in the *Get* the exact name of the man and woman and whatever other alias or description they may have[4]; (4) that a vow, in whatever way[5] orphans may impose it on their father's wife, shall suffice for the recovering of the *kethubah*[6] (Git. 34*b*).

It is also quoted on the authority of R. Gamliel the Elder that an important *takkanah* was enacted that the witnesses should write their names in full[7] in the *Get*[8] (for the general good) (Git. 36*a*).

JOSHUA B. GAMLA, a High Priest,[9] according to statements in Yoma 18*b* and Yebamoth 61*a*, enacted that there should be teachers in all the cities (of the Holy Land) for children (over five years of age) (B.B. 21*a*).[10]

[1] These witnesses used to assemble in the large court, Beth Ya'azek, in Jerusalem, where their evidence was tested by the *Beth Din*. Prior to this enactment if they arrived on the Sabbath Day, and had already exceeded the Sabbath limit of 2,000 cubits, they could not leave the place at all that day.

[2] Bill of divorce.

[3] Prior to this enactment the husband could set up a court of three persons wherever he happened to be, and cancel it before them; and the bearer in ignorance of the annulment might then give it to her, and she might subsequently, on the strength of the *Get* received, remarry whilst it was, in fact, cancelled.

[4] Prior to this enactment, if for any reason they had adopted any other names, they gave in the *Get* their newly adopted names only, and not those by which they had formerly been known, and that could lead to abuses, e.g. people might spread rumours after the woman had remarried, that the first husband had never divorced her and thus expose her children by the second husband to be regarded as illegitimate.

[5] Even in a somewhat harsh manner, e.g. 'Forbidden be to me the fruit of the earth, if I received my *kethubah*'.

[6] Before this she could only recover the *kethubah* from orphans by taking an oath; and, since she was under suspicion that she might feel herself justified in swearing falsely, on account of the trouble she had had with the orphans, in order to become entitled to compensation, the Rabbis refrained from imposing an oath on her, and thus she might lose the *kethubah*. Hence R. Gamliel's enactment which had made the recovery of her *kethubah* easier for her.

[7] i.e. their names and that of their father, e.g. Jacob b. Izhak.

[8] At first the witnesses used simply to write, 'I, so and so, subscribe as witness,' when, according to Rashi, they did not specify even their names, but relied on their writing as a means of identification (see Strashon ad loc.), a matter which led to abuses, since their writing could not always be found in other documents for purposes of identification. R. Gamliel, therefore, announced that the Rabbis had enacted the said *takkanah* to prevent abuses.

[9] About the last decade before the destruction of the Temple (64 c.e.).

[10] In Judaism the education of children lay, from the very beginning of Jewish history, in the hands of their fathers, who were regarded as the child's natural instructors (Deut. VI, 7; XI, 19). Later it was found necessary to provide teachers for fatherless children. This was carried out by the State which employed teachers in

RABBAN[1] JOHANAN B. ZAKKAI enacted nine *takkanoth* which are given in detail in the Babylonian Talmud[2] (R.H. 31*b*). They are as follows:—

(1) After the Temple was destroyed he enacted that the *Shofar* should be blown (when the New Year fell on the Sabbath day) in every place where there was a *Beth Din*.[3]

(2) That the *Lulab* should be waved in the provinces throughout the whole seven days.[4]

(3) That new produce should be forbidden during the whole of the day of the waving.[5] This I have also mentioned earlier amongst the *Gezeroth*.[6]

(4) That the evidence regarding the new moon (at the New Year) should be accepted throughout the day.[7]

Jerusalem to whose care such children from the provinces were entrusted. This scheme was afterwards extended by the establishment of district schools limited to youths of sixteen and seventeen years of age who obviously could go from home by themselves, and so younger children were still threatened with deprivation of the necessary instruction. Then came Joshua b Gamla and introduced the duty incumbent upon each community of setting up public schools in every town for children over five years of age, and, although prior to this great work Joshua b Gamla had not been too popular amongst his contemporaries because of his irregular appointment to the office of High Priest which was regarded as the result of a political intrigue, and as a conspiracy against the will of the religious authorities—indeed most of the incumbents of that office during that time were not of the worthy type required (see Yoma 9*a*)—yet, on account of his great achievement in the furtherance of Jewish education, he earned the highest praise of posterity, as the man who saved the Torah from oblivion.

[1] In San. v, 1, he is quoted without the title Rabban. Apparently he taught this *Halachah* before his ordination. See San. 41*a* and *b* on this point.

[2] Five of the *Takkanoth* are quoted in the Mishnah R.H. IV, 1–4, the other four in the Gemara R.H. 31*b*.

[3] Earlier this practice was limited, according to Rashi, to the Temple alone, or according to Maimonides (*Yad*, Shofar 2, 8) to Jerusalem.

[4] Originally this duty of taking (waving) the *Lulab* during seven days was confined to the Sanctuary, while in the remaining parts of the country the practice was observed on the first day only. After the Temple was destroyed, R. Johanan instituted this *takkanah* in remembrance of the Sanctuary, and in order to invest the new centre with a similar authority.

[5] The 16th day of Nisan on which the *Omer* (lit. sheaf), a sheaf of barley, was offered, after which offering the new corn could be used (Lev. XXIII, 10). Formerly in Temple times the new produce could be eaten immediately after the *Omer* had been offered, but when the Temple was destroyed and, consequently, there was no *Omer* offering, the new produce could, according to Biblical law, be used from dawn. The *takkanah* was enacted in anticipation of a speedy rebuilding of the Temple, out of fear that people might be led to continue the practice to which they had become accustomed since the destruction (see Men. 68*a*).

[6] Because the regulation leads to a prohibition.

[7] Originally during the Temple period, it was ruled that the day should be kept holy from the sunset of the 29th of Elul, as a precautionary measure lest the witnesses might arrive some time on the 30th day, and report on the visibility of the moon on the previous evening. Even where they did not arrive on that day, although in such

(5) That even though the head of the *Beth Din* is somewhere else, the witnesses for the moon may, nevertheless, proceed to the place of the Assembly[1] to deliver their testimony.

(6) That the priests should not ascend the platform[2] wearing their shoes.[3]

(7) That the witnesses (testifying to the rise of the new moon) should be allowed to desecrate the Sabbath, except in Nisan and Tishri.[4]

(8) That a proselyte was not obliged to set aside a quarter of a coin[5] for his nest of pigeons[6] as it might lead to wrongdoing.[7]

(9) That there was no need to bring the (fourth year) fruit[8] to Jerusalem; it was sufficient to bring its value in money.

R. GAMLIEL OF JABNEH,[9] the grandson of R. Gamliel the Elder,

a case it had been decided that the New Year should begin from the following day, yet the rest of the 30th of Elul was kept holy, in order to prevent the public from treating the whole of the day in future years as a week-day on the assumption that the witnesses would not now come, or would come very late. As a result, however, of the acceptance of evidence during the whole of the day, the Levites came to doubt whether, during the evening daily offering, they should recite the festive psalm (see Tamid 7, 4) or that of the week-day, and so omitted the daily hymn altogether. The rabbis, therefore, were led to limit the acceptance of evidence until the time of the evening offering. After the destruction of the Temple, however, R. Johanan b. Zakkai reintroduced the right of accepting evidence throughout the day.

[1] i.e. of the *Beth Din*. In spite of the absence of their chief, the Court would sanctify the new moon (see R.H. 2, 7). The privilege of proclaiming the new moon sanctified was earlier vested in the Chief of the Court, but R. Johanan b. Zakkai enacted this rule seeing that, in order to avoid inconvenience, the witnesses might refrain from bringing the required evidence (see R.H. 31*b*).

[2] On which the Levites stood when chanting their daily hymns, and from which the priests uttered their priestly benedictions.

[3] Cf. Sot. 40*a*, lest a shoe lace become loose, and the priest going down to retie it would lay himself open to suspicion that he was disqualified for priestly service.

[4] Cf. R.H. 21*b*. This concession was given on account of the superior sanctity of these months.

[5] It is not certain whether the coin in question was a shekel or a dinar. The quarter of one of these two was fixed as the price of the bird offering (lit. nests), viz., two pigeons.

[6] The offering is prescribed in Lev. v, 1–10, as obligatory in expiation of certain offences, and the convert was not only obliged to bring this, the smallest offering, during the Temple days but even after its destruction the Rabbis continued to impose upon him the setting aside of the cost of the offering in case the Temple should be rebuilt. R. Johanan b. Zakkai, however, abrogated that obligation.

[7] Lest the money set aside might be used for secular purposes, and so unlawful use be made of sacred things.

[8] According to the Rabbis, the law that the fourth-year fruit was to be consumed in Jerusalem (Lev. xix, 24) was applicable also in the case of trees which were distant from Jerusalem one day's journey by foot (40 miles) (one mile = 2,000 cubits). R. Johanan's view was that since there was no longer a Temple, there was no point in bringing the fruit to Jerusalem merely to decorate the streets with it. He thus ordained that they should bring its money value instead.

[9] Known as R. Gamliel II.

introduced the benediction known as *Birkhath ha-minim*[1] (Ned. 28*b*). Actually in the *Gemara* it is stated that Samuel ha-Katan (the smaller, i.e. the younger)[2] composed it, but Maimonides (*Yad*, Berachoth 2) attributes its authorship to R. Gamliel and his Court. The reason for this may be found in the facts that R. Gamliel II was Nasi at that time, and Samuel ha-Katan a member of his Court (San. 11*a*); and as the words of this benediction could only be established as a definite formula by the sanction of the Nasi, it is, therefore, quoted as having emanated from him. I have given a similar explanation in connection with the *takkanoth* enacted by the Great Assembly which are quoted on the authority of Ezra.

Rabbi (our holy master), the grandson of R. Gamliel of Jabneh, called a meeting of the *Beth Din* and they decided on a vote that in the case of a field which had been in the possession of *sicarii*[3] for twelve

---

[1] The 12th benediction of the *Amidah* (lit. standing, referring to the *Shemoneh Esrei* eighteen benedictions, the chief portion of the morning service). It is directed against slanderers and informers who by their treacherous machinations and intrigues have wrought havoc in Israel.

[2] An epithet given him on account of his extreme modesty, as illustrated in the incident quoted in Sanhedrin 11*a* where he exposed himself to humiliation in order to save another from embarrassment. Zacuto (1450–1510) in Sefer ha-Yuhasin, quoted by our author in a footnote, advances the view that the R. Gamliel who is associated with the *Birkhath ha-minim* is R. Gamliel the Elder, and not his grandson, R. Gamliel of Jabneh. At first our author disputes such a view on the ground that the place of origin given in the Gemara for the said *takkanah* is definitely Jabneh. Yet he finds some justification for it in the prediction, uttered by Samuel ha-Katan at the time of his death (Sanhedrin 11*a*), that Simeon and Ishmael were destined to perish by the sword, and if, according to Rashi, ad loc., Simeon was the son of R. Gamliel the Elder, i.e. the father of R. Gamliel of Jabneh, how could he (Samuel) be taken as a contemporary of R. Gamliel of Jabneh? Heilprin in Seder ha-Doroth on R. Gamliel ha-Zaken and on Simeon ha-Pekuli elaborates this point at length. To him the difficulty raised above by the Gemara's statement that Jabneh was the place where the said *takkanah* was enacted could be resolved by evidence given by the Yuhasin that R. Gamliel ha-Zaken had also worked there. There is, however, a difficulty in finding any historical support for the view held by Rashi (as above) that the Simeon referred to by Samuel ha-Katan at the time of his death was R. Simeon b. Gamliel ha-Zaken, who is generally supposed to have been martyred shortly before the destruction of the Temple. Firstly there is no historic evidence for the nature of his death (see Halevi, *Doroth* 1, p. 191, and Weiss, *Dor* 1, p. 200). Secondly Samuel lived nearly half a century after the destruction of the temple, whereas Simeon died before that event. We may, therefore, welcome Halevi's ingenious assumption, *Doroth*, pp. 180, 201, that the Simeon referred to by Samuel was the son of Hanina (the Segan of the Priests), known as Simeon b. ha-Segan (cf. Men. 100*b*) who witnessed the destruction of the Temple. According to this interpretation the view commonly held that *birkhath ha-minim* was composed by Samuel ha-Katan at the request of R. Gamliel of Jabneh is the more probable (*v.* Sanhedrin, Sonc. ed., p. 46, note 5).

[3] One who seized property by violence or threat, or who confiscated it in the absence of owners who were either killed or taken captive in war. Jews at the time of this *Takkanah*, about 200 C.E., were still suffering from the terrible effects of the Hadrianic persecution following the Bar Kochba revolt.

months, whosoever should first come to purchase it from him should acquire the title, but must also give a quarter of the price[1] to the original owner (Gittin 58b). Again he enacted for the people of the countryside[2] that if a woman noticed one day a discharge she should count for her cleansing six (clean) days in addition to that day (Nidda 66a).[3]

The *takkanoth* of Usha[4] are enumerated in our Talmud (Keth.49b and 50a). They are as follows:—(1) That parents should support their sons and daughters while minors. (2) Where a parent has transferred all his property to his sons during his lifetime the latter are obliged to support their parents, out of the estate. (3) One who gives extravagantly to charity should not give more than a fifth part of his income.[5] (4) A man is expected to be patient with his son (who is disobedient) until the age of twelve, when he may throw off his responsibility.[6] (5) Should a wife sell her *melog*[7] property during the life-time of her husband, he, if he survives her, may legally seize the property from purchasers.[8]

[1] On the assumption that the *sicarii* were generally reducing the sale price by a quarter of the real value.

[2] Who were not learned in the law (see R.H. 35a). In the text of the Gemara, the words are 'in the fields', but Alfasi's version, Shevuoth, chap. ii, reads 'Savadith', the name of a place.

[3] According to rabbinic interpretation of the Biblical law, women undergo two categories of uncleanness, (1) that of 'nidda', menstruation, (2) of the *Zabah*, 'flux'. When a woman begins to have her normal discharge she is deemed unclean for seven days, irrespective of whether the issue has occurred once, or repeatedly during the seven days. This seven-day period is followed by eleven days, known as the eleven days between the menses. A flow of blood during these intervening days is regarded as a 'flux', and if repeated for three days in succession, the woman is termed a 'zabah', and must wait until seven clean days have passed before she can immerse herself, or be deemed fully clean. At the termination of those days of flux impurity she enters again into the period of menstrual impurity (see Nid. 72b and Yad, Issurei Biah 6, 1–4). But as the application of the laws during the two periods is different, particular care is required to avoid confusion, and learned persons only can be relied on. The folk of the countryside, however, were ignorant of the law, and thus liable to apply the law erroneously; for this reason Rabbi was led to enact that in the case of a discharge which had occurred during one or two days only, the woman may cleanse herself after the passing of six days besides the unclean days; but in the case of a discharge which had lasted three consecutive days, she cannot cleanse herself until seven fully clean days have passed. Later in the Talmudic period, the restriction necessitating a period of seven clean days was self-imposed by the daughters of Israel, even for a single blood issue occurring at any time.

[4] A Galilean city near Shefar'am, Tiberias and Sepphoris, where an important synod of rabbinical authorities met about the middle of the second century, after the Hadrianic persecutions had subsided.

[5] In order not to expose himself to dependence on assistance from others.

[6] Lit. in the Gemara 'come down upon his life'. He may, after that age, adopt severe corporal punishment and even cease to feed him.

[7] The capital of which belongs to the woman, while its usufruct is enjoyed by the husband.

[8] Our author in a footnote observes that the authority of one of these *takkanoth*

The fourth benediction in the grace after meals was enacted in Jabneh (Ber. 48*b*)[1] under the presidency of R. Gamliel II who assumed office after the death of R. Johanan b Zakkai and continued in office until after R. Akiba died a martyr's death.

(i.e. the second) is questioned in the Gemara, ad loc. ; and if they were issued by the Beth Din of R. Gamliel the Elder, who, as mentioned in R.H. 31, had transferred his Patriarchal seat from Shefar'am to Usha, how could the authority of such enactments be disputed, seeing that such as had the sanction of the Patriarch alone were never disputed? But since these *takkanoth* are not referred to either in the Mishnah or in the *Baraitha* and they were only familiar to the Amoraim, the Gemara, therefore, questioned the validity of the tradition that the *takkanah* in question was enacted in Usha, whereas if it had been referred to in the Mishnah or *Baraitha* they would not have questioned its authority. *V.* Jer. Peah, chap. i, with reference to the case of R. Yeshovav who had disposed of all his possessions to the poor, when R. Gamliel sent him a message that the distribution for charity is limited to a fifth; hence this *takkanah* of Usha must have had the sanction of a much earlier authority. In the *Seder Hadoroth*, s.v. R. Gamliel the Zaken, however, it is proved that the R. Gamliel who sent the aforesaid message was R. Gamliel I and not Gamliel II. (Yet Rashi, R.H. 31*b*, s.v. ומיבנה, seems to maintain that the R. Gamliel who was in Usha was R. Gamliel II.)

[1] After the defeat of Bar Kochba at Bethar (135 C.E.). Hadrian, it is said, forbade the interment of the slain. Later, when this prohibition was removed, this benediction ('who art kind and dealest kindly with all') was introduced into the grace after meals.

RABBINIC ENACTMENTS UNANIMOUSLY ADOPTED

WE find in the *Mishnah* and *Baraitha* and in both Talmudim practices with rabbinic authority, and ordained *takkanoth* of a general character, concerning which we cannot find any traces of dispute, and of which we know that they were accepted by all the people from ancient times and that their observance was received as a perpetual obligation.

The opinion of Rabbi Abraham b. David[1] in his *Sefer ha-Kabbalah*[2] is well known, where he writes to the same effect regarding the general acceptance of the main substance of the rabbinic observances. He takes, as an example, the kindling of the Sabbath light. It is only a rabbinic enactment for domestic welfare[3] but we find no dispute about the duty of kindling the Sabbath lamp in itself; the authorities differ only as to the kind of oil and the material to be used for the wicks.[4] Similar *takkanoth* were spread among, and accepted by, the people because they were sanctioned by the *Beth Din Hagadol* of Jerusalem by whose decisions the whole of Israel was bound to abide.

To this category belong the following *takkanoth*:—

The response of *Barukh Shem*, etc., following the first verse of the *Shema*[5];

The washing of the hands in the morning[6] and before prayers[7];

The final water[8] after the meal;

The obligation to erect a synagogue as soon as a place is inhabited by

---

[1] Known by the initials of his name, RaBaD I, astronomer, historian, and philosopher of Spain (1110–1180). Distinct both from Abraham b. Isaac of Narbonne (RaBaD II) and from Abraham b. David of Posquières (RaBaD III).

[2] Book of Tradition, Chronicles from the days of Moses to his own time.

[3] See Sab. 25*b*, where the mourner's words 'thou hast removed my soul far off from peace' (Lament. III, 17), are referred to the kindling of the Sabbath light, as loss of light causes loss of peace.

[4] See Shab. II, 1.

[5] Its origin is ascribed by the rabbis (Pes. 56*a*) to the Patriarch Jacob, but no Biblical source is found for its wording, except possibly Ps. LXXII, 19, where it appears with slight variations. At first it was recited in the Temple, but later it was introduced as a response to the opening verse of the *Shema*. See Midrash Rab. Deut., chap. ii, for the reason given why on the Yom Kippur Day alone it is to be recited aloud.

[6] According to Asheri (Ber. 60*b*) this ritualistic requirement is an elementary act of hygiene, since it is almost impossible to guard the hand against uncleanness during one's sleep.

[7] Just as the priests of old prepared for their daily service in the Temple by the washing of their hands (Ex. XXX, 20), even so does the Israelite when he is about to come into the presence of his God.

[8] The washing of the hands after a meal was for the purpose of removing any grease resulting from the meal. See also Hul. 105, Tos., s.v. מים and Yoma 83*b*.

the minimum quorum of ten[1]; the manner of imposing communal levies[2]: one half to be proportioned to means, and the other half in proportion to the number of persons;

The general rule of reading the *Haftarah*[3] on Sabbaths and Festivals;

The number of men to be called to the reading desk (almemar) for the portion of the Law was fixed at seven on each Sabbath morning, six on the Day of Atonement, five on the three chief festivals, and four on the first of the month and the days of the mid-festivals.[4] We find no trace of opposition to these enactments.

When a minimum of three men[5] eat together they must say the common grace.[6]

The sounding of the Shofar on the eve of the Sabbath to warn the people to cease from work.[7]

The rabbinic precepts followed on the first night of Passover[8] such as the eating of *Haroseth*,[9] the drinking of the four cups of wine,[10] the duty of reclining on the left side on couches round the table,[11] and many other

---

[1] See *Yad, Tefillah* 11, 1.

[2] For the various needs of the community, connected either with its welfare or arising in times of danger when its existence was threatened, see B.K. 116*b*; B.B. 7*b*. For the detailed regulations associated with this legislation, see H. Mishpat 163, as well as the Glosses of Isserlis and the commentaries.

[3] The reading from the prophets immediately after the reading of the Law during the morning service of the Sabbaths and feast-days. The portions selected were cognate to the Sidrah (weekly reading) of the week. The name הפטרה is derived from the verb פטר,, and means dismissal or leave-taking, i.e. conclusion or completion, signifying the end of the reading for the day. No definite date for its origin can be given. The view attributed by many to Abudrahem (see note 3, p. 82) that its institution goes back to the time of persecution under Antiochus IV or Epiphanes (165 B.C.) is not definitely given by him. On p. 63 of his work he refers only to days of religious persecution which are assumed by S. L. Gordon (*Otzar hatefilloth*, Wilna ed., p. 702), to have been the days of the Hadrianic oppression. Büchler, J.Q.R. vi, p. 7, advances the view that the background of the institution to read the 'prophets' was to counteract the Sadducees and the Samaritans who had denied the authority of the Prophets. The former view which is advanced by Elijah Tishbi in his Dictionary, s.v. פטר, is quoted by Heller, *T. Yom Tob* on Megillah 3, 4, s.v. לכסדר.

[4] See Megillah 4, 2 and the Gemara 23*b* and 24*a*, regarding reasons for these numbers.

[5] Ritually a boy over thirteen is reckoned as a man, the view being based on the term איש given to him on his reaching that age (see Rashi, Nazir 29*b*, s.v. ורבי יוסי.

[6] Where one of them leads the other two in saying the grace together (Ber. 7, 1). For the exegetical proof text see the Gemara 45*a*.

[7] Sab. 35*b* and Suk. 5, 5.

[8] During the ceremonial of the Seder, the home service held on the first night of the festival in Eretz Israel and on the first two nights in the Diaspora.

[9] A mixture of nuts, apples, and wine to symbolize the clay which the Israelites were forced to work into bricks. The bitter herb is dipped into it to mitigate its bitterness (see Pes. 115*b*).

[10] In commemoration of the four stages of redemption, as intimated in Ex. VII, 7–9.

[11] In allusion to an ancient custom symbolizing freedom.

unusual customs at the meal, intended to engage the children's attention and make them ask questions. Again the reading of the *Haggadah* as it was compiled in the days of the Temple. The waving of the *lulab*[1] (palm-branch) in all four directions. Views were divided with regard to the order of the waving, but not regarding the duty of the ceremony itself.

Again we have the precept to eat on the eve of *Yom Kippur*.[2] Although this was deduced from a Scriptural passage,[3] yet as I have shown elsewhere, it is actually a rabbinical law, and the Biblical text is only a support.

According to Maimonides, *Yad*, Tefillah 4, 4, the Beth Din that followed Ezra enacted that one who suffered from pollution[4] should not recite his prayer until he had had immersion. However, Karo[5] (*Kesef Mishneh*, ad loc.) had already expressed astonishment and doubt as to whether there is any proof text for this *takkanah*.[6]

Again, we have the duty resting upon the father of arranging for his sons and daughters to be married soon after the period of puberty,[7] and of training his children, while minors, in the observance of the precepts,[8] and of preventing them from eating prohibited food.[9] They[10] also said, if one has children in his youth he should marry in his old age.

The precepts of rabbinic authority are too many for us to quote them in detail. I shall refer only to those few that are quoted in the *Mishnah* and *Baraithoth* anonymously and unanimously without recorded opposition.

Thus they legalized the marriage of a girl minor[11] that prople might

[1] In the Temple the lulab, together with the other three species, was waved in all directions during the recitation of the passages expressive of thanksgiving or prayer, in acknowledgment of God's sovereignty over nature (see Suk. 3, 9).
[2] See *Orach Hayim* 604. Epstein, *Torah T'mimah* on Leviticus XXIII, 97, advances as a reason for this precept that the self-affliction which is preceded by a day of feasting is much more emphatic.
[3] Lev. XXIII, 32, 'And ye shall afflict your souls on the ninth day (of the month).' But does one fast on the ninth? Do we not fast on the tenth? Rather it seems to mean that, if one eats and drinks on the ninth, Scripture reckons it to him as if he had fasted on both the ninth and the tenth (Yoma 81b; Ber. 8b).
[4] See Lev. xv, 16.
[5] The codifier of the law who divides it into the well-known four sections.
[6] See Ber. 3, 4, 5, and the Gemara 21b and 22a.
[7] Yeb. 62b; *Yad*, Issure Biah 21, 25, Eben ha-Eezer, 1.
[8] Suk. 42a.
[9] Yeb. 114; *Yad*, M. Assuroth 17, 28; *Orach Hayim* 343.
[10] The rabbis, e.g. R. Joshua in Yeb. 62b.
[11] The marriage of a minor boy is invalid (Yeb. 10, 8; *Yad*, Yibum 6, 8) whereas in the case of minor girls whose fathers are dead or absent, and who were married by their brothers or mothers, in whose charge they were, their marriage is rabbinically valid and, therefore, מיאון (a declaration of refusal) would be needed for the dissolution of their marriage. See Yeb. 13, 1; *Eben ha-Ezer* 37, 14, 155.

not treat her as ownerless property,[1] and the marriage of a deaf mute woman.[2]

They gave the husband the full benefit of his wife's *melog*[3]-property during her lifetime as against his liability to ransom her (in case of capture). He was also obliged to support her because of the benefit which he derived from the work of her hands.[4]

They enacted that the woman who seeks to recover payment of her *Kethubah* from orphans is not paid unless she first takes an oath,[5] and that the husband is his wife's heir[6] and is responsible for her burial and wailing expenses.[7]

Again, that the *Kethubah* is to include provision that the sons born of that marriage shall inherit their mother's *Kethubah* in addition to the portion of their father's property which they receive along with their brothers (of another marriage).[8] The *Kethubah* is to contain also the provision that the female children shall receive support from the property of their father until they become betrothed or reach their majority.[9] Again, there is the enactment that daughters who are left unmarried after their father's death may claim (from their brothers) a tenth of the estate for dowries and trousseaux.[10]

Again, we have the classification of certain types of women who are

---

[1] Being fatherless she might be liable to be mistreated by unscrupulous people (cf. Rashi Yeb. 112b, s.v. שלא and *Yad*, Ishuth xi, 6).

[2] So that no liberties should be taken with her; see Yeb. 112b.

[3] See note 7, p. 94, e.g. the usufruct of the property which she has inherited from her mother.

[4] Keth. 4, 4; *Yad*, Ishuth 14, 3.

[5] To the effect that it had not yet been paid to her. Ket. 9, 8; *Yad*, Ishuth 16, 19.

[6] *Yad*, Ishuth 22, 1.

[7] Keth. 4, 4. It was customary at that time to hire women to bewail the dead, as referred to in Jer. ix, 16.

[8] M.Keth. 4, 10. This ruling had in mind the case of a father who was predeceased by the children's mother, and who had remarried and begotten new male children, in which case there might be a difference either in the value of the *Kethuboth* or in the number of the beneficiaries. This provision, therefore, aims at preventing another woman's children from benefiting by the first wife's *Kethubah*. See Keth. 52b for another important reason for this provision, viz., that a father should be encouraged to give dowry to his daughter as liberally as he treats his son, since he would then be assured that the property would not ultimately be lost to her sons.

[9] M. Keth. 4, 11.

[10] See Keth. 68a and Ned. 39b, where this *Takkanah* is more fully explained and is shown not to mean that if a man were to leave ten daughters and one son, the latter should receive nothing. Indeed, in such cases it was ordained that the first to marry should receive a tenth of the estate, and the second her tenth from what is left, and so on. In a case where they all marry at the same time a similar procedure is adopted, namely that after receiving their share in accordance with the *Takkanah* they pool the whole amount involved and divide it equally among themselves.

to be divorced without receiving their *Kethubah.*[1] Similarly regulations concerning a woman who refuses marital intercourse.[2]

The measure, again, not to declare valid the divorce of a mentally defective woman[3] in order that she should not be treated by unscrupulous people as a piece of ownerless property. Since her consent is not needed, actually in accordance with Biblical law she could be divorced.[4]

The *takkanah* that a man's four cubits should everywhere give him the right to ownerless property within that area[5] enacted in order that people might be prevented from quarrelling,[6] as well as the other ways of acquisition instituted by the Rabbis. In most of these *takkanoth* the details only were disputed, not the principal enactment. The purpose of these rabbinic precepts was, in some cases, to guard domestic peace, in others to introduce good habits of life in Israel or order in all religious matters; in others, again, to bring to memory as frequently as possible the miracles which God had wrought for us in the past, as also to recall the tribulations that passed over us, the remembrance of which the Jewish race has cherished.[7] All the anniversaries of *Megillath Ta'anith*[8] were fixed for these reasons (see Sab. 13*b*). As to the *takkanoth* of rabbinic origin, some of them were promulgated for the general good, others in the interests of peace or for the avoidance of ill-feeling or to prevent the bolting of the door against borrowers; some again to guard the honour of the woman, so that the husband should not find it easy to divorce her, and so that daughters of Israel should not be left, driven forth and abandoned like ownerless property. Two complete chapters in the Treatise of Gittin (fols. 32–42) are devoted to those *takkanoth* which were enacted by the rabbis for the general good and in the interests of peace.

In cases where the reasons for their promulgation appear at first sight to be somewhat remote, we are told by the rabbis that their enactment was prompted by actual events experienced by them, as I have already mentioned in connection with the particular *takkanah* that bills of divorce should be dated, lest the husband might shield a

---

[1] Such as those guilty of transgressions of Jewish observances enumerated in detail in M. Keth. 7, 6.

[2] Keth. 5, 7; *Yad*, Ishuth 14.

[3] Who is not capable of taking proper care of herself.

[4] But only in cases where she is capable of taking care of her letter of divorce, i.e. where she realizes the significance of her action; since, according to the law of the Torah, a woman even of sound mind may be divorced without her consent. See *Tur Eben ha-Ezer* 119 from Yeb. 112*b*.

[5] So that no other person could claim it if he picked it up.

[6] See B.M. 10*a*.

[7] i.e. they have celebrated their victorious end.

[8] See note 6, p. 88.

daughter of his sister,[1] that the Jerusalem Talmud and Alfasi refer definitely to a historical case of this kind. Similarly with regard to the *takkanah* that there should be an *Erub* for courtyards[2] in the interests of peace, the Jerusalem Talmud (Erub. chap. iii), quotes on the authority of R. Joshua an actual case of a woman who was hated by her neighbour but who once sent the *Erub* by her son to her enemy's house, whereupon the latter received it and kissed the son, etc., and this had the effect of making peace between them, according to the verse 'Her ways are ways of pleasantness'.[3]

Another point one needs to know is the difference between the term תקנו and התקינו,[4] both used for 'they ordained'. The first is employed for *takkanoth* which the Rabbis, by a majority vote, determined to enact for the general well-being, whereas the second term either in the singular or in the plural refers to cases where, prior to the particular enactment, another practice was in vogue, and only when they had seen that that practice was bound to lead to evil consequences did they think it necessary to alter the rule to a more appropriate form. (v. R.H. 31*b* where the Rabbis discussed the term התקין 'he had ordained'[5] and explained that he had interpreted [a Biblical text] and then ordained.[6]) I shall here quote just a few cases from this category. See Bik. 3, 7. Formerly all those who could recite (the declaration of the first fruits)[7] recited it and all those who could not recite it followed the recital by the Priest, but when out of embarrassment the latter refrained from bringing the first fruits, it was ordained[8] that all, including those who could recite them, should repeat the words after the Priest.

Formerly they used to say at the close of every benediction מן העולם (from everlasting), but after the heretics had corrupted the meaning[9] of

---

[1] See note 3, p. 72.
[2] See note 10, p. 82.
[3] Prov. III, 17.
[4] From תקן 'improve'; the first is the *Piel* or active, and the second is the *Hif'il* or causative.
[5] With reference to Ben Zakkai's *Takkanah*, following the destruction of the Temple, that the new cereals should be forbidden during the whole of the 16th of Nisan (Lev. XXIII, 10). Biblically, in the absence of the *Omer*, the new corn may be eaten even from daybreak on the said day (Men. 68). R. Judah, however, traces the forbidding of the new corn throughout the whole day to a Biblical law, hence the discussion of the term התקין 'he ordained' which was raised.
[6] Thus, although the enactment is attributed to him, yet it is regarded as Biblical, since it is based on a Pentateuchal text (see R.H. 31*b*). The author's references to this matter as proof of the suggested distinction between the piel תקן and the causative התקין are not very clear. The other quotations, however, given in support of his suggestion are more informatve.
[7] See Deut. XXVI, 5-11, and M. Sot. 7, 13.
[8] Here, and in the cases that follow, the Hebrew term התקין is used.
[9] By affirming that there is but one world or age.

the phrase, it was ordained that they should say מן העולם ועד העולם (from everlasting to everlasting) (M. Ber. 9, 5).

The fruit of the fourth year vineyard[1] was taken up to Jerusalem.[2] When the fruits became too cumbersome for transportation, it was ordained that they could be redeemed (even where the vineyard was close to the Wall of the City) (M. Ma'aser Sheni 5, 2).

Formerly when they used to bring food into the house of mourning[3] the rich would bring theirs in baskets of silver and gold, and the like,[4] so that the poor felt embarrassed. In consideration of the feelings of the poor it was ordained that all should bring it in baskets of (peeled willow) twigs (M.K. 27a).

Formerly when they were wont to serve drinks[5] in the house of mourning, the rich would serve white glass or the like,[6] so out of consideration for the poor it was ordained that all should serve them in painted glass.

Formerly they were wont to uncover the faces of the (dead) rich,[7] but out of respect for the feelings of the poor, who felt ashamed, they enacted that the faces of all dead should be covered (ibid.). Cf. loc. cit. for many other references to similar cases where the Rabbis instituted practices different from what they had been before, in order not to cause embarrassment to the poor. Anyhow, one can see from these cases the difference between the use of תקנו and התקינו.

---

[1] See Lev. xix, 24.

[2] From any place in the country which was not more than one day's journey distant from Jerusalem in any direction.

[3] For the first meal after a funeral, called 'meal of consolation' and prepared by a neighbour (see B.B. 16b).

[4] While the poor used to bring it in baskets of peeled willow twigs.

[5] See Pes. 110a; Keth. 8b.

[6] While the poor served in coloured glass.

[7] And cover the face of the poor.

CHAPTER XIII

ENACTMENTS THE BINDING FORCE OF WHICH WAS LATER RELAXED

AGAIN, in many cases, we find that what had been definitely prohibited by earlier authorities was later permitted by the *Beth Din*, as in the following instance. According to the Biblical law, where the levirate marriage[1] could be performed, *halitza*[2] was not regarded as the fulfilment of the precept. Yet it was later ruled that *halitza* was preferable to the levirate marriage[3] (Yeb. 39*b*).

Indeed, even things prohibited by Biblical law were occasionally permitted by the Rabbis where only passive violation was involved,[4] and, in cases which appeared to them at the moment urgent, or where they had grounds for apprehension that, in the absence of some guidance, the people would be led to more serious violations of the law, they felt prompted to set aside certain precepts, of which category the following are examples. They forbade the blowing of the *shofar* on a New Year's Day which fell on the Sabbath, lest one should inadvertently carry[5] the *shofar* four cubits in the public domain[6] (R.H. 29*b*).

They also forbade the taking of the *lulab* in hand on the Sabbath for the same reason[7] (Suk. 42*b*).

See Yeb. 90*b* for the following examples where the rabbis made their decisions in cases which would have entailed the punishment of *Kareth*,[8] even where there was involved only an abstention from per-

---

[1] See note 7, p. 9.

[2] See note 10, p. 6.

[3] Because it was noticed that the levirate marriage was not exercised for the fulfilment of the precept, but was prompted by other and selfish motives.

[4] Violation of the law by abstention, i.e. by passively not doing what one is commanded to do; this was in certain cases under the jurisdiction of the Rabbis (see Yeb. 90*b*), as distinct from active violation, i.e. by actually doing what one is commanded not to do, as this involved the defiance of a Pentateuchal law.

[5] As not all are skilled in the blowing of the *shofar*, some might be tempted to carry it to an expert to learn, and thus commit a transgression.

[6] The law prohibiting the transporting of things four cubits in the public domain comes down by tradition (see Sab. 96*b*).

[7] See Rashi, Suk. 42*b*, s.v. ללמוד, who shows that the waving of the *lulab* required some teaching.

[8] i.e. precepts the violation of which involved the punishment of *Kareth* could be suspended by rabbinical ordinances.

forming the act in question, viz. the cases of the uncircumcised,[1] the sprinkling,[2] the knife.[3]

Similarly they suspended Ezra's *takkanah* of immersion for those who had suffered pollution, see Ber. 22*b* and *Yad*, K. Shema 4, 8,[4] and also the *takkanah* that a virgin should be married on a Wednesday,[5] v. Shittah Mekubezeth,[6] Keth. 3*a*.[7]

Here belong also the 'fixed *takkanoth*' which are enumerated in the first Mishnah of the seventh chapter of Shebuoth and to which the Rabbis refer as 'great *takkanoth*'.[8] Rashi's elucidation of this phrase is that the Rabbis here were unmaking a Biblical law by the transference of the oath from the employer (lit. householder), i.e. the respondent who, according to Biblical law would take the oath and be exempt from payment[9] and its imposition upon the employee,[10] as a condition of his

---

[1] This refers to the proselyte who is circumcised on the Passover Eve. Although pentateuchally he would, as an Israelite, be obliged to keep the Passover, the rabbis pronounced him unclean (see Pes. 92*a*), and he was, in consequence, prevented from participating in the said celebration, even though failing to do so involved the violation of a precept carrying the punishment of *Kareth*.

[2] Sprinkling an unclean person on the Sabbath is only rabbinically forbidden (see Pes. 92*a*). If then the eve of the Passover fell on the Sabbath and also happened to be the seventh day of the purification of a person unclean according to Pentateuchal law, he would be permitted to participate in the *Paschal-lamb* celebration. Yet the Rabbis, by prohibiting the sprinkling, prevented him from fulfilling the Pentateuchal precept of the *Paschal-lamb*, even though its violation, as said before, involved the punishment of *Kareth*.

[3] i.e. circumcision, the violation of which involved *Kareth*. It was found sometimes necessary to postpone circumcision when it fell on a Sabbath, although it generally supersedes the Sabbath. That might happen through the rabbinic prohibition against carrying the knife on the Sabbath even along the roofs (see Sab. 130*b*).

[4] The author's reference in the text to the concluding paragraph of Tefillah is erroneous.

[5] See M. Keth. 1, 1, because the Courts sat on Mondays and Thursdays, so that in the event of a man having a case regarding his wife's virginity, he could bring it forthwith before the court. Although a similar reason could be advanced for a Sunday that day was nevertheless excluded on account of the Sabbath which would interfere with the necessary preparations.

[6] See note 1, p. 31.

[7] Which states that where the Courts meet every day, the restriction to a particular day is suspended.

[8] At first they referred to these as 'great *takkanoth*'. The designation 'great', however, was questioned by the rejoinder 'Why great? Are there also small enactments? Surely all *takkanoth* must be equal in importance,' and, in consequence, they designated them as 'fixed *takkanoth*'. See B.M. 112*b*, s.v. תקנות קבועות.

[9] That the oath is to be imposed upon the defendant, and not upon the plaintiff, is derived from Ex. xxii, 10, 'And the owner thereof shall accept it (the oath of the bailee), and he (the bailee) shall not pay.' It is upon him whose duty is to pay, in this case the bailee, that the oath devolves (see Sheb. 45*a*).

[10] e.g. in the case where a dispute has arisen between the employee and his employer, the employee is to take the oath and so obtain his due.

receiving payment, because there was reason to think that the employer, busy with his labourers, might be subject to forgetfulness.[1]

The Rabbis likewise made liable to a fine one who is suspected (of having taken a false oath)[2] or an informer[3] so that they are thereby put in a disadvantageous position

Similarly one who has been robbed,[4] or who has been wounded,[5] takes the oath and so recovers the damages.

Again, the Rabbis have imposed an oath of inducement upon the defendant who denies the whole claim[6] made against them (see Sheb. 40b). Again they imposed an oath upon a bailee[7] who offers to pay for the article he is accused of taking. He is to swear that the article in question is not in his possession (B.M. 34b).

In some cases they have even set aside a Pentateuchal law when doing so involved a direct violation, provided that there was a sound reason for the action such as we find in the following case. According to Pentateuchal law a woman who declares to her husband 'I am unclean[8] to you' is to be believed.[9] The Rabbis, however, later enacted that she is not to be believed because she might have set her affections upon another man,[10] and so she is permitted to continue cohabitation with

[1] An employer might have so many labourers that he might confuse one with another, whereas the employee deals, as a rule, with one employer only, and he can remember more easily whether he has received his wages or not.

[2] And enacted that his opponent should take the oath and receive the amount claimed, instead of the defendant doing so and being exempt from payment. See the Mishnah ad loc. on the transgressions which place him in such a category.

[3] One who gives information about someone's possessions whereby he exposes them to illegal seizure (see B.K. 117a; *Yad, Hobel Umazik* 8, and *Hoshen Mishpat* 388). In case of a dispute between the informer and his victim where the former is not certain of the extent of the damage, the latter is to take the oath, and so recover his loss from the owner (see Tos. B.K. 62a, s.v. עשו).

[4] This is illustrated in the Mishnah as follows—A man entered into another house to take a pledged article without authority, and it is proved that he carried nothing going in, but carried something when leaving, and so a dispute arose between him and the householder. The latter said 'you have taken my property' and he said 'I have not'.

[5] The illustration given here is similar to the above. It was proved that A went into B's house intact, and came out wounded; A claims that B has wounded him, and B denies it.

[6] Actually no oath is to be imposed in a case of complete denial. The Rabbis, however, put the defendant on oath to induce him to admit the truth. See B.M. 5a.

[7] The bailee in question is an unpaid one who would have been discharged if he had sworn that the article was stolen or lost. In this case, however, he offered payment rather than swear, yet to clear him of any suspicion that he might have coveted the article, and that he is only inventing a story of theft (in this case) he was put on oath in spite of his offer of payment (*Yad, She'elah Upikadon* 6, 1).

[8] i.e. unfaithful—In other words, 'I have committed adultery.'

[9] And therefore to be divorced and to receive her *Kethubah*.

[10] And so have purposely made such a declaration in order to obtain her freedom to marry the other man.

her husband, notwithstanding the fact that Pentateuchal law forbids her to be his wife.[1] Gerondi, ad loc., has raised the difficulty in connection with this enactment which follows from the principle that a *Beth Din* cannot promulgate a law which involves a direct violation of a Biblical law[2]; he meets it, however, by the argument that such a rabbinical measure was intended to guard something, and in cases where there was a strong reason for the enactment,[3] a Pentateuchal law could be abrogated even where the violation was direct (Tos. Yeb. 88a, s.v. מתוך). Thus the evidence of one witness was admissible to establish the woman's position, even though the evidence of one witness is Pentateuchally always inadmissible in cases where a prohibition has been declared,[4] but where there was a supporting argument for such an admissibility they admitted the evidence even though abrogating thereby a Pentateuchal law[5] in a way involving direct violation.[6]

Here again it is evident that they relied on the single witness because he would not lie in a matter the truth of which was bound to come ultimately to light.[7] See Tos. Naz. 43a, s.v. והדאי[8] and Tos. A.Z. 13a, s.v. ואת[9] and also *Kesef Mishneh* on *Yad, Nedarim* 3, 9,[10] which also deals with this subject. I am referring to this provision here very briefly

[1] See M. Ned. 11, 12.
[2] See Yeb. 89b.
[3] Such as the prevention of lawlessness.
[4] As in the case referred to in M. Yeb. 10, 1, where the woman's established position as a married woman can be altered by the evidence of a single witness that her husband has died.
[5] See Deut. xvii, 6.
[6] As in the case where the woman is permitted to remarry.
[7] They followed here an established principle that where a thing is bound to come to light later, men do not lie (see R.H. 22b). Besides this argument there were two other reasons, (1) a woman takes every precaution to verify the evidence of the single witness before she decides to re-marry, as she is aware of the many disabilities to which she would be subject in case of her first husband's return; (2) in view of the fact that she may remain in a state of perpetual desertion, i.e. perpetually tied to her absent husband, the Rabbis have, in her case, relaxed the rigidity of the law of evidence and permitted her to remarry on the evidence of a single witness (see Yeb. 88a).
[8] With reference to the rabbinic law (see Yeb. 89b) that the husband is the heir of a wife who died while a minor. (Biblically, in such a case, her father is her legal heir). He may defile himself by her corpse during burial, though he is a priest (see Lev. xxi, 2) .This involves an active abrogation of a Torah law; yet it was allowed, on the ground that she is regarded as a *Meth Mitzwah*, e.g. a corpse whose burial is obligatory upon anyone who discovers it where no one else is available to act; and, although she may have relatives who might be called in (in which case she would not come under the category of *Meth-Mitzwah*), yet the Rabbis reasoned that, since these relatives are not her heirs, they would not be interested in her burial, and they therefore classed her as a '*Meth-Mitzwah*'.
[9] Where the reference is given.
[10] Where Maimonides definitely rules that the vow of fasting cannot be enforced on the days of Hanukkah and Purim. Hence the Pentateuchal law of vows is abrogated in favour of a rabbinic ordinance against fasting on the said days.

but I have dealt with it at length in my work *Torath Nebiim* in the section *Horahath Sha‘ah*.

Ezra in punishing the Levites by depriving them of the tithe, as already mentioned, thereby abrogated a Torah law. RaDBaZ[1] in his Responsa, vol. ii, No. 787, raises an objection against the extension of Ezra's punitive measure to the sons of the Levites, on the ground of the ruling in connection with robbery and usury,[2] that the fine imposed on the transgressor is not to be extended to his son. His answer to this is that Ezra imposed the said restrictive measure upon his contemporaries only, but that the people themselves adopted the practice of extending the original refusal of the tithe to the Levites also to their descendants.

Nehemia b Hachaliah prohibited the handling of utensils (on the Sabbath day). The *Beth Din* that followed him permitted, and again (after a period of prohibition) repermitted their handling[3] and so it has remained (see Shab. 123*b*).

Johanan the High Priest[4] brought to an end the duty of confession at the presentation of the Tithe[5] and abolished the wakers[6] and strikers[7] (Sota 48*a*).

Rabban Simeon b Gamliel, the father of R. Gamliel of Jabneh, who was killed two years prior to the destruction of the Temple,[8] issued a ruling that where a woman was liable to bring five offerings for five ascertained births[9] she need bring only one[10] (Kerith. 8*a*). Rashi, ad loc., explains that

---

[1] Abbreviation of R. David b. Zimra, Spanish talmudist of the sixteenth century, who died in Palestine in 1589.

[2] This ruling is referred to in connection with various transgressions, and not only with reference to these two, see M.K. 13*a* and Git. 44*b*, and with reference to usury, see also B.M. 62*a*.

[3] In the first instance the permission was granted conditionally in cases where the object in itself was needed; in the later instance, in cases where the space it took up was needed.

[4] See note 1, p. 47.

[5] See Deut. xxvi, 13, and Sot. 48*a*, the reason being that the tithe, following Ezra's measure, was no longer given to the Levites.

[6] Every day the Levites ascended a *duchan* (stage) and exclaimed 'Awake, why sleepest thou, O Lord' (Ps. xliv, 24). It appeared to him unseemly to use such words towards God. See Sot. 48*a*.

[7] They used to make an incision between the horns of the beast, so that blood should flow into its eyes, and thus, by preventing it from seeing what was happening, avert a consequent struggling. In his opinion such an injury inflicted a blemish upon the beast.

[8] See note 2, p. 93, on this point.

[9] See Lev. xii, 2 ff. In the case in point, the woman had miscarried five times and in each case it was ascertained that there had been a human embryo.

[10] This ruling was issued as an extraordinary measure against those who took advantage of the large demand for doves made by women obliged to bring separate offerings for each birth, with the result that prices had risen tremendously. This ruling brought prices down. His exceptionally great authority was illustrated by the fact that the ruling was in direct opposition to a Pentateuchal law.

R. Simeon b. Gamliel had expounded this law not in agreement with the Torah but, because of the rise of prices, he here followed the teaching 'It is time to act for the Lord, they have broken thy law'.[1] Cf. *Responsa Zemah Zedek*[2] No. 28, and Responsa Beth Jacob,[3] No. 129.

R. *Johanan b Zakkai* abolished the *takkanah* that one must bring (fourth year) fruit to Jerusalem. He ruled that one can bring its money value instead. I quoted this earlier[4] with reference to the law that a prohibition that has been decided by a majority vote can be rescinded only by another majority vote[5] (see Betza 5*b*).

Again, R. *Johanan b Zakkai* is cited as having abolished the fastening of the tongue of scarlet to the door of the Temple Court on the inside[6] (R.H. 31*b*) (the fastening on the outside having been abolished earlier).

He is also quoted as having enacted that at a time when adulterers had increased in number,[7] the ceremony of the bitter water should be discontinued (Sotah 47*a*), and at a time when murderers had increased in number the ceremony of breaking the heifer's neck should be discontinued[8] (Sab. 49).

---

[1] Ps. cxix, 126. See Ber. 63 where it is interpreted as follows—It is a time to act for the Lord even when it involves breaking of the law; for, in this case, had such a measure not been adopted the poor women would have ceased to bring their offerings altogether, and thus would have eaten the sacrificial meat while in an impure state. It is observed by the historians that this is the only *halachah* connected with the name of R. Simeon b. Gamliel, which goes to support his policy as expressed in the pronouncement attributed to him (Aboth 1, 17) 'I have found nothing better for a man than silence; study is not the most important thing but *action*'. In this ruling he gave a practical example of his teaching which agrees with the statement made jointly by him and R. Eliezer b. Zadok, that no decree ought to be laid upon a community unless the majority are able to abide by it (see A. Z. 36*a*).

[2] By R. Menachem Mendel, Rabbi of Nickolsburg, Germany, of the seventeenth century. See *Magen Abraham* 242 with reference to this response in relation to this subject.

[3] By Rabbi Jacob, a contemporary of the famous author of the שׁ Shabetai b. Meir ha-Cohen of the seventeenth century.   [4] See note 8, p. 92.

[5] See *Yad, Mamrim* 22 for the principle that the later authority must surpass the former both in wisdom and in numbers. He thus holds that a majority vote alone obtained by the later authority is not enough. Again, even where the reason for the ruling of the first *Beth Din* no longer exists, it is still binding until it has been rescinded by another *Beth Din* which surpasses the former, etc. See M. Ed. 1, 5.

[6] After the High Priest had performed the Service on *Yom Kippur*, a tongue of scarlet was fastened to the door on the outside, and if it turned white the people used to rejoice; if not, they were cast down. In order to avoid a possible sorrow it was enacted that it should be fastened to the door on the inside. This also proved unsatisfactory, and the procedure was abolished by R. Johanan b Zakkai, who ruled that half of it should be fastened to the rock and half between the horns of the scapegoat.

[7] In the case of both men and women the water could no longer be used as proof. This view was supported by the rabbinic interpretation of Numb. v, 31, 'And the man shall be free from iniquity,' viz. when the man is free from iniquity the water is a test for his wife, but not when he is not free from iniquity (Sotah 47*b*).

[8] See Deut. xxi, 1–9. The ceremony was performed in a case of uncertainty only, but not at a time when murder had openly increased (Sotah 47*b*).

During the final war[1] they (Ben Zakkai's *Beth-Din*) enacted that a bride should not go out in a palanquin.[2] The Rabbis, however, permitted it.

Rabbi (the Holy One) decreed that Beth She'an[3] should be exempt from the duty of giving tithes[4] (Hul. 6*b*). This decree is also quoted in Jer. Demai, chap. ii, *hal.* 1, where it is stated that he also declared the produce of several localities, such as Kisrin,[5] Beth Guvrin[6] and Kefar Zemah[7] exempt from Sabbatical laws. Again see M. Oholoth 18, 9, for a statement that Rabbi and his court by vote declared the place Keni[8] clean,[9] although it was believed by the public to be unclean. In view of this we can now understand why his colleagues did not consent to his wish to abolish the fast of the ninth of Ab (Meg. 5*b*), although according to the view advanced by Tos., ad loc., he did not intend to abolish it entirely, but was concerned only to place it in the same category as the other fast days.[10] In spite of his authority as President they did not consent, because he had already shown lenient views in two other cases, namely in exempting Beth She'an from tithes, and in freeing the town of Keni from any suspicion of uncleanness, and they could not tolerate another such lenient measure, since after the third time they would have been branded as a permitting Court. See Ab. Zar. 37*a*.[11]

R. Judah II, the grandson of Rabbi (the Holy One), permitted the

---

[1] i.e. during the war of Titus, see Rashi, Sotah 49*b*, s.v. בפולמוס האחרון.

[2] In which she was conveyed to the husband's house, lest she should be assaulted by the Roman soldiers (Sotah 49*b*).

[3] A strongly fortified city in Canaan, which was not captured till the time of Solomon, and which later fell into the hands of the Philistines, and afterwards into the hands of the Greeks (Josh. xvii, 16; Judges i, 27; 1 Kings iv, 12). It changed hands several times during the wars of the Greco-Roman times, and because it was rarely inhabited mainly by Jews, it was granted the exemption from the duty relating to tithes.

[4] In the matter of tithes it was placed in the category of all the other territories and localities which, though they had been captured earlier, were not regained after the return from Babylon (see *Yad*, Terumoth 5).

[5] To be identified with Caesarea or Caesarea Philippi, on the coast.

[6] A city in south-western Judea identified with the present village Beit Jubrin.

[7] A variant quoted in the Jer. Demai is Beth Zemah, identified with Samakh, near the shores of the Sea of Galilea.

[8] Prof. Danby, note 14 ad loc., quotes a suggestion that it is to be identified either with Wady Kanah (in Samariah) or with Ain Keni (near Lydda).

[9] See Oholoth 18, 7, for the ruling that the dwelling places of the Canaanites are unclean because they were in the habit of burying abortions in the house. After examination, however, Keni was declared free of that suspicion.

[10] Where less rigorous restrictions apply, in that the fast does not begin on the preceding evening, and the wearing of shoes or the use of cosmetics, etc., is not prohibited.

[11] When a court has dealt leniently in its ruling in three cases one after the other, it is then classed as a 'permitting court'.

use of heathen oil (Ab. Zar. 35*b*).[1] He also granted permission to a woman to remarry in the case where her husband had given her a bill of divorce to operate if he died within twelve months (ibid. 36*a*, see Tos., ad loc., s.v. אשר).[2] Again, we find the sages of Babylon[3] permitting the use of heathen bread. They abolished in Babylon the declaration requested of the bearers of a bill of divorce, on presenting it to the wife, that it had been written and signed in their presence, but only after they (the Babylonians) had studied and had become expert in the laws of divorce.[4]

[1] Although this is found in the Mishna compiled by his grandfather, it is suggested by Tos. A.Z. 36*a*, s.v. אשר that it may be a later interpolation.

[2] His ruling was in opposition to that of the M. Git. 7, 8, according to which the divorce is invalid unless the husband declared her divorced from the very moment indicated in the bill of divorce, and consequently, in the case here stated if, the husband died childless, she must still fulfil the levirate law before she may remarry.

[3] There is difficulty in tracing this permission to the Babylonians. In the Babylonian Talmud (A.Z. 35*b*) it is deduced from a statement made on the authority of R. Johanan (a Jerusalemite). Indeed, the more lenient view on this point is quoted in the Jerusalem Talmud, ad loc., not in the Babylonian.

[4] This ruling is attributed to Rab, the head of the School of Sura (219 C.E.), a Babylonian centre of learning (Git. 6*a*; *Yad*, Gerushin 7, 10).

CHAPTER XIV

A SUMMARY OF THE VARIOUS CATEGORIES OF THE ORAL LAW

ALL the subject-matter in the Mishnah and Talmud is thus divided into six categories, viz.—

(1) Interpretations which have come down from Sinai and which can be supported, however remotely, by Scripture.

(2) *Halachoth* received by tradition for which no support can be found in Scripture.

Over the laws which belong to these two categories there has never been any divergence of opinion. Whenever a scholar stated that he had any law by tradition, it was accepted without challenge.

(3) Laws which were derived by exegetical rules such as the traditional hermeneutical principles.

(4) Cases where the ruling was not based upon Scripture, but was derived from common reasoning, and logical analysis.

It is in connection with these latter two categories that most of the controversies recorded in the Mishnah and the Talmud arose. One Talmudical scholar expounded his view and another rejected it. To one his reasoning appeared logical, whereas to another it did not, and so they remained in opposition.

(5) *Takkanoth* or enactments.

(6) *Gezeroth* of a universal character.

These were enacted by a vote of the Great Beth Din, and became established and fixed for all time, so that they cannot be annulled, in accordance with the principle laid down in the Mishnah (Eduyoth 1, 5) that no Court can annul the decision of another court unless it is greater than the former in wisdom and in numbers, except in cases where such *takkanoth* and *gezeroth* were not generally accepted, as in the case of heathen oil,[1] or in cases where Biblical support was found for setting aside the decision of the earlier court. In such a case the ruling of the former court can be annulled, even though it enjoys the status of the Great Beth Din, as I have shown at length in my treatise. Otherwise the decisions of a Beth Din are unassailable and permanent.

It was on the following ground than an Amora was not empowered to dispute a decision of a Mishnah or baraitha, viz. that when Rabbi (the Holy One) had concluded the compilation of the Mishnah, he gathered all the contemporary scholars and put its contents to the vote,

[1] See A.Z. 37*b*, and note 1, p. 110.

and by the majority decisions taken all the opposing views and con-
tentions of the minority were overruled.

In this principle lies the reason for the punishment of the rebellious
elder, viz. that the individual can no longer adhere to his opinion once
it has been overruled by the majority. Therefore when Rabbi found it
right to support the opinion of an individual he refers to it in the Mishnah
anonymously on the authority of the Sages, in order to have the *halachah*
in question confirmed as an accepted law, even though it was the view
of an individual (see Hulin 85a).[1] But if it is true that on several occasions we find the rabbis attributing an anonymous Mishnah to R. Meir
which afterwards was disputed by the rabbis and overruled; how, we
may ask, could they dispute an anonymous Mishnah, the contents of
which had been decided by a majority vote of Rabbi's Court at the
time when the Mishnah was being compiled, so that the view of
an individual rabbi was incorporated as an accepted law? On this
point I have already shown in the treatise cited above[2] that, in fact, it
was only R. Hiyya and Rab who, although they were, with others,
members of Rabbi's Court,[3] had the authority to overrule an anonymous Mishnah, and to base the Court's ruling on a single individual
authority, because the authority of Rabbi's decisions in the Mishnah
rested on the voting of his Court. If, therefore, they (R. Hiyya and Rab)
questioned the ruling of an anonymous Mishnah and showed it to
follow a mere individual's opinion, it must be inferred that they had
been absent at the time from the Court, and so had not participated in
the voting. Their views supporting a minority view had, therefore, not
been stated in the presence of all, and so they are competent to bring
forward their plea for the rescinding of the decisions obtained by a
majority vote in their absence, since the Torah's ordinance 'to incline
after the many'[4] applies only in cases where all the representatives of
differing views meet together and participate in the voting, in which
case the minority, on submitting its views, is overruled by the majority,
but not in the case where some are absent whose views the majority have
not had the opportunity of hearing, as I have clearly shown at length in
my work.[5] See Git. 59a and San. 36a where Rab is quoted as saying
'I was one of the voters in the Court of Rabbi and it was with me that the

[1] There a *halachah* held only by R. Simeon is quoted in the Mishnah anonymously
on the authority of the 'Sages'.
[2] Mishpat Ha-Horaha.
[3] The former, although he had studied in Rabbi's Academy, was regarded by
Rabbi more as a colleague than as a pupil. The latter was one of the youngest
members of his Court and became afterwards the head of the Sura Academy.
[4] Ex. XXIII, 21.
[5] It is assumed that, had they heard the views of all, they might have arrived at
a different conclusion.

SUMMARY OF THE CATEGORIES OF THE ORAL LAW 113

voting began'.[1] We see thus that they did join Rabbi's Court as voters when the Court submitted a decision to a vote, because he (Rab) had already attained by then a high status in the knowledge of the Torah, while R. Hiyya ranked still higher, being regarded by Rabbi as his colleague. Therefore, in cases where Rabbi has incorporated a ruling anonymously in the Mishnah which was universally accepted by all his contemporaries, without a single recognized authority being left out of the voting, the *halachah* of this anonymous Mishna is then fully adopted because it was passed by a full vote. Where, however, R. Hiyya or Rab or R. Hanina bar Hama or Levi,[2] or one of the other members of the Court maintains that the *halachah* of the Mishnah is to be traced to the opinion of an individual which is disputed by other authorities, it must then definitely be assumed that they were not present at the voting, and that they have thus the right to question that Mishnah's authority by opposing the decision at which Rabbi's court arrived, even though in some cases we find statements made by R. Johanan[3] or Samuel[4] regarding an anonymous Mishnah to the effect that it follows the opinion held by an anonymous teacher, such as R. Akiba or R. Menahem b Yosi[5] but that other scholars are in disagreement with them and the *halachah* rests with these others. Although they were at that time only in their student days they had, however, probably heard from their teachers, R. Hiyya or R. Hanina or Levi, viz. that they had not consented to the view anonymously mentioned, and these teachers, of course, were actually members in Rabbi's Court, as mentioned above.

The same applies to the following case quoted in San. 74a. In the upper chambers of the house of Nithza in Lud[6] it was resolved that, in the case of three laws in the Torah, one must suffer death rather than transgress them.[7] Yet we find R. Ishmael[8] in opposition to this decision.

---

[1] As he was the youngest, the voting began with him in accordance with the procedure of commencing with the lesser judges (see San., loc. cit.).

[2] Both were R. Hiyya's contemporaries and members of the school of Rabbi. R. Hiyya, however, and Rab were their seniors.

[3] b Nappaha, cited generally as R. Johanan, a Palestinean scholar, disciple of the last Tannaim. The reference mentioned is given by his pupil Rabbah bar bar Hana, a Babylonian Amora of the second generation.

[4] Generally known as Mar Samuel or Yarhinai, a Babylonian Amora of the first generation and head of the Nehardean Academy.

[5] Whose opinions are usually quoted anonymously in the Mishnah. See Meg. 2a and 26a, and Rashi, Keth. 101b, s.v. זו דברי.

[6] Identified with the present-day Lydda in the south of Israel.

[7] There are divergent opinions amongst the historians regarding the date when these measures were adopted and also on the grounds for them. It is agreed that they were prompted by the Hadrianic persecutions during the first half of the second century. See Graetz IV, pp. 155 and 428 ff. and Halevi *Doroth* i, p. 371.

[8] R. Ishmael b. Elisha of the third Tannaitic generation, a prominent member of the Sanhedrin at Jabneh (Eduy. ii, 4) before it had moved to Usha.

His attitude is indeed startling, for surely in a case where the decision was taken by a majority vote, the disputant is to be judged as a rebellious elder and punished accordingly.[1] How then did R. Ishmael take the liberty to challenge it? It must be assumed that he had not participated in the voting, and so had the right to dispute the decision. Indeed R. Samson (of Sens)[2] in his commentary on the Mishnah (Oholoth 18, 9) on the authority of the Tosephta (ad loc.) states that in order to arrive at a clear decision, the Rabbis, as a rule, took a majority vote, and that in some cases R. Ishmael refrained from participating in the voting.

Similarly we find a statement quoted that 'in early days there were no disputes in Israel for, on every law over which some had doubts and a controversy was raised, they took the matter to a vote and decided it in accordance with the view held by the majority' (Sanhedrin 87b). It was only from the time of Jose b Joezer,[3] a contemporary of the Hasmoneans, that controversies began to remain unsettled, because the scholars of that time had been exiled to various places as a result of decrees issued by Antiochus.[4] They could not assemble in one place and consequently could not ascertain the opinion of the Court by a majority vote. It is for that reason that the question of the laying of hands on the heads of sacrifices[5] has since remained a controversy (Hag. 17b).

Yet after God favoured his people and restored the Sanhedrin to its former position we no longer hear of disputes over *halachoth* except over that of the laying of hands,[6] for every *Nasi* or head of the *Beth Din* supported the view of his predecessors and did not favour the subjecting of their rulings to a vote. But during the period of Shammai and Hillel there were difficulties over three other *halachoth* which are detailed in Sab. 15a.[7]

[1] Deut. XVII, 12; M. San. 10, 1.
[2] Known in the abbreviated form of *Ha-Rash*, one of the French Tosafists of the twelfth century, a pupil of the famous Tosafist R. Tam. His commentary on the Mishnah covers only that part which is not dealt with in the Babylonian Talmud with the exception of the two tractates *Berakoth* and *Niddah*.
[3] Referred to in Aboth 1, 4, as the man of Zeredah, the native town of Jeroboam, 1 Kings XI, 26. With him and Jose b Johanan began the period of the 'Zugoth' (duumvirates), the first of the pair occupying the office of president of the Sanhedrin, and the second that of vice-president.
[4] Epiphanes, King of Syria, styled in rabbinic sources 'the wicked'.
[5] The question as to whether it is permissible on feast days which was raised at that time.
[6] See M. Hag. 2, 2.
[7] The chief source for this reference is in M. Eduyoth 1, 1. There the dispute is referred to Shammai and Hillel themselves, and not to their school. The following are the three halachoth: (a) the amount of dough subject to the law of *hallah* (dough offering, Num. xv, 20; M. Hal. 2, 6); according to Shammai it is one *Kab* (equal to 24 eggs) whereas Hillel held that twice that amount would be required; (b) the

Even in earlier days we find disputes over certain *halachoth* among the authorities as, for example, the difference of opinion between David and Saul regarding the validity of *Kiddushin* (betrothal) where a loan and a *perutah* (a small coin) have been offered for it (San. 19*b*),[1] according as it was held that the would-be husband's mind was set on the loan or on the coin.

Again there is the dispute between Hezekiah, King of Judah, and the contemporary sages, whether the month of *Nisan* can be intercalated in Nisan. He held that it can, but the Sages did not agree with him[2] (San. 12*a*).

Again there was a dispute between two high priests who had survived the first Temple. The one said 'I (did the sprinkling on the inner Altar) by a circular movement of my hand', and the other said 'I did it by walking round the Altar'[3] (Yoma 59*a*).

An observation on these disputes was made by Tos. on Hag. 16*a*[4] where we read, 'They say in Hagigah that *Semichah* alone was the first disputed *halachah* in Israel', but whereas a similar claim is found in

amount of drawn water which, if it fell into the *Mikwah* (immersion pool) before it had its requisite 40 seahs of flowing water, makes it unfit for ritual purification; according to Hillel one *Hin* (Ex. xxx, 24, = 3 *Kabs*) is sufficient while Shammai held that only a measure of three times that amount would have that effect; (*c*) the time after which a woman who becomes menstruous is deemed unclean and so liable to transfer uncleanness to other things touched by her. According to Shammai this begins from the time she has discovered the flow, while Hillel extended the period backward to the time of her first examination.

[1] Saul held that in such a case the would-be husband thinks mainly of the loan, and consequently the woman cannot be betrothed (v. Kidd 6*b*; 47*a*), whereas in David's view his mind is set on the *perutah* and so the betrothal is valid. This dispute arose in connection with David's claim from Saul to deliver his daughter Michal to him for a wife, as was promised to him as a reward for the slaying of Goliath (1 Sam. xvii, 25).

[2] One of the principal rules of the Hebrew calendar is that of the intercalary month, i.e. an extra month was added once in three years, or seven leap years in every cycle (*Mahzor*) of nineteen years. The additional month is decided upon, according to the view of the rabbis, before the month of *Nisan* is proclaimed, and the month succeeding that of Adar is then called *Adar Sheni* (Second Adar). As soon as *Nisan* has been proclaimed, it cannot be reproclaimed as *Adar* so as to make the ensuing month *Nisan*.

[3] They are both referring to the procedure of the sprinkling of the horns of the inner Altar by the High Priest on the Day of Atonement when he came out of the Holy of Holies (Lev. xvi, 18). Although he began with the west, where he sprinkled the veil, yet he did not commence from the most westerly horn, because in accordance with the biblical expression 'he shall go forth', he had to make his exit, first by passing the north-westerly horn, and then commencing from the north-easterly horn (in spite of the principle that one should not forgo the opportunity for the performance of a religious act). He then returned to sprinkle the north-westerly horn, etc., but a dispute arose whether he should carry out the procedure by walking around or by a simple circular movement of the hand. The two high priests differed on this point of procedure.

[4] s.v. ‫יוסי‬.

Tosafoth Yeshanim[1] on Yoma for the dispute between the two high priests referred to above, to one who goes more deeply into this question, there is no problem. For only such a dispute as that over *Semichah* (laying on of hands) is actually regarded as such, because it continued for a long time without settlement, running as it did from Jose b. Joezer down to the Shammaites and Hillelites, whereas the above-mentioned disputes only lasted a short time because of some one point, but as soon as it (the point) had been settled, it ceased to operate, and the rabbis put the matter to vote and decided it in accordance with the decision of the majority, as I have shown in my treatise '*Mishpat Hahoraha*'.

There is yet another point which one needs to know in this connection, viz. that only those *takkanoth* which were promulgated either by the Presidents in Palestine, or by the Exilarchs in Babylon, who were conceded power and authority over the whole people and whose directions were loyally followed by all Israel, were generally referred to in the Mishnah and Talmud by the words 'They have ordained', or 'They caused to be ordained', as they were *takkanoth* universally accepted among the people; whereas such *takkanoth* as were issued by other Sages whose authority did not extend over all Israel, and who were only of standing in their own congregation and localities, are known always by the place in which or for which they were enacted. So, for example, R. Jose enacted in Sepphoris[2] that women while in the closet should talk to one another to secure privacy from the intrusion of men (San. 19a). So R. Abahu prescribed in Caesarea[3] the ritual of the *Tekioth*[4] (blowing of the ram's horn) at New Year (R.H. 34a). So again R. Assi prescribed in *Hutzal*[5] the manner of blowing the Shofar on a festival when it fell on the eve of the Sabbath[6] (Hulin 26b).

None of these sages, R. Jose, R. Abahu, and R. Assi, who, as Palestinians, were subject to the jurisdiction of the Presidents, had the power to promulgate *takkanoth* for the general acceptance of Israel without the

---

[1] A group of glosses left by the Tosafists and revised and compiled by R. Samson b. Abraham of Sens (1235) known either as the *Tosafoth* of Sens or as the *Tosafoth* of the ancients.

[2] See note 2, p. 85.   [3] See p. 109, note 5.

[4] Referring to the sound of the Shofar on the first day of the seventh month (Lev. XXIII, 24). The general term for the sounds is 'tekioth', in the Bible, however, there is also found the '*teru'ah*', so doubt arose as to the sound of the latter, regarding which R. Abahu came here to a definite conclusion.

[5] North of Jerusalem, described as an old fortress (see Jastrow s.v. הוצל).

[6] v. Sukka 5, 5. They used to blow six blasts on the eve of the Sabbath in order to mark the entrance of the Sabbath. This was observed even when a festival happened to fall on the same day, as there was still a distinction made between the festival and the Sabbath day. The subject of discussion, however, was the kind of blast to be used, whether it should be the plain *tekiah* or the tremolo *teru'ah* blast. R. Assi prescribed that both should be blown in one breath.

consent of the Presidents. Apart from their own locality they could not impose an acceptance of their rulings upon other communities, so the *takkanoth* issued by Rab and Samuel who ruled over all the exiles in Babylon are mentioned as applicable to Babylon only, since they could not enforce them on the Palestinians where the Presidents had authority. See Ber. 33*b* on the composition for us by Rab and Samuel of a precious prayer in Babylon,[1] a benediction beginning with the word ותודיענו.

Later when the Palestinian Academies declined in standing, whilst those in Babylon rose, reaching the position when all Israel followed the sages of Babylon alone, we find the general terms 'It was instituted', 'They ordained', and 'They caused to be ordained', applied even to the *takkanoth* promulgated by Amoraim, heads of Academies, without any indication of the particular place for which the *takkanah* was intended.

So, for example, in the case of R. Judah[2] who was the most prominent figure of his generation, to such a degree that even R. Nahman[3] the E——rch's son-in-law paid him honour,[4] we find that the references to his *takka...oth* are g.....n in general terms—viz. R. Judah laid down the formula for a ...e ' c ' sale of slaves (Git. 86*a*), or again, R. Judah instituted the formula for a deed of *halitzah* (Yeb. 39*b*), and so particularly in the case of Samuel who, both prior to Rab's arrival in Babylon[5] and after Rab's demise, was recognized as the leading authority of his age, and whose leadership the house of the *Resh Galutha* consistently followed,[6] his *takkanoth* were also referred to generally in the following form: Samuel laid down that a *get*[7] (Bill of Divorce) made by a man on a sick bed should run 'If I do not die this is not to be a *get*, but if I die it is to be a *get*'[8] (Git. 75*b*).

[1] Lit. a precious pearl. The prayer in question is the paragraph inserted in the *Amida* of the Sabbath evening service if a Festival happens to fall on it. It refers to the difference in the degrees of sanctity between Sabbath and Festival. Owing to its fine composition the rabbis called it a pearl.

[2] bar Ezekiel, head of Pumbeditha, the famous seat of learning in Babylon, a disciple of Rab, whose *halachoth* he often quoted.

[3] bar Jacob, head of the School of Nehardea.

[4] v. Kid. 70*b*, R. Judah was summoned before R. Nahman to defend himself against an accusation, whereupon R. Nahman said to him, 'If I do not understand even the ordinary language of the Master, how is it possible that I should send a summons to the Master?'

[5] v. Meg. 22*b* for the facts that Rab happened to visit Babylon on a fast day, and that at that time Samuel (as mentioned there) already occupied his position as head of the academy in Sura.

[6] I can find no proof of this statement.

[7] In the Hebrew text the author actually refers to a writ of emancipation; the reference in the Gemara, however, is to a Bill of Divorce given by a husband on a sick bed to his wife.

[8] That is, the conditions in such a case, if it is to be binding, must be duplicated or expressed both affirmatively and negatively. Here he commences with the negative first, because a man does not like to commence with evil.

CHAPTER XV

RULINGS ESTABLISHED BY THE USAGE
OF THE PEOPLE

WE again find various rulings, mostly in the Order of Nezikin,[1] for which there is no Biblical support and of which the Rabbis have not stated that they were transmitted to them by tradition. These rulings were established purely by the usage of the land, as for example, the rulings of the first Mishnahs of the seventh and ninth chapters of Baba Metzia and that of the first chapter of Baba Bathra, where the Rabbis asserted that the matter depends entirely on the custom of the land.[2] At times a still more significant point may be seen in the fact that the Rabbis designed certain laws in the Mishnah by the general term *halachoth*, subsequently interpreting it as the accepted laws of the land; v. Kid. 39a, where *Orlah*[3] is designated an *halachah* and the Gemara explains this to mean that it is an accepted law of the land.[4] See B.M. 93a for the ruling that those who guard fruit may eat thereof. This, it is stated, is in accordance with the general custom of the land and not based on Scriptural law.

A case of the same category is found in the Mishnah, B.M. 4, 11, where we read: 'It was truly said that strong wine may be mixed with light wine because it (the latter) improves it.'[5] From this, the Gemara states it may be concluded that, wherever the Rabbis assert 'It was truly said', it is a *halachah*.[6] Maimonides in his Introduction to the Mishnah classes this *halachah* with the Sinaitic Laws. This is presumably in view of the principle stated in the Jerusalem Talmud[7] that all rulings introduced with the expression 'Truly' are Sinaitic. The author of the

[1] The fourth of the six Orders of the Talmud, devoted mainly to civil and criminal laws.
[2] For instance, the length of a day's work is regulated by custom, or again, if partners have agreed to divide a piece of land among themselves, they are obliged to contribute equally to the building of the fence. Again if a man leases a field not on a rental basis, but for an agreed share in the produce, he is to follow the custom of the land in the method of cutting the crops.
[3] Uncircumcised produce, Lev. xix, 23–24, 'When you come into the land and plant trees for food, ye shall count the food thereof as uncircumcised three years it shall not be eaten of.'
[4] Referring to the law of *Orlah*, as applied outside the land of Israel. v. M. Orlah, 3, 9.
[5] And adds to the advantage of the purchaser. But with other produce, one is not allowed to mix the produce of one field with that of another.
[6] i.e. the words indicate a decisive and undisputed ruling.
[7] Kilaim 2, 2; T'rumoth 2, 1. Sab. 10, 4. All these refer to *halachoth* introduced by the expression 'Truly'.

Responsa *Havoth Yair*[1] (No. 192)[2] challenged Maimonides' ruling.[3] However, in the case of the intermixture of wines mentioned above, the meaning of the statement 'wherever, etc.' (as above) is that it is an accepted law of the land, for so men acted from early times in commercial matters. We can similarly explain the Mishnah, B.B. 2, 2: 'No one should open a bakery or a dyer's workshop under his neighbour's storehouse, though truly the Rabbis did permit this in the case of wine.'

In this Mishnah, too, they are dealing with generally accepted laws of the land. It may be observed, however, that the author of *Havoth Yair* does not make reference to this Mishnah.

Indeed, if you search through the treatise of Baba Bathra, which is larger than any other, you will not find any *halachoth* based on the written law or received by tradition from Sinai, except in its eighth chapter in which the laws of hereditary degrees, as set out in the Torah, are dealt with, and a few other such *halachoth*; otherwise all the decisions and rulings discussed in it belong to the category of laws whose main grounds, as given by the Rabbis, were either common reasoning or the customs of the land followed by the people in their commercial transactions or in their efforts to prevent damage to neighbours. All are expansions of the chief ordinance in the Torah, 'The Court shall judge in cases of damage and lawsuits with a just judgment',[4] i.e. legal cases, both civil and criminal, as also of the general ordinance 'and thou shalt do that which is right and good.'[5] Even in the case of the principle established by the Rabbis that mere occupation of a property for three years (where there was no protest by the owner) acquires *Hazakah* (the right of ownership) without any other legal proof by document, they endeavoured to find Scriptural support (vide B.B. 28*b*, 29*a*) by

[1] By R. Yair Haim Bachrach of Worms (1638–1702).
[2] This responsum is renowned as a scholarly treatise on oral tradition.
[3] From *Yad*, M. Asuroth 10, 10, where although the prohibition of *Orlah* outside the land is a Sinaitic law, yet, in this case, he derives it direct from the Mishnah (Orlah 3, 9) where the term *Halacha* alone (without 'truly') is mentioned. Indeed most of the rabbinic authorities in their discussions on this point have concluded that the statement of the Jerusalem Talmud must not be understood literally to mean that all such *halachoth* are laws transmitted from Sinai. It is merely meant to emphasize that wherever the *halachah* is preceded by such words as 'truly it was said' it ranks as being as decisive and undisputed as the 'Sinaitic laws' even though not actually so. See Rashi on B.M. 60*a* s.v. באמת; Bartenura, T'rumoth 2, 1; T. Yom-Tob B.M. 4, 11; *Kesef Mishneh* Matnoth Aniim 6, 5; and Asheri in his compilation of the *Mikwah* laws. There is, therefore, no ground for the challenge in question since the wording of Maimonides can be interpreted in the same way. One wonders how the author with his remarkable knowledge of the facts came to omit the aforesaid references.
[4] Deut. xvi, 18.
[5] Deut. vi, 18.

analogy from the Biblical case of the *Mu'ad* ox,[1] but without success,[2] until they ultimately applied common reasoning as the chief basis for this ruling. They penetrated the minds of men and noted their conduct and judgments, so in this case they realized that for one year or two or even three years a man is careful of his title-deeds, but beyond that time he is careless (B.B. 29a).

Many of the presumptions[3] established by the Rabbis as basic principles in their legal decisions originated in the fact that they had observed the nature of man and his endeavours and habits in human society. They made a profound study of his condition in relationship with his neighbour and came to understand the laws of nature in virtue of which they were able to lay down and apply such principles as that of presumption or that of 'majority' as solid foundations in the administration of justice which indeed became important factors in Jewish law. The following are examples:—(a) It is presumed that a thing which is in one's possession is the property of the possessor,[4] (b) that no man will pay his debt before it falls due,[5] (c) that no woman will dare to make a false assertion in the presence of her husband,[6] (d) that no man will be so brazen-faced as to deny a debt in the presence of his creditor,[7] (e) that a man will not make a claim against another unless he has a claim,[8] (f) that witnesses will not sign a document (of sale) unless the

[1] Lit. forewarned, applied to an ox that has gored on three successive occasions; v. Ex. xxi, 29. The number three, with which the analogy is made, is based on the text 'from yesterday and the day before' which with to-day makes three.

[2] The arguments brought forward in refutation of the analogy could not be met.

[3] Known by the familiar Hebrew term חזקה, lit. taking hold or possession. In certain cases it is used for a presumption arising from the fact of possession, and in others, one arising from the nature of man or from certain actions and circumstances (v. Keth 75b).

[4] In the Talmudic legal terminology it reads 'leave the money in the possession of its master', hence the general principle in Jewish law that the onus of proof is on the plaintiff (see B.K. 35a; B.M. 100a; Keth. 20a).

[5] v. B.B. 5b, i.e. if a lender fixes a date for the repayment of a loan and the borrower pleads that he paid the debt before it fell due, his plea is not accepted, because it is presumed that, etc. . . . .

[6] See Yeb. 116a, Git. 89b; i.e. when a woman says to her husband 'you have divorced me' she is to be believed because of the presumption that no woman will dare, etc.

[7] It was on the basis of this presumption that we have the requirement that the man who admits part of the claim must take an oath, even though he could have been believed by reason of the fact that he could have used the plea of 'entire denial' which would legally exempt him from an oath, for in view of the presumption that no one would be so impertinent as to use such a plea in the presence of a creditor, the entire denial cannot be regarded as probable (see B.M. 3a, Tos., s.v מפני).

[8] This view is advanced by R. Nahman as a ground for the imposition of an 'oath of inducement', in case of an utter denial of the claim, even though the defendant in such a case should be exempt from an oath. On account of the said presumption this equitable oath was imposed (see Sheb. 40b).

vendor has attained his majority,[1] (g) that no man will go to the trouble of preparing a meal (wedding feast) and then waste it,[2] (h) that no man will drink out of a cup unless he has examined it first[3] (i) that no man will remain indifferent where his property[4] is threatened,[5] (j) that the agent will carry out his commission.[6]

Also in connection with some other legal restrictions or relaxations the Rabbis relied on such presumptions, for, not having scriptural support for them, it was purely on the basis of their knowledge of the nature of things and the nature of men, of the circumstances of each, and of the relative worth of some compared with others that they established such legal principles as we find in the following examples. It is to be presumed that when a woman commits adultery she has not attempted to ascertain[7] the pedigree of the adulterer.[8] It is taken for granted that

[1] In this case the age of twenty (see B.B. 155a), and not thirteen, as in the case of religious responsibility.

[2] v. Keth 10a and Yeb. 107a for examples of how this presumption was applied as a basis of various marriage laws. (1) A husband's allegation of unchastity immediately following the nuptial relation is taken into consideration on the ground that no man would go to the trouble, etc. (2) According to Beth Shammai minors should not be given the right of mi'un (refusal) because of the objection of people to marry them under the cloud of such a probability, since if the woman exercises mi'un after the marriage, he will have wasted his wedding feast and it is established that no man would, etc.

[3] This is applied in connection with the detection of physical defects by the husband in his wife where he claims nullification of the marriage, because his marriage was entered into in error. If she had already come under the husband's authority by betrothal, he is then charged with the duty of producing proof that she had the defects stated before the betrothal. In the absence of such evidence his plea would be overthrown by the said presumption that no man would drink out of his cup, etc.

[4] The author here employs the term נפש soul, i.e. life, for the Rabbis found in human nature an anxiety about the loss of money similar to that when life itself is threatened. In fact, in Jer. San. 8, 8, on this subject, the sentence 'One's money is as important to him as his life' is used.

[5] See San. 72b for the reason of freeing a house-owner from liability to the death penalty for having killed a thief who broke in, i.e. that they were certain of the thief's determination to kill the owner in case he should oppose him. He was prepared for the owner's resistance by reason of the presumption in question.

[6] Several laws were based on the application of this presumption, (a) the law in connection with the instruction to be given to a messenger regarding an erub (marking a spot as an abode for the Sabbath). See Er. 31b. (b) the law with regard to the appointment of an agent to secure one's betrothal to a woman (Git. 64a, Naz. 12b).

[7] The author here had omitted the negative, see below.

[8] v. Keth 14a, where this is mentioned in a retort to Abaye who raises a point of contradiction on a ruling of R. Joshua as compared with another of his rulings. In Keth. 1, 8, R. Joshua rules that if a woman is suspected of having had illicit intercourse, her statement that the man was a priest is not to be believed, whereas in Eduyoth 8, 3, he taught that the widow of doubtful stock is eligible for marriage with a priest. The answer was that one cannot compare a doubt which arises out of adultery with that arising out of marriage since in the latter case a woman would usually go to the trouble of investigating, but not so in the former case.

the guest[1] arrives in time.[2] It is assumed that an artisan will not harm his profession.[3] A *Haber*[4] is presumed not to let anything not properly seen to pass out of his control.[5]

Again it is presumed that a blood flux is normally sensed when it issues.[6] Similarly in the case of the adoption of the '*Miggo*'[7] by the court as a plea in favour of the defendant,[8] it is assumed that he has spoken the truth, because had he wished to deceive, he could have made use of a better defence; and there are many other lines of reasoning which are the fundamental grounds on which rests the legal principle of *Miggo*.[9]

[1] A euphemism for menstruation, Nid. 16a.

[2] Therefore in cases when a woman had failed to examine herself in time, even where subsequently she found herself clean she is deemed to be unclean because it is presumed that the guest, etc.

[3] This statement as here worded is found in later rabbinic legal literature. It is a derivation from several decisions in the Gemara. (1) See Men. 42b where it is permissible to buy *tzitzith* (fringes, Num. xv, 38) from a non-Jew provided that he is known as a business man who, it is presumed, will not discredit himself by making a false statement regarding the source of the *tzitzith* (see Hul. 98b). (2) It is permissible to employ a professional cook to taste food suspected of being mixed with an amount of prohibited food, v. *Orach Hayyim* 20, 5; *Yoreh Deah*, 114, 5.

[4] Lit. an associate, the opposite of *am ha'aretz*, illiterate and so untrustworthy. The *haber* was a member of an association which was scrupulous in the observance of the laws, particularly in those relating to cleanness and uncleanness and to those of the tithes. See Dem. II, 3, 'one who undertakes to live as a *haber*.' The title is based on Ps. cxix, 63. 'I am an *associate* to all that fear thee.' Collectively the association is called חבורה; cf. Tos. Dem. ii 'he has taken the pledge in the presence of a חבורה,' see also Ber. 31a 'he is to be cast out of the חבורה.'

[5] Applied to a case where a *Haber* having died and left fruit (not known to have been tithed), it is presumed to have been properly treated because it is taken for granted that a *Haber* would not allow, etc. (A.Z. 41b; Erub. 32a).

[6] Biblically the issue does not come under the category of fluxes which cause uncleanness except where the woman has sensed the issue. The Rabbis, however, imposed uncleanness upon her even on her observing a stain, either on her body or clothing, without having sensed its flow. They thus relied on the presumption that there can be no flow without its being accompanied by some slight sensation, and in case she is unaware of it, this must be ascribed to individual constitution. V. Nid. 57b for the statement by Samuel and the Gemara's conclusion there; 58b, 59a, and *Yad*, Issure Biah 9, 1.

[7] An Aramaic word used as a legal term connoting 'for this reason', composed of מן and גו, the equivalent of the Hebrew מתוך ('since, because, or whilst').

[8] When one of the litigants advances an assertion in support of a plea and it is known to the court that he has a still better reason for his plea, his assertion is accepted, on the assumption that he has spoken the truth, because had he wished to perjure himself he would have put forward a better case. Examples of its application are to be found in B.B. 33a and in Keth. 2, 1. If, for example, A claims ownership of B's property and B in his defence says 'this property belonged to your father and I bought it from him', B is to be believed, for had B wished to appropriate what was not his he could have advanced a better plea, viz. that he had purchased it from the claimant himself, and had held it by use, producing documentary proof for the necessary period of occupation, i.e. three years (see B.B. 3, 1).

[9] i.e. many arguments are tested in the Gemara as to whether this principle should be applied or not, as shown later in the text.

(1) A *Miggo* involving an impertinent plea.[1]

(2) A *Miggo* in a case of a conjectural plea.[2]

(3) A *Miggo* in a case which implies exemption from an oath.[3]

(4) A *Miggo* where it contradicts the established principle of *hazakah* (presumption).[4]

(5) A *Miggo* in a case where there are witnesses.[5]

---

[1] The following is the illustration: According to Scripture the defendant always takes the oath that he does not owe the amount claimed from him by the plaintiff and then is exempt, except in those cases detailed in the Mishnah Sheb. 7, 1, where the plaintiff takes the oath and vindicates his claim. Giving, as one example, the hired labourer, Samuel in Sheb. 45a points out that, in a case where the labourer has no witness that he was hired, the defendant's plea that he has paid him his wages is accepted, because of the *Miggo* that, had he desired to deceive him, he could have used a better plea, viz. that he had never hired him. This reasoning, however, is not upheld by the Codifiers (Maimonides, Sechirut 2, 8, and Asheri, Sheb. ad loc.), since to apply the *Miggo* in this case would be to contradict the established principle that no one is so brazen-faced as to make an utter denial in the presence of the claimant.

[2] This category of *Miggo* is elucidated by the following ruling in M. Yeb. 15, 1, and in the Gemara 115a. If a woman who went overseas in time of war later came back and stated that her husband had died, her evidence as to this is not accepted, because in time of war she can speak only from conjecture. In a case, however, where the fact that there was a war was established only by her evidence, the question is then raised whether her evidence should not be accepted on the ground of a *Miggo*, for had she desired to deceive, she need not have disclosed the fact that there was a war at all. In the Gemara the question remains undecided, but Maimonides (*Yad*, Gerushin 13, 2) and Karo (*E. Haezer*, 17, 49) have decided not to accept her evidence in such a case, since to them hers is still a conjectural plea.

[3] In the case of a paid bailee who pleads that the article deposited with him was lost by an unpreventable accident where an oath is imposed upon him and he is then exempt (Ex. xxii, 10; Sheb. 8, 1). This ruling is applied even in a case where the owner cannot produce witnesses in whose presence he handed over the article, even though in such a case the bailee should be exempt from the oath by the argument of a *Miggo* to the effect that had he intended to deceive the owner, he could have pleaded that the article had never been deposited with him. Yet as this would result in exempting the defendant from an oath, it is not applied. (v. *Yad*, S'chirut 2, 8; Hos. Mish. 296) Asheri on Sheb. 45a disputed this conclusion.

[4] For an illustration of this, see B.B. 5b, where a creditor claims payment at the time when payment is due, and the debtor pleads that he paid the debt before it fell due; the latter is not believed in view of the presumption that no man pays before his debt falls due. A question, however, arose over the case where the creditor claims payment some time after the debt falls due, and the debtor pleads that he had paid before that date, whether one should accept his plea on the ground of a *Miggo*, since he could have pleaded that he had paid the debt when it fell due, or whether if we will accept this plea, it will contradict the said 'hazakah'. In the Gemara the question remains undecided, but Maimonides, *Yad*, Malveh 4, 1, and Karo, Hosh. Mish. 78, 1, summed up in the negative.

[5] For this, see illustration in B.M. 81b. A man hired an ass to his friend and warned him not to go by the way of Nehar Pekod, a place which is exposed to river floods, but to go by the way of Naresh, where there is not any water. The ass died, and when the borrower returned he himself admitted (without witnesses) that he did go by the way of Nehar Pekod, but claimed that the river bed was dried up. Even though, had he wished to deceive, he could have pleaded that he had gone by the way of Naresh,

(6) A *Miggo* based on the argument that the defendant could, if he had so wished, have remained silent,[1] which indeed is stronger than any other of the *Miggo* arguments.

All these principles are rooted deeply in the ground of common reasoning alone; there is no basis for them either in Scripture or in oral tradition; but as we have already explained above, rulings derived from common reason are equal in authority to those derived directly from the Torah. Similarly with regard to the 'majority' rule,[2] the Rabbis acted in accordance with the normal relations of man with man, as, for example, they issued rulings on the basis of the fact that most women marry as virgins, and that, in most of the cases of those who marry as virgins, the fact is known.[3] So too in the matter of the fact that most of those engaged in Shechita are experts (Hul. 3*b*).[4] Although there was no Biblical support to be found for these assumptions of the 'majority' and 'presumption' rules, yet they were applied as recognized principles. It is true that the Rabbis sought a Biblical basis for the majority principle in a case where the numbers are not actually ascertainable (Hul. 11*a*) and after suggesting various Biblical cases as proofs they concluded with the argument that the state of an object needs to be determined only in cases where it is possible[5]; so too Rashi, ad loc.,

nevertheless his evidence was not accepted, because in a case like this, where there were witnesses that Nehar Pekod was never free of water, one does not apply the *Miggo* reasoning (v. *Yad*, Sechirut 4, 4).

[1] See Keth. 2, 3. If witnesses testify that a document is in their handwriting, but they were minors, or otherwise ineligible to be witnesses, they are believed; and the document is invalid, because had they wished merely to upset the validity of the document, they could have remained silent and not borne any testimony.

[2] A principle by which the Rabbis were guided in regulating the administration of justice, and which was followed in legal as well as in ritual enactments. Its Biblical basis is in Ex. XXIII, 2; v. San. 3*b*.

[3] v. Keth. 16*b* and B.B. 92*b* which show how these principles are to be applied. It quotes a case where a woman's claim to her full two hundred zuz Kethubah (see p. 88, note 9) is disputed by her husband on the ground that he had married her as a non-virgin. The ruling in this case is that although there is, in her favour, the fact that the majority of women marry as virgins, nevertheless she would be entitled to her claim only when witnesses are forthcoming to verify her plea, whilst in the absence of this there would be another fact which would impair that of the 'majority', the fact that whenever a woman marries as a virgin the marriage is known.

[4] So that in case the shochet is not available for examination, the principle here quoted is applied, viz. that most of those engaged, etc.

[5] This was in a discussion of the last suggested source for the deduction of the majority principle from the case of the *Shechitah*, from whence an assumption can be made that most beasts do not suffer from defects in their 'pipes' (wind or food) otherwise it may be asked, 'Is it not possible that if one of them, particularly the food pipe, had an injury, the tiniest injury would make it t'refah at the spot where the knife made the cut of severance; and since this is not even considered the case, does it not prove the application of the majority principle?' On this comes the rejoinder that we are out to determine the state of an object only where it is possible; consequently the said deduction need not necessarily be made.

states definitely that the 'majority' principle must have been a Sinaitic law. Earlier in the Gemara they also attempted to demonstrate a Biblical basis for the principle of *hazakah*. They suggested here the Biblical law regarding the plague of leprosy in relation to houses,[1] but they are dealing there with a presumption regarding a thing existing already in fact,[2] and also with a principle of majority depending on the actual nature of things. For the application of these two principles we have Biblical support, hence where a doubt arises we rely, for example, on the principle of *hazakah*,[3] viz. the presumption that the state of the object has not undergone any change from what it was earlier. Whereas in cases where the said two principles are not based on the nature of objects, they are simply the outcome of the position of men in society and their relationships with it, such principles being only capable of establishment by logical reasoning and profound reflection. Yet although they found no Scriptural basis for such, they followed these fundamental guiding principles in their rulings, since they regarded a view based on factual experience as being equally authoritative with one derived from the hermeneutical rules. Both principles where based on common reason had the same authority as Biblical law, provided both had been voted on and decided regularly, for they were *halachah* which had been decided by a majority vote and could not be annulled.

Again, we find that in some cases the Rabbis applied the principle that whichever one (amongst the litigants) is the stronger will prevail[4] (B.B. 34*b*). Asheri at the beginning of the first chapter of B.M. quotes authorities to the effect that these words 'whoever is the stronger' mean, not that he is actually superior in physical strength, but a claimant who will spare no endeavour, either in force of argument or physical effort, to acquire the property, thereby gives proof of owner-

---

[1] Cf. Lev. xiv, 38. If the priest, on his examining the plague sore, found it of a certain size, he locked up the house for seven days, postponing further examination till after the conclusion of this period. Is it not possible that while he was locking the door the plague sore grew smaller? Since therefore no notice of this possibility is found in Scripture, we may argue the validity of the principle of presumption, i.e. we presume that the plague-sore remained in the condition in which it was.

[2] Such as an existing sore of a certain size.

[3] As well as on the majority principle.

[4] This principle is advanced by R. Nahman in regard to a case where two men claim the same property and each pleads that it belonged to his father and neither can produce evidence. At first sight this gives the impression that mere force is adopted as the deciding factor, and although Rashi, ad loc., includes also the strength of argument as a means towards acquiring possession, yet physical force, too, is not excluded by him as a potential or decisive factor. See also Git. 60*b* regarding fields which adjoin a river. Rab and Samuel differ in their views, whether the owners lower down may draw up water first, or whether this right is to be assigned to the owners higher up. Seeing that no decision is given on the matter, the Gemara concludes that whoever is the stronger will prevail.

ship.[1] Again we find that in several cases they left (the settlement) to the discretion of the judges (Keth. 85b).[2] All these rulings are based on the principle of assessment[3]; and in monetary cases assessment is a definite factor, as is shown in the following case (Sheb. 34a):—If there is a lustful camel among others and a camel is found dead beside it, it is taken for granted that he killed it.[4]

Similar is the principle adopted in all cases where two statements are made, one within the minimum time[5] of the other, viz. that it is to be taken as though the latter was made simultaneously with the former,[6] except in the cases of betrothal,[7] divorce,[8] blasphemy, and idolatry[9] (B.B. 129b; Ned. 87a). Maimonides on the Mishnah (Tem. 5, 3) adds to these the cases of dedicated[10] and substituted offerings.[11] The special

---

[1] i.e. it is because he is the real owner that he concentrates all his efforts to regain it.

[2] Reference to this legal principle is made in several cases. The case in the text refers to a man who on his death-bed expressed the wish that his estate should be given to Tobiah without determining who he was, and, after he died, two Tobiahs presented themselves to claim the property, both having the same relationship, rank, and scholarship. The decision was left to the discretion of the judges. Another case in Keth. 94a refers to two holders of a deed relating to the sale or a gift of the same property, bearing the same date, both of whom appear before the court to claim the property. The matter is decided by the discretion of the court.

[3] i.e. judgment following upon calculation and assumption, therefore based on circumstantial evidence.

[4] Hence the conjectural evidence is applied for the purpose of issuing a definite judgment against the owner of the camel that is assumed to have been guilty.

[5] The period of the minimum time fixed by the Rabbis was the length of time needed for the utterance of the three Hebrew words of greeting used by a disciple to his Rabbi שלום עליך רבי (v. B.K. 73b; Naz. 20b).

[6] So, in case the speaker immediately cancelled or modified his first statement, the change is valid.

[7] In the Gemara the order is reversed.

[8] If a man betrothed or divorced a woman, but within the minimum time of his utterance retracted, the retraction is unavailing. Similarly if the woman whose consent for the betrothal is needed should withdraw her consent, it is invalid.

[9] If a man declares an idol as god or utters a blasphemy, and immediately, i.e. within the minimum time of his statement, withdraws it, his withdrawal is not valid. The reason for the exception, as given by Girondi on Ned., ad loc., is that these instances are cases involving most serious consequences and therefore particular care is demanded in making any statement upon them.

[10] v. Tem. 5, 3, if after one has dedicated a beast for a peace offering he changes his mind and says that its eventual young should be made a whole offering, the young are none the less still taken as the young of the peace offering, even although the later statement was made within the minimum of the time needed for the greeting utterance.

[11] v. Lev. XXVII, 10, for the prohibition of replacing a beast which was dedicated as an offering, where if one substitute one beast for another, both are sanctified and the offerer has transgressed a negative law. If after one had said 'this should be the substitute for a whole offering' he bethought himself and said 'this should be the substitute for a peace offering', it is still taken as the substitute for a whole offering, so that the original statement is the decisive one, even though the latter was made within the minimum of time of the first utterance.

ruling adopted in these cases is founded on the argument that in these cases the first utterance is equivalent to an act, and no later utterance had the power to supersede an act (see Shach[1] on *Hosh. Mish.*[2] 255) even though in the cases given the matter involves liability to the penalty either of flagellation or death.[3] Again there are several other rulings in laws relating to diet which are not deduced from Scripture nor is there any mention that such rulings had been derived from Biblical law or established tradition. The Rabbis only told us that these rules were known to them simply as laws of nature. They knew, for example, that it is inherent in the nature of salt that it extracts the blood in the meat; they consequently ordained that the meat should be salted in order to draw out the blood, and so the Rabbis established the following list of rules:—(1) What is preserved in salt is to be ritually considered as having reached the highest possible temperature.[4] (2) What is pickled (in brine or fermented juice) is to be ritually considered as having been cooked.[5] (3) Blood slips off the meat.[6] (4) Any substance whilst engaged in discharging does not absorb.[7] (5) When it discharges its own blood, it also discharges that which it had absorbed from without.[8] (6) The salt cannot in the case of vessels effect the discharge of what they have once absorbed.[9]

---

[1] Abbreviation of *Sifthe Cohen.*

[2] Where he questions the addition of the above two by Maimonides to the four exceptional cases.

[3] As in the cases of betrothal or divorce, where the difference between regarding the woman as married or as unmarried may involve the severest penalty.

[4] This is applied in the case where two articles of food, one permitted and the other prohibited, come into contact, and where one of them is heavily salted. v. Hul. 111*a*; Pes. 73*a*; *Yoreh De'ah* 91, 5.

[5] In the same way where a prohibited article of food has been mixed in the said substance with a permitted article, they are to be treated as if they had been boiled together (Hul. 111*a*; Pes. 76*a*).

[6] This theory is given in connection with a case where liver and meat have been roasted on one spit. Here the blood of the liver dripping on the meat does not matter in view of the said theory that blood slips off (Hul. 111*a*; *Yoreh De'ah* 73, 4).

[7] This refers to the liver which is considered as an exception in the following case, viz. if the liver touches meat, the latter becomes prohibited in view of the blood which it absorbs from the liver. On the other hand, if liver touches forbidden meat, it does not become prohibited because the liver, whilst it is discharging, cannot absorb anything from without (M. Ter. 10, 11; Hul. 111*a*).

[8] This theory applies to the case where meat, before it was actually salted, came into contact with meat which was still in the salt; although the former is liable to absorb blood from the latter and thus become forbidden, yet since it is yet to be salted, we apply the said principle, viz. that when, etc., v. Karo, *Beth Yosef*, 70, on the authority of R. Jonah; he is quoted also in the Code 70, 6.

[9] For this reason, therefore, a vessel once used for prohibited food cannot render permissible food which has been salted in it forbidden. See Tos. Hul. 113*a*, s.v. טהור *Yoreh De'ah* 105, 12.

(7) Permissible food will fatten forbidden food.[1] (8) A substance which, in itself, is affected by something else and so forbidden, cannot turn and cause a similar effect on the other.[2] (9) There is a special application of the dietary laws to prohibited substances which adhere to other unprohibited substances.[3] (10) A pungent element improves the taste of a substance whose flavour has been impaired.[4] (11) Vessels become satiated and are no longer receptive.[5] (12) Fat penetrates.[6] (13) Boiling liquid that is poured on brings the substance up to a cooking grade in heat.[7]

(14) The liver discharges its blood but does not absorb (the juice of the other element (M. Ter. 10, 11; Yoreh Deah 73, 2).[8] (15) When only part of an iron vessel is heated the whole of it is affected by the heat.[9] (16) An unbroken stream of liquid poured from one receptacle

[1] This has reference to the ruling not to have forbidden dishes and permissible ones roasted in one oven because the flavour conveyed by steam from one to the other is competent to affect it. This is so even in a case where it is the permissible dish that is flavoured with fat, as it is understood that it may fatten the other and thus in turn become affected by it (Pes. 76b; Yoreh De'ah 108, 1). Although this looks somewhat contradictory to the principle that follows, viz. that nothing which is affected by another thing can turn to affect it, in this case, however, the flavour conveyed by the steam is quite sufficient to do so (v. Shach, 108, 1).

[2] This has reference to pungent substances such as salt or spices which, if they have been rendered forbidden in themselves, even the presence of the largest quantity cannot neutralize (Orlah 2, 4; Yad, M. Assuroth 16a). If, however, they have been rendered forbidden by absorbing something which is prohibited they can then be neutralized by the usual quantity of sixty parts, because being, in themselves, only affected by other things they cannot be more potent than the thing which caused the effect. v. Tos. Hul. 108, s.v. אמאי; Yoreh De'ah, 105, 14.

[3] An exception was adopted here to the effect that the whole piece must be neutralized and not merely the actual substance joined to it, and even if it has been neutralized it still remains forbidden, because of the adhering of the prohibited substance.

[4] See A.Z. 67b. An element which imparts an impaired flavour is permitted. The later authorities made a provision that where the prohibited element is mixed with another element having a spiced taste, it improves the impaired flavour. v. Yoreh De'ah 103, 6.

[5] Lit. able to absorb. For the source, see A.Z. 33b where earthenware cups used for drinking wine, if the heathen have drunk from them permissible liquid, even two or three times, are no longer in a receptive state to absorb more. See also B.M. 40b 'vessels laden with absorption can absorb no more'. See Yoreh De'ah 135, 5, and Ture Z. Yore D. 93, 2.

[6] As a rule in the case of a forbidden substance, dripped on roasted meat (while on the fire) it would be sufficient to take the part away; if, however, the latter is a fat substance it penetrates and spreads throughout the whole piece. (Hul. 97a; Yoreh De'ah 105, 5).

[7] v. Tos. Zeb. 95b, s.v. עירה ; Isserlis, Yoreh De'ah 95, 3; Shach, 105, 5.

[8] See p. 127, note 7.

[9] This is applied in connection with several ritual laws, see Yoreh De'ah 94, 1. In case only part of an iron spoon used for milk has been dipped in a pot containing boiled meat on the fire, it is held that the whole of it was inserted. See Yoreh De'ah

into another makes full communication of conditions.[1] (17) (The forbidden substance) reawakens itself.[2] (18) The blood which is discernible on the surface of the meat is removed neither by salting nor by roasting.[3] (19) Again there is the ruling advanced by the *Geonim*[4] to the effect that meat which has been kept three days without salting from the time the animal was slaughtered has the blood dried within it and cannot discharge it by being salted.[5] (20) Here, too, belongs the dispute over a taste-giving substance in the second degree.[6]

(21) Also the dispute whether the flavour (of a forbidden thing) is a recognized factor[7]; (22) and whether the lower or upper of two substances prevails.[8] (23) Again the question whether we are to adopt the possibility of squeezing the forbidden substance out.[9] And so here, too, belong several regulations which were accepted by the rabbis in the administration of the law without their having any basis for them in Scripture nor claiming support for them from tradition; they merely studied and sought to comprehend the nature of meat, salt, blood, fat, the liver and the like, and by experiment came to lay down sound foundations for these practical decisions which were subsequently adopted among us as definite rulings.

Again one ought to be aware that, although Maimonides pointed out

121, 6. So a vessel only partially used for forbidden food requires *hag'alah* (a cleansing with boiling water) for the whole.

[1] From the lower vessel to the upper so as to affect the upper with the conditions in which the lower receptacle happens to be, either with regard to uncleanness or to the ritual laws of food (see Git. 16a; and Machshirin 5, 10).

[2] So that even in the case where it has already been neutralized, it may reassert itself, see *Tur O. Hayyim* 447, with reference to *Hametz* (a leavened element) which was neutralized before Passover (see also *Orah Hayyim* 447, para. 1).

[3] Hence the duty of soaking the meat in water before salting or roasting it, to make it ritually fit for use, since the effect of salting or roasting is only on the blood which the meat contains within it and not on blood discernible on the surface. Tos. Hul. 14a, s.v. ונסביך ; *Yoreh De'ah* 69, 76, 1, 2.

[4] An ancient title applied to the heads of the Sura and Pumbeditha Academies in Babylonia between the sixth and thirteenth centuries.

[5] Consequently, cannot be cooked unless it is roasted before an open fire (*Yoreh De'ah* 69, 12).

[6] An illustration is given in Hul. 111b where roasted fish from the fire, having been on a plate which had absorbed the taste of meat, may not be eaten with milk, even though the taste absorbed by the fish is already only of the second degree. This view of Rab is disputed by Samuel.

[7] i.e. in affecting ritually the substance which receives it (A.Z. 66b; Pes. 76a; *Yoreh De'ah* 108).

[8] This refers to two substances, one warm and the other cold, which are in contact. Whether the lower one prevails over the upper one or vice versa is a matter of dispute between Rab and Samuel. See Pes. 76a; *Yoreh De'ah* 105, 3.

[9] And thus subject only the forbidden substance to the law of neutralization and not the whole piece in which it has been absorbed (see Hul. 108b; *Yad*, M. Assuroth 9, 9).

(*Yad*, Shechita 10, 12), with regard to the *t'refah* indications, that even where the injury is found by medical investigations of nature and by the results of practical experience not to be dangerous to the life of the animal, yet only those injuries matter that have been listed by the rabbis on the Biblical principle (Deut. xvII, 11) 'According to the law which they shall teach thee, thou shalt do,' yet even he could not avoid being influenced by science in his decision to declare *te'refah* a beast whose lower jaw has been removed, even though there was no support for this decision in the Gemara and it was based on natural science alone,[1] as he had made clear in his responsum to the scholars of Lunel[2] as quoted by Karo in *Beth Yosef* on Tur, Yoreh Deah.

See also for the same point of view Hul. 54*a* with reference to the hunter striking the animal in the regions of the kidney, where the rabbis do not regard this injury as a *t'refah* indication, because it may be healed (by the application of a drug), just as similarly in the case of a *Pezua Dakkah*,[3] they rely on the existence of methods of healing (Yeb. 76*a*).[4] Also in the case where the animal's womb has been cut out (on the question whether it is to be pronounced *t'refah*) they acted on the authority of Theodorus, the physician, who stated that no cow or sow was allowed to leave Alexandria without first having its womb cut out (Sanhedrin 33*a*).[5] So, too, the investigation by the rabbis in the Talmud (Nazir 39*a*) as to the point from which the growth of the hair begins, i.e. whether beneath the scalp or from above it, an investigation which was important for the decision of the (relevant) *halachah*.[6] So too with reference to menstrual women, they had to investigate the different natural kinds of blood[7] (Nid. 20*b*); and so with several other cases.

[1] i.e. the fact that owing to the inability of the beast to take its food, its life will ultimately be endangered.

[2] French town with an important and scholarly Jewish community during the eleventh and twelfth centuries. Among the scholars of Lunel (and known as such) were Judah b. Saul Ibn Tibbon, physician and student, and Samuel Ibn Tibbon, the translator of Maimonides' *More Nebukhim* (Guide to the Perplexed).

[3] Where man's organs of procreation have been injured. See Deut. xxiii, 2.

[4] Abaye once received a question from R. Idi b. Abin as to how we are to proceed in healing a wounded membrum and he gives in his reply a detailed description of the method of healing. See loc. cit.

[5] So as to limit the Egyptian breed to that country alone. Hence the reliance on a physician in the matter of a pronouncement as to whether the animal is t'refah or not.

[6] The following case will explain the necessity for such an investigation. An unspecified Nazirite vow lasts 30 days, as derived from the numerical value of the word יהיה 'he shall be holy' (Numb. vi, 5). If he or others cuts off his hair before this period has elapsed, he will have to observe another such period. If after the said cutting there was still left a seven days' growth of the hair, it can be argued, if the growth is from the scalp, that it was new hair (unconsecrated) which was cut, while if growth is from the roots, the hair which was cut was the old (consecrated) hair. Only in the latter case will he require to observe another 30 days' period.

[7] Which menstrual women are liable to discharge, resulting in uncleanness.

CHAPTER XVI

MISCELLANEOUS RABBINICAL ORDINANCES

THE Rabbis had another important principle, namely that no action could be traced to the Torah which could cause even the slightest injury to the individual or still less to the community. Many legal decisions and definite *halachoth* were formulated by virtue of this principle. This is so even in connection with the death penalty for criminals, the severity of which towards transgressors is held to be an act of mercy to the world at large, v. *Yad*, Sanhedrin 11, 5. Yet, even in reference to this type of punishment, the Rabbis have deduced from the passage 'Thou shalt love thy neighbour as thyself',[1] known by them as the great positive principle in the Torah, that we are to choose an easy death[2] for the condemned (Torath Cohanim, Lev. xix, 18), and wherever the Rabbis were in doubt as to the kind of penalty to be imposed (upon the guilty) they deduced from the said passage that it is the Court's obligation to reduce it to a minimum and, in the case of the death penalty, to choose the easiest and least humiliating death (San. 45a, 52a). Similarly, the Rabbis deduced by common reasoning alone that the living bird of the leper[3] and the scapegoat[4] are free for profitable use[5] because the Torah did not order them to be sent away to cause a stumbling-block (Yoma 67b; Kid. 57a). Since it could not enter anyone's mind that our holy Torah, whose main purpose is to do us good and to protect us from falling into evil, should, even in the remotest way, charge us with such observances as would result in the falling into sin of those who practise them, the rabbis of necessity ruled that the body of the scapegoat is not forbidden for profitable use (other than eating), and that the living bird of the leper is free even for eating, so that one who picks them up unwittingly may have benefit from them. They also had another guiding principle, viz. that the Torah always wished to spare Israel (unnecessary) expense and did not wish to burden the people with great cost or strain, and so when the Rabbis discussed the reason why the mouthpiece of the *shofar* used on communal fast

---

[1] Lev. xix, 18.
[2] i.e. as little painful and humiliating as possible.
[3] To be sent forth into the open field, Lev. xiv, 7
[4] One of the two goats (Lev. xvi, 7) after the High Priest had laid his hands upon its head, confessing over it the sins of the people, was handed over to a man who led it to a precipitous and flinty rock from which it was cast down, Lev. xvi, 22.
[5] The bird is permitted as food by him who finds it, while any pieces of the scapegoat that may be picked up are permitted, for profit only, but not for eating.

days was to be overlaid with silver[1] and saw that there was no Scriptural source for the kind of metal with which it should be overlaid, they decided the matter on the basis of the general rule that the Torah wishes to spare the wealth[2] of Israel (R.H. 27a). So also where they discuss the urn in which was performed the casting of the lots for the two goats on the Day of Atonement, in meeting the question, why the casket was not made of silver or gold, they answer that the Torah had consideration for the wealth of Israel (Yoma 39a). Elsewhere they say that on the other days (not Yom Kippur) the ministrant raked out the cinders with a silver pan,[3] because the Torah wishes to spare Israel unnecessary expense (ibid. 44b). Further, the Torah always takes into consideration man's bodily sensations, so that the practice of its commandments should not be the cause of physical pain.

So, too, when they question (Suk. 32b) the opinion that the biblical text, 'bough of thick trees,'[4] refers to the myrtle,[5] for it is possible, they say, that it is the oleander.[6] On this point Abaye quoted as a refutation the passage: 'Her (Wisdom's, i.e. the Torah's) ways are ways of pleasantness,'[7] for the oleander will prick, scratch, and tear the hands of the user,' and Raba, taking the same view, quotes the passage: 'Therefore love ye Truth and Peace,[8] for this plant is poisonous.' For a similar view, see Yeb. 87b, where the eventuality is considered of the death of the child of a remarried widow on whose account she had been exempted from the obligation of the levirate marriage. This, it is held, does not subject her to halitza because it is stated in Scripture that 'Her ways are ways of peace', consequently if the subsequent death of the child obliged her to the performance of halitza it would cause grief to both her present husband and herself. See also Rashi, ad loc., and Ramban on Yeb., ad loc.

At any rate, as we have seen, all these rulings branched out from the general principle which serves as a basis throughout the whole Torah, that the purpose of all its commandments, whether in general or in particular, was the well-being of man and not the loading of him with a heavy yoke. In fact they set up a special ruling that men are not to

[1] Whereas that of the *shofar* used in the Temple on New Year's Day was overlaid with gold (M.R.H. 3, 3).
[2] Lit. the Torah had mercy on the money of Israel.
[3] See M. Tamid 1, 4, whereas on Yom Kippur he did this with one of gold.
[4] Lev. XXIII, 40.
[5] The author, by error, refers to 'fruit of a goodly tree', viz. the *Ethrog*, but in the Gemara reference is here made to the myrtle.
[6] A tree with bitter and prickly leaves.
[7] Prov. III, 17.
[8] Zech. VIII, 19. If such a plant were used as one of the four species, both the peace and the love intended by God's commandments would be upset.

perform precepts in batches, so that the precepts may not appear to be reluctantly borne by man as a burden (Sot. 8a). Several important rulings were derived from this, such as the ruling not to give two suspected women the water to drink[1] at one and the same time, nor to break the necks of two calves[2] at the same time[3]; and a similar reason is given in connection with the ruling not to refer, at the conclusion of a benediction, to two things at one time (Ber. 49a). See Tos. Sota 8a, s.v. והא for the statement that all these rulings are only rabbinically ordained.

At first sight it might appear as though the Rabbis put forward also another principle contradicting the above, one which does view the precepts as lying like a yoke on the shoulders of Israel. They say,[4] for example, that 'Precepts were not meant for enjoyment', and Rashi[5] interprets this to mean that the precepts were not intended for men to derive pleasure from, but that they lie like a burden about men's necks. On penetrating more deeply into their meaning, however, this (apparent) contradiction will be straightened out. Indeed, it never entered into the mind of the Rabbis to affirm definitely that any precepts were meant for our detriment, merely to burden us with various tasks which were unnecessary for the betterment of man's moral and social level of life. There cannot be attributed to Him (Blessed be He) an intention to harm us, when it is actually forbidden that one should do the least harm even to dumb creatures, and when many of the Talmudical authorities favour the opinion that the duty to avoid causing living things suffering is a Biblical law (B.M. 32b, and see *Mid. Rabbah*, Deut. vi, 1, where it is stated that just as God extends His mercy to man, so is it extended to the beast and the bird. See also *Moreh Nebukhim* iii, chap. 28, and Ramban on Deut. xxii, 6).

The chief fact is that the Torah precepts originated in grace and have as their object to purify mankind and to endow us with noble virtues. Furthermore, the Rabbis stressed this in the *Midrash Rabbah*, Lev. xxvii, in the words (God says thus to Israel), 'I did not trouble you to bring your offerings from among the animals that are found on the hills and not in domestic areas,' and so again 'I did not trouble you to bless me standing bareheaded'.[6]

---

[1] Numb. v, 22.
[2] Deut. xxi, 1 ff.
[3] v. Sota, ad loc., for references to other rulings of the same character.
[4] See R.H. 28a.
[5] s.v. לא ליהנות
[6] See Lev. R. Ch. 276, Tanhuma Emor, 10; Yalk. Micah 554, 6, God says 'I have not wearied you and have not said unto you, read it standing and with uncovered heads.'

Consequently, in a case where doubts arise as to the manner of observing the precepts of the Torah, we are to be guided by the aforesaid general principle that the Torah's tendency is towards leniency and not towards severity and its intention was not to make heavy the yoke, since her-ways are ways of pleasantness and all her paths are peace, and hence she has consideration for the wealth of Israel and still more for their bodily welfare. Therefore the statement referred to above, that precepts are not meant for pleasure, does not mean to convey that they were intended as a heavy burden, but signifies that the precepts were not intended to afford physical pleasure, for such a view would, indeed, prevent one from performing them at all, as in the case where one interdicted himself by vow from deriving any enjoyment from a particular object[1] which its use might give; again, we have been taught 'To-day is for the doing of them and to-morrow for the reward (for doing them)'.[2] One should not fulfil the commandments merely to receive reward,[3] or in expectation of benefits to come, but one should practise them with a sense of spiritual pleasure and joy, that he was found worthy to carry out the will of his Creator and not for bodily pleasure; for in reality these precepts were intended only to perfect our minds, and in following this principle their practice cannot be regarded as aimed at physical enjoyment.

Similarly the dispute between the Amoraim in the Gemara (R.H. 28a, Pes 115b), whether religious precepts need be performed with deliberate intention or not, is a consequence of the above question, viz. whether or not the performance of religious precepts is a burden with the sole end in view of doing God's will, so that if we can show that His will has been carried out the goal has been achieved. If so there is no need for particular intention in the performance of any precept since the primary object in view is achieved (by the performance alone). One who holds the view, however, that religious precepts need to be performed with deliberate intention must favour the opinion that there is nothing of a burden in the performance of the precepts, since their practice has the object only of perfecting the mind, as it is through those actions that man is awakened to meditate on the ideas of the unity and omnipotence of God; therefore, their performance without deliberate intention will

---

[1] With which the particular precept is to be performed, such as the *shofar* or *Ethrog*, etc. . . . See R.H. 28a.

[2] See Erub. 22a, on Deut. VII, 11. 'Thou shalt therefore keep the commandments, etc., which I command thee this day, to do them,' i.e. to do them to-day and receive the reward to-morrow, in the future, in the world to come. This is based on the suggestion that the words לעשותם and היום should be construed together; in fact the word היום immediately precedes לעשותם.

[3] Cf. Aboth 1, 3.

nullify the main action because the very thing, viz. the concentration of thought, which is so essential for the intensification in one's heart of the ideas which are meant to be taught or awakened by the practice of the external precept is in that case entirely missing.

A similar reconciliation is to be found between the ruling of the Rabbis that disused accessories of religious observances may, if necessary, be thrown away (Meg. 26a), and another ruling of theirs that one should not cover the shed blood with his feet,[1] so that he should not appear to others to treat the precepts with contempt[2] (Sab. 23a).

For in the case of such precepts as the *Lulab*, *Sukkah*, and *Shofar*, it is not the objects in themselves that have importance, they are only the means through which the hearts of the observers are to be rightly awakened, so that when no longer used they may be thrown away, even where this may expose them to disrespectful use. Yet in view of the exalted ideas gained through them, we are not to let them be exposed to disrespect. Maimonides has conveyed this idea felicitously in *Yad*, Shechita 14, 15, where he says, 'one is not to cover (the blood) with his foot so as not to show contempt for the precept, since the honour we so bestow is not directed to the precepts themselves, but to Him Who commanded them, Blessed be He! He has saved us from groping in the darkness and provided us with a lamp to make clear what is obscure, and light to show us the paths of uprightness.'

---

[1] See Lev. XVII, 13, where the blood of the beast (excepting cattle) or fowl killed for food is to be covered with dust. The Rabbis have deduced that with that with which one pours out (the blood) he must cover it, i.e. with his hand, not kick the dust over the blood with his foot (see Hul. 87a).

[2] This latter ruling appears to contradict the former.

אגדה

THE AGGADAH

CHAPTER XVII

THE *AGGADAH*¹—A GENERAL OUTLINE OF ITS MAIN ASPECTS

IT now remains for us to deal with the Aggadic element which forms a great portion of the Talmud and is an important branch of the Torah. This material is scattered throughout the *Mishnah* and the *Baraithoth* and the two Talmudim; and although its substance was not necessarily required for arriving at practical or legal decisions, its value is considerable from another standpoint. The passages are intended to perfect us in the ways of a pure faith and in all the fundamental principles on which the religion of Moses and Israel rests. Their chief object and purpose is to instruct us in knowledge, wisdom, and understanding of true ideas and right life.

The sayings in question are all charming and select, and in them much wisdom in matters of the highest import is condensed in short sentences, and this view is expressed by the Rabbis in the *Sifre*² on Deut. XI, 22, 'If you desire to know Him by whose utterance the World came into being, study the *Aggadah*, for through it you will discern Him Who by His utterances called the World into being.' Maimonides, in his commentary on the Mishnah (Ber. 9, 5), says, 'There is no point in quoting here the ideas advocated by the Philosophers unless it be for the purpose of thereby elucidating something in the domain of our Creed; since it is more precious to me to teach some of the fundamentals of our Religion than any of the other things which I study.'³ And just as

---

¹ Denoting all Scriptural interpretation which is pre-eminently non-*halachic* in character.

² Midrash on Numbers and Deuteronomy.

³ Maimonides interprets the verse Ps. CXIX, 126, 'It is time to work for the Lord. They have made void the Law.' which is quoted in the said Mishnah, as follows: 'When the time arrives for God to carry out His judgment on the evildoers, the latter are prompted by various factors to practise their evil so as to justify the judgment brought upon them.' In this elucidation he touches upon the great problem of Predestination and Freewill which he maintains to be capable of solution, though at first sight they seem irreconcilable. In this connection he quotes Is. LV, 8, 'For my thoughts are not your thoughts', and at the same time lays stress upon the futility of man in engrossing himself in the contradictions which result from the sharp contrast between the fore-knowledge of God and the freedom of will. He affirms, however, that true philosophers have given this matter profound thought, and have found a useful support for this doctrine of free will in Deut. XXX, 19, 'I have set before thee life and death, etc.' In the same context he refers to his Commentary on *Aboth* (seemingly in reference to the Mishnah, Aboth, 3, 15 'Everything is foreseen but the right of choice is granted'), where he quotes opinions of philosophers in support of his views and then concludes with the statement quoted above in the text.

rulings in *halachah* were intended to direct the practical observance of the precepts as duties to be carried out by the bodily faculties, so the Aggadic sayings on their side were intended to teach us clearly the mental side of our religion, as also the particulars of the doctrines of our faith, such as those of the Unity of God or of reward and punishment, or of the freewill of man; or again of angelology and the mysteries of prophecy; of God's providence over all created things or the nature of the human soul and its immortality; of the Messianic hope and the resurrection of the dead, and of many other such matters of faith. In particular the Aggadic sayings were mainly intended for the interpretation of such passages in the Torah and the Prophets as, at first glance, seemed mysterious or obscure. The Rabbis dealt variously with this secret material. In some cases they treated it at length and in an explanatory manner, in others they dealt with it briefly by slight allusions only. Maimonides, in his *Moreh*[1] i, chap. 70, says: 'You may observe that truly great topics on which the most eminent philosophers have meditated are scattered throughout the Midrash.' Note also the following statement in the *Moreh* iii, chap. 22: 'In attending to what I just mentioned let us take note of an utterance of our sages (blessed be their memory), men who are indeed worthy of that title, by which utterance the doubtful is explained and the hidden is revealed, and through which the secret things of the Torah are made clear, viz. that Satan and the evil prompter and the angel of death are all one.[2] In this saying is condensed the whole point of view which I have already set out,[3] a point of view the validity of which no reasonable man will doubt.'

In particular we find that the purpose of the several *Mishnayoth* and *Baraithoth* and the great bulk of the teachings of the two Talmudim was to instruct and direct us how to cultivate and acquire the pure and genuine virtues of uprightness, e.g. how one should conduct himself towards his fellow-men and towards society in general, particularly towards those charged with government. These authorities were conversant with all these subjects, partly from experience and partly from a profound study of ethics and of the way to administer the affairs of state. Thus Maimonides, in the Eight Chapters which he wrote as an

---

[1] *Moreh Nebukhim* or 'Guide of the Perplexed' which, in accordance with its author's own statement of purpose, aimed at promoting the true understanding of the real spirit of the law.

[2] Quoted from B.B. 16*a*, i.e. one and the same personality is active in destroying man, first by inciting him to do evil, and then initiating the accusation against him, and finally bringing death upon him, or in the words of the rabbis (ibid) 'He, Satan, comes down to earth and seduces men and afterwards ascends to heaven and stirs up wrath.'

[3] In his discussion of the Book of Job with special reference to the accuser Satan.

introduction to Aboth, dealing with Ben Kappara's[1] dictum[2]: 'Which is the shortest sentence of the Law on which all the essentials of the Torah depend?[3] The one which reads: "In all thy ways acknowledge Him",'[4] says: 'The Rabbis have comprised all that subject-matter in a few words which cover it completely,[5] so that, if you examine the meaning of these words of theirs and see how the Rabbis conveyed a matter of such weight and significance in so short a statement, you will conclude that they must undoubtedly have been uttered by divine inspiration.'

Indeed, the chief purpose of all the teaching of the Rabbis was without distinction to equip the people with such qualities of mind and character as thereby to deserve the designations 'the Congregation of Jeshurun'[6], 'Jacob the lot of His inheritance,'[7] or 'the people of Israel in whom God is glorified'[8] (v. Yoma 86*a*, *Yad*, Yesode Hatorah 5, 11).[9]

We entertain no doubt that all the Rabbis' teachings which have reference to the foundations of our faith and principles of the Torah were orally transmitted to them from Sinai, only from time to time they deduced these fundamentals by means of their exegetical rules, as it was always their method to support their teachings by Scripture, in order that the subject-matter might be kept easily in their memory. But the one sure fact undoubtedly remains, and that is that all these came down orally from the words of God to Moses our teacher; for if, in respect of the practical observance of the precepts and the physical duties required by them, which are but a preliminary (to the purity) of religious life they had halachoth traditionally received from Sinai, teaching how they were to be applied in various conditions and situations, how infinitely more is this view to be applied to matters of faith and the fundamentals of religion, such as the immortality of the

---

[1] So written in Aramaic, but Ben-Hakappor in Hebrew, Palestinian Amora of the beginning of the third century. His own personal name was Eleazar. He conducted his school at Caesarea.

[2] Ber. 63*a*.

[3] i.e. with the idea of which all the essentials of the Torah must be consciously associated.

[4] Prov. III, 6.

[5] The great ideal which Maimonides advocates in his fifth chapter is that all our efforts should be concentrated upon achieving the one object of reaching the goal set before man, namely 'to know God'. This exalted idea is embodied in the three Biblical words chosen by B. Kappara 'in all thy ways acknowledge Him'.

[6] Deut. XXXIII, 5.

[7] Deut. XXXII, 9.

[8] Cf. Isaiah XLIX, 3. 'Thou are my servant, Israel in whom I will be glorified.'

[9] Where these actual words are found: 'See how fine are the ways of him who has studied the Torah and how righteous are his deeds. Of him Scripture says: Thou art my servant, etc.'

soul and the life beyond; or, again, the mysterious nature of prophecy, and such other cardinal principles of our faith as have no direct references to them in the written Torah, but concerning which tradition has faithfully told us what was transmitted by the fathers to their children in order to fill the gap. Now the Rabbis have left us these traditions scattered throughout the Talmud and Midrash, in some cases fully explained, and in others hinted at by a brief reference, because where the information could be conveyed briefly they thought it inappropriate to deal with it at length.

Now since the style which the Rabbis adopted in the *Midrash* and *Aggadah* is not understood by the average student, so that at first glance many strange idioms and extravagances appear to be contained in their statements, such as have afforded the critics opportunities to pass censure upon them, and to conclude that the Rabbis presented us with strange, at times shocking, utterances, for the support of which they have needlessly deprived passages of their natural or primary meaning, I have set myself the aim to show the reader the methods employed by the Rabbis in these subjects, and to explain the many categories and definitions as well as the idioms and modes of expression which are used by them in the *Aggadah*, as also the various subjects which come under this category, and the reasons which prompted them to adopt such a style. All this I shall endeavour to present to the reader in a concise and at the same time intelligible way.

But first of all I find it necessary to make a small but useful observation, viz. that it is important for us to recognize and bear in mind that the various sages, i.e. the spokesmen quoted in the *Mishnayoth* and in the two Talmudim as well as in the *Baraithoth*, whether those of Palestine or those of Babylon, did not always hold uniform views, and what is more, were not all of the same standing in piety or wisdom.

They differed from one another in capacity and quality and, as it is only natural that people's views should be dissimilar, so also as regards other important attributes which adorn those who possess them. Consequently, we cannot compare the standing of one of the later *Tannaim* with that of Hillel the Elder,[1] the *Nasi* in Israel, or with that of so great a personality as was R. Akiba, or with that of Rabbi (the Holy), renowned for his great wisdom and piety. See B.B. 12a which says: 'The proof[2] is this, viz. that a great man here makes a statement which is afterwards quoted in the name of R. Akiba b. Joseph,' and Rashi

[1] Also named the Babylonian, because he was descended from a family of Babylonian exiles. He is celebrated not only for his prominence as a teacher, but also for his patience and humanity.
[2] That prophecy had not been taken away from the wise.

maintains that in this case we cannot argue that this is because they were both born under the one star,[1] since R. Akiba was certainly the greater man.

A fact to be recognized is that the *Nesi'im*[2] beginning with Simon the Just,[3] when prophecy ceased,[4] down to Rabbi (the holy)[5] had power and authority which extended over all Israel, as also the heads of the academies in Palestine, such as R. Johanan,[6] R. Ammi and R. Assi,[7] and the heads of the Academies in Babylon,[8] such as Rab and Samuel,[9] R. Nahman, R. Judah, Rabbah, R. Hisda, R. Huna, and R. Ashi,[10] whose competence and authority in Torah, and whose sagacity are known and familiar to us. With their rulings all the communities of the Diaspora complied, and their orders they all obeyed. All these were versed in Scripture, *halachah* and *aggadah*, and all their teachings, quoted in either *halachah* or *aggadah*, give signal testimony to their sagacity and piety, to the breadth of their mind and the depth of their intelligence on all subjects and matters which had direct bearing on the conditions of the people and on the understanding of religion. Therefore, we ought to accept their words with respect and reverence.

You will, however, find that some of the Sages of the Talmud specialized in *halachah* alone, and were thus not expert in Scripture. This is confirmed by the definite statement made in Tos. (B.B. 113*a*, s.v. תרוייהו) that it is found at times that the *Amoraim* were not versed

---

[1] i.e. under the same planetary influence, as Asheri on Ned. 39*b* explains the meaning of the Talmudic term *Ben-gil* (man of affinity).

[2] Plural of Nasi, see p. 88, note 1.

[3] High Priest—the son of Onias I (end of the fourth century B.C.). The title 'Just' was conferred upon him on account of his piety. He is reported (Aboth 1, 2) to have been one of the last survivors of the Great Assembly. Historians differ greatly over his identity and the time in which he flourished.

[4] According to the Talmud (Yoma 9*b*) Malachi was the last of the Prophets.

[5] See p. 55, note 3.

[6] Identical with Johanan b Nappacha (the Smith) (190–279 C.E.), head of the Academy at Tiberias. He is often referred to as the Compiler of the Palestinian Talmud (cf. Maimonides, Introduction to his Commentary on the Mishnah).

[7] Disciples of the former and successors to his Office.

[8] Such as those in Sura, Nehardea, and Pumbeditha.

[9] The former known as Abba Arikha (the tall), on account of his extraordinary stature (160–247 C.E.) was the founder and first principal of the College at Sura, and the latter called Yarhena'ah, the astronomer, of that at Nehardea.

[10] All these were successors of Rab and Samuel as heads of the Babylonian seats of learning. R. Nahman, the son-in-law of the Exilarch, was looked upon as an authority in civil law, and was a disciple of Samuel. R. Judah, known as Bar Yecheskel, was a pupil of Rab and was characterized by the epithet 'the acute'. R. Huna was the most eminent disciple of Rab. R. Hisda was one of his younger pupils, while R. Ashi was credited with the compilation and redaction of the immense material of traditions and commentaries accumulated in the Babylonian Academies, later embodied in the Gemara. He died 427 C.E.

in Scripture, as may be seen in the following question and answer (B.K. 55a): 'Why is there no mention in the first Decalogue[1] of the words כי טוב ("it is well")?'[2] (presumably implying that they do occur in the second).[3] The reply given was: 'Ask me rather whether they appear at all, for I am not aware of it.'[4]

See again A. Zar. 4a, where R. Safra, although commended by R. Abbahu as a learned man, could not answer the Minim[5] on a difficult Biblical passage. R. Abbahu afterwards said to them: 'When I told you he was a learned man I meant that he was learned in Tannaitic law, but not in Scripture'. On the other hand, you will find many Amoriam who concerned themselves with the aggadah and Biblical exegesis alone, and not at all with halachah. These sages were designated the teachers of the Aggadah. See also Jer. Maaseroth 1, 2, where R. Jonah suggests that a certain view[6] might have come from the teachers of the aggadah who translated the passage, 'our brethren המסו (have melted) our heart,'[7] as meaning (in accordance with Onkelos's translation of the word) פלגון 'they have split our heart in two'.[8]

Yet again, in Jer. Yeb 4, 2, a dispute is quoted between the teachers of halachah and those of aggadah over the question whether a pregnant woman is liable to have her original conception contributed to by having intercourse with a second male,[9] the aggadists affirming that she is. Thus, for example, the subjects in which the following teachers were chiefly occupied were the Midrash and the Aggada, and they are seldom or never mentioned amongst the halachists, viz. R. Levi,

---

[1] Ex. xx.   [2] In connection with the Fifth Commandment.
[3] Deut. v.
[4] This question was put to R. Hiya b Abba who was generally known as an exponent of halachah (v. Sot. 40a) and seemingly was indifferent to anything not involving halachic points. Yet the view advanced in the Tosafoth above mentioned is not very convincing, since it is difficult to attribute to R. Hiya such crass ignorance of the Scriptures. Since the words כי טוב appear in neither Decalogue, it is reasonable to take this retort to mean 'Why do you ask about the omission of כי טוב in the first decalogue, seeing that it is not even in the second?' where only the words למען ייטב appear but not כי טוב.
[5] Sectarians, or Dissenters. Some authorities are of the opinion that the designation refers to the Judaeo-Christians. Cf. Kohut, Aruch Completum, s.v. מין, for references to various views on this sect.
[6] Quoted, loc. cit., in connection with the criteria established in the Mishnah for determining the liability of pomegranates to tithing.
[7] Deut. 1, 28.
[8] The determining point in the Mishnah for the liability of the pomegranates to tithes is 'after they soften', and the term employed for expressing that is משימסו which is derived from מסס to melt, to dissolve (Ex. xvi, 21, Ps. lxvi, 3). Another view advanced on the authority of R. Joshua b Levi is 'when they become half ripe', and upon this latter view R. Jonah gives the suggestion referred to in the text.
[9] The question is important for establishing the legitimacy of a child in connection with the law of the levirate marriage (Deut. xxv, 5–10).

R. Samuel b Nahman, R. Abin Halevi, R. Tanhuma, R. Berachia,
R. Simeon Hahasid, and R. Pinchas b Yair, and others.[1]

If so, the following passage in the Talmud (M.K. 15*b*) can be
explained: 'R. Samuel b Nahman got upon his feet and said that even
a ban imposed by a domestic in Rabbi's house was not so lightly to be
removed by the Rabbis. R. Zera then said: 'It is surprising that this
venerable scholar should just now (after an absence of years) turn up at
the College'.[2] Since R. Samuel b Nahman was one of the Aggadic
teachers,[3] and as a rule did not attend the meeting-place of the
halachists, the Rabbis laid all the more stress on his attendance on this
occasion, and gave heed to his view on this *halachah* refusing to release
the man.

Again, I have noticed a novel feature, viz. that several teachers who
are otherwise rarely quoted in both Talmudim, except in connection
with one particular *halachah* or *aggadah*, are then known by an additional
name suggested by the contents of that *halachah* or *aggadah*. The
following are examples—R. Isaac Migdala'ah,[4] quoted in B.M. 25*a* is,
I believe, thus designated from the view which he advances in connection with the ruling that requires a proclamation of the finding of

[1] Here are some details regarding the identity of these *aggadic* teachers.
R. Levi. A Palestinean Amora of the third generation. His fame in *aggadic* lore
became so great that R. Johanan appointed him lecturer on the subject in his
Academy (Jer. Sukka 5, 1) and R. Ze'era who, as a rule, did not favour the aggadic
teachers (see Jer. Maasroth 3, 4) yet urged his disciples to give particular attention
to R. Levi's aggadic discourses on the ground that they always contained something
instructive (Jer. R.H. 4).
R. Samuel b Nahman. A Palestinean Amora of the third and fourth centuries, a pupil
of R. Jonathan (B.B. 123*a*).
R. Abin Halevi. Palestinean Amora. Several aggadic sayings are quoted on his
authority in the final folio of Berachoth.
R. Tanhuma b Aba. Palestinean Amora of the fifth generation and a well-known
aggadist of his time.
R. Berachiah. A Palestinian Amora of the fourth century and an acknowledged
master in the Aggadah.
R. Simeon Ha-Hasid. A Tanna quoted in Hagigah 13*b*.
R. Pinchas b Jair. A Tanna of the fourth generation and a fellow student of Judah I.
[2] This discussion took place over the annulment of a ban imposed upon a man by
R. Judah who had afterwards died.
[3] See a similar reference by the author in his glosses on M.K., ad loc. Nissenbaum,
author and writer of Warsaw, in some critical observations on the glosses in the
Annual Keneseth published by Suvalsky, 1890, rejects the suggestion, seeing that
R. Samuel b Nahman is quoted twice in connection with *halachic* subjects in Meg.
2*a*, and in Shab 58*b*. Indeed we find R. Samuel b Nahman's views quoted in connection with several other *halachoth*. See Hul. 45*a*; Keth. 17*a*, 49*b*, and B.K. 46*b*.
Therefore the designations *aggadists* and *halachists* must be understood as denoting
men who specialised mainly in the one or other particular branch of Talmudic
learning, but who did not necessarily devote themselves exclusively to it.
[4] i.e. pyramid man, from מגדל pyramid or tower (Gen. XI, 4, Cant. V, 13), a
Palestinian Amora of the third generation.

coins[1] for the purpose of their identification. This, R. Isaac says, is only when they lie like a *migdal* (pyramid).[2] Similarly, we find a scholar with the additional name of Zohamai[3] because of the *halachah* he advanced that, just as an unclean, unwashed man is unfit for priestly service, so an unwashed person is likewise unfit[4] to recite the grace (after the meal) (Ber 53*b*). Again, we find a scholar called Ben Rehumi[5] (Naz 13*a*) on account of the question he put to Abaye about one who, on hearing his companion exclaim: 'I undertake to become a Nazarite when I have a son,' added 'and I undertake it likewise', which saying implies a question and the answer: 'I am as good a friend to you as you are to yourself.'[6] Again, in Jer. Meg. 1, 11, on the query how Elijah came to offer sacrifices at a time when the use of '*Bamoth*'[7] had already been banned, R. Samlai Debura[8] justifies his action as permitted by God, as is shown in Elijah's prayer: 'I have done all this at Thy words,'[9] reading וּכְדַבְּרֶיךָ 'Thy instructions', instead of וּכְדָבָרֶיךָ 'Thy words'. Thus, we see that R. Samlai obtained the nickname (Debura) from his exposition of the text וּכְדַבְּרֶיךָ, and so with several others.[10] It is a novel idea which has not been touched upon by anyone else, and the Divine Being has helped me to discover it.[11]

[1] B.M. 2, 1.

[2] i.e. cone-shaped, a large coin being at the bottom and a smaller one above it, in which case it can be easily identified. If our author's suggestion is to be tenable we must then assume that this was one of the first accepted *halachoth* propounded by R. Isaac by which he later became known, for R. Isaac is quoted with the same designation in connection with other *halachoth* (cf. Yoma 81*b*; Nid. 33*a*). Again there is the suggestion that he was so called because he was born at Magdala in Galilee. See Jew. Enc., s.v. 'Yishak of Magdala' and 'Magdala'.

[3] i.e. man with filthy hands, from זהם contamination, froth.

[4] Probably one who had not dipped his hand in rose-water after the meal.

[5] Lit. son of my friend. רחם is Aramaic for 'friend'.

[6] Indicating thereby that 'I shall become a Nazarite when my friend has a son', hence the phrase in the *halachah* 'son of my friend' gives him his name.

[7] High place devoted to and equipped for service by sacrifice, cf. Zeb. 14, 4. Until the erection of the Tabernacle 'Bamoth' were legitimate, but they were prohibited after its construction. Elijah's action, however, on Mt. Carmel was justified by the need of the hour (v. Yeb. 90*b*). [8] From דבר utterance, saying. [9] 1 Kings XVIII, 36.

[10] In his glosses on B.M. our author refers also to a Midrashic saying quoted on the authority of R. Aba Meromania (מרומניה) in reference to Ps. LXXV, 7, 'Nor yet from the wilderness cometh הרים; the term הרים throughout Scripture indicates mountains, except in this passage where it denotes a lifting up, derived from רום. Here, too, our author finds support for his suggestion that R. Aba's by-name Meromania, which denotes lifting, came from his interpretation of this passage. Einhorn in his Commentary on the Midrash favours this view, though others have generally adopted the view that Romanya was the name of R. Aba's native place.

[11] Margulies in an essay annexed to his second edition of the Mebo ha-Talmud confirms this suggestion from many other sources. See also Mekor Baruch by B. Epstein (Wilno 1928), where the subject is treated elaborately, and the essay 'A Peculiar kind of Paronomasia in Talmud and Midrash' by J. D. Wynkopp in J.Q.R. 1911 on the subject.

We also find amongst the Talmudic teachers men distinguished by their piety and saintliness, men of (great) deeds, but from whom no *halachah* or *aggadah* has been left; men who were mostly known as miracle workers, or as active in intercession on behalf of the people or in invoking God's intervention on the people's behalf in time of adversity, such as Honi ha-Meaggel (the circle maker),[1] R. Hanina b Dosa,[2] Abba Hilkiah, and Hanan ha-Nehba.[3] Some of the rest were famous in rhetoric and worked for the deliverance of Israel, such as R. Joshua b Hanina (who, in my opinion, is not R. Joshua b Hananiah, the contemporary of Rabban Gamaliel II, and R. Akiba, as the author of the *Seder ha-Doroth*[4], assumed him to be, but is a R. Joshua b Hanina who lived at a later period[5]), or again Gobia b Peziza[6] and R. Reuben b Strobilus or Esterbeli.[7] Others again were skilled in refuting the arguments of the *Minim*. Many other Rabbis are mentioned in the Talmud as not frequenting the meeting place (the College) more than once a year (see Shab. 49b[8] and Hagiga 5b) and so were called 'one day scholars of the school'. Therefore when one meets a Talmudic saying one must ascertain its author and then investigate first his outlook from other quotations of his and also the conditions of his life and their causes. Then only will one be able to arrive at a better understanding of his utterances elsewhere, which may, at times, appear strange at first sight.

[1] The suggested reason for this name is that when he was once asked to intercede for rain, during a time of drought, he drew a circle and stood in prayer within it until his call was answered (Taan 3, 8).

[2] A pupil of Ben Zakkai, of the first century. His reputation as a saintly man spread far and wide, so that even his teacher asked him to intercede on behalf of his disciple who became sick (Ber. 34b).

[3] Both these latter were grandsons of Honi, the latter's name 'Nehba' (from חבא hiding) was given to him because he was wont to hide himself out of modesty (Taan. 23b).

[4] R. Yehiel Heilpern, one of the most eminent Talmudists in Lithuania of the seventeenth century. He is best known for his Seder ha-Doroth.

[5] The author, who seems to have thought of this R. Joshua b. Hanina as the one who was conspicuous for his rhetorical power, distinguishes him from the famous Tanna, R. Joshua b. Hananiah, the disciple of Ben Zakkai who, apart from his great fame in debates with the Roman Emperor Hadrian, was one of the most prominent *halachists* of his time. Cf. *Imre Binah*, part ii of his response, p. 23b, for a most interesting exchange of views on this novel suggestion between R. H. N. Dembitzer and the author.

[6] A sage, contemporary of Simon the Just, who, as quoted in Sanh. 91a, showed great wisdom in meeting various charges against the Jews in the time of Alexander the Great, whom he finally satisfied with his refutation of them.

[7] Eminent not only as a scholar, but as one who was actively engaged in the public affairs of his time, in the second century, the reign of Hadrian (see Me'ila 17a).

[8] Support for this cannot be derived from Sab. 49b where the reference is to a student who came to the College on that day for the first time. It is derived, however, from the reference in Hagiga to R. Idi whom the Rabbis called 'one-day scholar' because, owing to the length of his journey to the school, he could not remain there for longer than one day.

CHAPTER XVIII

AGGADOTH RECEIVED BY TRADITION

IT is well to recognize that just as the Rabbis received by tradition many *halachoth* dealing with the observance of the precepts so, too, many *aggadoth* that are found scattered in *baraithoth* and in the Talmud were received by the Rabbis by tradition from ancient times; and particularly such as relate to events in the life of the people in general, or touch upon the events in the lives of the great and distinguished men of the nation, whose names stand out amongst us as of men whose righteousness and godly fear were at the roots of their wisdom. Thus, the foundations of religion and the principles of faith as expounded in the *Aggadah* were transmitted from Sinai like the rest of the oral tradition which interprets the written Law. For all the events in the life of the people were transmitted by parents to children from the early generations. So, for instance, Hanania b Hezekiah, of the family of Garon,[1] wrote the Chronicle *Megillath Ta'anith*[2] to record the calamities which befell Israel and the wonders which they experienced. So, too, R. Jose[3] compiled the *Seder Olam Rabbah*,[4] a single baraitha which deals only with events throughout the ages.

In some cases the Rabbis employed the expression 'We have it by tradition', or the term *Masoreth*[5] when referring to *aggadoth* such as those in which events of the past are narrated; as in the following cases: 'We have it by tradition that Abraham was fifty-two years old at the time when he had gotten souls in Haran'[6] (A.Z. 9a); 'We have it by tradition that the deaths of Benjamin (son of Jacob), Amram (father of Moses), Jesse (father of David) and Kilab (son of David) were due to the

---

[1] A scholar who lived at the beginning of the first century.
[2] Lit. 'Scroll of Fasts'—an account of eventful days on which glorious deeds were performed, and which it is not lawful to keep as fast days. On the question of its authorship see Sab. 13b.
[3] R. Jose b. Halafta, the Palestinian *Tanna* of the second century, generally referred to as R. Jose.
[4] The earliest post-exilic chronological record, quoted several times in the Talmud. It covers the history from Adam to the revolt of Bar Kochba (A.D. 131–135). Reference to its authorship is made by R. Johanan (Yeb. 82b) who says that the *Tanna* of the *Seder Olam* was R. Jose. Modern scholars are divided on the subject of its authorship, cf. A. Marx, Introduction to his edition of the *Seder Olam*; B. Ratner *Mebo L'Seder Olam*, and *Dor*, ii, p. 257.
[5] From מסר, handed down.
[6] See Gen. XII, 5. According to aggadic lore this refers to the heathen men and women whom Abraham and Sarah had won over to the worship of God.

counsel of the Serpent'[1] (Shab. 55b); 'We have it by tradition that the women of that generation were sterilized'[2] (Yeb. 17a); 'We have it by tradition that so long as the Ark and the *Shechinah* are not at rest in their appointed place[3] conjugal intercourse is forbidden' (Erub. 63b); 'We have it by tradition that six miracles were wrought on that day when they were thrown into the furnace[4]: the furnace floated upwards and its walls burst, etc.' (San. 92b).[5] Again, 'We have it by tradition that Nebuzaradan[6] survived along with Sennacherib'[7] (San. 95b). In the same way, the Rabbis also introduce with the word *Masoreth* several statements which were handed down to them by tradition as, for example, where they say 'A *Masoreth* from our ancestors is in our possession that the Ark took up no room'[8] (Meg. 10b); or 'A *Masoreth* is in our possession from our forefathers that Amoz and Amaziah were brothers'[9] (Meg., ibid.); 'A *Masoreth* is in our possession that the names given to the spies were intended to indicate their conduct' (Sot. 34b). Again 'A *Masoreth* is in our possession that the *Cherubim*[10] took up no room' (Jer. B.B. 6, 2).—Several such reliable proofs as these establish the fact that *aggadoth* which relate occurrences of the distant past were all in the possession of the Rabbis as traditions from our ancestors.

To this category belong all *aggadoth* which tell us of happenings in former generations, even if they are not introduced with the phrases 'It is a Masoreth, etc.', or 'We have written it by tradition'. For they

---

[1] Cf. Gen. III, 13. This brought death on mankind, otherwise they were entirely sinless.

[2] Referring to the women of the ten tribes which Shalmaneser had carried away into ptivity (2 Kings XVIII, 11) where they were exposed to intermarriage with the he. ᵉⁿ. They were sterilized to prevent them from bearing children lest they should intermarry with the heathen.

[3] As, for example, when a battle is in progress, since the Ark was not merely a depository of the Tables of the Law, but was also a Divine protection against the enemies and a source of inspiration in time of danger.

[4] Referring to Hananiah, Mishael, and Azariah who were thrown into the fiery furnace by Nebuchadnezzar (cf. Dan. III).

[5] (1) Although it was originally built in the earth, the furnace floated upwards so that all might see the miracle; (2) Its walls fell in for the same reason; (3) Its foundations crumbled; (4) Nebuchadnezzar's image, i.e. his pride, was overthrown; (5) Four royalties were burned; (6) Ezekiel resurrected the dead in the valley of Dura.

[6] Nebuchadnezzar's Army Commander who was delegated to conquer Jerusalem. Cf. 2 Kings XXV, 8.

[7] King of Assyria, 705-681 B.C., whose armies invaded Judea during the reign of Hezekiah and besieged Jerusalem, but were discomfited by a sudden and serious calamity, as a result of which 185,000 men were destroyed in a single night (2 Kings XVIII–XX).

[8] According to the dimensions given in the Bible (Ex. XXV, 10) the Ark could not be accommodated except in some way which remains incomprehensible to us.

[9] The former was the father of Isaiah, and the latter the King of Judah.

[10] Cf. Ex. XXV, 18.

certainly did not fabricate these stories, rather they were transmitted to them as true stories. The following examples may be cited: 'There is the reference made by the Rabbis (Pes. 56a) to the fact that Jacob, at the time of pronouncing his blessings over his sons, recited the words 'Blessed be His name whose glorious kingdom is for ever and ever'.[1] Similarly, there is the reference to the things that Hezekiah enacted with some of which the Rabbis agreed and with some of which they did not.[2] Again, there is what we are told of Wahab and Sufah,[3] viz. that they were two lepers[4] who followed in the rear of the Israelite camp (Ber. 54a); also the incidents related in Sot. 13a of the time when Jacob was about to be buried, regarding Husham, a son of Dan,[5] and how Naphtali had to go to Egypt to fetch the document of sale, and so forth. And particularly the references to the events which took place during the last days (of the first Commonwealth) in relation to Nebuchadnezzar and Zedekiah (Ned. 65a)[6] and to the incident of Eliezer b. Puerah[7] who advised the King (John Hyrkanus) to lay aside the royal crown (and appropriate for himself the priestly crown) (Kid. 66a), and also all the stories of the time of the destruction of the first and second Temples. All these had come down to them by tradition from parents to children.

The author of *Me'or Enayim*[8] in chapter 5 of his *Imre Binah*[9] has given

[1] This doxology, which accompanies the opening verse of the *Shema* to emphasize the belief in the sole sovereignty of God, is not of Biblical origin.
[2] See M. Pes. 4, 9, where six things which King Hezekiah did are enumerated. With three the Rabbis agreed, and with three they did not.
[3] Num. xxi, 14. 'Wherefore it is said in the book of wars of the Eternal, Waheb, etc.'
[4] Who, while stationed outside the Camp, saw the miraculous destruction of the Amorites and went and reported it.
[5] The story tells of the claim which Esau made for the one remaining sepulchre in the Cave of Machpela, and how Naphtali was sent for the document of sale which was in Jacob's possession, but how before Naphtali had returned, Husham, who could not endure to see his grandfather lying in contempt until Naphtali's return, struck Esau on the hand, thus removing the one obstruction in the way of the burial (Sot. 13a).
[6] How Zedekiah violated an oath made to Nebuchadnezzar on the ground that the Sanhedrin had absolved him from it, and how the latter when called to account for his irregular act kept silence and said nothing in their own defence.
[7] Who incited the King against the Pharisees to such an extent that there was a mass murder of the Rabbis by the King.
[8] R. Azariah b Moses de Rossi, a distinguished Italian scholar of the sixteenth century. According to tradition he was descended from a family brought over by Titus from Jerusalem.
[9] Which is the main section of *Me'or Enayim*. The work is divided into four parts. In *Imre Binah* the author follows scientific methods of inquiry, touching upon many Biblical subjects in a manner which his contemporaries often regarded as irreverent, so that they declared it a heretical work. The severest of his critics was the Codifier, R. Joseph Karo.

us clear proof that many details related in the Talmud and *Midrash* in connection with the life of the Patriarchs are to be found quoted by Yedidiah the Alexandrian,[1] who lived about 200 years before the close of the Mishnah and about thirty years before the destruction of the second Temple. This is one of the strongest evidences that these facts came down to us by trustworthy tradition. I can here adduce further decisive proof from the books written for the Romans by Josippon[2] who lived at the time of the destruction of the Second Temple, and was a contemporary of R. Simeon b Gamaliel I, the father of R. Gamaliel of Jabneh, and who accordingly lived four generations before Rabbi our Holy Teacher who compiled the *Mishnah*, for he relates in his Antiquities several narratives from the times of early generations which are also recorded for us in the Talmud and Midrash. From this we can see that all these matters were received by the Rabbis by tradition, and from the part available to us we can judge regarding the whole, that in what concerns the acts of the Patriarchs, Prophets, Monarchs, Princes, and Priests, the Rabbis conveyed the facts to us as they had received them from their ancestors. I shall refer briefly to some instances.

In Josippon's Antiquities, Book i, chap. 14, the author relates that many of the children of Israel perished in Egypt during the three days of darkness. This agrees with what the Rabbis relate in the Midrash.[3] Again, in Book ii, chap. 4, Josippon relates that Potiphar's wife (Gen. xxxix) pretended to be sick on the day of the Egyptian feast when they all went to their place of prayer.[4] Again, in Book ii, chap. 1, he tells us that the bones of all the Tribes[5] were carried up out of Egypt for reburial in the land of Israel, and that the bones of Reuben[6] rolled about in the coffin. This also agrees with a statement of the Rabbis.

In Book ii, chap. 9, he tells the story of how the magicians of Egypt

---

[1] Philo Judaeus, the celebrated Alexandrian philosopher. His works were not acceptable to contemporary Judaism because he allegorized the facts of the Biblical narrative and often ignored the traditional interpretation of the text.

[2] The author obviously refers to the Antiquities of the Jews by Josephus Flavius (Joseph b Mattathias) (37–105 C.E.), one of the military leaders of the Jews in their struggles for independence against the Romans, who surrendered after the fall of Jerusalem, and not to the so-called 'history' of Josippon reputedly written by Joseph b. Gurion which appears to have been written some time in the tenth or eleventh century and is regarded by critical historians as of doubtful authority.

[3] Cf. *Midrash Tanhuma*, Ex. R. 14, for the statement that the wicked in Israel, who had no desire to leave Egypt, died during the days of darkness so that the Egyptians might not see their destruction and say 'See, these Israelites, too, have been destroyed'. Cf. also Rashi on Ex. x, 22.

[4] Cf. *Tanhuma*, ad loc., and Rashi on Gen. xxxix, 11.

[5] i.e. the sons of Jacob.

[6] The Talmud (Sot. 7b) gives it as Judah, by a deduction from the text, 'And this is for Judah' (Deut. xxxiii, 6).

warned Pharaoh that an Israelite boy was to be born soon who would
deliver his people and bring upon Pharaoh terrible calamities and, as
a result, he decreed that 'every son that is born to them ye shall cast into
the river'.[1] All this is related also by the Rabbis in Talmud and
Midrash.[2] Josippon also tells us[3] that it was made known to Amram by
prophetic vision that a son was to be born to him who would be the
saviour of the people.[4] He also tells us[5] how Moses was handed round to
all the nursing mothers but would not suck from any other breast except
that of his mother, as is also told in Sotah (12*a*). Further, he tells us[6] the
story of the daughter of the Ethiopian king who became the wife of
Moses, and how he (Moses) captured the road to Ethiopia by a ruse
with a stork, though it was full of serpents and scorpions, as is related
to us in detail in the *Yalkut*.[7] Similarly, in his book *The Wars of the Jews*,
Joseph ha-Cohen[8] tells us how during the building of the Temple by
Herod[9] no rain fell except during the night, so as not to interrupt the
building, even for a moment; a reference to which is also found in the
Talmud (Ta'an.23*a*). So, too, he tells of the Sanhedrin's unwillingness
to give Herod permission for the pulling down of the older Temple,
giving as their reason their apprehension lest he should neglect its
rebuilding,[10] as is also recorded in B.B. 3*b*. So, too, he has a reference to
the remarkable case of the sons of Kimhith, all of whom served as High
Priests, and two of whom actually ministered as such on one and the
same Day of Atonement,[11] as is also recorded in Yoma 47*a*.

Such instances are many, and it would need a special work to com-

---

[1] Ex. I, 22.
[2] See Sot. 12*b* and Ex. R., ad loc., also quoted by Rashi.
[3] In ch. ix, par. 3.
[4] In the Talmud (Sot. 13*a*) this is attributed to Miriam who prophesied when
Aaron was her only brother before the birth of Moses saying, 'My mother will bear
a son who will be the saviour of Israel'.
[5] Ibid., par. 5.
[6] Ch. x, par. 1.
[7] In the legend recorded in the *Yalkut* (a haggadic compilation on the Bible),
Ex. 168, and also in the *Sefer Hayashar* reference is made to this daughter of the
Ethiopian King as his wife (Cf. *Myth and Legend of Ancient Israel*, vol. ii, p. 248).
[8] Obviously Josephus.
[9] See note 4, p. 181. Being anxious to ingratiate himself with the Pharisees, whose
sentiments he had so often outraged, and whose authority he had many times flouted,
he rebuilt the Temple on a much grander scale, so that it became known as the Temple
of Herod.
[10] Cf. the ruling that a Synagogue should not be demolished before the new one
has been built to take its p[lace] (cf. Meg. 26*b*). Baba b Buta, however, advised Herod
to reconstruct the Temple as it stood, on the ground that the ruling in question did
not apply in the case of Royalty since a King could not go back on his word.
[11] It happened that one of them, R. Ishmael, contracted uncleanness from the
spittle out of the mouth of an unclean person which flew upon his garments, whereupon his brother Jeshebab entered and took his place.

pare all the incidents quoted by our Sages of Blessed Memory with those of the *Antiquities* and the *Jewish Wars of the Jews*, or with those that are to be found scattered throughout the ancient books of the other peoples, such as those of Aram,[1] Syria,[2] or Greece. For example, the story which the Rabbis tell us about Manasseh,[3] trying Isaiah and sentencing him to death, and how he (Isaiah) disappeared within a cedar-tree by pronouncing an ineffable name (Yeb. 49b).[4] I have it in a translation of an old Syriac book.[5] Again, the story of Manasseh repenting and how his prayer for forgiveness was accepted (San. 103a) is also mentioned in the Apocrypha.[6] Also the account of the power which Solomon exercised over Ashmedai (King of the Demons), mentioned in the Talmud (Git. 57), is also found in other literatures of much earlier date than the completion of the Talmud. This is not the place to treat this subject at length, but from the few examples which I here set out the reader can easily judge for himself that the narratives which have come down from ancient times to Israel, with their miraculous events, were not pure inventions, God forbid, but were handed down to the Sages from early days, and that the latter recorded for us what their ancestors had told them of the actual things God had wrought for His people in ancient days.

[1] Or Aramea, corresponding generally to Mesopotamia.
[2] The territory round Damascus.
[3] King of Judah, son of Hezekiah.
[4] He met his death while inside the tree, as the King ordered that the tree be sawn asunder. See J.E. VI, p. 636, for the assertion that the legend of Isaiah's martyrdom was transmitted from Talmudical circles to the Arabs (Ta'rick, ed De Goeje, i, 644).
[5] Unfortunately no definite source is given by the author for the story.
[6] A series of Jewish writings of the last two centuries B.C., and the first two A.D., which though akin in form to the Bible were not received into the Canon.

CHAPTER XIX

THE THIRTY-TWO MIDDOTH (RULES)
EMPLOYED IN THE *AGGADAH*

ANOTHER thing must be recognized, namely that just as the exegetical interpretations of the *halachah* were governed by thirteen middoth (hermeneutic rules) formulated by R. Ishmael[1] so, too, the interpretations of the *aggadah* were formulated under the guidance of the said thirteen *middoth*. You will find throughout that the Rabbis did not hesitate to employ the *Kal V'homer*[2] and the *Gezerah Shavah*[3] in expounding the *aggadah*, as I shall soon clearly indicate with examples, but in addition to these methods, they were in possession of other methods of exposition for the *aggadah*, such as the set of the thirty-two *middoth* formulated by R. Eliezer b. R. Jose the Galilean.[4] These were recognized just as definitely as the thirteen *middoth* of R. Ishmael, for the Rabbis say (Hul. 89a) 'wherever thou hearest words of R. Eliezer b. R. Jose the Galilean in the *aggadah*, turn thine ear into a hopper'.[5] These methods were precisely defined and followed wherever they were prompted to magnify, adorn, and praise goodly virtues, so as to influence others to persevere in or appropriate these virtues with still greater persistence. By using these exegetical methods they found Biblical support for the virtues in question as, for instance, in their praise of the virtue of charity, they said: 'He who gives charity in secret is greater than Moses our Teacher'[6] (B.B. 9b); and again, 'Great is charity since it brings nearer deliverance'[7] (ibid. 10a). Again, in speaking of hospitality to wayfarers, they say that it is greater than

---

[1] Known as the *'Baraitha* of R. Ishmael'.

[2] An inference from the light (less important) to the heavy (more important) and vice versa. For examples, see B.B. 9, 7; Sanh. 6, 5; Aboth 1, 5.

[3] An inference by analogy, by a similarity of phrasing in two Pentateuchal passages. Examples Ar. 4, 4; Pes. 66a.

[4] The thirty-two rules were set out with explanatory notes by Einhorn in his Introduction to *'Perush Maharzaw'*, his Commentary on Midrash Rabbah (Wilno ed.). In his Commentary he very often indicates which of the thirty-two rules the Aggadists employed for the interpretation of the particular *aggadah* expounded. Later critical historians contend that the thirty-two *middoth* apply quite as much to *halachic* interpretations. See S. Krauss, *Schwartz Festschrift* 57, 2.

[5] A container which is wide at the mouth and narrow at the outlet. Hence, receive his words avidly, but be slow in losing them.

[6] This is deduced as follows: Of Moses it is written 'For I was afraid because of the anger and the wrath' (Deut. IX, 19); and of him who gives charity in secret it is written: 'A gift in secret subdues anger' (Prov. XXI, 14). It should not of course be inferred that Moses lacked that virtue, for the *aggadic* teacher is concerned merely with finding whatever support he can for his praise of the worthy act.

[7] Deduced as follows: 'Thus saith the Lord, Keep ye judgment and do *Zedakah*

the welcoming of the Presence of the Shechina[1] (Shab. 127a). Indeed, they often expound Scripture in extolment of hospitality (Ber. 63b). They also showered high praise on him who helps the *talmid hacham* (the scholar)[2] with his wealth, comparing the deed to the offering of the *tamid* (daily sacrifices) (Ber. 10b), and they compare one who 'fills the throat of the scholars with wine'[3] to one who offers a libation on the Altar[4] (Yoma 71a).

Again they say that all (the glories) that the prophets have foretold of the future are for him who marries his daughter to a *talmid hacham*, or who associates him with his business, or who helps him with his wealth[5] (Ber. 34b). So, too, they repeatedly commend and praise the observance of the Sabbath, saying: 'He who observes the Sabbath according to the law[6] will be given an unbounded heritage,[7] and even if he practise idolatry like (the generation of) Enosh[8] he will be forgiven' (Shab. 118b). Similarly, they extol the man who engages in the study of the sacrificial chapters,[9] saying that it is reckoned to him as though he had actually offered the sacrifices[10] (Men.110a); so, too, they

(lit. righteousness, used in Hebrew for charity) for my salvation is near to come and my righteousness to be revealed' (Is. LVI, 1). The deduction is based on the theory that 'in the measure with which one measures it is meted out to him'—hence, God will be righteous to Israel when they themselves practise righteousness (Sot. 8b).

[1] Deduced from the fact that Abraham addressed himself to God, saying 'My Lord, if now I have found favour in thy sight, pass not away' (Gen. XVIII, 3), thus asking Him not to withdraw His Presence while he was seeing to his guests.

[2] The Talmudic term *talmid hacham* denotes not only scholarly attainments, but also the qualities of piety and venerableness regarded as the reflection of the qualities of the divine. The hospitality, therefore, extended to him is compared with that extended to God through the daily offerings. This was stressed in particular after the sacrificial services had ceased to function, so that the people were thus directed to another laudable practice as a worthy substitute.

[3] An expression used for inviting scholars to banquets for the purpose of ennobling the gatherings.

[4] Expressing a thought similar to that in note 2 above.

[5] All such statements aimed at influencing the people to take part in, and encourage the study of the Torah.

[6] The version in the Gemara text is different 'He who delights in the Sabbath'.

[7] Since spiritual delight, by its very nature, knows no limit.

[8] In whose time, according to tradition, idolatry began to spread, see Rashi, Gen. IV, 26, on the text 'Then it was begun to call idols by the name of the eternal', viz. making them the objects of idolatrous worship and calling them deities. The essence of this statement lies in the fact that since the Sabbath is associated with the creation and the divine covenant, the observer, by his observance of the 'day', bears testimony to both the 'creator' and His creation.

[9] Studying the Tractates of laws in connection with the sacrificial offerings in the Sanctuary.

[10] In the Talmudic text the statement runs thus: 'To him who occupies himself in the study of the "sin offering", it is reckoned . . .', i.e. the devout study of the subject and its fundamental purpose of effecting a change in the sinner's thoughts and an improvement in his conduct will be as effective as the actual bringing of the offering.

eulogize the great virtue of studying the Torah, saying that whosoever teaches his neighbour's son[1] Torah is regarded as though he had himself received the Torah on Mount Sinai (Kid. 30a). Again, they mention as a reward for him who recites the grace after meals over a full cup (of wine) that he will be given an unbounded heritage (Ber. 51a). They also eulogize the deed of escorting a guest, saying that as a reward for the four paces which Pharoah had accompanied Abraham, he got the benefit of Israel's labour in Egypt for 400 years[2] (Sot. 46b). For all these views and many others like them, the Rabbis found Biblical support in accordance with the traditional exegetical methods, such as the *Kal Vahomer*, the *Hekesh*,[3] the *Ma Mazinu*,[4] and the *Gezerah Shavah*, and chiefly in order to gain support for their efforts at inspiring those who heard them so that they should, in view of their great importance, concentrate upon appropriating such virtues.

On the other hand, wherever they had occasion to discountenance evil practices and to speak of them with abhorrence, they would overawe and terrify the people in order as far as possible to drive them away from following crooked ways, for when men realize the enormity of their evil doings they are vigilant to keep from all such practices.

In this matter also they buttressed their statements by the accepted exegetical methods. Thus, for example, they said: 'Whoever turns his eyes from the practice of charity[5] (should be regarded) as though he were an idolater'[6] (Keth. 68a) ; 'Whosoever indulges his anger by breaking vessels in his rage (should be regarded) as though he were an idolater' (Shab. 105b); 'Whosoever is dominated by a haughty spirit is as though he worshipped idols,[7] i.e. as though he had denied the

---

[1] In the Talmudic text as it is given in a parallel passage in Ber. 21b, there is no mention of his neighbour. In the text of Tr. Ber. the reference is to his own son, and in that of Kid. to his grandson, which is the more likely, as the Rabbis laid great stress on the durability of the 'triple cord' (Eccl. IV, 12). See B.M. 85a on Is. LIX, 21, and Keth. 62b.

[2] The deduction is made from Gen. XII, 20, 'And Pharaoh gave men charge concerning him', i.e. he gave him an escort.

[3] Lit. clapping together, comparing, from the Chald. word נקש, Dan. v, 6, akin to נגש, to draw an analogy based on the close connection of two subjects in one and the same passage. It is not included amongst the thirteen rules of R. Ishmael.

[4] Lit. 'as we find here', a method by which an analogy is made from one case to another (see Yeb. 7b.)

[5] i.e. from one who appeals for his help.

[6] The deduction here is based on the occurence of the word בליעל (base) in two Biblical contexts, one (Deut. xv, 9) dealing with the duty of helping the poor, and the other (Deut. XIII, 4) with inciting to the service of idols.

[7] Since it is written with reference to haughtiness (Prov. XVI, 5) 'Everyone that is proud in heart is an abomination to the Lord', and with reference to idolatry (Deut. VII, 26) 'Thou shalt not bring an abomination into thine house'.

fundamental principle[1] of the faith and broken all the laws of sexual morality[2] (Sot. 4*b*).

Again, they based on Scripture the view that the insolent stumbles in the end into adultery and, because of him, the rain is withheld[3] (Taan 7*b*). They similarly emphasized the gravity of evil speech, so far as to liken it to the three most serious sins, idolatry, adultery, and murder[4] (Jer. Peah i), a view quoted also by Maimonides, *Yad,Deoth* 5. They also state, in Jer. Hag. i, that whosoever seeks honour for himself by the degradation of his fellow-men has no share in the world to come. Again, they declare the use of flattery to be utterly detestable. The flatterer, they say, draws down anger upon the world, and even the unborn children in their mother's wombs curse him (Sot. 41*b*). Yet again, they emphasized the prohibition of accepting hospitality from men of a niggardly spirit[5] (Sota 38*b*). Similarly, they say: 'Whosoever does not escort his friend (guest) on his way is as though he were to shed (his) blood'[6] (ibid. 46*b*).

They also give utterance to the following aphorisms: 'He who does not help a scholar with his wealth will never see a trace of blessing'; 'He who leaves a whole loaf on the table is as though he were an idolater'; 'He who is changeable in his speech is as though he were an idolater' (San. 92*a*). They have many other similar exaggerated expressions of warning to overawe the people.

In this connection, cf. Maimonides, *Commentary on the Mishnah*, San. 7, 4, where he says that the Rabbis have warned us against impure thoughts[7] and have urged upon us to keep aloof from such things as may draw us to them. They have, he says, elaborated this subject at considerable length, to scare us against such things. See also *Ribash*,[8] responsum 171, who, in the course of his reply to the questioner says: 'As regards your quotation from the *Geonim*,[9] that "he who disobeys

---

[1] This is deduced from the single passage (Deut. VIII, 14) 'lest thine heart be lifted up and thou forget the Lord thy God'.

[2] Again deduced from the similar use of the word 'abomination' in the passage (Prov. XVI, 5) quoted above, 'Everyone that, etc.,' and in Lev. XVIII, 27, 'For all those abominations.'

[3] Both these statements are deduced from Jer. IV, 3, 'Therefore the showers have been withheld and there hath been no latter rain, yet thou hast a harlot's forehead.'

[4] The three crimes which must be avoided even on pain of death.

[5] Cf. Prov. XXIII, 6, 'Eat thou not the bread of him who hath an evil eye.'

[6] For the Gemara continues 'had the men of Jericho escorted Elisha they would have prevented him from stirring up the bears against the children'(see 2 Kings II, 23).

[7] v. Yoma 29*a*. Sinful thought, i.e. the planning of sin, is more injurious (physically and morally) than the sin itself.

[8] The initials of Rabbi Isaac Ben Sheshet, Spanish Talmudic authority of the fourteenth century. His responsa, under the above name, four hundred and seventeen in number, are of both halachic and historic significance.

[9] See note 4, p. 129.

the *Herem*[1] falls under the Biblical warning 'He will not clear the guilty'[2] and he is to be treated like an idolater", I answer that, though the Rabbis have exaggerated (the seriousness of) the matter at issue, as was their way in all such cases, and though, in connection with the serious sin of swearing falsely, they say that with reference to every other transgression it is said (in the Torah) "he will hold guiltless"[3] but here "will not hold him guiltless"[4], and again that in all other cases the sinner alone is punished, while here both the sinner and his family are punished (Shab. 39a); yet, notwithstanding all this, they did not include this among the three laws[5] which one should suffer death rather than transgress; for, indeed, that had not entered any man's mind, nor had any one thought so. It was, simply, the method of the Rabbis to exaggerate the seriousness of sins so as to lead men to be on their guard against falling into them. For example, they say that he who speaks evil of his neighbour raises his sin to the level of those three transgressions in the Torah.[6] Similarly, R. Akiba has stated in a lecture that "he who does not visit the sick is comparable to a shedder of blood" (Ned. 40a). Again, they affirm that he who rends his garment in anger is comparable to an idolater. But could anyone seriously maintain that in connection with these sins the principle of suffering death rather than transgress them should apply?' So far the statement of the *Ribash*.

It would, indeed, take too long to quote in detail all the cases where the Rabbis magnified their abhorrence of sinful ways. They did so with great understanding and wisdom, in order to attract people's attention, so that they might beware of being any longer snared by evil.

Again, in their exaggerated praise of those who practise kindness[7] or visit the sick, and in their lofty exaltation of these virtues, they were prompted by a similar aim, that of awakening the people and stimulating them to keep to the straight path.

[1] The 'ban' or an accursed thing or man. In ancient times it was applied to spoil taken from the enemy, later it denoted excommunication as a punishment for an offence which was detrimental to the Community. The Geonim viewed seriously disobedience to their Herem regulation, since the Herem was used by them as a weapon against wrongdoers.
[2] Ex. xxxiv, 7. One of the 'Attributes' of God.
[3] See note 4.
[4] Ex. xx, 7. 'The Lord will not hold him guiltless that taketh His name in vain.' Actually in Ex. xxxiv, 7, we also read 'He will not hold guiltless', but this, however, is preceded by 'He will hold him guiltless' thus showing that repentance does remove guilt (v. Yoma 86a).
[5] Idolatry, incest (including adultery), and murder. v. Sanhedrin 74a.
[6] v. Ara. 15b for this and many other aggadic sayings in which the seriousness of the evil tongue is condemned to the point of exaggeration.
[7] Gemiluth Hasadim.

They trod this path because it seemed the most appropriate to them and to all succeeding teachers of each generation for showing the people the kind of deeds which they ought to practise. This they did by setting before the eyes of the people the evil consequences of any negligence in the performance of these deeds, and all their statements, exaggerated as they were, were supported from Holy Writ with the help of the Hermeneutic rules, in order that they might be easily remembered by all the students or others who heard them. So Maimonides asserted in his *Moreh Nebuchim* iii, 43, that 'the exegetical expositions of the Rabbis, particularly those which are based on rule *Al tikre* ('Do not read so but so'[1]), were merely expressed in poetic form to urge upon men the appropriation of virtues, and warn them against the practice of vices. They supported, he says, their views from Scripture, simply because they had no other early written records at all besides the Holy Scriptures; the recording of other things had been forbidden by the prohibition that the oral tradition should not be written down.[2] So when they came across something suitable, they devised support for it from Scripture in order that men might remember the moral lesson contained in it.

In a similar way the Rashba[3] quoted by the Kotheb[4] on B.B. 78*b*, with reference to the exposition by the Rabbis of the passage 'wherefore come ye Hamoshelim[5] (they that speak in parables) come to heshbon', where they say that 'hamoshelim' means 'those who master their evil inclinations', and 'Come to heshbon'[6] means 'Come and let us consider the accounts of the World', maintains that the intention of the Rabbis in connecting these ideas with Scripture in this way was that men might always remember them, but they did not actually intend to interpret the words of the text in a sense so extremely remote from its

---

[1] Under this rule, which originally involved a changing of letters or vowels, the changes were suggested merely for the purpose of the homily and did not impair the integrity of the text.

[2] v. Git. 60*b* on the text 'For according to the mouth of these words' (Ex. XXXIV, 27). The oral tradition was regarded as too sacred to be committed to writing. This was not uncommon with other nations who claimed the possession of verbal communications from Supreme Beings.

[3] The initials of Rabbi Solomon b Abraham Aderet, Spanish Rabbi of the thirteenth century. As an opponent of both the external and the internal enemies of Judaism he was led to write a commentary on the Aggadah of which fragments only are extant.

[4] A work of Annotations by R. Jacob b Habib on the 'En Yakob', a collection of all *aggadic* passages which he had edited. Ben Habib left Spain in the year 1492 with the other exiles and settled in Salonica, where he edited and compiled the En Yakob.

[5] From משל parable. It can also be derived from מָשַׁל ruler. Here it actually refers to those who speak in parables.

[6] They rendered the word not as the name of a place, but as meaning 'reckoning' from the root חשב.

literal meaning. See also, in this connection, the statement of the author of the *Shiltei Ha-Gibborim*[1] on Alfasi, chap. i, of A. Z.: 'It was the method of the Rabbis to expound a passage in any way possible to them.' In this, they relied on the *aggadic* principle, deduced from the verse 'Once God hath spoken, twice have I heard this',[2] that one Biblical verse may convey several meanings, which is in accordance with the tradition as it was taught in R. Ishmael's school that the verse 'And like a hammer that breaketh the rock in pieces'[3] means that just as the hammer splits[4] the rock into many fragments, so may one verse be split into (i.e. convey) many meanings (San. 34*a*). Another example is where they say in *Ta'an.*, chap. i,[5] 'that Jacob our patriarch did not die.' 'Was it then for naught (it is retorted) 'that he was mourned?' and the reply is that the statement is inferred from a verse of Scripture.[6] The Talmudic teacher here means to convey that the sages are given permission to expound passages in any way they deem proper in order to attain their object, which is to impress (some idea) upon the multitude. They could accordingly go on multiplying deductions from Scripture and expound and elucidate quotations in various ways, merely for the sake of following the Rabbinical advice, 'Study and receive a reward,'[7] and the chief reason for basing an idea upon a Biblical passage[8] was to preserve it in memory. The rabbis (Erub. 54*b*) had this in mind where they urged upon us that 'The Torah can only be acquired with the aid of mnemonics', and again where from the verse 'Set thee up waymarks',[9] they deduced the similar idea 'devise signs for the Torah'.[10] See also Erubin 21 on the text 'and besides that Koheleth was wise, he

[1] R. Joshua Boas, an Italian Talmudic Scholar of the sixteenth century. Halpern, *Seder ha-Doroth* assigns the authorship of *Shilte ha-Gibborim* to R. Isaiah di Trani the Younger, possibly on account of the fact that the latter is very frequently quoted in the book.

[2] Ps. LXII, 12.

[3] Jer. XXIII, 29.

[4] The Talmudic text actually reads מתחלק (is split), i.e. the hammer is split by the rock and not מחליק (splits). The amendment was made by the Tosafist, R. Samuel (cf. Tos., ad loc., s.v. מה), as against the view of R. Tam, who retains the textual reading, because he holds that a hammer would be split when striking on an extraordinarily hard object.

[5] Ta'an. 5*b*.

[6] Jer. XXX, 10. 'Therefore fear thou not, O Jacob. . . . I will save thee from afar and thy seed from the land of their captivity,' i.e. as his seed will then be alive so he, too, in spirit, will be alive.

[7] Sot. 44*a*; San. 51*b*, i.e. one is rewarded by the mere study apart from any other practical benefit derived therefrom.

[8] Regardless of its connection or otherwise with its literal sense.

[9] Jer. XXXI, 20.

[10] Referring to the mnemonics frequently employed by the Rabbis to assist the memory.

also taught the people knowledge',[1] where they infer that he taught it to them with the aid of mnemonics. Rashi, ad loc., comments that he had instituted a *massoreth* (a record of the minutest details of the text) with signs, both in the scriptural texts and in the study of the *Mishnah* (*Halachah*). See also Shab. 104*a* for the instruction 'devise for yourself (mnemonic) signs for the Torah and you will (i.e. by memorization) acquire her'.

Both earlier and later scholars have elaborated this subject at length, in a manner sufficient to justify the above methods as applied by the Rabbis in their exegetical expositions. It cannot seriously be suggested that they purposely departed from the literal sense of the text, for assuredly they were aware of the important principle that the text cannot deviate from its literal meaning.[2] They say, for example, in the Gemara (Git. 7*a*): 'Am I not aware that the text is here enumerating towns in the Land of Israel,'[3] yet R. Gebiha, of Argiza, derives the following lesson from these names: If a man has cause for indignation[4] against his neighbour and yet remains silent[5], He who abides for all eternity[6] (God) will execute judgment for him. Here the Rabbi has attached a moral lesson to the text, viz. that a man should not hasten to revenge himself upon his neighbour, but should rather wait patiently until he be avenged by God. Although this inference from the text is very far-fetched, yet owing to the prohibition against recording the oral tradition in writing, the Rabbis endeavoured to discover even remote points of contact with the text (to support thereby their moral teachings as based on the oral tradition).

Indeed, in the case of those parables which contained moral teachings and were quoted by the masses in their ordinary conversation, and which they understand only through their everyday experiences of life, even for these the Rabbis have sought textual proofs and Biblical support as, for example, where they ask in the Talmud: 'Whence can we derive Scriptural proof for such and such a proverbial saying' (San. 7*a*, and B.K. 92*a*).

---

[1] Ecc. XII, 9.

[2] v. Shab. 63*a*.

[3] This is a retort by an *Amora* who inquired from another the point of the verse (Josh. xv, 22) 'Kinah and Dimonah and Adadah'. On his reply that the text was merely enumerating towns in the Land of Israel, he made the above retort.

[4] From the Hebrew word קנאה, Deut. XXIX, 19.

[5] From דמם, Lev. x, 3.

[6] From שכן (to rest), with reference to the divine glory, Ex. XXIV, 16 (Rabbinic שכינה).

CHAPTER XX

THE PRAISE OF THE RIGHTEOUS AND THE CONDEMNATION OF THE WICKED IN *AGGADAH*

THE Rabbis had likewise a tradition, as far as possible to praise the conduct of godly men, to demonstrate their worth and weigh it against their failings in the scales of merit, and to endeavour in every way possible to justify the doings of the good. It is in view of this principle that they state that anyone who maintains that David sinned is in error,[1] and similarly anyone who maintains that Solomon sinned.[2] Again, anyone who maintains that Reuben sinned is in error,[3] and likewise anyone who maintains that the sons of Eli sinned,[4] and similarly anyone who maintains that Samuel's sons sinned.[5] Likewise anyone who holds that Josiah sinned is also in error[6] (Shab. 55*b*, 56*a–b*). They also say (A.Z. 4*b*) that David could not have been a man of such a character (as to commit such an act of immorality as that with Bath-Sheba); the whole incident was related for the purpose of leading men to repen-

---

[1] Since we read (1 Sam. XVIII, 14) 'the Lord was with him', and it is impossible to imagine him as a sinner and the Divine Presence with him. Even the express statement (2 Sam. XII, 9) that he despised the Word of the Lord 'to do what was evil in His sight' is interpreted as meaning that he only wished to do evil, but did not actually do it. This is deduced from the wording in the text 'to do' which is not 'he did'.

[2] The fact that Scripture states (1 Kings XI, 4) 'his heart was not perfect with the Lord, as was the heart of David, his father', does not necessarily imply that he sinned. 'His heart was not as perfect as that of his father, but he did not sin.'

[3] Here, too, the Scriptural statement (Gen. XXXV, 22) that he lay with Bilhah, his father's concubine, ought to be interpreted as meaning that he had merely transferred his father's couch to his mother Leah's tent. The author has inverted the order of the Gemara which begins with Reuben, continues with the sons of Eli and Samuel, and then refers to David and Solomon, which is the correct chronological order.

[4] Notwithstanding the express statement (1 Sam. II, 22) telling how they lay with women. This, they claim, is to be interpreted as meaning that they merely delayed the women's bird offerings after childbirth (Lev. XII, 6–8) so that the women had to wait in Shiloh until their offerings had been sacrificed on the altar and were thus prevented from returning to cohabit with their husbands. Hence the form of the charge made against them.

[5] It is true that, according to Scripture (1 Sam. VIII, 1–3), Samuel's sons walked not in his ways, but that does not necessarily imply that they sinned. It means merely, as it says, that they did not walk in the ways of their father, i.e. that they did not act just as he had done.

[6] Although it is expressly stated (2 Kings XXIII, 25) that he returned to the Lord with all his heart, from which it seems to be implied that he had sinned before repenting. Yet the verb שוב, return, may be interpreted to mean that he was revising his judgments, and so can be translated 'returning to judge over again all cases on which he had pronounced judgment between his accession and the finding of the Torah' (cf. 2 Kings XXII, 1–8).

tance.[1] We can thus see that even in cases where the misdemeanour of Biblical worthies was definitely recorded, the Rabbis sought exegetical means of justifying the acts in question, or of minimizing their guilt.

It also goes without saying that they used exaggeration in the praise of those good deeds of the righteous which are expressly recorded, and employed exegetical methods to show that such persons observed the laws of righteousness in a higher degree than is even required in Scripture, and so endeavoured to reveal by exegetical interpretation what the text left unrecorded. See for example the Midrash, Genesis Rabbah, chap. 47, where one of the Midrashic teachers (R. Levi) deduced from the use of the word נימול[2] he was circumcised, rather than מל (he circumcised himself), that Abraham had found himself circumcised (from birth); on which point R. Berachyah observes that R. Aba on that occasion rebuked R. Levi with the words: 'You are a liar and a cheat,' for the fact, he said, was that Abraham had given himself this pain in order that God might double his reward.[3]

This is a typical case where the Rabbis teach us that we ought to stress the good deeds of the righteous and show that all their acts were performed in the most perfect manner. Hence, when R. Levi wished to show by exegetical methods that Abraham did not undergo any pain by circumcision, because he had found out that he was already circumcised, so that no merit could be imputed to him for it and so, according to the above principle, was not exegetically regular, Rabbi Aba objected to his method as very improper and reproached him severely, using the offensive epithets of 'liar and cheat', because, in accordance with the Midrashic precept, it is the duty of the lecturer to praise and magnify the deeds of godly men even beyond the record. Consequently, R. Aba made a counter deduction that Abraham did, indeed, suffer great pain, and yet carried out the command of God in love, undergoing the physical affliction in order to fulfil the divine precept.

R. Moses Hayyim Luzatto[4] in his short Treatise on the *aggadoth*,

---

[1] The wording, as quoted here by the author, is not the exact wording of the Talmudical text, which is to the effect that if an individual sins, he may be referred to him (David) to learn the way of repentance.

[2] In Gen. xvii, 26, referring to Abraham's circumcision.

[3] The following is a more accurate account of the Midrash. We read נימול 'he (Abraham) was circumcised', thus, says R. Aba b. Kahana, Abraham underwent this pain in order that God should double his reward. R. Levi, however, retorted that we do not read מל 'he had circumcised himself', but נימול, which means that he had examined himself and found out that he was already circumcised. On this point R. Berachya observes that R. Aba, on hearing R. Levi's interpretation, could not refrain from calling him liar and cheat, since נימול implies that he had inflicted upon himself the pain of circumcision.

[4] Italian Cabbalist and poet, born at Padua, 1707, died at Safed in his fortieth year. The short Treatise referred to is מאמר על האגדה.

cites this Midrash to prove that one of the duties of a lecturer employing the Midrashic method is to praise the worthy deeds of the righteous so far as possible.

On the other hand, they follow a similar important principle when referring to the evil doings of the wicked, viz. they charge them with all other possible abominable deeds, deducing their charges from the context in each case. Thus, for example, they charge Achan[1] also with the desecration of the Sabbath[2] and with the violation of a betrothed damsel (Sanhedrin 44a).

In a similar way they have drawn a deduction from the verse 'And Esau came in from the field',[3] that on that day he committed five sins. He had dishonoured a betrothed damsel, committed murder, and denied the existence of God, denied the resurrection of the dead, and he despised his birthright.

Again, with reference to Ahaz[4] they deduced by Biblical exegesis (B.B. 16b) that he had violated his mother and had put a lizard upon the Altar (Sanhedrin 103b).[5] Similarly, where they refer to Balaam they charge him with having had intercourse with his ass[6] (A. Zarah 4b).

It is particularly to be noted that when they relate abominable deeds of the wicked, in their desire to render them more horrible, they often illustrate them by the most detestable of all deeds known to them, viz. the violation of a betrothed damsel on the Day of Atonement (v. B.M. 83b). So, too, they deduce from Scripture that Elisha saw that the mothers (of the children killed by the bears) had all become pregnant on the Day of Atonement[7] (Sot. 46b). In the Jer. Hag., ii, they

---

[1] v. Joshua, VII, 1.

[2] This act is not quoted in the Gemara; on the other hand, there are others there given which are omitted by our author, such as his transgression of the whole five books of the Torah, and his effacing the sign of the Abrahamic covenant.

[3] Genesis xxv, 29.

[4] The son of Jotham and eleventh King of Judah, a corrupt ruler who violated the law of God and had no respect for the prophets (see 2 Kings xvi).

[5] Here the author has erroneously ascribed these crimes to Ahaz, whereas in the Gemara they are attributed to Amon (son of Manasseh) while Ahaz is accused of causing the sacrificial service to cease, of permitting adultery with blood relations, and of sealing up the Torah.

[6] From the words of the ass 'Ever since I was thine' (Numb. xxii, 30): 'I have carried you by day and have been your companion by night'. See the discussion that follows for the extent of the Gemara's interpretation.

[7] In Scripture (2 Kings II, 24) it is stated that 'he saw them and he cursed'. On the question of what he actually did see, they answer that he saw as above, i.e. in the case of those children who mocked at him, saying, 'Ascend, thou bald head, ascend thou, etc.,' telling him thus tauntingly to ascend into heaven as his Master had done, he traced (in these young delinquents) an admixture of rudeness and impiety inherited from their idolatrous parents; hence the Rabbis' charge of a guilt most abominable in their sight.

charge Elishah Ben Abuyah[1] with the sin of riding (ostentatiously through the streets of Jerusalem) on a horse on a Day of Atonement which fell on the Sabbath, and similarly on several other occasions[2] refer to a violation of the Day of Atonement which falls on the Sabbath as an aggravated transgression.

However, they have laid down a principle for us in Tractate Sanhedrin[3] to the effect that in the case of all others[4] one should not seek to expound the Biblical passages, referring to them in ways discreditable to them, whereas in the case of the wicked Balaam one may expound the Biblical passages referring to him as far as possible to his discredit. They mean to say that in the case of the three Kings[5] one should not endeavour to expound the Biblical passage relating to them in any way more unfavourable than is actually implied by the text, but that when dealing with the wicked Balaam one may expound them as much as one likes to his dishonour, showing how he was continually engaged in evil and in the most abominable crimes, and make these well-known to the public, since a wicked person of such an exceptionally low moral standard as Balaam was capable of committing every sort of transgression, and therefore such an exposition as the above that Balaam had had intercourse with his ass should not be regarded as too far-fetched. The compiler of the *Ein Yaakob*, Ber. 7*a*, has also taken it in this far-fetched way, and has given some peculiar interpretations of Scripture to support the *aggadah* as, for example, where he argues that while the analogy employed in the *Gemara*, as based on the similarity of the verb הסכנתי[6] used here (with reference to Balaam's ass) with סוכנת[7] used elsewhere, is fallacious, in view of the statement in the latter passage[8] that the King knew her not, yet, following the above-mentioned principle ascribed to the *Aggadic* teachers, that they should

[1] A Palestinian teacher of the law of the first and second centuries, who, later, became unfaithful to Jewish tradition. He aroused the hostility of the Rabbis against him to such an extent that they refrained even from pronouncing his name, referring to him as *Acher* (the other), i.e. the one outside the fold, the apostate.

[2] I have so far traced only one other source, viz. Pes. 49*b*, where R. Eleazar speaks so bitterly of an *Am ha-Aretz* as to permit his being killed on a Day of Atonement which falls on the Sabbath—a statement which can scarcely be taken literally.

[3] San. 106*b*, with reference to people who have no portion in the world to come (see note 6).

[4] i.e. those not there enumerated.

[5] To whom the Mishna (San. XI, 1) refers as having no portion in the world to come, viz. (1) Jeroboam the son of Nebat, a King of Israel, who is stigmatized in Scripture as one who sinned and caused others to sin (1 Kings xv, 30; Aboth 5, 18); (2) Ahab, the son of Omri, a King of Israel (1 Kings xxi, 21); (3) Manasseh, the son of Hezekiah, a King of Judah (2 Kings xxi).

[6] 'I was wont' (Num. XII, 30).

[7] In the verse 'Let her (Abishag) be his סוכנת (companion)' (1 Kings I, 2).

[8] Ibid. I, 4.

expound the passage to Balaam's discredit, in so far as that is possible, they have naturally laid to his charge this abomination, finding for it Scriptural support, even if it be far-fetched, because they did this in dealing with other passages in their accustomed manner. Maimonides again, in his *Commentary on Aboth*, with reference to the statement of the Mishnah 5, 19, that the disciples of Balaam the wicked (inherited from him) an evil eye, a haughty mind, and a proud spirit, says that 'the man who was so perverted as to seek to persuade the daughters of Midian to abandon themselves to prostitution was, no doubt, capable of committing all other possible loathsome deeds'.

In particular you will find the said principle expressed in the words of the Jerusalem Talmud (San. 51*a*), where we read that R. Levi had for six months expounded the Biblical text: 'Because thou has sold thyself to the work of evil in the sight of the Lord,'[1] as blaming Ahab for his misdeeds[2], until Ahab actually appeared to him in a dream and complained: 'What wrong did I ever do to you, and what evil did I ever commit in your presence?'[3] R. Levi subsequently spent six months expounding the later verse of the passage 'but none was like Ahab, who did sell himself to work wickedness, whom Jezebel, his wife, led astray', in a manner that was favourable to Ahab. We see, therefore, that it mostly depended on the lecturer, as is seen in this case, where at first he construed Ahab's deed to his discredit so far as to attribute to him all possible evil, though this could only be deduced in a very far-fetched way, yet afterwards he made similar deductions to his credit. Indeed, he found some mitigation even for the sins and outrages expressly set out, in emphasizing that they were committed only at the instigation of his wife, Jezebel. One may take this as a guide to all similar expositions and see how all depended on the lecturer, and how there was no definite tradition in these matters.

The motive which prompted the Rabbis to adopt this method in these *aggadic* expositions was their desire to strengthen in the people's minds the great principle, which the authors of the Mishnah had laid down, that 'precept draws precept in its train, and transgression draws transgression'.[4] Consequently, the Rabbis charged the public lecturer with the duty of inculcating this idea as thoroughly as possible, and of teaching the people that the man who walks in the way of the Torah

---

[1] 1 Kings XXII, 20.
[2] With particular reference to his outrageous dealing with Naboth the Jezreelite.
[3] The Jer., ad loc., states that Ahab (in the dream) had directed his attention to the end of the passage (ibid. XXII, 25) where it expressly states that it was his wife, Jezebel, who had instigated him to that cruel act.
[4] Aboth 4, 2.

finds it become second nature to him, so that it is easy for him to practise all other good deeds and nothing causes him any difficulty any longer. Even when we find these people doing something wrong we should try with the help of the exegetical method to put a favourable construction on their action and to adduce such mitigating circumstances as to show that there was, indeed, no crime at all committed as, for example, in the case of David and Bath Sheba.[1] They even put forth the plea that everyone of the house of David who went out to the War wrote a bill of divorcement for his wife.[2] In a similar manner they exonerated Solomon on the ground that he did not, in fact, sin, and that where he did fail was in not restraining his wives from sin.[3] So, too, they judged the cases of Reuben and the sons of Eli favourably.[4]

They wished, in the second place, to teach by this method another important lesson—viz. that as soon as a man deviates, however slightly, from the way of the Torah, he at once needs more caution and more encouragement, because of the threatened danger that one transgression will draw after it another and, if he is not on his guard to resist the temptation to evil that threatens him, and which has already seduced him to taste of the forbidden fruit, he will expose himself to the practice of all sorts of abominations. Consequently the best line to follow is to teach the people and show them the way in which they should walk, the way which was laid down by past experience in the events which occurred in the life of former generations, as it is written: 'Remember the days of old. Consider the years of many generations.'[5] Thus, from the way of life of men of earlier generations we see and learn that any virtue to which a man has begun to habituate himself takes such deep root that it exercises a good influence upon him wherever he may turn in the course of his later life.

On the other hand, in the case of a man with evil inclination, even if at first he deviate only slightly from the way of goodness, in the course of time this deviation will draw after it more serious transgressions, since it comes to be fixed as habit and permanent nature and, therefore, it will be difficult for such a man to abandon the path which he has chosen. Particular caution, therefore, is necessary in the early stages, to prevent the evil from taking deep root and becoming a fixed habit.

[1] The latter, who was the granddaughter of Ahitophel and wife of Uriah, was seduced by David during the absence of her husband, who was then engaged in the siege of Rabbah (2 Sam. XI, 4-5).

[2] So that on this view Bath Sheba was, at that time, a woman divorced by her husband.

[3] On account of which Scripture treats him as though he had himself sinned.

[4] See notes 3, 4, p. 162.

[5] Deut. XXXII, 7. A reference to the lesson to be drawn from the lives of those who have passed before us.

See the Responsum of Ralbach,[1] No. 126, in connection with the principle laid down earlier: 'It was the method of the Rabbis to accentuate the guilt of the guilty, so weighing him down in the scale of culpability as, for example, they allege of Anah[2] that he was the offspring of an incestuous union and that he reared such offspring even in the animal world'[3] (Pes. 54a). Similarly, they heightened the misdeeds of Laban and Balaam. It was likewise their method to justify all the deeds of the righteous man and to place him in the category of merit, as we see clearly in their statements about persons who are referred to in the Bible as guilty of some misconduct, but who, according to their view, did not in fact commit any sin. In view then of this rabbinical theory the questioner asks for an explanation of the deduction of the Rabbis (Meg. 14b) from David's words to Abigail, 'listen to me.'[4] Surely, David was a pious man and, following the above theory, we are required to construe things in his favour, even where the literal meaning of the text implies that he did wrong; yet here the Rabbis made a deduction to the contrary, namely that David intended to commit a grave sin with Abigail, who was a married woman, whereas the text, in its literal sense, does not say this. Similarly, he continues, in the case of Joseph, who is accepted as righteous, the actual text testifies that he did not respond to the lustful request of his master's wife, but fled from her; why then did the Rabbis infer (Sot. 36b) from the text, 'and he (Joseph) went into the house to his work,'[5] that he went in for the purpose of the immoral act, but in seeking to carry it out found himself (physically) incapable, just as the Rabbis in the *Yalkut* on Kings interpreted the words 'thou camest in to me',[6] which the Zorphathite woman said to Elijah the prophet, to mean that he went in to associate with her immorally? How did they come to suggest a sin against God detestable even in an ordinary person, and especially in such a saintly man as Elijah, and why should they seek to weigh these (righteous men) in the scales of guilt, when there is nothing which indicates it of

[1] Rabbi Levi b. Habib, a Spanish Rabbi, born in 1480, died at Jerusalem in 1545. His collected responsa number 147.
[2] The son of Seir the Horite who, in Gen. xxxvi, 20, is referred to as the brother of Zibeon, and in verse 24, as his son. The Rabbis deduced from this inconsistency that he was the offspring of the incestuous marriage of Zibeon and his mother.
[3] He reared the ימים mentioned in Gen. xxxvi, 24, i.e. mules, the offspring of an ass and a mare. v. Hul. 7 for the statement that ימים signifies dreadful beings because they cause fear to people. The author in the text has added the words 'and he had intercourse with his mother', but the Gemara reads: 'in view of his brother Zibeon's intercourse with his mother.'
[4] 2 Samuel xxv, 31, which hint, according to the Rabbis, at an indecent request.
[5] Gen. xxxix, 11.
[6] 1 Kings xvii, 18.

them? Of what value, in fact, are such exegetical expositions, and what prompted their authors to depart from their guiding principle of judging the actions of the righteous, under all circumstances, on the side of merit?

Such are the arguments advanced by the questioner in Ben Habib's Responsum, and I myself have found one other similar passage, where the Rabbis inferred from the words 'and David was come to the head'[1] that he wished to worship idols (San. 107*a*).

Ben Habib, in meeting the difficulty raised by the questioner, wrote that even where the Rabbis found fault with the actions of the just, their intentions were good, since even in doing this they meant to show some praiseworthy aspect in their lives, and thereby to teach the truth of that which the Rabbis had laid down as a fundamental principle, viz. that the greater the man the greater the power of his evil inclination.[2] And so they show how the evil inclination within David overpowered him at times so far that he was about to commit an immoral act with a married woman; but this did not, in fact, happen, because of his determination to control his inclination. Again, the frequent tribulations which befell David caused him almost to deny Providence. The Rabbis interpreted this disposition as an inclination towards actual 'idolatry', but it may be taken, as they have interpreted the term *Abodah Zarah*[3] (B.B. 110*a*) elsewhere, as meaning a service which was strange to him but not actual 'idol worship'. Similarly, he adds, in the case of Joseph, although his intention was already towards evil, and he had actually entered the house to consummate the sinful deed, yet he succeeded in repressing his evil inclination and did not commit the sin; and in the view of the Rabbis, this was an outstanding achievement, for had he not been passionately tempted to the immoral association in question, in view of the difference in status, since a humble slave as a rule would not have raised his eyes to his master's wife, Joseph's conduct would by no means have been an outstanding achievement, whereas in this case where he had already been assailed by temptation and yet had made himself master of it, the Rabbis have chosen his act for special praise; for was he not wholly set on the sin, and what mighty efforts were needed to suppress his evil inclination, as his thoughts were fully occupied with the sinful deed, and these thoughts would, indeed, have condemned him, but for the principle adopted for Israel that an evil thought is not to be viewed as an evil deed, as is stated in the Jerusalem Talmud,

---

[1] When he fled from Absalom his son. 2 Sam. xv, 32.
[2] Suk. 52*a*.
[3] Lit. 'strange work', implying either idolatry or any kind of work or thought which is alien to the spirit of the Torah.

Peah i.[1] The stories are embellished to bring out the worth of the pious, how they were saved from falling into sin, in line with what was said before (in the case of Abraham) that it is the lecturer's duty to prove that Abraham had not been born circumcised but had undergone the great pain of the operation, yet endured the trial. So, too, in the case of Elijah, the Rabbis, in their deduction mentioned above, had the special object of manifesting his greatness by showing that in spite of the Zorephathite's allegation against him, she yet regarded him as a godly and saintly man, and had no doubt of his virtue and, therefore, ventured to entreat him to pray to God for her son. (Here the Responsum ends.)

Again, there were questions which the questioner posed in the said Responsum, viz. with reference to several of the *aggadoth* which not only are unrepeatable[2] but are even inappropriate for a written record at all, such as the description given in B.M. 84a of the membrum genitale of R. Johanan.[3] Indeed, he says, decent people ought not to speak except on worthy matters, and particularly so in the case of pious and saintly men like them; and besides, he asks, of what use are these *aggadoth* to the people, they contribute neither to the love of God nor to the fear of Him. On the contrary, he continues, the Rabbis themselves said that in the case of one who speaks obscenely, even if a decree of seventy years' happiness has been issued for him, it is reversed for evil (Sab. 33a). And again, what about such *aggadoth* as at the outset appear to be obscene, like those referred to in Sab. 140b[4] and in San. 82b?[5] Indeed, for what purpose have the authors of the Talmud included such *aggadoth*? Ben Habib, however, does not here give an adequate answer. But some famous Rabbis have actually endeavoured to give a justification for their inclusion, as, for example, R. Judah Löw ben Bezaleel, of Prague,[6] who, in his *Beer Hagolah*, has striven to prove the propriety and justness of the words of the Rabbis. And there is a point which he makes here that may be used for the elucidation of these *aggadoth*.[7] It is to the effect that the Rabbis wish to show how, in spite of the perfect vigour of many of them, which was such that they had no

[1] And also in the Babylonian Talmud, Kid. 40a.
[2] On account of their seemingly obscene contents.
[3] Given in a humorous and exaggerated manner. Others translate it the 'waist', referring in the context to the bodily figure of various Talmudical teachers.
[4] Quoting the advice given by R. Hisda to his daughters on how to excite their husbands' sexual desire.
[5] The detailed description of the position of Zimri ben Salu and Cozbi during their commission of the immoral act (Num. xxv, 8), as also the description of Zimri's excessive lust.
[6] Bohemian Talmudist and mathematician of the sixteenth century, held in high regard, and the centre of a whole cycle of legends.
[7] Such as that referred to before from B.M. 84a.

ailments, they yet withstood the power of passion and overcame it. Furthermore, there were some of them famous for their outstanding beauty[1] who used to stand purposely at the gate of the place of the ritual immersion,[2] and (on being challenged) said that the women were like so many white geese in their sight[3] (Ber. 20*a*). This is specifically recorded as a praiseworthy act of these Torah students, who were so confident of themselves that, even in the riskiest of moral situations, they came out safe and intact, with no ill-effects.

[1] See B.M. 84*a* and B.B. 58*a*, 'The beauty of R. Kahana is a reflection of that of R. Abahu, etc.,' i.e. each was more beautiful than the other.
[2] So that he might be met by the women as they came up from the bath. 'Let them,' he said, 'see me at that moment in order that they may bear sons as beautiful as I am.'
[3] i.e. they did not excite any passion in them.

CHAPTER XXI

THE QUOTING OF VARIOUS PERSONS UNDER ONE AND THE SAME NAME

FOR the reason stated above, namely that the Rabbis had the definite principle in their homiletic interpretations of praising, so far as possible, the deeds of the virtuous and of disparaging the doings of the wicked in every available way, they further adopted as one of their methods that of calling different personages by one and the same name if they found them akin in any feature of their characters or activities or if they found a similarity between any of their actions. Even where there was only some resemblance in the names of different persons, they blended the two in one, as we see in the following cases (Meg. 15a): 'Malachi and Ezra are one and the same person, for, in the prophecy of Malachi, it is written "He hath married the daughter of a strange God",[1] while in the book of Ezra, it is written "We have broken faith with our God and have married strange women!"[2] Similarly, they held that Hathach[3] and Daniel are one; that Pethahiah[4] is the same as Mordecai, and Sheshbazzar[5] the same as Daniel.[6] Again, they said that Cyrus, Darius, and Artaxerxes are all one (R.H. 3b).[7] V. Tos, ad loc., s.v. שנת, and also the further statement made there that Sihon, Arad, and Canaan were all one. Similarly, in Pes. 54a they said that Anah is the same as the Anah mentioned earlier,[8] which indicates that Zibeon had an immoral association with his mother[9]; and we find a

---

[1] Mal. II, 11.

[2] Ezra x, 2.

[3] Est. IV, 5.

[4] A Levite who was appointed over the bird offerings. The literal meaning of the name is פתח־יה 'God has opened', and Mordecai was able to 'open' a discussion upon the complicated problems of the said offerings and expound them.

[5] A Prince of Judah, Ezra I, 8.

[6] The statement with reference to Hathach is indeed in Meg. 15a, as quoted by the author, but not the other two, that about Pethahiah being in M. Shek. 5, 1, and Men. 65a, and that about Sheshbazzar, being quoted in the Yalkut Shimeoni 1068, 5, from the Chronicle Seder Olam of R. Jose b. Halafta.

[7] Critical students of the history of the Persian Kings have found the Biblical accounts in Ezra, Nehemiah, and Daniel, upon which this statement is based, a subject requiring scrutiny and examination, for in their view, the facts of the history of the ancient Persian Empire do not agree with those in the Bible. Again, that the name of each of those three might denote more than one monarch is possible, but that all the three names belonged to one Monarch is very unlikely; the author's contention, however, is that the Rabbis only intended to express their view that the character of the one was identical with that of the other.

[8] i.e. the Anah of verse 24 in Gen. XXXVI is the same as the one in verse 20, ibid.

[9] See p. 168, note 2.

similar statement in the *Midrash Rab. Sidrah Vayeshev*, on the verse 'and his name was Hirah',[1] that the Rabbis state that Hirah and Hiram[2] are one man, and that he lived almost 1,200 years. See also Jer. Sotah 25*b*, where R. Akiba expounds verses to show that Elihu b Barachel[3] and Balaam are one person.[4]

De Rossi,[5] in his *Me'or 'Enayim*, chap. xviii, has collected the statements quoted above, showing how the Rabbis identified several different persons with the name of one man who was outstanding either in virtue or vice. To them I may add some further cases; thus, for example: Memucan,[6] in their view, is the same as Haman (Meg. 12*b*); Nebat,[7] Sheba b Bichri,[8] and Michah[9] are one and the same (San. 101*b*); Beor[10] and Cushan Rishathaim[11] and Laban the Aramaean are identical (San. 105*a*). In Jer. Naz. 42*b*, too, we read 'Laban and Cushan Rishathaim are identical.' Again, in the *Midrash Rab.*, on the portion *Lech Lecha*, the Rabbis state that Amraphel[12] and Nimrod[13] are one and the same. They also state in Ber. 29*a* that Jannai and Johanan (the High Priest) are one and the same.[14]

The main reason for this method is to be found in the chief principle which the Rabbis laid down as a cornerstone or basis for their exegetical expositions, viz. that the lecturer may in all possible ways enhance the praise of righteous and pious men, and wherever he finds reference in Holy Writ to the worthiness of a particular righteous man he should

[1] See Gen. xxxviii, 1, referring to the Adullamite who was visited by Judah.

[2] Who is stated in 1 Kings v, 15, to have been loved by David all his days.

[3] The youngest of the friends who came to comfort Job in his distress (v. Job xxxii, 2–6).

[4] He based this on his designation הבוזי (the Buzite) which literally means 'despised'. On the other hand, his opponent R. Eleazar b. Azariah who maintained that Elihu and Isaac are one inferred it from the word ברכאל which in the literal sense means a blessing of God. Both Rabbis, it seems, aimed at showing the character of the one to be identical with that of the other.

[5] See p. 150, note 8.

[6] One of the seven princes of Ahaseurus (Est. i, 14).

[7] The father of Jeroboam who revolted against Rehoboam and became the first King of the Northern Kingdom (1 Kings xii).

[8] Who had revolted against David immediately after the collapse of Absalom's rebellion (2 Sam. xx).

[9] Also called Micaiah, who had established an idol-worshipping centre and engaged a Levite to minister therein (v. Judg. xvii–xviii). All these three were Ephraimites.

[10] The father of Balaam.

[11] The King of Aram referred to in Judges iii, 8.

[12] King of Shinear, one of the four Kings who invaded Canaan in the time of Abraham (Gen. xiv, 1–2).

[13] Son of Cush and grandson of Ham (Gen. x, 8–10). His name, which denotes rebellion, marked him out as the prototype of a rebellious people (Pes. 94*b*).

[14] This is the view of Abaye which was opposed by Raba, see page 47, note 1.

attribute any other virtue to him which is found in any other out-standing personality, if only this can be given Biblical support, however far-fetched. In this way we find the 'righteous' adorned with every worthy quality and virtue.

Similarly in the case of the wicked man, the Rabbis strove to expatiate upon his sinfulness as far as they could and, even in cases where wicked-ness was not expressly stated, they derived it from other cases where wickedness was categorically affirmed, to prove that an evil man is capable of anything, and they supported their expositions even with the slightest and remotest of indications, as we have seen in the *aggadic* state-ment: 'The phrase "son of Beor" denotes that he had had connection with an animal' (in this case his ass[1]) or that Laban is identical with Cushan Rishathaim, deriving this from the dual of *Risha*[2]; and these expositions were derived in very remote ways, in accordance with their regular method, and expressed thus[3]: 'I derive this from a Scriptural verse.'[4] For further references, see *Me'or 'Enayim*, chap. xviii, which elaborates this subject at great length.

For the decisive proof, however, of this theory, I shall produce clear and positive evidence from the categorical statement in B.B. 91a, that Ibzan[5] is Boaz. This is received by the Gemara with the question 'What does this teach us?'[6], which the *Rashbam*[7] interprets to mean 'of what benefit is it' or 'what good can be derived from it?' At the outset, the raising of this question seems a difficulty. Why, indeed, should this case be different from all the other cases in the Talmud, for nowhere else is this actual question asked? According, however, to the above explana-tion, the observation here is quite appropriate after all. In all the other cases there might be a considerable benefit from combining various virtuous men under one name in order to identify the characteristics of one with those of another, and this is the great advantage of magnifying the laudable deeds of the righteous, but not so in this case of Ibzan, for of him nothing virtuous is recorded in Scripture. What advantage is it to

[1] San. 105a. A play on the Hebrew word בעור which can be read as בעיר cattle, Ex. xxii, 4.
[2] He had committed two evils upon Israel, one in the days of Jacob, when he pursued him with the object of capturing him (Gen. xxxi, 23), and the other in the days of the Judges (see Jud. iii, 8).
[3] With reference to the statement, made on the authority of R. Johanan, that Jacob our Patriarch did not die.
[4] Which actually may offer a very slender proof for the statement. For a sample case, v. Ta'an 5b.
[5] The tenth judge, who succeeded Jephthah in judging Israel. See Jud. xii, 8.
[6] The author's quotation, 'of what consequence is it?' is inaccurate.
[7] R. Samuel b. Meir, grandson of Rashi, who completed his unfinished com-mentary on B.B. from fol. 29b.

Boaz to identify Ibzan with him? The Gemara's question is thus appropriate, and the answer given is that there is another motive behind the statement, viz. that although he had many children already,[1] yet he[2] fulfilled the precept 'in the evening withhold not thine hand'[3] by marrying Ruth in his old age. See *Rashbam*, ad loc.

Again they state in the same context that Elimelech[4] and Salmon[5] and Peloni Almoni[6] and the father of Naomi were all the sons of Nahshon (b Aminadab),[7] and on this the Gemara again asks 'What does this statement teach us?' since there is not, in this case either, any relation to the guiding principle which we have mentioned above, viz. the magnifying of the righteous. The answer given is that there is a moral lesson to be inferred from it, viz. that the sin of one who leaves the land of Palestine for a foreign country is so great that any merit possessed by his ancestors is of no avail for him. At all events one can see that the lecturer always had the particular intention of impressing the people and arousing their minds by giving praise to the righteous and blame to the wicked, or of teaching a moral lesson or some laudable habit.

[1] Ibzan is stated in Scripture to have had thirty sons and thirty daughters (Jud XII, 8 and 9).

[2] Boaz, i.e. if Ibzan is identified with him.

[3] Eccl. XI. 6. The Rabbis, Yeb. 62b, deduced from this that if a man married in his youth, he should marry again in his old age, and if he had children in his youth, he should also have children in his old age.

[4] Husband of Naomi of Bethlehem who withdrew in a time of scarcity into the land of Moab where he died (Ruth I, 1–3).

[5] Father of Boaz, also called Salmah (cf. Ruth IV, 20).

[6] The literal meaning of these words is such a one, or so and so (Ruth IV, 1).

[7] Cf. Ex. VI, 23; Numb. X, 14.

CHAPTER XXII

THE METHOD OF EXPOUNDING THE NAMES OF PERSONS

IN their homiletic interpretations the Rabbis also adopted a special method of expounding the names of persons. They maintain that a name has its influence[1] (Ber. 7b). Thus, it is reported of R. Meir that he paid close attention to personal names[2] (Yoma 83b). Cf. also the following remark upon Delilah's name[3] (Sot. 9b): 'If her name had not been Delilah, she ought to have been called so, since she weakened[4] his strength and his vigour.' In several individual cases they are found quoting such *aggadoth* as traditions that had been received from their ancestors. Thus, in Sot. 34b we read: 'It has been received by tradition from our fathers that the names of the spies[5] were in accordance with their actions, but only one such name has come down to us, viz. Sathor (b Michael), so called because he tore down the works of God.[6] Michael (his father), again, was so named because he regarded God as powerless[7] (against the inhabitants of the land).

They had a special tradition expounding the names of men referred to in the Chronicles. The contents of the Book of Chronicles, they say, were intended solely for homiletic interpretation.[8] (See beginning of *Canticles R.* and of *Eccl. R.*[9]) Yet although the whole of Scripture was a subject for Midrashic interpretation, and although in particular the Scroll of Esther is to be interpreted homiletically, just like the Torah itself (Jer. Meg., chap. i), there was, nevertheless, in existence the definite ruling that no text ever loses its literal meaning and, in fact, both (the Midrashic and the literal interpretations) are true, as is maintained by *Ramban*[10] in his critical notes on *Sefer ha-Mitzvoth*, root ii, where he points out that the Rabbis did not say 'the text had only its

---

[1] i.e. a person's name has an influence or bearing upon his character or fate.

[2] Once the name of an innkeeper, Kidor, made him very suspicious of his honesty, in view, he said, of the phrase כי דור in the Biblical verse, 'for a generation (כי דור) that is very froward.' (Deut. XXXII, 20).

[3] The woman of Sorek loved by Samson (Judges XVI, 4–20).

[4] A play on the name Delilah from דל weak, poor (Is. XIX, 6; Ps. LXXIX, 8).

[5] See Numb. XIII, 33.

[6] From סתר to upset, tear down (in Talmudic Hebrew), by bringing back a discouraging report of the land which had been promised to our forefathers by God.

[7] From מכך to bring low, Lev. XXV, 25; Ps. CVI, 43.

[8] Lev. R. I, 3.

[9] Where fanciful interpretations of the several names attributed to Solomon are found.

[10] See p. 23, note I.

literal meaning', they said that 'no text loses its literal meaning', which means that both the inner and the external meanings can be true, and that the '*text*' in this case carries both. See Yeb. 24*a* for the statement that although throughout the Torah the text does not lose its literal meaning,[1] nevertheless, in this case the *gezerah shavah* has come and completely deprived it of its natural meaning.[2] Again, with regard to the claim of R. Kahana (Shab. 63*a*) that though he had studied the whole *Shas*[3] (Talmud) he had nevertheless failed to learn (as he should) that the text never departs from its literal meaning, his reference is only to the proverbial and poetical passages of Scripture, such as that quoted in the context in the Gemara, 'Gird thy sword upon thy thigh,'[4] not to the precepts of the Torah, where there can be no doubt that this principle of the literal meaning has its deep roots in the Law, for otherwise one might come to interpret such a law as that of circumcision in the same sense as that in which we understand the words 'And ye shall circumcise the foreskin of your heart'[5] (i.e. metaphorically), or one might interpret the precept of *tefilin* (which is conveyed to us) through the words 'And thou shalt bind them for a sign upon thine hand, etc.',[6] merely to mean that one should effect a remembrance in the heart and mind (without the physical act), and so men might, God forbid, do away with the actual carrying out of the precepts; and what would then become of the Torah as a whole. See Responsa of *Rashba*, No. 415, with reference to his pronouncement of excommunication against the heretical sect which removed the literal sense (from the names) in the biographical parts of the Torah, and according to whom, for example, Abraham and Sarah represent only such elements as matter and form. Thus, R. Kahana held that the rule that 'the text does not lose its literal meaning' applied only in cases of Torah precepts, since in these cases such a principle was a matter of great importance as affecting the conduct of man to be regulated by the Torah commandments, but not so in the case of the proverbial or poetical passages of Scripture, since in them it was the homiletical exposition which mattered, Mar b R. Huna, however, retorted that the rule applied in these cases also. This view was generally accepted for the Torah as a whole.

---

[1] By the fact that it has been homiletically interpreted.

[2] So that, for example, in spite of the ordinary meaning of the text that the child of the levirate union should be named after the deceased (Deut. xxv, 6) it was ruled that the succession in the name mentioned in the text refers to the inheritance only. See p. 9, note 3.

[3] ש״ס an abbreviation of ששה סדרים, the six orders of the Talmud.

[4] Ps. xlv, 4.

[5] Deut. x, 16.

[6] Ibid. vi, 8.

With regard, however, to the Book of Chronicles, the Rabbis had a special tradition that that book was given only for homiletical purposes, i.e. that homiletic interpretation was the main theme there. See Meg. 13a, where we read that R. Simeon b Pazi introduced his exposition of the Book of Chronicles as follows: 'All thy words are one[1] and we know how to expound them.'

Indeed, an indication of the abundance of such homiletical expositions on the book of Chronicles may be found in the statement of the Rabbis (Pes. 62b) that the expositions given of the names between Azel and Azel[2] had the same weight as 'the loads of 400 camels',[3] or again, in Jer. San.,[4] where R. Simeon b Lakish is quoted as saying: 'In former days if a man said to me that there is a Book of Chronicles in Babylon I would go and fetch it from there ; now, however, if all our Rabbis went together, they could not bring it.' He certainly did refer to homiletic expositions on the Book of Chronicles, which he thought he might bring in book form from Babylon, for the written recording of such expositions was already permitted during the lifetime of R. Johanan and R. Simeon b Lakish (v. Git. 60a),[5] and not to the actual volume of the Book of Chronicles in the Bible, for it was just as procurable by the Palestinians as any other of the Holy Books; and he indicated that the Babylonian scholars were more conversant with homiletical interpretations of the Book of Chronicles, and he was eager, therefore, to bring them to Palestine. He meant that the writing down of such *aggadoth* was already permitted, and in view of their great number it would be impossible to carry such a heavy load, since enormous quantities of expositions had been collected on every tip (of the letters of the Book).

Prior to the time when the writing down of the *aggadoth* was publicly permitted, the expositions of the Book of Chronicles were recorded in the same manner as those recorded in the *Megillath Setharim*[6] and were not so large in quantity. But in virtue of this principle which they held by tradition (that Chronicles was for homiletical use only) the Rabbis

---

[1] i.e. all the names of this Book can be interpreted as referring to one and the same person. As an example of this, he gave the passage 'Jered the father of Geder and Heber the father of Socho and Jekuthiel the father of Zanoah'(1 Chr. IV, 18), all which names, he says, refer to Moses.

[2] Referred to in 1 Ch. VIII, 43, and again in VIII, 44.

[3] One of the fanciful or exaggerated Aggadic statements which aimed at giving a conception of the abundance of expositions even on such a small portion of the Book as one verse.

[4] Helek X, 1.

[5] They and their contemporaries had found out that the recording of the *aggadoth* could not be dispensed with for fear that they might be doomed to oblivion.

[6] Concealed scrolls containing *halachoth* and maxims which the scholars were accustomed to write on scrolls and which were, at first, hidden owing to the prohibition against committing *halachoth* to writing (see Rashi Sab. 6b, s.v. מגילת).

had not missed any opportunity of expounding in the book of Chronicles any of the names of men and the reasons why they were thus named. See Meg. 13*a* and 14*a*[1]; San. 21*a*[2]; Tem. 16*a*[3]; and B.B. 91*b*.[4] And similarly in Jer. Yeb., chap. Hearel,[5] and other scattered *Midrashim*, one can find a variety of exposition of names of men referred to in the Book of Chronicles, and all prompted by the aforesaid guiding principle which the Rabbis had received by tradition to the effect that the (names of the) Book of Chronicles are given only for expository purposes.

The Rabbis also were in possession of a special principle in reference to the Book of Canticles, that nothing should be inferred from it which could be regarded as disparaging, but that on the contrary all interpretations should be eulogistic. This must be due to the view at which the Tannaim of the Mishnah (Yadaim 3, 5) had arrived, that while all the Writings[6] are holy, yet the Song of Songs is holy of holies, and the whole contents of the poem are to indicate the relations between God and the congregation of Israel, and therefore nothing in it ought to be interpreted in such a way as to reflect dishonour upon Israel.[7] See *Shir Hashirim R.* on the verse 'he brought me to the banqueting house'[8] to the effect that R. Meir, who had expounded the words as meaning that the people of Israel had confessed that they were dominated by an impulse of evil, was reproached by R. Judah on the ground that the Song of Songs was always to be interpreted eulogistically. Similarly, when R. Meir sought to interpret the passage 'while the King sitteth at Table, my spikenard sendeth forth its smell'[9] as referring to the making of the Golden Calf, R. Judah retorted that the Song of Songs was not to be interpreted disparagingly, and this principle was like a guiding light to all subsequent Preachers, so that where it was possible to attach to the contents of the Poem credit and praise for the people of Israel, they did not rest until they had found some sort of basis or support for this line of thought, in order that they might make effective the principle stated above.

[1] Dealing with the exposition by R. Simon b Pazi of the Book of Chronicles.

[2] On the name of Eglah, assumed, according to Rab, by Michal.

[3] On the variation of Caleb b Jefunneh's name as referred to in Num. XIII, 6, and in I Chron. II, 18.

[4] On the names of Mahlon and Chilion (Ruth I, 2) and of Joash and Seraph I Chron. IV, 22, who are assumed to be identical pairs.

[5] In 48*b*, on names referred to in I Ch. VIII, 8, and ii, 17, see *Korban Ha-Edah* (by R. David Frankel of Dessau, 1704–1762), ad loc., for the view that such expositions were prompted by the tradition that the names in the Book of Chronicles were material for exposition only. See Introduction to Hamidrash V'ha-Maase (Pietrkov 1913) by R. E. Libshutz of Kalisch (Poland) on this subject.

[6] Actually *Kethubim*, i.e. Hagiographa.

[7] See San 101*a* for a severe reprimand for anyone who treats the Song of Songs as a secular poem.   [8] Cant. II, 4.   [9] Ibid. I, 12.

CHAPTER XXIII

SUPPORT IN HISTORY FOR 'TRADITION' HANDED DOWN BY THE GREAT ASSEMBLY

AGAIN, they had another tradition handed down to them from the men of the Great Assembly, viz. to interpret the term *Vayehi* ('and it came to pass') wherever it is found in Holy Writ as an indication of the approach of trouble (Meg. 10*b*). This rule is also quoted in the *Midrashim*,[1] not, indeed, as coming from the men of the Great Assembly but as a tradition which came down from the (time of the) exile. Along with this they have also a further rule that wherever the term *Vehayah* ('and it will come to pass') is found, it is to be interpreted as introducing a welcome event. While this is a chief principle among guiding rules which were received by tradition and by which the *aggadah* is to be interpreted, yet we find also great support for it in the history of the people of Israel. Indeed, my attention was early called to this by a certain eminent scholar.[2]

If one looks closely into the conditions of the people of Israel, he will find that their political situation in the past was usually not very favourable. Their early ancestors sojourned as strangers in the land of Canaan, and their offspring later became slaves in Egypt, forced to make bricks and mortar. Even after they had been delivered from slavery they were forced to wander in the desert for a period of forty years without rest. As soon as Joshua b Nun died, their neighbours subjugated them and made them tributary. The Philistines, in particular, never ceased to fight against them, overpowering them time and again, so that at length even the Holy Ark was taken captive. Again, during the days of Saul and David, the people were divided in their allegiance, some following David and others Saul, and after the death of the latter there were many who still supported his sons. Later, even when David had firmly established his Kingdom, he was pursued as a fugitive by his son Absalom, and had to face the opposition of Sheba b Bichri. Even though King Solomon actually enjoyed peace on all sides without and within the land during the days of his reign, he had yet imposed such a heavy burden upon the people as later was the cause of the ten tribes abandoning his son, Rehoboam, and so of bringing about the division of the Kingdom between Judah and

[1] See *Midrash Gen.* R. 42; Esther 1, and *Midrash Ruth* 1, 7.
[2] It is assumed that the scholar referred to is Nachman Krochmal (1785–1840), one of the founders of Jewish Science who lived at Zolkiev (Galicia), the seat of the author's rabbinate.

Ephraim, under Rehoboam and Jeroboam. Later still the King of Assyria overcame the ten tribes and carried them into exile, and ultimately Nebuchadnezzar, the King of Babylon, destroyed Jerusalem, burned the Temple, and carried off its vessels to Babylon, when many of the Sons of Judah went into exile as captives. Although Cyrus later issued a brief edict (for the rebuilding of the Sanctuary), the Samaritans arose and obstructed the work, and even though the Jews later obtained permission for its construction they subsequently became subject to the Persian and Egyptian empires. Later the Greeks, under Antiochus Epiphanes, with the assistance of apostates and traitors from the worst elements of Israel, forced the people to transgress against their faith and break the covenant, until the Hasmoneans arose and fought heroically for the cause of their religion and smote the enemy with the sword. Yet immediately after this, new sects arose among them, namely, Sadducees and Boethusians,[1] in opposition to the Pharisees and their teaching founded on the Oral Law. Rivalry also grew strong between the brothers Hyrkanus and Aristobulus[2] for the crown, and the Romans were ultimately called in to settle the dispute,[3] an invitation which brought Pompey into the Sanctuary of God. Indeed, as a result of the Roman suzerainty Herod[4] and his children, who were actually of Idumean stock and so were hated by Israel, rose to be rulers of the land. Herod, who was under the domination of the Romans, set up statues and idols in the land of Israel, and honoured the Roman kings by naming cities after them. The end was that Vespasian and Titus[5] invaded the land, burned the Temple, and destroyed Israel root and branch. Fifty-two years after the fall of Jerusalem the spirit of revolt once more came upon Israel with the rising of Bar Kochba[6] and

[1] The author, in identifying the Sadducees as the followers of Zadok, the disciple of Antigonus of Socho (Ab. 1, 3) and coupling with them the adherents of Zadok's associate, Boethus, is here following the Aggadah in Ab. de R.N. 5, the historical value of which, however, is seriously doubted by critical historians.

[2] The grandsons of John Hyrcanus I, son of Simon the Maccabee.

[3] It was the younger and more attractive brother, Aristobulus, who asked for the Romans' help, whereupon Pompey, the Roman Consul, at Damascus, answered the call by marching into the country and settling the dispute in his own fashion by reducing Judah to a mere vassal state.

[4] Generally known as Herod the Great, and by the Jews as Herod the Wicked (73–4 B.C.), the son of Antipater the Idumean, who had been appointed by the Romans as Governor of Judaea, jointly with Hyrcanus. Herod was pro-Roman and Roman nominee for the rulership of Judaea. He married Marianne, the grand-daughter of Hyrcanus II. His career was stained by the ruthless murder of the Hasmonaean princes, including even his own wife and children. See p. 152, note 9.

[5] Roman Generals, father and son, who commanded the armies against Judaea in the Roman Judaean War. The former became emperor and the latter succeeded him.

[6] The name 'Son of a Star' was given him as a title, his real name being Simeon. After the suppression of the revolt, it was altered to Bar Coziba (Son of Lies).

his comrades. They rebelled against Rome and attacked her, inflicting many casualties on the Roman army in the battle of Bethar, but they were at last overcome by Trajan and Hadrian, who ruthlessly suppressed the rebellion and passed a ploughshare over the Temple site. Since then the children of Israel have passed from exile to exile, and we still find ourselves sunk deep in the evil state, filled with yearning and hope that God will once again favour us and restore our ancient glory.[1]

Thus, the true observer ought and must come to the conclusion that all these severe trials which have come upon us in the space of this long period had as their divine object to teach us to improve our ways, in accordance with the great principle in the Torah that it is owing to our sins that we have been left sunk in captivity, and that as soon as we change our conduct God will gladly grant us perfect deliverance. There is an abundance of Biblical testimony for this fundamental hope. See the *Responsa Besamim Rosh*[2] No. 251, the author of which dwells at great length upon the proof of the principle of the Torah that all the tribulations which were inflicted upon us were only intended as a means of curing us of a disease and of fitting us for the Messianic age, that we might be adorned with every worthy quality and virtue, and so attain perpetual prosperity as well as bodily and spiritual perfection. Thus, the present days are but days of test and trial, and it was this idea which the Rabbis condensed in the axiom quoted above: 'Wherever the term *Vayehi* (it came to pass) is used, it indicates the approach of trouble,' meaning thereby to convey that all which is recorded of the days that have passed consists but of trials which we as a race experienced, and in spite of which we are still alive and still remain staunch adherents of the authority of the Torah of Moses and the Talmud of Rabina and R. Ashi,[3] and 'no weapon formed can succeed against us'. The Rabbis were influenced by this idea in their adoption of the method in their homiletical expositions of magnifying the trials of the past and describing them in exaggerated forms. Take as an example the *aggadah* that Pharaoh slaughtered 150 Israelitish babies in the morning and 150 in the evening for the purpose of bathing in their blood,[4] or that he used

---

[1] The partial realization of this age-long hope and yearning has taken place in our days when on the 4th of Iyar, 5708 (15th May, 1948), the State of Israel was publicly proclaimed in a part of ancient Eretz Israel and has since been recognized by the nations of the world. Praised be the Rock of Israel and his Redeemer.

[2] Assumed to be a collection of 392 responsa from the *Rosh* (R. Asher b. Yehiel) edited by R. Izhack de Molena. The authority, however, for this identification has been questioned. See *Shem ha-Gedolim* by Azulai (1724–1800), bibliographical section, s.v. *Besamim Rosh*.

[3] Accepted by historians as the editors of the Talmud.

[4] As a cure for the leprosy with which he was stricken, according to the *Midrash Ex. R. 1*, and *Targum Jonathan Ex. 11, 23*.

the bodies of Israelitish children to fill out the walls when there was a shortage of bricks (*Midrash* Ex.*R.* 1, quoted also in Rashi on San., on the authority of a *Sefer Aggadah*).[1]

In a similar way they exaggerated in describing the great slaughter and destruction wrought by Nebuzaradan when he conquered Jerusalem and destroyed the Sanctuary, or again, the actions of the Greeks or the Romans when they set fire to Jerusalem (see Git. 57*a*; Jer. Ta'an., chap. iv, and the Midrash on Lamentations).

As for the second part of the aforesaid rabbinical principle in their homiletical rules, viz. that wherever the term *Vehayah* (and it will come to pass) is found it indicates the approach of gladness, this rule aims at showing that the homilist has a duty to glorify the good life which awaits us in the future, and that he is under obligation to enlarge upon such anticipations in every possible way in order to gladden depressed souls and inspire their hearts and strengthen them in the conviction that their loyalty to their exalted faith was not in vain, but they are to be compensated in the future many times over for all the sorrows and hardships which they may have suffered. It was for this reason that the Rabbis did not miss any opportunity which came to hand of over-emphasizing the future which God has in store for His people, after their deliverance from exile, as one may see in the following quotations: 'The women of the future will bear children every day,' or 'The future soil of the land of Israel will yield cakes and silken robes'.[2] They similarly magnified the splendour of the walls of Jerusalem and the future sanctuary[3] (B.B. 75*a* and *b*), and the same is true of many other homiletic expositions of the future deliverance which appear to be exceedingly far-fetched, but all such expositions were solely due to the guiding principle of homiletical exegesis that wherever the term *Vehayah* (and it will come to pass) is found it indicates happiness,[4] so that where one dealt with the future he had the duty of anticipating nothing but good for Israel in general and for each individual Israelite in particular.

[1] See Rashi San. 101*b*, s.v. נתמכמך.
[2] See Sab. 30*b*.
[3] As an example may be given the following exposition of R. Johanan in the Gemara, ad loc. 'The Holy One will in time to come bring precious stones and pearls which are thirty cubits long by thirty broad and will set them up in the gates of Jerusalem.'
[4] Such as 'Trees are destined to yield fruit every day' (Shab. 31*b*) or 'All the fruitless trees are destined to bear fruit' (Keth. 112*b*).

CHAPTER XXIV

DIVINE PROVIDENCE IN THE *AGGADAH*

AGAIN, I must mention that the Rabbis of the *Aggadah* recognized rules laid down as fundamental principles in relation to the Providence of God and His administration of the world. Some of these rules were deduced from Scripture; others were handed down by tradition, and these fundamental principles which came to be regarded as unquestionable axioms served for the inference of new teachings, so that from ideas already revealed new ideas, hitherto unrealized, were brought forth, as, for example, the great principle deduced from Scripture that God completes the years of the righteous from day to day[1] (Kid. 38*a*, R.H. 11*a*),[2] and in case of doubt they availed themselves of the same principle as a means of fixing the times of death of the Patriarchs as falling in the month of Nisan. Where they had Scriptural evidence that they were born during that month, they took it for granted that they must have died in the same month, because God completes the years of the righteous, etc. (R.H. 11*a*).

They also had it by tradition that a good man never turns wicked[3] (Ber. 29*a*), and acting on that principle they refrained from removing Samuel ha-Katan[4] (the younger) from the reader's desk, in spite of the error he had made in the *Birkhat ha-Minim*.[5]

Again, they said, 'we have it by tradition that the evil impulse

[1] The proof text for this principle is 'The number of thy days I will fulfil' (Ex. xxxiii, 26), and another, 'I am hundred and twenty years old "this day"' (Deut. xxxi, 2). The argument is that by the words 'this day he meant to stress that on 'that day', his (Moses's) years had reached full measure (Sot. 13*b*).

[2] To the effect that the day of the death of Moses was also his birthday, which is derived from the principle in question.

[3] i.e. he ought not to be suspected of having changed his ways.

[4] *Tanna* of the beginning of the second century, known specially as the author of the additional benediction to the *Shemoneh Esreh* (eighteen benedictions, familiarly known as the Amida) which is the anathema against the sectarians, slanderers, and informers of that and subsequent times who caused great sorrow to the people, composed at the request of the Patriarch, R. Gamliel II. The suggestion that this pronouncement was directed against the Judaeo-Christians is definitely baseless, in view of the fact that their number was insignificant in Samuel's time.(See *Halachoth Gedoloth* edited by Hildesheimer (1890). Its designation 'the benediction against the Minim', indicates that it was intended to be used against all those who refuse or defy the teachings of God. See *Abodath Israel* by R. Israel Kimhi (Smyrna 1736) for the suggestion that the description מינים is derived from מאן (dissenter) supported by the words, Jer. xi, 10 מאנו לשמוע who refused to hear.

[5] See the Gemara, ad loc., 'if one errs in the Birkhat ha-Minim he should be removed from the reader's desk' lest he arouse suspicion of affiliation with the Mineans, and so be loth to join in this solemn pronouncement against them.

dominates man only[1] in relation to what his eyes see'[2] (Sot. 8*b*), on the basis of which they framed the law that a woman (sentenced to death by stoning) is to be stoned (half) naked for there is no fear of impure thoughts arising.

Similarly, they possessed other principles concerning God's way of administering this lower world, such as, 'The Merciful One does not strike first against human beings'[3]; 'The Holy One, blessed be He, does not exact punishment from a people till he has first exacted punishment from their Guardian Angel' (Mak. 12*a*). See also Rashi, ad loc.[4] Again, 'The Holy One, blessed be He, does not exact punishment of a people until its measure is complete'[5] (Sot. 9*a*); 'The Holy One, blessed be He, does nothing without consulting his Heavenly Court'[6] (Gen. R., chap. Bereshith)[7]; 'Where it is a case of censure we begin with the least

---

[1] The important word 'only' is omitted by error in the citation by the author.

[2] This statement is made with regard to the procedure for testing the chastity of the suspected woman (Num. v, 12–28). One of the provisions was that her bosom was not to be uncovered, lest the young priests be dominated by an evil impulse through this exposure. An objection was, however, raised against this argument from the procedure in connection with the execution of a woman by stoning where only the lower part of the body of the sentenced woman was covered. To this the rabbis replied that in the former case she might go forth from the Court innocent and might thus remain a means for exciting the passion of those who had seen her exposed, whereas in the latter case her life is to be ended by stoning. But on the question raised that the latter might be the cause for arousing evil impulses for other women, the answer was given that the evil impulse sways men only in relation to what his eyes see, viz. the one woman in question, and she would no longer be alive.

[3] This is not found in the Aggadic section of the Talmuds, but is in the Midrash Lev. R. 17, 4, and is deduced from several cases:—(1) from what happened in the case of Job, where the messenger brought news that first the oxen and asses were slain and only afterwards the servants (Job i, 14, 15); (2) from what is related of the plagues upon the Egyptians, that first their possessions were destroyed and only afterwards their firstborn were smitten (see Ps. LXXVIII, 47–51).

[4] This statement of the Gemara is loosely paraphrased by the author. The passage in the Gemara runs as follows:—'Resh Lakish said that the Prince of Edom (Rome) was destined to fall into three errors.' He refers to the time of retribution for Rome's cruelties, as forecast by the Prophets (Is. LXIII). Rashi interprets Prince as Guardian and suggests that the punishment will be exacted from Rome's Guardian Angel first, i.e. the latter will have to be defeated first. In support of this, he quotes the passage of Is. XXIV, 21. 'And it shall come to pass in that day that the Lord shall punish the host of the High Ones (i.e. their Guardians) in Heaven and the Kings of the earth upon the earth.'

[5] The author has here confused two sayings which occur on one and the same page in the Gemara. One is 'God does not exact punishment of a people until the time of their banishment into exile', and the other is 'God does not, etc., of a man until his measure (of guilt) is complete.'

[6] The term used is פמליה which means the family, i.e. group of counsellors. This saying is derived from Dan. IV, 14. 'The matter is by the decree of the Watchers and the sentence by the word of the Holy Ones.'

[7] It is found in San. 38*b* and Pirke de R. Eliezer 24, and thence in *Midrash ha-Gadol* on Gen. i, 26 and xi, 7. In Gen. R. 8, 3 there is a similar statement, but quite differently worded.

important being'¹ (Taan.15*b*). In all these and all other similar principles found in the *Aggadah*, they derived the main basis from Scripture, founding their deductions in similar cases on this.

In addition to the above we can cite other examples from the sayings of the Rabbis which were transmitted by tradition, viz.:—

'There is a tradition that once a thing is given in heaven, it is never taken away again'² (Ta'an.25*a*). Again, they said: 'There is a tradition that no tribe will become entirely extinct'³ (B.B. 115*b*). And again, 'There is a tradition that nothing which descends from heaven is unclean'⁴ (San. 59*b*).

These principles help to solve many difficulties in the Talmud. In Sab. 10*b*, for example, the Rabbis state that a man should never single out one of his sons for differential treatment, because it was on account of two sela's weight of silk which Jacob had given to Joseph beyond what he had given to his other sons⁵ that his brothers became jealous of him, and so caused the enslavement of our forefathers in Egypt. Now a

---

¹ This is deduced from the Scriptural account (Gen. III, 14–18), viz. that at first the Serpent was cursed, then Eve, and after her, Adam.

² This is stated in connection with a story from the life of R. Hanina b Dosa who lived in extreme poverty. In response to his prayer, the legend goes, a leg of a golden table was stretched out to him from heaven. When, however, he saw in a dream that this would impair his table in heaven, he prayed to God that He should take it away from him, and his prayer was answered. Upon this the Tanna says that the latter miracle was even greater than the former, because of the above-mentioned tradition.

³ This is cited in reference to the order of succession in the laws of inheritance. In the case of a man who has died without issue and of whom no surviving descendants can be traced, inquiries are to be made for the rightful heirs in descending order, as for example whether the deceased has left behind him a nephew, a niece, or any descendants of such. Once it has been established that such descendants are non-existent, inquiries are then to be instituted in the ascending order. They are to be searched for from the father and the father's father, until the first ancestor of the tribe is reached; and if only a single member of the tribe can be traced, his relationship to the deceased can be established for the purpose of inheritance. A question is, however raised here in the Gemara 'Why not go back as far as Jacob, the father of the founder of the tribe'. To this Abaye replied as above. His view is supported by Mal. III, 6, 'Ye sons of Jacob are not consumed.'

⁴ This is given in reference to a legend concerning R. Simeon b Halafta who on being roared at by lions and threatened with being devoured alive, recited the Scriptural passage 'The young lions roar after prey' (Ps. CIV, 21) whereupon two lumps of flesh descended from heaven, one of which the lions ate. R. Simeon brought the other piece to the lecture-room and on inquiring from the scholars whether it was fit to be eaten they answered that 'nothing which descends from Heaven is unclean'. A similar question was propounded in Men. 69*b* concerning wheat which had descended from the clouds, whether it was fit for the offering of the two loaves (Lev. XXIII, 17). R. Tam in Tos., ad loc., s.v. חיטין maintained that in neither case could the event be rationally interpreted.

⁵ Referring to the garment of fine silk he had given Joseph (Gen. XXXVII, 3).

difficulty is raised in Tosafoth[1] concerning this statement. 'Surely,' they ask, 'the enslavement of the Israelites in Egypt was decreed as far back as at the "Covenant" concluded between the pieces.'[2] The answer given is that in accordance with the important principle laid down by the Rabbis to the effect that 'Evil is brought about through the agency of the guilty, and good through that of the good',[3] we are able to conclude that the reason why the additional though insignificant thing given by Jacob to Joseph was instrumental in bringing about the descent of his children into Egypt was that this differential treatment of one of his sons must be imputed to Jacob as a misdemeanour which became the cause of the great evil (of the Egyptian enslavement); for had there been no guilt in this special love shown by Jacob to Joseph, the fact could not have been used as the divine instrument for their descent to Egypt which would in that case have been brought about by something else.

A similar light is thrown on the statement that the case of Kamza and Bar Kamza was the cause of the destruction of Jerusalem,[4] in referring to which the Gemara (Git. 57*a*) concludes by saying, 'note, from this incident, how serious it is to put a man to shame, for God took up the cause of Bar Kamza and destroyed His own holy house.'

Though we all know that other causes brought about the destruction of the House in question, such as the division of opinions, the separation of hearts, the causeless hatred and rivalry of many sections in Israel, as

---

[1] s.v. הוֹן.

[2] Where it is written: 'Thy seed shall be a stranger in a land that is not theirs' (Gen. xv, 13).

[3] v. Sab. 32*a* on the verse 'if any man fall from thence' (Deut. xxii, 8) in connection with a house which was built without a parapet. Such a man, the Tanna of the school of Ishmael says, deserves to fall to his death, for he is designated in Scripture הַנּוֹפֵל, i.e. he that is to fall (i.e. as an act of retribution for a crime committed) but good things are brought about through the agency of good men, and evil things through the agency of evil men. According to this theory one who commits wrong, as in this case the man who had built his house without a parapet, is used as a divine instrument to bring about the predestined punishment on another guilty man. Other references to this principle are made in connection with the inclusion of two special sections in the Torah, one relating to specific laws of inheritance (Num. xxvii, 36) and the other to the supreme penalty for gathering sticks on the Sabbath (Numb. xv, 32). The former, it is pointed out, was added at the instance of the daughters of Zelophehad who were righteous women, and the latter at the instance of the guilty man who committed the offence (see B.B. 119*b* and San.8*a*). In any case it was a definite theory of the Rabbis that 'guilt of any kind or degree is instrumental in bringing about evil'.

[4] A trivial incident indeed. There was a man who had a friend Kamza and an enemy, Bar Kamza. Once he gave a party and invited his friend, but by error the invitation was sent to his enemy. On the latter's arrival at the party the host, in spite of Bar Kamza's appeals not to put him to shame, obstinately insisted upon his leaving (Git. 55*b*).

well as the wickedness of the 'Parhedrin'[1]; yet since the slight to Bar Kamza was a contributory factor in the destruction, we must recognize the seriousness of putting another to shame, in view of the fact that such a tremendous calamity was caused by it.

---

[1] Government assessors with jurisdiction over the market places, with a bad reputation for their oppressive measures, which they employed against the dealers at the market place (see Yoma 9a).

CHAPTER XXV

ALTERATIONS IN TEXTUAL READING AS A SPECIFIC DEVICE IN HOMILETIC EXPOSITIONS

THE homiletical expositions in the Gemara are frequently based on the hermeneutic rule 'al tikre,' 'do not read so but so', and they are mostly subject to the transposition of the consonants שׁ *sh* and שׂ *s* or to the substitution or alteration of vowels or punctuation, as in the following examples: 'Do not read "Shamoth" desolation, but read שמות "Shemoth" names' (Ber. 7b),[1] or 'Do not read "v'savea" (satisfied) but read "Sheva" (seven)'[2] (Ber. 14a). Or again, on the words 'there is none biltekha (beside Thee)'[3] they say 'Do not read "*biltekha*" but *ballothekha* (to wear Thee out)'[4] (Ber. 10a). Again, 'Do not read *we-sam derekh*[5] but *we-sham derekh*'[6]; and there are many other examples like these.

And as I have already said, Maimonides maintains in his Moreh Nebukhim[7] that all the exegetical expositions based on the hermeneutic rule, '*al tikre*,' were merely poetical expressions in a particular style to aid the memory in retaining the morals and warnings of the

---

[1] See Gemara, ad loc., where on the question raised, whence comes the importance attached to a name. R. Eleazar answered 'It is said (Ps. XLVI, 9) "Come look at the deeds of the Lord Who has made 'Shamoth' on the earth." Do not read 'Shamoth' from שׁמם (see 1 Ch. VII, 37), but read 'Shemoth' from שׁם. The spelling is alike, so that the actual text is left intact.' R. Eleazar possibly wished to teach us that names carry with them serious implications; the same thing under a different name thus may lead to 'ruin'.

[2] The Talmudic passage runs as follows: 'He who has passed seven nights in succession without having had a dream is to be called "wicked", for it is written (Ps. XIX, 23) "And he (that hath fear of God) shall abide satisfied, he shall not be visited with evil." Do not read, etc. Again both words "Saveah" and "Sheva" are spelt alike.' The moral inherent in this statement is that one should at least once a week think of the material aspect of life as a transient dream. He who fails to do so, and consequently indulges too much in bodily pleasures, deserves to be classed as 'wicked'.

[3] 1 Sam. II, 2.

[4] This is followed by the following statement: 'the nature of the Holy One, praised be He, is not similar to that of a mortal, for whilst the works of a mortal wear out their maker, God wears out His works.' Here, too, they have taken advantage of the similarity in the spelling of the two words to derive a moral from the altered vocalization.

[5] Ps. L, 23. 'To him, who ordered (we-sam, from שׂים, to place, to set out) his way, will I show the salvation of God.'

[6] From שׁום appraise, estimate, value. Upon this the *aggadic* teacher bases his statement that whosoever rightly appraises his way enjoys the privilege of beholding the salvation of God. See M.K. 5a; Sot. 5a.

[7] Part II, chap. xliii, see page 159.

Rabbis, by connecting them with various indications in the different Scriptural writings in which they found support.

Also since no visible distinction was to be found in Holy Writ between the right שׂ and the left שׁ,[1] and there were likewise neither vowels nor punctuation marks, it was quite easy for the reader to render the text as it suited him, in order to provide himself with mnemonics in connection with such subjects as appealed to him. An example of such rendering is the following exposition (Ber. 30*b*): 'None may engage in prayer except when in a serious mood, for it is written: "Worship the Lord *behadrath Kodesh* (in the beauty of holiness).[2] Do not read *behadrath* (in beauty) but *beherdath* (with the trembling of)." '[3] In this case there is an evident interchange of letters (ד and ר), and in Jer. Sab. 44*a* the ruling is given that there need be no hesitation to expound words in a manner involving a transposition of the letters ר and ד.[4]

A similar method is found in their exposition in Ned. 90*a*, when they read the words וחפרה הלבנה (the moon shall be confounded)[5] והפרה חל-בנה (he shall nullify it—unvow—when ready made).[6]

Similarly the passage[7] 'Nought comes from them nor from their multitudes, neither shall there be a נֵהַּ (wailing) for them,'[8] they interpret as though it read 'Neither shall there be נֹחַ (Noah) amongst them (San. 108*a*).[9]

Again, in M.K. 2*a* the Rabbis explain the term בית השלחין (an

---

[1] The letter שׁ is usually taken as having a diacritical point on the right side and sounded as sh; a diacritical point on the left hand side gives it the sound of *s*.

[2] i.e. with awe or with reverential fear. ה and ח are here also interchanged owing to the similarity of their forms.

[3] Ps. xxix. 2.

[4] They deduce the number of 39 labours prohibited on the Sabbath from the numerical value of the word אלה (these) in Ex. xxxv, 1, the א being one, the ל, 30, and the ה strictly speaking accounting for five but taken here as eight owing to its similarity in form with the ח (8).

[5] Is. xxiv, 23, with reference to the question whether the husband has the authority to nullify his wife's vow (Numb. xxx, 9) before it becomes operative, or only after it has become operative. R. Nathan's view is that he cannot nullify it before, and his deduction is from a play upon these words. See next note.

[6] In view of the comparison drawn between making a vow and the building of a 'Bamah' (Ned. 22*a*) they played on the word הלבנה of which the second syllable בנה denotes 'to build' and so expresses the view that the vow must exist before it can be abrogated. Here they transposed the gutturals ה and ח in both words, the ח in וחפרה into a ה and the ה of הל into a ח for the sake of deducing the following *halachah*: 'The husband can disallow his wife's vow only חל בנה when the edifice of the 'bamah'— i.e. the vow—has already begun.

[7] Ezek. vii, 11.

[8] From נהי Ezek. xxxii, 18.

[9] It is from this verse that the school of R. Ishmael infers that the decree of destruction had been issued also against Noah but that he was rescued because of the favour which he had found in the eyes of God (Gen. vi, 8).

irrigated field) on the basis of the term מַשְׁלְהִי, used by Onkelos as equivalent to the words עָיֵף וְיָגֵעַ (weary).[1] Here Rashi observes that the gutturals ח and ה are interchanged, producing the form הַשְׁלְהִין not הַשְׁלְחִין.[2]

The *Ritba*,[3] ad loc., quotes the statement in the Jerusalem Talmud quoted above, that the Rabbis had no hesitation in transposing the gutturals ה and ח, and the author of the *Me'or Enayim*[4] has endeavoured to show that the Babylonian rabbis also adopted this device in their homiletical expositions, quoting numerous examples to substantiate his opinion.[5] The reason for this transposition is I think to be found in the statement in Jer. Meg. 1, 9, that in the earlier written text of the Torah the ה was not closed, from which we may infer that in later days the form of the ה was closed like that of the ח.[6]

Maharik,[7] in his *Responsum* No. 71, does actually quote the said statement of Jer. Meg. as proof of the similarity in form of the two guttural letters; and he also quotes the statement in Men. 29*b* that the careful scribes left the left-hand stem of the ה hanging in the air, implying thereby that the less careful scribes closed it with the stop, like the letter ח. For that reason the two letters were generally transposed for homiletical purposes.

Again, the Rabbis say in Kid. 30*a*: 'Do not read *we-shinnantam*[8] (thou shalt impress or repeat it to them) but read '*we-shillashtam*'[9] (treble it— i.e. teach it to them threefold), in which case there is a clear variation from the Scriptural text. Here we must recognize that the variant in question is adopted by the expositor only to interpret the text as referring to the duty of twice making a break between one study and another, the consequence of which is a study of three different subjects. See, however, Rashi, ad loc., who offers a different explanation of this homily.[10] At all events, the rule '*Al tikre*' is found only in cases where a

---

[1] Deut. xxv, 15. Hence an irrigated field, i.e. exhausted and thirsty.

[2] As is the Aramaic rendering.

[3] R. Yom Tob b Abraham Ashbili, famous Spanish Talmudic commentator of the first half of the fourteenth century, disciple of the Rashba, R. Solomon ben Adereth.

[4] See p. 150, note 8.

[5] See also *Torah T'mimah* on Ex. xx, 12, note 82.

[6] A more plausible explanation is perhaps the fact that the two letters belong to the guttural section group אהח"ע, in all of which there is a similarity of sound.

[7] R. Joseph b Solomon Kolon, an eminent Talmudist of the fifteenth century. His responsa under the above name occupy a foremost place in rabbinic literature.

[8] Deut. vi, 7, in the *Shema* with reference to the duty of transmitting our heritage to the children.

[9] From this the rabbis deduced the duty of dividing studies into three parts, *Torah —Mishnah—Gemara*.

[10] Rashi finds in the verb *we-shinantam*, which is derived from שנן, the intention of indicating the duty, not only of teaching, but of sharpening, i.e. impressing, and this

change of vowels or punctuation alone is involved, such as can serve as a mnemonic for scriptural interpretation.[1]

Further, one should note that in the Palestinian *baraithoth* and the Jerusalem Talmud they made use of the rule in question in support of their homilies, but whereas in some cases the words '*al tikre*' are expressly mentioned, in others they are omitted, although one can see that they have the device in mind. The following may be cited as examples:—

'Do not read *haruth*[2] (inscribed) but "*heruth*" (freedom).'[3]

Again, the statement in the *baraitha*: 'Scholars advance peace in the world,' is deduced from 'all *banaikh* (they children) shall be taught by the Lord', reading, however, not '*banayikh*' (thy children) but '*bonayikh*' (thy builders).[4]

See also Mechilta[5] on the Scriptural verse: 'And ye shall observe the "Matzoth",'[6] from which the Rabbis have deduced that a commandment which comes within one's power to perform should not be put off.[7] For this deduction they employed the above device of reading not הַמַצוֹת (the unleavened bread) but הַמִצוֹת (the commandments).

Similarly, in the Jer. Ber. 4*a* we read: 'Angels have no limbs that bend,' for it is written: 'I came near unto one of them קמייא (before me),' but we read קיימא [8] (standing). So, too, in the Jerusalem

---

can be achieved only by using also the two means of interpretation, *Mishnah* and *Gemara*. Were the word intended to denote mere teaching, the verb ושניתם from שנה would have been more appropriate.

[1] Cf. Shab. 104*b* and Er. 54*b*. The Torah is to be acquired by mnemonics.

[2] Ex. XXXII, 16. 'The writing of God "haruth" (graven) upon the tablets.'

[3] Aboth 6, 2. From this the Rabbis deduced that no man is regarded as free unless he is occupied in the study of the Torah, which is the best means of self-restraint from worldly temptations. See also Aboth 3, 6.

[4] Ber. 64*a*, cited by R. Eleazar on the authority of R. Hanina. The moral which he intended to convey was that scholarship is indeed the building material of the world and the scholars are the master builders. A similar idea deduced by a similar exegetical device is found in Taan 4*a*, on the phrase 'whose *avaneah* (stones) are iron' (Deut. VIII, 9). Do not read 'Avaneah' (stones, from אבן) but *boneha* (from בנה) builders.

[5] A Midrashic collection dealing with portions of Exodus. The term is the Aramaic equivalent of the Hebrew word מדה 'measure' which, in the Rabbinic language means a Hermeneutic rule, or method of interpretation. See Targ. on the word משורה, Chr. XXIII, 29.

[6] Ex. VII, 17.

[7] Lit. should not be allowed to become 'leavened'.

[8] This is the reading as given in the Jerusalem Talmud. The Scriptural reading is קאמיא (that stood by) from קאם (Onk. Ex. xv, 18) standing firm, so that no alteration in the structure of the word is called for. V. Rashi, ad loc., who quotes the Jer. statement, translating the קאמיא 'those who are standing' as referring to the passage in Zech. III, 7, 'among those who *stand* as evidence.' The author's oversight of all this is to be regretted.

Talmud Ber. (beginning of chap. v) we find: 'Do not read *b'hadrath Kodesh* but "*b'cherdath Kodesh*".'[1] Again, in Jer. Sheb. 12a: 'Abortions have also a portion in the future world,[2] for it is written (Is. XLIX, 6) "and to restore נְצוּרֵי (the preserved) of Israel", but we read "to restore the נְצִירֵי (the created ones) of Israel".' The interpretation which reads 'yod' in place of *vaw* derives the word from יָצַר, i.e. all that were created of Israel, whereas if both 'vaw' and yod are absent, the word will mean נֵצֶר (a branch), i.e. every branch of Israel shall be restored.[3] The author of the *Yefeh Mareh*,[4] ad loc., has not correctly interpreted it.

Again, the statement in Jer. Naz. 20a, that *Shehitah* is not clearly set out in the Torah.[5] It is only inferred from the word in Scripture וַיִּשְׁטְחוּ (and they spread abroad for themselves)[6] but reading not וַיִּשְׁטְחוּ but וַיִּשְׁחֲטוּ (they killed) for themselves,[7] on the basis of an interchange of letters employed in certain words, such as כֶּשֶׂב for כֶּבֶשׂ or תַּחַת for חָתַת, and the like.[8] This case is also quoted in the *Sifre* on Num. XXIII, and again in Yom. 75b.

Now with regard to the view advanced by Maimonides, referred to above, that the main purpose of this exegetical device was only to offer support to Torah precepts by confirming the homiletic exposition of Holy Scripture, and guarding it against being forgotten; if this be the case how can he justify the objection raised in the *Gemara* Ber. 30b[9] where the question is asked: 'Does not Scripture say "*be-hadrath*" (with beauty)?' Or again, the objection in the case of the deduction in R.H. 13b where the *Gemara* bids us read not '*lishelosh*' (for three) but '*lishelish*' (to a third),[10] i.e. when the crop has ripened a third it is to be

[1] See p. 190, note 2.

[2] In the text, ad loc., the reference is made to the resurrection and R. Eleazar states that abortions will also rise at the resurrection.

[3] Is. LX, 21. The statement in Jer. Talmud may be interpreted still more simply thus: 'Since the קְרִי (reading version) in the text is נְצוּרֵי from נָצַר a word akin to נָטַר to preserve, guard (cf. Is. XXVII, 3), and the כְּתִיב (the written version) is נְצִירֵי from יָצַר to fashion, create, the Rabbis direct us to read here in accordance with the כְּתִיב or the written version.

[4] R. Samuel Jaffe (Constantinople, sixteenth century).

[5] It is only inferred in a far-fetched way.

[6] Numb. XI, 33, from שׁטח in connection with the gathering of the quails which came down like the manna.

[7] From שׁחט. The version quoted by the author is a fusion of both the Babylonian (Yoma 75b) and the Palestinian, since in the Jer. Talmud, alteration is only suggested in the word for the purpose of intimating that there came down to Israel, besides the manna, a species which required killing, hence there is here a remote reference for the duty of shehitah.

[8] Such as שַׂלְמָה Ex. XXII, 8, for שִׂמְלָה Deut. XXII, 5.

[9] Against the interpretation 'do not read *b'hadrath* (beauty) but read *be'herdath* (trembling)'.

[10] Lev. XXV, 21, with reference to the promise of abundance of produce for a period of three years.

considered ripe, with reference to the obligation of tithing. Why does the *Gemara* then raise the objection: 'Is the true reading not *"lishelosh"*,'[1] for surely, according to the view of Maimonides mentioned, there is, after all, no proper homiletic exposition involved here, but a matter of finding a slight support in a scriptural verse; why then should it matter whether we read *'b'hadrath'* and *'lishelosh'* or not? After all, this method is only utilized here to provide remote support from Scripture. I have referred to this observation of mine also in my commentary on the Talmud, and it still needs consideration.[2]

[1] i.e. how can one alter the word from its literal meaning for the mere sake of an exegetical deduction?

[2] Rabbi Baruch Epstein in his Mekor Baruch, pp. 497 seq., treats this subject exhaustively and deals with this point at great length.

CHAPTER XXVI

AGGADOTH AIMED AT INSPIRING AND STIRRING THE CURIOSITY OF THE PEOPLE

IN my work, *Darkhe Horaah*,[1] I have furnished proof that even in the case of homiletic expositions which tended to conclude with halachic rulings, the expositor was always mindful of the effect of such rulings in inducing good behaviour in the listening public. In some cases he did not publicly set forth the *halachah* fully in consonance with the accepted decisions, but this was meant as a precaution against a possible lack of serious regard for rabbinic prohibitions, and for that very reason he stated the *halachah* in public in a very stringent form (v. Hul. 15*a*).[2]

Similarly, in *Aggadic* interpretations the lecturer's aim was to inspire the people to the service of God and to awaken them to a realization of the emptiness of their vain life, so that they should be compelled in this world of forgetfulness to fit themselves for entering the banqueting hall (of immortality), adorned and graced with a pure heart and good deeds. Thus, the chief object of the lecturer was to awaken the slumbering soul from its foolish sleep and stir it up to do what was right. If at times he noticed that his simpler utterances made no impression upon the audience he sought to find another method for his purpose by telling them stories which sounded strange or terrifying or which went beyond the limits of the natural and so won the attention of his audience for his message.

The *Rashba*,[3] making reference to this in his commentary on *Berachoth* (chap. ix), in the Aggadic section, where he speaks of the stone which Og, King of Bashan, attempted to cast down upon Israel,[4]

---

[1] Lemberg 1842, treating of the procedure adopted by rabbinic authorities for arriving at halachic decisions. It also deals with the category of observances known as *minhagim* (customs or usage).

[2] e.g. with reference to the dispute between R. Meir and R. Judah over food cooked on the Sabbath. According to R. Meir if it was done by inadvertence, one might partake of it the same day, while according to R. Judah, he might partake of it only after the expiration of the Sabbath.

Rab, in deciding the *halachah* for his disciples, favoured the view of R. Meir, which was more lenient. In his discourses to the public, however, he set forth the *halachah* in accordance with the view of R. Judah, in order not to lead the ignorant into a more serious breach of the law.

[3] See p. 159, note 3.

[4] Ber. 56*a*. The legend narrates how Og had planned to destroy Israel. 'The camp of Israel,' he said, 'extends three miles.' He then planned to uproot a mountain three miles in size, throw it upon them and kill them. He uprooted the mountain and raised it above his head, but God sent ants which bored holes in it, causing it to fall upon his

says of this matter: 'Maimonides, in his introduction to the *Mishnah*, has referred to the two ideas which the *Aggadic* teachers had in mind (when relating these outlandish *Aggadoth*).[1] But, in my view, there was besides these another motive behind some of the *Midrashim* of the *Aggadists*, namely that since there were occasions when, as the *Aggadists* were delivering their discourses publicly and elaborating matters useful to the audience, the listeners fell asleep, the lecturer, in order to awaken them, had to make use of queer and astounding tales to rouse them from their sleep.'

The reason is clearly shown in the Midrash *Hazitha*,[2] par. הִנָּךְ יָפָה where we read that Rabbi was delivering a discourse and the audience had dozed off, so in his desire to arouse them he told them of one Israelitish woman who in Egypt gave birth herself to 600,000 children.[3] Similarly, the story told of Og, how he uprooted a mountain three parasangs in extent, was meant to convey that Og's object was to deprive the children of Israel of their rights based on their three ancestors. The *Aggadists*, however, put the idea in the form of this astounding tale in order to arouse the public to follow the lecture with greater interest.

Such are *Rashba's* observations. I have also found another reference which supports this suggestion, viz. Mid. Rab. on the Scriptural story of Noah, Gen. XXXIII, 7, where we read that R. Akiba gave a discourse in *Ginzak*[4] of Media on the misdeeds of the generation of the flood, yet they were not moved to tears, but later when he discoursed on the sufferings of Job they were moved to tears.

We also find in Gen. R. LVIII, 3, and in Est. Rab. i, that R. Akiba noticed once while delivering a public lecture that his audience was dozing. In order to rouse them he said: 'How did it come to be that Esther was raised to be queen over 127 states? It was because she was a descendant of Sarah, who reached the age of 127.'[5] We can here see R. Akiba's method of using striking illustrations in his public lectures in such a manner as to stir his audience to tears or to arouse them to pay

---

head and rest on his shoulders, and when he tried to throw it off, his teeth became interlocked, thus preventing him from throwing it off, with the result that Moses was able to strike the mighty blow which killed him.

[1] They were intended to sharpen the intellect of the students, or else to open the eyes of fools hastening to find fault with the scholars as soon as they found their words difficult to follow.

[2] The exegetical *Midrash* on Canticles.

[3] He meant this to refer to the birth of Moses who equalled all the rest of the people in importance. The number 600,000 is given in Ex. XII, 37.

[4] A city in the north of Media (north-western part of Iran) (see Neubauer, *Geographie*, p. 375).

[5] The oddness of the comparison helped to awaken his listeners from their slumber.

more attention to his homiletic expostions. In this way all the homilies in the Talmud and Midrashim, which at first glance appear to be very strange, may be explained, for they were made as occasion or necessity arose to impress the gathering attending the lecture.

Following this explanation, we can understand the following exposition of R. Akiba[1] (Sot. 11*b*): 'The Israelites were delivered as a reward for the righteous women of that time. It happened by a miracle that they (the babies which they bore) were swallowed by the ground, and the Egyptians brought oxen and ploughed over them, etc. Yet they broke through the earth, sprouting (like herbs from the soil), and came in flocks to their homes.'[2] Although in the Gemara version this is reported in the name of R. Awira, in Cant. Rab.[3] it is quoted in the name of R. Akiba.[4] One who knows R. Akiba's true genius and intellectual capacity, aptly described[5] in these words in Yeb. 16*a*: 'A man whose name is known from one end of the world to the other,' and also as indicated by Maïmonides, who in his commentary on Aboth[6] upon R. Akiba's saying: 'Everything is foreseen but the right of choice is granted,'[7] declares that this statement suits R. Akiba,[8] may find it difficult to reconcile such an odd Aggada with him; but from what we now know of his method, as shown in the two *aggadic* expositions which we have dealt with above, viz. that when he noticed his audience uninterested or drowsy he would relate to them sensational legends to arrest their attention, we may, I think, unhesitatingly accept this *aggadic* homily as another of those which had as their object the impressing of the masses and the impelling of their hearts towards the things which are right. See San. 101*a* for the statement that R. Akiba (one of the four elders in question) had replied: 'I interpreted a verse.'[9]

---

[1] Who behaved heroically in those days of oppression.

[2] The *Aggada*, in its own fanciful style, pictures the scenes elaborately. First, it tells us how the women used to obtain and carry the food to their husbands, the slaves, and remain with them in secluded spots, and when the time of their delivery arrived, how the babes were attended to and fed by God's Ministering Angels, and how they were preserved in subterranean caves, and how when the babes were grown up, the earth opened its mouth and returned them to the light of day. Like the grass of the fields they sprouted from the soil and moved away in herds to their homes.

[3] The author ascribes to Cant. Rab what is in fact recorded in Ex. R. 1, 16.

[4] See also *Yalkut Shimoni* on Ezekiel, par. 354, cf. also R. Is. Pick glosses, ad loc.

[5] By R. Dosi b Horkinas.

[6] Ch. III, 15.

[7] By which he lays down the basis of the Jewish doctrine of free-will.

[8] i.e. it is fitting that such a philosophical mind should give us such an epoch-making maxim.

[9] R. Akiba, one of the four elders who visited R. Eliezer when sick, made the observation that 'suffering is precious' and, on being questioned as to the source of his statement, he replied that he had interpreted a verse. The author quotes this in support of his view of R. Akiba's homiletical method.

And methods similar to that adopted by R. Akiba were used also by other Aggadists in their homilies in order to attain the objects which they had set before them.

With regard to the questions found in Num. R. and Deut. R., and in the *Midrash Tanhuma* and the *Pesikta Rabathi*, with which these books often begin their homilies, namely the *halachic* dissertations which are introduced with the words 'There is a ruling that an Israelite, etc.', or with the words 'May our teacher instruct us', and followed with *Aggada*, we cannot trace the use of a similar formula in the Talmudim (Babylonian or Palestinian), except once in the Babylonian Talmud (Sab. 30*a*), as follows: 'The question was put to R. Tanhum of Neway, as to what was the ruling about extinguishing a lamp burning for a sick man on the Sabbath, whereupon he began his answer, "O Solomon, where is thy wisdom and where is thine understanding?"' and the *Aggadist* goes on to indulge in sophistry, changing one subject for another until he closes his homily with the words 'and as for the question which I have been asked in your presence, a lamp is called lamp (and the soul of man is likewise called lamp)'. It is better to extinguish the material lamp[1] than the lamp of God.[2] Rashi, ad loc., observes that this ruling[3] is actually deduced not from the passage cited but from the verse: 'He shall live by them,'[4] as referred to in Yom. 85*b*; but as his discourse was attended by women and other unintelligent folk, he conveyed this *halachah* to them with the help of *Aggada*.

The chief object, however, of the Babylonian and Palestinian Talmudim was to enlighten us either on *halachic* and legal decisions or upon matters of *aggadic* or ethical character. For this reason the redactors of the Talmud (except in the one case) did not embody such a form of teaching in the *Gemera*, but dealt separately with the homiletical expositions in relation to the particular purpose for which they were needed, and separately also with the *halachoth*, which were systematically set out on the basis of religious and legal fundamentals; but they did not think it necessary to associate *halachic* dissertations with *aggada*, which would imply arriving at final rulings by *aggadic* methods, because they knew it would be futile to do so, since the *Kabbalah*[5] or the hermeneutic rules, or again common reason, were

---

[1] Made by man.
[2] i.e. the soul. Cf. Prov. xx, 27, 'the soul of man is the lamp of the Lord.' This goes to prove that where life is endangered, the laws of the Sabbath are suspended.
[3] i.e. that the laws of the Torah are suspended where life is endangered.
[4] Lev. xviii, 5. The author of this deduction is Samuel who concludes 'He shall live, not die, because of them'. This was adopted by the Rabbis as an irrefutable principle.
[5] The doctrines received by oral tradition.

sufficient to help the scholar to reach his final conclusions in *halachah*. The above method was, indeed, applied by the Rabbis, but only when required for the purpose of elucidating certain rulings to the masses or the womenfolk, as already mentioned on the authority of Rashi, and so they thought it proper to avoid associating such a method with the *Gemara*. Such formula, indeed, is left in Tractate Sabbath, the case quoted above being a sample of the style of the homiletic expositions of those days. But it was not so with the *Midrashim*, which were not recognized as being for the teaching of *halachoth*, or for the publication of legal rulings needed for actual practice. In these *Midrashim*, the Rabbis at times left us their homilies either introduced with the words: 'There is a ruling that an Israelite, etc.,' or with the words: 'May our Teacher instruct us,' as indeed homilies were introduced when delivered to the masses in those early days.

One may also note that the Passover *Haggadah*,[1] the compilation of which is thought to have taken place during the time of the Temple, as recorded in the Mishnah, Pes. 10, 4,[2] also introduces subjects with questions in the same way as the *Midrashim* of the earlier days. At first the children are made to ask four questions about the difference between this (the Passover) and other nights, and then the celebrant begins to narrate the succession of events and to expound the Exodus and various passages in the Scriptures relating to this subject, and finally he turns back to reply to the questions which had been put to him. So, for example, in reply to the question: 'Why are we eating this matzah?' he says: 'Because the dough of our forefathers did not have time to be leavened.' And there are similar replies regarding the *Pesach* (sacrificial lamb) and the *maror* (bitter herb). In this way the familiar difficulty which is raised as to why the narrator does not proceed at once with his proper answers to the questions on the reasons for the eating of *matzah* and *maror* is met, if we bear in mind the above elucidation of the methods adopted by the *Tannaim* and *Amoraim* in their

---

[1] The ritual recitation for the Passover Home Service. Its name is derived from the word והגדת 'and thou shalt tell'. Ex. XIII, 8, and it includes the narration of the Exodus.

[2] Where first mention is made of the ritual and where R. Gamaliel is reported (*Mishnah* 5) as saying that 'one who has not said (i.e. not understood the spiritual implications of) these three words, Pesah, Matzah, and Maror' has not done his duty. The opinion is held by many scholars (see J.E. VI, 141) that this R. Gamaliel was the first of that name (who lived during the Temple) because he speaks of the Passover lamb. But even according to the view held (Weiss, *Dor*, II, 74) that he was R. Gamaliel II the mere fact that R. Gamaliel II speaks of a familiar ritual proves that the Haggada was already in existence before his time. The proof however which the author has probably also considered was R. Tarfon's statement (*Mishnah* 6) in connection with the order of the Haggadah. R. Tarfon had lived during the Temple time (see Jer. Yoma III, 7). See also glosses on Nid. 6*b* by the author.

homiletical discourse, as we have seen them exemplified in connection with the question referred to above (Shab. 30a), viz. that their way was to pass from one subject to another related to it, until they came back finally to reply to the main question asked.

Again, we can still trace in the Babylonian Talmud the formula for an 'introduction' which expositors had used in Eretz-Israel. We find examples in the *Midrashim Lament.R.* and *Est. R.*, of one lecturer choosing one text for his introduction, and of another choosing a different text for his purpose. But in the dissertations upon complete Scriptural passages which have come down to us in the Babylonian Talmud, there are no such formulas of introduction, except in a very few cases as, for example, in their discourses on Esther (Meg. 10b, 11a). Again, R. Simon b Pazzi, in Meg. 13a, 'introduced' his discourse upon the Book of Chronicles with the sentence: 'All thy words are one.'[1] Similarly, in Sot. 2a, when Resh Lakish began to interpret the Chapter on the *Sotah*, he said: 'The marriage of a woman with a man is brought about in accordance with the behaviour of the man.'[2] Two such introducing formulae are also to be traced in the chapter dealing with murderers, Mak. 10b.[3] But beyond the ones here mentioned, we find no other such formula in the Talmud, for they were employed merely as required orally in exposition, and the Talmudical teachers did not see the necessity of including them in the *Gemara*. A very few examples here and there were found sufficient to preserve a record for coming generations of the particular method which early expounders had adopted.

[1] i.e. all the various names in the Book of Chronicles refer to one person.
[2] As a reward for righteous deeds he gains a faithful wife.
[3] The formulae used by R. Hama bar Chaninah and Resh Lakish.

CHAPTER XXVII

AGGADOTH EXPRESSING PROFOUND IDEAS IN FIGURATIVE STYLE

THERE are several subjects in the *Gemara* whose meaning cannot be taken in a literal sense, because the text expounded literally would depict God as a corporeal being, and would also at times involve an act of blasphemy. We should, and we are, indeed, in duty bound to believe that the transmitters of the true *Kabbalah*, who are known to us as righteous and saintly men and also as accomplished scholars, would not speak merely in an odd manner. We must therefore believe that their words were uttered with an allegorical or mystical sense and that they point to matters of the most elevated significance, far beyond our mental grasp.

The Rabbis deemed it proper not to expose to the masses the mystical doctrines that were hidden in their words, and so they uncovered only one handbreadth, leaving ten handbreadths covered. The literal sense of such words of theirs was only as it were a mere outer garment beneath which lay precious ideas observed only by the wise and understanding student. Such *Aggadoth* were long ago alluded to by Maimonides and *Rashba*. Thus, Maimonides, in his commentary on the *Mishnah* (San. x, Introduction) alludes to errors which characterize the two classes of students. One class, he says, consists of those who take the words of the *Aggadoth* literally and do not even imagine that they contain a hidden inner meaning. The impossible is thus an actual fact to them. They do so because they do not understand the ways of wisdom and are thus deprived of its perfect quality, which would enable them to be on the alert to understand them. See also the Introduction to the *Moreh*, where Maimonides writes in this connection: 'We have noted that the unenlightened man of the mass of students meets no difficulties in the homiletical expositions,[1] since the uncultured and hasty man who is void of knowledge does not pass beyond the surface meaning of the word which nevertheless remains impossible.'[2] Again, see *Moreh* i, 71, where he speaks of these brief observations and intimations in the Talmud and *Midrashim* as a grain-sized heart round which there is a multitude of shells, and some err so far as to occupy

---

[1] The term המעיינים (students) as quoted by the author here varies substantially from הרבנים (masters) as in the original text of Maimonides.

[2] Here again the text המציאות is inadequately quoted from the original, which reads טבע המציאות הנמנעות.

themselves solely with the outer shells, because they think that there is
no kernel beyond the shells.

The second class consists of those who despise the *aggadoth* and scoff
at the words of their masters. These are foolish men, void of understanding; and, indeed, what a distance there is in human qualities
between them and the truly wise men. These are a detestable sort of
people who are critical of the great and the exalted,[1] of men whose
wisdom has been tested and proved by the wise (of every age). So far
Maimonides, *Commentary on Mishnah*. In his Introduction to the whole
Mishnah he states that so far as has been revealed to us it was by their
upright and righteous conduct that the Rabbis came to be known as
great scholars and righteous men, and it behoves us, therefore, to admit
that the failure on our part to understand their words is to be attributed to our own weakness of mind,[2] because actually there are four
evil conditions which hinder us from the attainment of wisdom:
(1) Feebleness of intellect; (2) Being overcome by lust; (3) Being too
lazy to seek wisdom; (4) Being easily tempted to the pursuit of material
possessions. It is this moral that the rabbis intimated in the following
words (Git. 57a): 'He who mocks at the words of the Sages is doomed to
punishment by boiling dung.'[3] No boiling dung could be worse than
the foolishness which leads a man to scoff at the words of such great
sages, and you will find no one who will regard the wisdom of the wise
as unreal, except one who is lured by his appetites, who gives preference
to the sensual pleasures; one who does not endeavour to enlighten his
mind with illuminating words.

The third (commendable) class consists of students of full intelligence
to whom the fine quality of the sages has become evident. They know
full well that the Rabbis did not indulge in jests, and it is clear to them
that whereas some parts of the statements of the Sages are revealed (to
ordinary minds) other portions are concealed, and that in this latter
part the Rabbis sought to express ineffable things by means of riddles
and parables. Such is the opinion of Maimonides. Compare also what
Rashba says in his *Novellae* on the *aggadoth* of Berachoth,[4] viz. 'Note that
the Midrashim and the *aggadoth* of the Rabbis contain hidden ideas and
thoughts faintly hinted at, and if these appear as worthless words to the

---

[1] נשיאים (princes, leading men) in our text is slightly misprinted because in the
original text the reading is נשואים (of exalted position).

[2] I cannot trace this statement in Maimonides's *Introduction*.

[3] Which creates a place to be avoided by people. The reason is evident, for the
ignorant man also creates deserted places in that people shun his company.

[4] With reference to the *aggadah* (Ber. 6a) 'Whence do we know that the Holy One,
Blessed be He, puts on *tephillin*?' These Novellae were published with the *En
Yaakob* (Wilno, 1912).

ignorant, to those of understanding who are acquainted with the "hidden wisdom" these words deal with subjects demanding a high intelligence. There are some of these *aggadoth* which can be expounded only by those versed in mysticism, but to the master in this domain they contain "hints" of the structure and foundations (of creation). In some of them there is both a revealed and a concealed part, as in the leaf or the fruit (of the tree)[1]; others again are written in a cryptic language. But in no case do they mean merely what the words literally convey.' See also on this topic the *Novellae* of *Rashba* on the *Aggadoth*, Ber. 32*b*, in connection with expositions by the Rabbis on the verse, 'Can a woman forget her עוּלָהּ[2] (suckling child)?'[3] to the effect that it means עוֹלָה[4] (burnt offering).[5]

I shall now give a list of *aggadoth* which cannot, and ought never to be explained literally:—

'The Holy One, Blessed be He, dons *Tefillin*[6] (Ber. 6*a*).'
'The Holy One prayeth' (ibid. 7*a*).[7]
'The God of Israel says "Who rules me? The righteous man rules

---

[1] i.e. what is revealed has only the value of the leaves. The essential part of the tree, the fruit, is concealed.

[2] Akin to עוּל or לוּע suckle, cf. 1 Sam. VI, 1, עָלוֹת milk-giving cows.

[3] Is. XLIX, 13.

[4] From עוֹלָה ascending, since it ascends wholly in the fire.

[5] It would be helpful to quote here more fully both the text of the *Aggadah* and the observations of *Rashba*. 'Can a woman, etc. "Can I, said the Holy One, praised be He, forget the burnt offering which thou didst offer me whilst thou wast in the desert?" Upon this Israel pleaded: "Since there is no forgetfulness before Thee, Thou may'st not then forget the incident of the golden calf." "No", answered the Lord, גם אלה תשכחנה even this can be forgotten (referring to the word אלה of the text, Ex. XXXII, 4, "These are thy gods, O Israel.") Again Israel pleaded, saying "Since there is forgetfulness, may'st Thou not forget the events at Sinai". "No," He replied, ואנכי לא אשכחך "And I will not forget thee" (referring here to the word אנכי of the first command of the Decalogue, Ex. XX, 2).' Upon this the *Rashba* comments that there are some students who erroneously think that the Rabbis have, in these and in similar *Aggadoth*, merely indulged in interchanging the meaning of words, and so arbitrarily substituting עוֹלָה suckling for עוֹלָה burned offering, and so too with אלה and אנכי of Ex. XXXII, 4, and XX, 2. Such students, however, are divided into two categories. One class believes naively that this mode of interpretation actually represents the style and method by which the Rabbis normally interpret Scripture, the others cite such *Aggadoth* as proof of their allegation that the Rabbis, in general, expound Scripture erroneously. The *Rashba* refutes the incorrect impression of the former and the groundless allegation of the latter.

[6] This is inferred from Is. LXII, 8, 'The Lord hath sworn by the arm of His strength,' where *by His strength* is taken to mean Tefillin.

[7] Inferred from Is. LVI, 7. 'I will make them joyful in my house of prayer.' The text does not say in their houses, but in my house. The prayer reads as follows 'May it be my will that my mercy should overcome my anger, and may my compassion rule over my attribute (of justice), so that I may deal with my children according to the measure of kindness, and may I, in regard to them, overlook the measure of judgment.'

me." The Holy One, praised be He, issues a decree and the righteous man annuls it.' M.K. 16b.[1]

'The Holy One, Blessed be He, later admitted that Elijah was right (Ber. 31b).[2]

'Moses stood in prayer until he had won over (lit. weakened) God' (Ber. 32a).[3]

'The Holy One, Blessed be He, sheds two tears into the Ocean' (Ber. 59a).[4]

'When Moses ascended on high, he found the Holy One, Blessed be He, putting crowns[5] on the letters of the Torah, and He said to Moses "Is there no Shalom (greeting) in thy town?"'[6] (Shab. 89a).

'The Holy One, Blessed be He, called Jacob El (God)'[7] (Meg. 18a).

'Bring an atonement for Me,' says the Holy One, Blessed be He, 'because I have diminished the (size of the) moon'[8] (Hul. 60b).

'What is the Holy One, Blessed be He, now doing?' Elijah was asked once, and he answered that He was issuing halachoth in the name of the Rabbis, but He was not doing so in the name of R. Meir (Hag. 15b).[9]

'The Holy One, Blessed be He, seized Jeroboam by his garment and said to him "Let us both walk in the Garden of Eden"'[10] (Sam. 102a).

'The Holy One, Blessed be He, went and appeared before him

---

[1] Deduced from 2 Sam. xxiii, 3. 'To me (David) spake the Rock of Israel, a ruler over man shall be the righteous. He ruleth through the fear of God.' The text is taken to mean that the Rock of Israel spake to David saying, 'I rule man, who ruleth me, etc.'

[2] The passage begins thus: Elijah addressed himself to God in a reproachful manner, quoting 1 Kings xviii, 37, 'Thou didst turn their heart backward,' thus attributing Israel's failings to God for having created 'man' with inclinations towards evil; and, in a later utterance, Micah iv, 6, 'and that I have afflicted,' He admitted his own guilt.

[3] Deduced from the fact that Moses uses the term ויחל Ex. xxxii, 11, 'besought' which is from חלה 'Supplicate' and not the usual term ויתפלל from פלל.

[4] The passage in full is as follows: 'Once, on the occasion of an earthquake, Rab Ketina inquired from a magician as to its meaning. He replied: "When the Holy One, blessed be He, calls to mind His children, who are plunged in distress amongst the nations of the world, He sheds, etc., and the noise (caused by the tears) is heard from one end of the world to the other."' It would appear that R. Ketina took his words seriously.

[5] Generally known in Aramaic as 'taggin', three small strokes on the letters.

[6] i.e. why do you not wish me good fortune in my work?

[7] Lit. 'mighty', but also used for 'God'. This saying is deduced from Gen. xxxiii, 20, 'and (Jacob) called it (the Altar) El-Elohe-Israel,' but the Aggadist expounds it as follows: 'and He called him El,' i.e. the Elohe-Israel (called Jacob so).

[8] For this reason, continues the Aggadah, you find the addition 'For God' in connection with the new moon offering (Numb. xxviii, 15).

[9] Because R. Meir was a pupil of Elisha b Abuyah, afterwards known as Acher (the other), who was charged with heresy and desertion of Judaism (Hag. 15b). See p. 165, n. 1.

[10] i.e. promising him a reward if he would repent.

(Sennacherib) as an old man'[1] (San. 95*b*), etc. 'Bring me a razor and I will shave thee.'

There are many *aggadoth* similar to these which, according to the ordinary literal meaning, would associate a grotesque corporeality with God, such as it is blasphemous to ascribe to Him; but the Rabbis have used these *aggadoth* to reveal profound secrets, discernible only to the very few who have gained access to the courts of wisdom, and have reached the high degree of scholarship necessary to comprehend the mystical ideas enshrined in these words.

The editor of the *Ein Ya'akob* in '*Kotheb*' on Ber. 59*a* quotes the observation of R. Nisim Gaon[2] on the passage in the Gemara 'What does an earthquake signify?' It signifies, he says, 'that the Holy One, Blessed be He, is shedding two tears into the great sea.' On this he observes: It is well to make it clear at the outset that, whether due to common sense or to what the Rabbis taught us, no one doubts that it is wrong to compare God to any creature, and consequently there cannot be with Him any (such physical manifestations as) laughter, weeping, sighing, or the shedding of tears; and if this is clear to us, it is then obvious that, in every case where the Rabbis have used such terms they did not mean them in the literal sense, but employed them only as a figure of speech or illustration to make clear the measure of the thought, through objects which are well known to us by sight. For as the Torah spoke in the ordinary language of man and as the Prophets employ terms in relation to God which apply to a human being, such as, for example, 'Behold the eye of the Lord,'[3] 'Behold the hand of the Lord',[4] 'And the anger of the Lord was kindled',[5] 'Smoke rose up from His nostrils,'[6] 'And fire out of his mouth devoured"[7]; and as all these expressions were nevertheless necessarily metaphorical; so were also the similar utterances employed by the *aggadists*.' In his conclusion the author of the '*Kotheb*' incorporated in the *Ein Ya'akob* also quotes the views of *Rashba*, which are similar to those of R. Nisim, and he goes on to cite further Scriptural passages, the actual words of which appear

---

[1] And He said to him 'When thou goest to the Kings of the East and the West, the death of whose sons thou hast caused, what wilt thou say unto them?' 'What then shall I do?'asked he. 'Bring me, etc'. This mystical and allegorical *Aggadah* is supported by a Scriptural verse, Is. vii, 20.

[2] Nisim b Jacob b Nisim, an eminent Talmudical exegete and moralist, who lived in Africa during the twelfth century. See p. x.

[3] Ps. xxiii, 18.

[4] Ex. ix, 3.

[5] Num. xi, 10.

[6] 2 Sam. xxii, 9.

[7] Ibid. xxii, 9.

strange for they depict God as a corporeal being, passages such as 'My soul shall weep in secret for your pride',[1] 'My heart yearneth for Him,'[2] 'For a fire is kindled in my nostrils.[3]' He also quotes R. Hai Gaon[4] as making similar observations on this subject.

In this category belong also those *aggadoth* in the Talmud and *Midrashim* which relate to the banquets (for the righteous) in the time to come from the flesh of Leviathan[5] and a gigantic beast that consumes the grass of a thousand mountains in one day,[6] as well as on the wine which has been preserved (for the scholars) in its grapes since the days of creation.[7] All these were figurative expressions. See Maimonides, *Commentary on the Mishnah*, San. 10, 1, and the observations of *Rashba* in his novellae upon the *aggadoth* in Ber. 34*b*, where dealing with the exposition by R. Joshua b Levi of the verse 'the eye hath not seen', etc.,[8] which takes these words as referring to the wine preserved in its grapes, etc., he makes the following comment: 'The expression "wine preserved in its grapes" indicates a secret as well as a literal meaning and may be explained as follows: since wine is a means of making man's heart to rejoice and of causing man to forget his cares, the *aggadist* has here symbolized therewith the gladness and delight which will be enjoyed in the world beyond, and the fact that the joy will not be marred by distress and care. He further tells us that wine is stored in the grapes for scholars because the Torah is symbolized by wine, as it is written: Drink the wine which I have mixed.[9] They, therefore, forecast joy (figuratively) by wine for scholars (since scholarship is likened to wine) and measure for measure.' See *Rashba*, ad loc., where he treats this subject at great length. See also his observations in his Novellae on the *Aggadoth*, B.B. chap. v.[10] After first explaining the matter of the future banquet for the righteous in the literal way, he then begins to hint at the deep secrets as, for example, that the Leviathan

---

[1] Jer. XIII, 17.

[2] Ibid. XXXI, 19.

[3] Deut. XXXII, 22.

[4] Hai Ben Sherira, Gaon of Pumbedita in the tenth century.

[5] Name of a monster referred to in Is. XXVII, 1, and also described in Job XL. For the *Aggadah*, see B.B. 75*a*.

[6] Lev. R. Ch. 22.

[7] Ber. 34*b*; Shab. 63*a*.

[8] Is. LXIV, 3.

[9] Prov. IX, 5. See Genesis R., chap. xliii, on the text 'And Melchi-Zedek brought forth bread and wine' and Canticles R., chap. i on 'For thy love is better than wine'. In Taan. 7*a*, however, the reason given for the likeness of the Torah to wine is that as wine is preserved in inferior earthen vessels, so the Torah abides only with the humble-minded.

[10] i.e. upon the *Aggadoth* relating to the Leviathan and the gigantic beast referred to in the Gemara 74*a*.

and the '*Behemah*' allegorize the intellect and soul of man. See also on this point Maimonides, *Yad, Teshuba* 8 and Nachmanides, *Sha' ar Hagemul* x.[1] In any case, all these authorities of necessity agree that the *aggadoth* to which we have referred in this paragraph and which, according to ordinary reason, seem to have no sense and are at first glance contradictory to the principles of our religion and the fundamentals of our faith, contain important intimations on matters of high worth, and these profound thoughts are merely enveloped in a covering of many outer shells, the inner meaning being left for those alone who can penetrate into the hidden things of God.

[1] The last chapter of the thirty chapters of his work *Torath ha-Adam.* It deals with eschatology.

CHAPTER XXVIII

AGGADOTH RELATING THE PERFORMANCE
OF MIRACLES

WE shall now deal with the many incidents cited in the Talmud or in *baraithoth* which are of a miraculous character, and we shall recall the views of the earlier Rabbis, and their clear and conclusive judgment on this subject. Thus, for example, we shall refer to the story of Nakdimon b Gorion for whom the sun broke through (the clouds)[1] (Taan. 20*a*) and that of R. Phineas b. Yair for whom the river Ginai was divided (Hul. 7*a*)[2], as also to the miracles performed by R. Eliezer b Hyrkanus to support his argument about the oven, known as the Oven of Aknai[3], when he called on the walls of the school and the aqueduct for proof[4] (B.M. 59*b*), and so also to all the miracles which were wrought for Honi ha-Meaggel[5] and for R. Hanina b Dosa[6] as related in Tractate *Ta'anith* in the chapters dealing with the deeds of the pious saints. And there are many other supernatural events and wonders which are beyond our powers to explain, but of which we are told at considerable length in the Talmud, the enumerating of which, however, would take too long.

I shall only observe here that in the view of many of the sages it is right to take these accounts in their ordinary literal sense, and believe that they actually occurred exactly as recorded, that is, they actually took place in the lives of these just and saintly people; and that just as it is the duty of any man who calls himself an Israelite to believe literally the miracles which are recorded in the Bible, so is it right and proper for him to believe that God altered the course of nature for the sake of the saints and the devout who were *Tannaim* or *Amoraim*. And such was the view of R. Hai Gaon, according to *Ha-Kotheb*, in *Ein*

---

[1] To enable him to prove that when he discharged his pledge of twelve wells of water to the heathen, it was still daylight, and that he had, therefore, carried out his promise on the day fixed by him. See Gemara, ad loc., for the details of the case.

[2] He was on his way to ransom some prisoners and the miracle enabled him to cross the river on dry ground.

[3] An oven made in separate pieces joined by cement. R. Eliezer holding the view that it was not liable to uncleanness was in direct opposition to the ruling of the majority, for which action he was excommunicated. The meaning of *Aknai* is 'snake', and this name was applied to the oven in question because, in the words of the Gemara, it had become as encompassed with arguments as a coiled snake.

[4] i.e. he said 'let the walls of the school-house and the stream of water prove that the *halachah* is with me'. Whereupon the walls bowed and the water flowed backwards. But even so, the Rabbis did not accept his view.

[5] Lit. the circle-maker, see M. Ta'an.3, 8, for the reason for this surname.

[6] See ibid. 24b, also Ber. 71*b* and Yoma 53*b* for his saintliness and the miracles he worked by his prayers.

Jacob, Hag. chap. ii, who is there quoted as saying[1]: 'It is as well for you to know that the above view[2] was accepted by all the early authorities and none of them had denied the fact of miracle, for they maintained that God performs wonderful signs through the righteous, as he did through the Prophets. He causes the appearance of wonderful phenomena through the Saints as He did through the Prophets, since there is some profit to the world from those things, and nothing at all to do harm; for surely God knows that He cannot be challenged as having done something useless; and, therefore, all that was recorded as happening to R. Hanina and others is held to be literally true. When R. Samuel b Hofni,[3] of blessed memory, and others came forward, they maintained that these supernatural phenomena had appeared to the prophets alone, and that no such miracle would occur except to a prophet, and rejected any occurrence in the lives of the saints which was of a miraculous nature, and were emphatic that even the reference to R. Akiba as having looked upon the *hekhaloth*,[4] as also the similar references to R. Nechunya b ha-Kannah (and to R. Ishmael[5] and others) were not accepted as facts. We, however, hold the view that God does perform supernatural things for his Saints, and does show them His Heavenly Halls.' Such is the view of R. Hai Gaon.

R. Samuel b Hofni's views are quoted in *Re-Dak*[6] (on 1 Samuel XXVIII) with reference to the case of the 'Mistress of Ob',[7] who had summoned the spirit of Samuel from the underworld.[8] R. Samuel, he says, advocated the opinion that this Biblical account cannot be accepted literally as it is taken by the Rabbis, since it is irreconcilable with reason.[9] But in face of the views quoted above from the venerated

---

[1] Of the entry of the four Rabbis into Paradise (Heb. פרדס); see Soncino translation of Tr. Hagigah, p. 90, note 10, on the meaning of the term.

[2] i.e. the details related in connection with the aforesaid entry into Paradise.

[3] The last Gaon of Sura, who died in the year 1034 C.E., and who was known as a rationalist because he put reason above tradition.

[4] Heavenly halls, as described in the mystical writings *Hekhalot Rabbathi*, the authorship of which is attributed to Ishmael b Elisha.

[5] Referred to in the said work as *Yoredei Merkabah*—i.e. riders, those who had achieved the privilege of disclosing the mysteries of heaven.

[6] Abbreviation for R. David b Joseph Kimchi, well-known Italian Hebrew Grammarian and Commentator of the twelfth century. His commentary on the Prophets and Psalms is of great exegetical value, and has been translated into classical and modern languages, having exercised a great influence upon Biblical scholars.

[7] Necromancer (*ba'alath ob*) of En-dor, a woman believed to be capable of consulting 'ob', the spirits of the dead. See 1 Sam. XXVIII, 7.

[8] At the request of King Saul on the night before the fateful battle of Gilboa in which he lost his life.

[9] By such a view he placed himself in opposition to many contemporary theologians, among them Saadyah Gaon who held fast to the belief that the spirit of Samuel was, indeed, brought to life again. See J.E. XI, 19.

R. Hai Gaon, which have been generally accepted, we have no concern with R. Samuel b Hofni.

It is true that many scholars[1] have thought fit to interpret such stories as those of Rabbah bar bar Hannah[2] (B.B. 73*a*) or that of R. Eliezer ha-Gadol,[3] in which it is told how he called upon the walls of the school-house and the aqueduct to prove his case (B.M. 59*b*), or the story related of a saintly man who overheard a conversation on affairs of this world between the spirits of two young girls who had been buried wrapped in reed mats (Ber. 18*b*), as having been seen only in dream visions and not in actual fact; none the less, the occurrence related of Nakdimon b Gorion[4] and the miracles attributed to R. Hanina b Dosa, as similarly all the miracles which we are informed happened in the Holy of Holies to Simon the Just (Yoma 39*b*)[5] and others like these, are related by the Rabbis as things which had been actually experienced, and they become familiar to all the generations, early and late. Thus, for example, Josephus, in his *Wars of the Jews*, also relates similar occurrences, e.g. how during the last few years preceding the destruction of the Temple the gates of the Temple Court closed of themselves, and how there appeared terrifying signs in the sky. How then could one interpret all these as things which appeared merely in dream vision or, again, as mere figurative or allegorical expressions?

Ritba,[6] in his Novellae on B.B. chap. v, speaking of stories told by Rabbah bar bar Hannah, cited by *Kotheb* on *Ein Jacob*, ad loc., says: 'There are in the stories in this chapter things that are odd to all ordinary men, since they cannot be adapted to human comprehension. And there are also in these stories indications that they were not things seen by the physical eye but only the product of imagination in dream. This may be because of the fact that the scenes which the sages had witnessed during their journey on the Ocean had made them meditate

---

[1] Quoted later by the author.

[2] Babylonian *Amora* of the second generation whose grandfather Hannah was R. Hiyya's brother. The stories of his experiences on the sea and in the desert are strange, fantastic, and exaggerated.

[3] R. Eliezer b Hyrkanus, one of the most prominent *Tanaim* of the first and second centuries, a disciple of R. Johanan b Zakkai. His individualistic views, opposing majority rulings such as over the Oven of *Aknai*, see p. 208, note 3, led to a rupture between him and his colleagues.

[4] See p. 208, note 1.

[5] The Gemara, ad loc., gives a full account of seven miracles which took place regularly during the forty years of Simon the Just's ministration as High Priest, and which cannot be explained by human reason, viz. (1) the lot cast 'For the Lord' (see Lev. xvi, 8) came up always in the right hand; (2) The red strap tied around the neck of the goat (see Yom. 6, 6) invariably turned white, indicating the full forgiveness of sins (cf. Is. 1, 18); (3) The light in the Temple never failed; and so forth.

[6] R. Yom Tob b Abraham Ashbili, eminent Talmudical scholar of Seville in the fourteenth century.

during their solitude on the wonderful sights they had seen, so that in their sleep they appeared to them so vividly that there was no distinction between what they had been thinking of and the scenes they beheld in their dreams.' The Geonim went on to interpret the meaning of the words 'I saw', employed in the Gemara,[1] as referring to a vision in a dream and not to something actually seen. See *ha-Kotheb* on *Ein Jacob* on Ber. chap. iii with reference to the story told by the saintly man who overheard the two dead girls talking together, who quotes the views of *Ritba* mentioned above and adds his own view that when we are told of R. Eliezer B. Hyrkanus that he called on the school walls to provide proof for his argument, this means only that the sage fell asleep in the school-house and saw all this in his dream. *Ha-Kotheb* thus arrives at the conclusion that the above story told of the saintly man and those told of Ze'iri[2] and the father of Samuel,[3] who went to the graveyard (on different occasions to make inquiries of the dead) (Ber. 18b),[4] must also be interpreted on similar lines, as likewise various other miracles and wonderful occurrences mentioned in the *Gemara*. These views of *Ritba* are also found associated with the name of R. Hananel,[5] whose view is quoted in *Shittah Mekubbezet*[6] on B.M. at the end of chapter '*Hazahab*' (60b). The author of *Shittah Mekubbezet* also has interpreted the story told in B.M. 84a of a dispute[7] between the Heavenly Academy and the Holy One, when it was suggested that Rabbah bar Nahmani should be called upon to decide the matter; and this was all revealed in a dream to Rabbah bar Nahmani, prior to his death, so that he might depart this life in comfort of mind. A similar interpretation is given by Alfasi in a *responsum*, where he makes reference to the story told in B.B. 58a of R. Banaah, how he used to mark caves[8] and how in one of them he found Abraham asleep in the

---

[1] By Rabbah bar bar Hannah.
[2] *Amora* of the third century, born in Babylonia.
[3] Abba b. Abba, a Babylonian *Amora* of the second and third centuries, always referred to as the father of Mar Samuel, the principal of the Academy of Nehardea (see Ber. 18b).
[4] Ze'eri had deposited some money in trust, and the trustee died without leaving word of the place where the money was hidden. The father of Samuel was a trustee of money belonging to orphans and on the money being claimed after his death, his son went to inquire of his father where it could be found.
[5] Biblical and Talmudical commentator (990–1050), Rabbi of Kairwan (Tunis). Believed to have been a disciple of Hai Gaon, whose method of giving simple interpretations and avoiding mysticism he followed in his commentary on the Talmud.
[6] See p. 31, note 1.
[7] Over the law of leprosy in a case where it was doubtful whether the bright spot preceded the white hair, or the reverse, v. Lev. XIII, 1–3.
[8] In which dead were buried, to guard people against contracting uncleanness by walking over them.

arms of Sarah,[1] that it was merely a dream. I also read many years ago in a very ancient book, *Kaftor-va-Ferach*,[2] by R. Yitzhak ha-Parhi,[3] that the Geonim were of opinion that various strange accounts in the Talmud can be explained by the assumption that the Talmudical teachers simply fell asleep in the lecture-room and saw these strange things in their dreams. See also Maimonides, Commentary on the Mishnah, San. 10, 1, where in the course of his observations he refers with approval to this suggestion. He says: 'I hope yet to compile a work which will comprise all the aggadic expositions of the Talmud and explain them logically, showing their appropriateness to the subject-matter. I intend to make clear how some of the expositions can be understood literally and others only figuratively, while others, again, were only dream visions, though they are stated in a clear and simple manner, as though they had been seen whilst awake.'

Indeed, the Talmudical teachers themselves say of visions and of the hearing of a *Bath-Kol*[4] which had come to their ears that these all happened in dreams. See Hag. 14*b*, where we read how R. Jose ha-Kohen went and related the events[5] in question to R. Johanan b Zakkai, and how the latter said: 'Happy are ye and happy is she that bore you! Happy are my eyes that have thus seen! Indeed, in my dream you and I were reclining on Mount Sinai and a *Bath-Kol* came to us from heaven, saying "Ascend hither! Ascend, there are great halls prepared for you!"' We thus see that the sound of the *Bath - Kol* reached their ears as in a dream vision. In the same way the *Bath-Kols* mentioned in the story of R. Banaah and in those of Rabbah bar bar

---

[1] The *Aggada* relates how during his search for such caves he had found the Machpelah cave where the patriarchs are buried, at the entrance of which stood Abraham's servant, Eliezer. On inquiring, 'What is Abraham doing?' he replied, 'He is sleeping, etc.'

[2] Being researches into the history, geography, and other antiquities of the Holy Land. The author also deals with those laws which can only be practised while dwelling in the Land, such as the laws of *Terumah* and of the tithes, etc. First published at Venice between 1545 and 1548. A second edition appeared in Berlin in 1849, edited by Hirsch Edelman, while a third edition was published by Luncz in Jerusalem in 1897. Our author apparently refers to the first edition, since the second edition was printed after the publication of the *Mebo*.

[3] Scholar, traveller, and Palestine explorer (1282–1357), born at Florenza, Spain. The family name, it is suggested, was taken from that of his native town (Perah—flower). His name was not Yitzhak but Ishtor. See J.E., v, 343; Otzar Israel I, 315.

[4] Lit. daughter of a voice, i.e. a resonance, an echo, a reverberation caused by the human voice, or any other sound proceeding from an invisible source and considered by the Rabbis as a heavenly or divine voice proclaiming God's will.

[5] Which had happened to him and R. Joshua while on a journey. According to the Talmudical account the latter began to expound the work of the Chariot, and, as soon as he had begun, although it was a day in Tammuz when the sky in Palestine is generally absolutely cloudless, the heavens became overcast with clouds, a rainbow appeared, and the ministering angels gathered together to listen to the exposition.

Hannah can be explained as having been heard in dreams. Yet in several other instances, where reference is made to a *Bath-Kol*, it must be interpreted as the divine voice coming down to men direct from heaven, as I have said already elsewhere.

But if, as I have submitted to the reader, the Geonic view is true that a number of *aggadoth* will have to be interpreted as scenes seen in dreams, it is nevertheless to be recognized that in the case of many other *aggadoth* the only way to understand them intelligently is to take their words in their literal sense.

This is in accordance with the view of R. Hai Gaon (quoted before), who says: 'The Holy One, Blessed be He, never ceased bestowing upon us His kindness and His truth; and just as He bestowed upon the band of prophets His divine care by doing for others through their agency, or for themselves, miraculous things in supernatural ways, He also does similar things through and for the righteous, who have devoted their lives to His ministry, and who are endowed by Him with the power of knowledge and understanding needed for His divine and holy service.' This agrees also with the views expressed by *Rashba* in his Novellae on the *aggadoth* quoted by the '*Kotheb*' on *Ein Jacob* Hul. 7*a*, in reference to the miracle performed by R. Phinehas b Yair, when he passed through the River Ginai[1] on dry ground, where he writes: 'A view which has been very widely expressed in both the Torah and the Talmudim is that we are bound to give credence to the wonderful occurrences which have happened, when required, either to the entire people through the agency of the prophets, or even to a single one of the saints. This belief has been transmitted from fathers to sons, so that you will find it mentioned by the Rabbis on several occasions, as, for example, in reference to the difference which arose between R. Eliezer b Hyrkanus and the other Rabbis regarding the oven of Aknai, or again, the references to Rabbah and Raba (he is probably alluding here to the *Aggada* found in B.M. 86*a* mentioned above, where Rabbah b Nahmani was suggested as one to decide in a dispute between the Almighty and His heavenly academy and to the sending of greetings to Raba from the heavenly academy),[2] etc.' We can see, therefore, two different schools of thought regarding this subject, and I am unable to judge which is the truer, but any man with a keen eye can discriminate between the rabbinic sayings in question, as to which of them should be understood in their literal sense and which explained as referring to things seen only in dream or vision.

[1] Which he had to cross on his way to ransom prisoners. According to another view (Jer. Demai 13) he was on his way to the school to deliver a lecture.

[2] Raba was not exceptional in this respect; see Taan. 21*a* where it is stated that Raba held only third place in the attainment of this distinction.

CHAPTER XXIX

THE PARABLES OF THE *AGGADAH*—ILLUSTRATIONS POINTING A MORAL

THE form of parable[1] used by the Rabbis is one of the thirty-two methods of interpretation compiled by R. Eliezer, the son of R. Jose the Galilean, for the interpretation of the *Aggadah*.[2] The Rabbis employed this form mostly for the purpose of elucidating Biblical passages or for meeting challenging criticisms against the Torah put forward by pagan philosophers or heretics. In most cases even this outer garment in which the Rabbis clothed their words is intellectually charming and artistically delightful. Consult, in this connection, the beginning of *Midrash Koheleth*[3] and of *Midrash Hazitha*,[4] where the Rabbis pointed out the value of the parable and where they say: 'Let the parable not be esteemed lightly, since it is through the parable that one can penetrate to the depths of the Torah.'[5] See also Maimonides' introduction to the *Moreh*, where he deals at length with the subject of parables.[6] I shall mention only a few attractive parables from the Talmud and Midrash as examples.[7] Thus, in Ber. 33*b* we read: 'To what can the matter be compared?—To a man who complimented a King on his ownership of

---

[1] From the Hebrew word 'Mashal', to compare, denoting a fictitious narrative intended to convey a moral in a more convincing form. V. Jud. IX, 7–15, and of Nathan, 2 Sam. XII, 1–14. Students of the subject are referred to Guttman, Hamashal Bitekufath Hatalmud, Jerusalem, 1940.

[2] The parable is method no. 26.

[3] An homiletical Midrash on Ecclesiastes.

[4] Or *Midrash Shir ha-Shirim Rabbah*, a homiletical *Midrash* to Canticles called *Hazitha* after the proemial verse, Prov. XXII, 29, quoted at its beginning.

[5] The saying is not to be traced in the *Midrash Koheleth* as it has come down to us, while in *Midrash Hazitha* the word 'depths' is not in the passage.

[6] Generally with the parables employed by the Prophets. He regards an understanding of the parables, their ideas and meaning, as a key to the understanding of all the Prophets. He quotes the parables of Holy Writ, and the beautiful illustration given by the Sages, viz. that if a man loses in his house a *sela*, or a pearl, he can find it by lighting a taper worth no more than a single *issar*. Hence, although the parables in themselves may not be of great significance, great ideas can be made understandable through them.

[7] By way of illustrating the manner in which they were employed by the Talmudists as a means of conveying a correct understanding and a better elucidation of their arguments.

millions of silver coins, etc.'[1] On this passage, see *Moreh* i, chap. lvi,[2] where Maimonides points out the profundity of the parable.

Again, in Ber. 61*b* we have the parable of the fox walking along the river bank, etc.[3]

Again, in Taan. 5*b*, there is the parable of the tree which the traveller addresses: 'O Tree, with what shall I bless thee?'[4] Similarly, in A.Z. 4*a* we read the parable: 'To what can the matter be compared? To a man who is the creditor of two persons, one of whom was his friend, the other his enemy. From his friend he accepts payment in installments, whereas of his enemy he exacts payment in one sum.'[5] See further, A.Z. 54*b* and 55*a* for several beautiful parables,[6] particu-

---

[1] Actually the King owns millions of gold coins. Hence it was detraction rather than a compliment. This parable is quoted in reference to a disciple who, reading prayers in the presence of R. Hanina, showered a variety of epithets on God, such as great, valiant, tremendous, powerful, strong, etc. When he had finished the Rabbi reproached him, saying, 'Have you now finished the praises of your Master? Your conduct may be compared to a man, etc.'

[2] It is, in fact, cited in the fifty-ninth chapter and not in the fifty-sixth, when Maimonides admonishes those who are extravagant of praise in the prayers they compile although they are ignorant of the true attributes of God, and so treat God with a revolting familiarity.

[3] It is the well-known Aesop fable of the fox which, noticing the fishes swimming to and fro, asked them why they were moving so fast. 'Because we are afraid of the nets,' they replied. 'Come to shore then and live with us.' 'What a foolish suggestion,' the fishes exclaimed. 'If we are in danger here in the water, where we live, how much greater would our danger be on shore, where we die?' This illustration was used by R. Akiba in answer to Pappos b Judah, his fellow prisoner, during the Hadrianic persecutions. When Pappos suggested that he should desist from holding sessions with his pupils, thus imperilling his life, R. Akiba proved to him by this parable that since the Torah is life itself to the Jewish nation, the fear of death is no reason for deserting it.

[4] The story is told of a man who was journeying in the desert, hungry, weary, and thirsty, and who found a tree with a pleasant shade and sweet fruit, by which was flowing a stream of water. He ate the fruit and drank the water and rested in the shade. When he rose to continue his journey, he said 'O Tree, O Tree, etc. Thou art already blessed with sweet fruit, pleasant shade, and a stream of water. God grant that all the shoots taken from thee be like thee.' This parable was used by R. Isaac when he was about to part from R. Nahman, in whose company he had spent a most pleasant time. 'With what shall I bless you?' said R. Isaac, 'With knowledge of the Torah or with riches or with children? You have already been blessed with all these. God grant that your offspring be like you.'

[5] This parable was employed by R. Abbahu as a reply to a question put to him by the *Minim* on the Biblical passage, 'You only have I known of all the families of the earth, therefore I will visit upon you all your iniquities' (Amos III, 2). 'Why,' they asked, 'should the anger be vented on a friend?' His answer was given in the above parable showing that it is because Israel is like this friend that God punishes them only by intermittent visitations.

[6] Employed by the Rabbis in their replies to the questions put to them by philosophers and General Agrippa, e.g. 'Why does God not abolish such things in creation as are worshipped by the idolators?' Again, 'Why is He so jealous of the idols to which by this very gesture he concedes an importance comparable to Himself?'

larly the illustration given by R. Akiba to meet the challenge of Zunin (that crippled pagans actually enter the shrine and come out cured), where he explains how affliction comes upon men that are faithful in carrying out their commissions, by a charming parable of how once there was a trustworthy man in a town with whom the townspeople used to deposit their money without witnesses, etc.[1] See also B.B. 10a for R. Akiba's reply to the question put to him by Turnus Rufus[2]: 'Why, if your God loves the poor, does He not support them?'[3] and also the reply which he gave by means of a beautiful parable to the same inter-locutor's question regarding the holiness attaching to the Sabbath Day, as quoted in Gen. R. chap. xi[4]; also the reply given by 'Rabbi' to the question put to him by the Emperor Antoninus,[5] who argued that both body and soul can escape judgment (San. 91b).[6] See also Lev. R.

[1] And not *with* witnesses, which is a slip of the author's. One man, indeed, the parable continues, always entrusted his money to him *with* witnesses. One day, how-ever, this distrustful man forgot his caution and deposited his money with him *without* witnesses. The wife of the trustworthy man attempted to induce her husband to deny the deposit, as punishment for his suspicion, but he replied, 'Shall I lose my reputation of trustworthiness because this fool has acted in an unseemly manner?' So it is with the Heavenly afflictions upon men. They are intended to stay for a certain length of time and have a day and hour appointed for their end. If, at the time appointed for their departure, the man should enter an idolatrous shrine, the suffer-ings are tempted not to leave him, yet they answer that the fool's acting in an un-worthy manner is no reason why we should act against the directions of God, and fail to fulfil our obligation.

[2] Roman Governor of Judea in the second century at the time of the outbreak of Bar Kochba's revolt; also called Tinnius or Tyrannius. Several conversations on religious topics are recorded between the two.

[3] R. Akiba illustrated his reply by the following parable: Suppose a King was angry with his son and put him into prison, ordering that no food should be given him; yet if the King heard that someone had gone and given him food, would he not send that man a present?

[4] Turnus Rufus asked R. Akiba regarding the Sabbath Day, 'If God has conferred such honour on this day, why then does He allow the winds to blow, the rain to fall, and the grass to sprout up on it?' R. Akiba answered 'Let me illustrate it with a parable. Suppose two householders occupy a single courtyard and one of them does not contribute towards the *erub* (see p. 41, note 4), they would certainly be forbidden to move anything from the house into the courtyard; whereas, if there is only one householder in the courtyard, there is no such restriction. Thus God who is the only owner of the whole world knows no restriction upon movement in His case.'

[5] A Roman emperor, hero of Jewish legends in the Talmudim and Midrashim, particularly on account of his friendship with Rabbi. It is not certain which emperor is meant by this name.

[6] Arguing that each of them could plead 'not guilty' on the ground that neither without the other could have committed any sin, for no sooner are they separated than they commit no sin. Rabbi answered him with the following parable: 'A King once appointed two watchmen over his beautiful garden. One was blind, and the other lame. The latter said to the former "I see luscious fruit in the garden and if you will carry me there, I shall get them, and we can eat them together." The blind watch-man consented, and both ate the fruit. At the king's investigation into what happened

chap. iv for the way in which R. Joshua b Korchah disposed of the question put to him by a *min* —'Since the Biblical law is to incline after the majority, and we are in a majority, why do you not follow the faith of the majority?'[1] Again you find several sound rejoinders made in a similar style by R. Akiba, R. Joshua b Korchah, R. Jose, and R. Joshua b Hananiah. Amongst the *Amoraim* there was R. Abbahu, who excelled in illustrating his replies to monarchs and *minim* by attractive and artistic parables. It would, indeed, take too long to refer to all such parables; here I am only calling the attention of the student to the subject.

R. Johanan b Zakkai was particularly complimented by the Rabbis on the fact that he did not omit from the scope of his studies even the fables of the foxes and the parables of the fullers[2] (B.B. 134*b*; Suk. 28*a*). In the Tractate Soferim they attribute this interest in parables also to Hillel the elder. Of R. Meir the Sages reported (San. 38*b*, 39*a*) that he had 300 parables of foxes as well as fuller's parables. However, we have only three of them left. Thus, it is recorded in the Mishna (Sot. 49*a*) that they said when lamenting his death: 'When R. Meir died the authors of parables ceased.' See Rashi on San., ad loc., where he gives in detail the three parables referred to.[3] Actually there are many other fox parables scattered throughout the Talmud, such as the parable of the fox walking by the river, which I have quoted above, in Ber. 61*a*, and, in addition, I have found many other parables scattered in the Midrash, for example, the beautiful parable in Eccl. R. 5, para. 14, on the verse: 'As he came forth out of his mother's womb, naked, so shall he return.' There, Geniba[4] compares man in this world to a fox that has found a vineyard surrounded on all sides with a high fence (except

to the fruit, each attempted to clear himself of guilt, one by pleading his blindness, the other his lameness. The king, however, made the blind man carry the lame, and thus passed judgment on both. So God will reunite their souls with their bodies and punish them both for their sins.'

[1] He illustrated his reply by asking him whether he had any sons; to which the *min* replied that by asking this he had reminded him of his troubles; for indeed he had several sons, but when they sat together at table, each of them wished to praise his own God and so they came to blows. Thereupon R. Joshua asked him whether he himself could get along with them, and he said 'No'. 'If so,' R. Joshua retorted, 'why should you urge upon us to unite with them? rather go and unite with them first yourself.'

[2] The fuller is several times referred to in the Gemara as a well-known figure. See J.E. 221, s.v. *Aesop's Fables among the Jews*. See Guttman, Hamashal Bi-Tekufath Hatanaim, pp. 70–73, for treatment of the fullers and their parables.

[3] Rashi gives the three parables in question combined into a single story. The reference to the fuller's parables given here is not in the Talmudic text.

[4] Babylonian scholar, contemporary of Rab (Ber. 27*a*) but at variance with Mar Ukba the Exilarch (Git. 7*a*) and so regarded as of a quarrelsome nature (Git. 31*b* and 62*a*). The verse is Eccl. v, 14.

for a small opening at one point).[1] See also Gen. R. chap. lxiv, which tells of R. Joshua b Hananiah, the famous Torah scholar, (how he turned the excited people from thoughts of revolt by his fable concerning) a lion in whose throat a bone got stuck as he was devouring his prey, and how an Egyptian crane extracted it.[2]

Place and time do not permit me even to refer to all the parables scattered through the Talmud or to enumerate them, since they cover such a wide range of subject. In Tractate Berachoth itself I have found as many as ten[3] parables, all of them fascinating and delightful. They are found particularly in the *Tosefta*, the *Torath Cohanim*,[4] and the *baraithoth,* and they are far too many to be dealt with individually. I am here merely directing the attention of the student to this type of rabbinic interpretation, since the parable forms an important part of the means employed by both the *Tannaim* and the *Amoraim* for their regular (*aggadic*) expositions. The Palestinian scholars, during the later periods when they gave less attention to halachic studies, perfected their methods of *aggadic* exposition and made a still greater use of the form of the parable for every kind of exposition. The student will find a large collection of these in the *Pesikta*[5] and the *Tanhuma*,[6] and in the many other later *Midrashim* which were collected and have come down to us through the later Palestinian sages. But these parables can compare

---

[1] The parable runs that the fox wished to enter, but finding the hole too small to squeeze through, he starved himself for three days, until he became thin enough to enter. Once in the vineyard he indulged in the tempting fruit, and so regained his former size. He had therefore to starve himself again for another three days to reduce his size. When he finally got out, he looked at the vineyard, and exclaimed: 'Vineyard, vineyard, how pleasant art thou, and how desirous thy fruit. But of what benefit is it to me, since I depart from thee as thin as I entered?' Such, says Geniba, is the fate of man in this world: As man came forth, etc.

[2] R. Joshua b Hananiah was the leader of the people at the beginning of Hadrian's reign, who had given permission to rebuild the Temple, and afterwards, influenced by the evil report given by the Samaritans, had withdrawn it. This raised the anger of the people who began to plan a rebellion. R. Joshua b Hananiah skilfully made use of Aesop's fable concerning the lion who had a bone caught in his throat and who offered a reward to anyone who would extract it. The crane appeared and put his long bill into the lion's throat, thus relieving him. When he asked for his reward, the lion replied that he had already received his reward by escaping unscathed from the lion's mouth. 'Similarly,' says R. Joshua, 'we can now be happy in knowing that Hadrian is permitting us to live undisturbed.'

[3] They are found in the following folios: 7*b*, 9*b*, 11*a*, 13*a*, 32*a*, 61*b*.

[4] An exegetical Midrash on Leviticus.

[5] A collection of Midrashic discourses for the festivals and the special Sabbath-days. There are three such collections: (1) Pesikta Rabbati, (2) Pesikta Zutri, (3) Pesikta de R. Kahana. The author does not indicate to which Pesikta he refers.

[6] A homiletical Midrashic work covering the whole of the Pentateuch. Its name is derived from the Palestinian aggadist R. Tanhuma b. Aba (fourth century). This Midrash is also referred to as *Midrash Yelammedenu* because of the fact that its introductions commence mostly with the words Yelammedenu Rabbenu.

neither in quality, beauty, nor thought to those handed down to us by the early *Tannaim*, which are scattered throughout the *baraithoth* and to which I have referred above.

The Rabbis also adopted a special form in their parables of seeking to introduce the facts to the reader in the form of a dialogue between two persons. Thus, they put in the mouth of each disputant arguments with which he defends his case and justifies his action. They sometimes pursued this method in dealing with monarchs and princes of the nations, such as Nebuchadnezzar, Nebuzaradon, Haman, and Ahasuerus, who are profusely treated in this way in the tenth Chapter of Sanhedrin and in the fifth of Gittin and in the first of Megillah. There is nothing in the suggestion that the Rabbis had received by tradition this material and the pleas put forward by the monarchs. For in fact the arguments thus represented as used by such persons are to be understood in the same way as the parallel cases of the arguments put into the mouths of beasts, birds, and fishes, and even of inanimate things, such as hills and rocks, and even the letters of words; which must necessarily be interpreted not as real but as merely one of the methods of the parable and as similar to the devices of poetry where the poet puts words into the mouths of people who are concerned in the same subject, showing how each person might state his case, as against the other, if only he had sufficient intelligence to understand the essence of the matter involved and its causes. Thus, for example, in the fox fables referred to above we have the fox or the lion arguing and so forth, and it is through the parable, as such, that one can penetrate thoroughly into the ideas which it is intended to convey. So also the debates in those imaginary dialogues were found very helpful for the clarification of ideas and were designed to bring to light ethical principles in support of the fundamentals of the Faith. It was by this mode of teaching that the Rabbis made their way to the heart of the masses, to awaken and lead them towards the desired goal.

This idea has already been expressed by *Tosafoth* on A.Z. 17a[1] and Hul. 7a.[2] Thus, in the answer of the mountains: 'Before we pray for thee, we must pray for mercy for ourselves,' they observe: 'You are not

---

[1] s.v. עד with reference to the incident related of R. Eliezer b Dordia how during an experience of profound repentance he sat between *two hills and mountains* and called upon them to pray for him.

[2] s.v. אמר with reference to one of the miracles performed by R. Phinehas b Yair who when he was about to pass the River Ginai approached the river saying, 'River, divide thy waters for me, so that I may be able to cross over.' The river replied 'Thou art going to do the will of thy Creator, and I am going to do the will of my Creator'. Upon this *Tosafoth* again makes the same observation as above and quotes the Ben Dordia incident as an example.

to assume that this reply came directly from the hills and mountains. It was Ben Dordia himself who imagined the possibility of such a retort coming from them.' And *Ritba*, on *Ein Jacob*, ad loc., also observes at a later point: 'Not that the hills had to pray for mercy for themselves, but the *Baraithah* simply illustrates the actual fact that Eliezer b Dordia understood in his own mind that the hills, were they endowed with the faculty of speech, might well answer that they needed mercy for themselves.' This is also borne out by the Scriptural parables, which are not to be understood literally as though there was actual speech and answer, as, for example, in the parable: 'And the vine said unto them, "Should I leave my wine?" '[1] The author of the *Perek Shirah*[2] had the same idea in mind where he sang the praise of God through the mouths of birds and animals. This, he says, did not mean that they were uttering words, but was to teach the simple idea that if they had been capable of talking they would have had to express themselves in such a way.

Rashba, quoted by *Kotheb*, on *Ein Jacob*, Hul. *7a*, with reference to the dialogue between R. Phinehas b Yair and the River Ginai, deals similarly with this subject, and says: 'What should not be overlooked by you is the fact that the Rabbis were fond of dwelling upon the miracle and its resulting phenomena in the form of dialogue making the matter clear or vivid by arguments of the disputants. They even go so far as to use such forms of expression as the dialogue also in connection with the story of creation, as if God had created all creatures at their express wish. See R.H. *11a* for the statement that all the creatures of Genesis were made with their own consent; though it is quite inconceivable that the nothing from which the creatures were produced should offer its consent prior to their being brought into being. How then could the Rabbis represent the creatures' consent as a condition for the creation when they were not even potentially, much less actually, in existence? Similarly, we have the Rabbinic story in

---

[1] Jud. IX, 7–15. The Hebrew quotation ואת מתקי is erroneous since מתקי (my sweetness) is mentioned in connection with the fig tree, and in relation to the vine the term תירושי (my wine) is used and not גפני which can only be translated 'my vine' and not 'my wine'.

[2] Lit. 'Chapter of Song', an ancient *Baraitha*, composed of Scriptural verses which the author put into the 'mouths of heavenly bodies' as well as of plants and dumb creatures, and in which they praise God, and from which we are to derive moral lessons and draw religious inferences of great value. Many indirect references are found in the Talmud to this *baraitha*. Joseph Albo, *Ikkarim* III, speaks at considerable length of the value of the lessons which we can derive from the composition in question. *Kenaf Renanim* (Warsaw, 1888), by R. Enoch Zundel Luria (Russian preacher and author of the first half of the nineteenth century) is the best-known and most enlightening homily on this famous *Baraitha*.

Hul. 60b with reference to the plea of the moon that it was impossible for two kings to use the same crown,[1] where we are told that God said to her: 'Go and reduce thy size!'[2] All such *aggadoth*, found as they are in a number of places, merely use the form of the parable in an extended way for the purpose of conveying much useful knowledge which would help to direct us to the truth of our faith that it was by God that the world was created and that it is under His Providence, as also to other matters of real benefit to us.

In the present case the dialogue between the pious R. Phinehas b Yair and the river Ginai had the purpose of making it widely known that even ordinary men, and still more pious men, ought to avoid changing things from their natural condition to an unnatural one, and that even where they possess the spiritual power to perform such a miracle they should exercise that power in an emergency only for the sake of a religious act which is required at the time.

Of this class of parables we find several examples where the Rabbis represented inanimate things as well as plants and animals as speaking and arguing with men. We have an example in the saying of Resh Lakish (San. 108b). The raven[3] gave Noah a triumphant retort, saying: 'Your master hates me[4] and you hate me.'[5] Similarly, we have the plea of the dove[6] to Noah: 'May my food be as bitter as the olive, but from the hand of God'[7] (Erub. 18b). So also even the letters of the alphabet were made to plead with God, as where is related in Jer. San. 2, 6, on the authority of R. Hoshea, that the letter '*yod*' went up and prostrated itself before the Holy One, blessed be He, and said: 'Master of the worlds, Thou hast torn me from that good woman (Sarah).'[8] They also relate there how the Book of Deuteronomy went

[1] As there was jealousy between her and the sun.
[2] i.e. the moon, not the sun, was to be reduced.
[3] Sent forth by Noah to find out the state of the waters of the Flood (Gen. VIII, 7).
[4] Evidenced by the fact that He had commanded seven pairs of the clean creatures to be taken into the Ark and only two of the unclean (the raven is an unclean bird).
[5] For instead of choosing one of the clean species for that risky journey, you are choosing me of whose species there are only two.
[6] Which was also sent forth again and again until she returned to Noah in the evening with an olive leaf plucked off a tree in her mouth (ibid. VIII, 11).
[7] Rather than depend on mortal Noah.
[8] Sara was originally called שׂרי which means 'my princess'. Her name was changed later, v. Gen. xv, 15. God, however, promised the yod a place with Joshua, whose name was originally הושע, but was later changed to יהושע (with a yod) v. Num. XIII, 16. The name of the author of this homily, 'Hoshea,' may not be a mere coincidence. There are several sayings in Talmud and Midrash, the topics of which bear some similarity to the authors' names. Attention has already been directed to the treatment of the subject by J. D. Wynkoop in the JQR 1911, by B. Epstein, *Mekor Baruch*, and by R. Margulies in his essay annexed to the second ed. of the Mebo ha-Talmud (Chajes).

up and prostrated itself before God (and pleaded with Him).[1] And so also we find it stated on several occasions that the 'attribute of justice[2] spoke before the Holy One, blessed be He'. See Jer., ibid.[3] Again, we find such statements as the following, 'the intercessory spirit[4] spoke before the Holy One, blessed be He' (San. 44b); and so, too, in Gen. R. chap. viii, we find quoted a dispute between the virtues:[5] Kindness favoured the creation of man, whereas truth did not, righteousness favoured his creation and peace was against it.

Similarly, we have the homily in Jer. Mak. chaps. ii, 6, of a question put to wisdom (and prophecy) by the Rabbis, as to what kind of punishment should be imposed upon the sinner. Now surely kindliness, truth, and wisdom in these stories are only qualities which have been personified, and not speakers who can argue in debate. The Rabbis merely ascribed to these virtues fictitious arguments such as might have been put forward with regard to the creation of man, in view of his attitude to good and evil according to the natural inclinations found in him, and expressed these in a poetical form. To this category belongs also the expression found in Gen. Rab. chap. ii, 2,[6] and quoted in the *Moreh* ii, 5, that 'the earth mourned her evil lot, saying: "I and the heavens were created together and yet the heavenly beings are animate while we are inanimate" '. But if the lower creatures (including herself) are inanimate, how could she lament over her evil lot? What the Rabbis really meant was that had the earth been able to speak she might have put forward such an argument. See also *Moreh* ii, 29.[7]

Again, where the Rabbis tell us of the decisions and arguments advanced by the Sodomite litigants (San. 109b) or of the criticisms levelled by Korah and his party against Moses (San., 110a), or the

---

[1] Saying, 'Thou hast written in Thy Torah that any written deed of which the least point is omitted (the first and best proof in the Torah of this is the minuteness of the details of the purchase of the sepulchre for Sarah by Abraham) (Gen. XXIII, 3, 20) becomes *ipso facto* void. Now Solomon attempts to obliterate a "*yod*" of mine, for in place of the words לא יסור "he shall not depart" (Deut. XVII, 17), he has said ולא אסור I will depart and yet not let my heart be perverted,' thus removing the *yod* which forms the main basis for the law in question.

[2] One of the attributes assigned to God in Ex. XXXIV, 6–7, which are called in Hebrew 'Middoth' lit. measures. Those of justice and mercy are often personified.

[3] Which refers to the statement of R. Aha that there were three kings at whom the 'attribute of justice' laughed. See also Shab. 55a; Meg. 15b; San. 94a.

[4] פסקנית in Hebrew lit. splitting, i.e. an arguing spirit; see Rashi, ad loc., for the view 'that it is an additional name of the Angel Gabriel, who always interceded on behalf of Israel'.

[5] Which were consulted by the Creator regarding the creation of man.

[6] On the passage 'and the earth was "*tohu*" (empty) and "*bohu*" (formless)'. Tohu and bohu, the Rabbis in question say, mean 'mourning' and 'crying', implying that the earth was crying, etc.

[7] Maimonides elaborates the theme of the figurative language of the Prophets.

discussion which Sennacherib had with his commanders (San. 95*a*), or
the conversation of David with Yishbi Be-nob (San. ibid.), as also the
advice given by Nebuchadnezzar, the scribe of Merodach-baladan,
to his master, or again, the words attributed to Nebuzardan[1] (San. 96*b*),
or similarly, the allegations which Haman made against the Jews, in
speaking to Ahasuerus (Meg. chap. i)—all these, if we wish, we can take
literally and say the facts were handed down by tradition. That is to
say they can be interpreted in accordance with the principle elaborated
in chap. xviii (i.e. literally). But there is also the more probable view
that the Rabbis gave those details in an allegorical or poetic style,
according to their method of showing in a vivid way what arguments
each of these persons might have put forward in conformity with the
position they occupied, in justification of their actions. The Rabbis
adopted this method as one that was found helpful in gaining the
understanding of the people and in implanting in their hearts the
lessons of morality and the fear of God; thus selecting any incident
which had occurred in the past with all its possible circumstances and
setting it up as an example for recommending the practice of
virtue or for the repudiation of the practice of evil. One who looks into
this subject with an open and penetrating eye will find many other
Aggadic saying which go to prove my point. I have merely endeavoured
to arouse the student's interest in the subject.

[1] In reference to the seething blood of Zechariah, and the means by which it found
rest and its effect on Nebuzaradan's mind.

CHAPTER XXX

THE *AGGADIC* USE OF HYPERBOLE AND THE EMPLOYMENT OF NUMBERS FIGURATIVELY. ALSO BIBLICAL QUOTATIONS IN THE *AGGADA* WHICH ARE AT VARIANCE WITH THE MASSORETIC TEXT

THERE is still another important principle which the Rabbis have laid down for us (Hul. 90*b*), viz. that our sages made use of hyperbolical expressions.[1] Thus, in Arachin 11*a* we read: 'Your mnemonic sign is that it was the *Baraitha* which employed hyperbole.'[2] So, again, in Erub. 2*b*: 'It is reasonable to hold that Bar Kapara's "limit"[3] was only a hyperbolical expression.' Again, the Rabbis in Hul.[4] bring forward as evidence of hyperbole in the Talmud three cases where they gave the exaggerated number of 300.[5] To a similar category may be ascribed the passage (in Bech. 57*b*) regarding the egg of the Bar-Yokni[6] which, it is stated, destroyed 300 cedar trees. Here, too, belongs the statement of Jonathan[7] (Yeb. 16*b*) that he had 300 arguments to prove that the daughter's rival is permitted (to marry the brothers),[8] or that

[1] As an example they quoted the statement in Taan. 2, 2, that the ash-pile, in the middle of the Altar, on which the ashes were collected, accumulated at times as much as 300 Kors of ashes, estimated in our measure at about 2,830 bushels.

[2] This occurs in reference to the *magrefah*, an organ-like and shovel-shaped instrument which had ten pipes with ten holes in each pipe. The Rabbis differed, however, with regard to the manner of production of the musical notes. On the authority of Samuel, it was stated that each hole produced ten different kinds of notes—a hundred together, and a *baraitha* was quoted to the effect that each of the holes produced one hundred notes—a thousand together. In order to remember whose view was represented by the thousand they gave the mnemonic sign mentioned.

[3] i.e. Bar Kapara, in saying that a weight, even up to a hundred cubits, does not necessitate the lowering of the entrance into the alley, intended only to show that R. Judah's extension of the limit up to forty and fifty (in opposition to the limit of twenty given by the Rabbis in the Mishnah) was to be regarded merely as a hyperbole.

[4] Ibid.

[5] They are (1) the ash-pile as referred to in the note above; (2) a golden vine stood over the entrance to the sanctuary, and whosoever gave a golden leaf, berry, or cluster as a freewill offering had it hung thereon by the Priest. It once happened, says R. Eliezer b Zadok, that three hundred priests were required to clear them away; (3) three hundred priests were needed to handle the *Parocheth* (veil) in case of uncleanness.

[6] A bird of a fabulous size, the eggs of which were exceedingly large.

[7] Or rather what R. Dosa b Harkinas said to the Rabbis, when they visited him to ask him about a rumour that he was the author of the decision that the daughter's rival is permitted to marry the brothers.

[8] See Yeb. 2*a*, 13*b*, regarding the levirate marriage (Deut. xxv, 5–10). The law only applies in the case where the widow is not amongst the 'Forbidden degrees', in

boast of Doeg the Edomite[1] that he could count 300 *halachoth* while sitting in a tower flying in the air[2] (San. 106*b*), or the statement of Eliezer b Hyrkanus,[3] prior to his death, that he had studied 300 *halachoth* on the subject of planting marrows (by magic)[4] (San. 68*a*), or the statement that R. Johanan b Narbai[5] would consume 300 calves at a meal and drink 300 jars of wine (Pes. 57*a*). See, too, *Rashbam*[6] on Pes. 119*a* regarding the statement that Korah's treasure house was a load for 300 white she-mules, where he says that this is not to be taken literally, and that this view is to be taken also of the other occurrences the number 300 in the Gemara.

In another passage we read that Nebuchadnezzar sent to Nebuzaradan 300 mules laden with iron axes which could break iron[7] (San. 96*b*). See in connection with this passage R. Isaiah Berlin's[8] marginal notes, ad loc., who refers to the statement of *Rashbam* quoted above. Again, there is the passage in Git. 68*a*, where R. Johanan is quoted as saying that there were 300 kinds of demons in Shichin. See also Keth. 111*b* (where R. Hiyya b Ada tells how from a vine left to him by his father he cut 300 clusters—of grapes—per day).

The author of the *Me'or Enayim*[9] chap. xx includes in this category also the 300 fox fables attributed to R. Meir (San. 38*a*) and the 300

which case both she herself and her rivals are exempt from the obligation in question. The ruling of the Shammaites was that only the widow herself is exempt, not her rival (i.e. her husband's other wife).

[1] Who held the office of overseer of King Saul's flocks. As a result of the information which he had brought to the King of the assistance given to the fugitive David at Nob by the High Priest Ahimelech, he obtained the Royal authority to kill Ahimelech and his priests, a task which he carried out with cruelty; cf. 1 Sam. xxii.

[2] Rashi, ad loc., offers various suggestions as to the meaning of this, viz. as referring to (1) the laws even on such a small matter as the upper stroke of the *lamed*, which is tower-like in shape; (2) the laws on the possibility of defilement by entering into a heathen land by a tower-shaped conveyance; (3) the laws regarding a tower which was actually suspended in the air by enchantment; (4) laws regarding the cleanness or otherwise of the contents of a tower which does not rest on the ground immediately, i.e. is supported by pillars (see M. Ohol 4, 1).

[3] Who had been placed under the ban (see B.M. 59*b*).

[4] Although sorcery was punishable by death (Ex. xxii, 17), R. Eliezer's action was in this case permitted since it was for the purpose of teaching. On the same occasion he made reference to his study of three hundred laws on the subject of one of the forms of leprosy, viz. 'The deep bright spot' (Lev. xii, 2), cf. Gemara loc. cit.

[5] Designated in the Gemara as the son of Pinkai. Heilprin, *Seder Hadoroth* makes the suggestion that he may be identified with Johanan the High Priest, who after serving as High Priest for eighty years became a Sadducee. See Ber. 29*a*.

[6] R. Samuel b Meir (1085–1174) grandson and disciple of Rashi, and one of the *Tosafists*.

[7] For the purpose of hewing down the gate of Jerusalem.

[8] An eminent critic among the German Talmudists, and Rabbi in Breslau (1725–1799).

[9] Azariah di Rossi, v. p. 150, n. 8.

halachoth which were forgotten during the days of mourning for Moses (Tem. 15*a*). We also find it related (Shab. 13*b*) that 300 jars of oil[1] were taken up to Hanania b Hezekia.[2] According to the above principle[3] there can be no ground for the difficulty raised in *Tosafoth* on Sot. 34*a*, s.v. יותר, over the reference made in the Gemara, ad loc., to more than 300 mils,[4] since this figure of 300 is to be taken, like the other Talmudic references to this number, in a sense other than the literal.

The Gemara also adopted the number sixty as a common hyperbolical expression. This is supported by *Tosafoth* in B.K. 92*b*, s.v. שתין, on the saying: 'Though sixty men pursue him who takes his meals early in the morning, yet they will not overtake him.' This number sixty, they say, is a common expression used in the Gemara, just as in the saying quoted on the same page: 'Sixty pains assail the teeth of him who hears the noise made by another man eating, while he himself eats nothing,' or in the saying (Hul. 58*b*): 'They suspended sixty manas of iron on the gnat's proboscis.' So R. Isaiah Berlin, in his marginal notes, ad loc., directs attention to Rashi (Shab. 90*b*, s.v. שתין, which refers to a number of sixty seals),[5] who states that it is not to be taken literally. See also *Maharsha*, Novellae on Ber. 57*b*, where he deals with the statement of the Rabbis that the Sabbath is a sixtieth part of the world to come, and sleep a sixtieth part of death,[6] and says that the number sixty in these two cases is not to be taken literally, and refers for support to *Tosafoth*, B.K. 92*b*, as mentioned above.

The statement that the egg of the Bar-Yokni destroyed sixty cities (Bech. 57*b*) belongs to the same class, as similarly the number sixty used (with reference to R. Eleazar b Simeon[7], viz.) that 'they spread

---

[1] Not 'wine' as erroneously stated by the author.

[2] They were supposed to have been taken to an upper chamber where he was engaged in reconciling with the Torah certain passages in the book of Ezekiel which were apparently in conflict with it.

[3] viz. that the number of three hundred is not to be taken literally.

[4] i.e. the water of the Jordan facing the Israelites was heaped up in stacks to a height of more than three hundred mils (a mil is 2,000 cubits). This, according to *Tosafoth*, contradicts another statement (B.B. 75*b*) that the cloud rose only three parasangs (a parasang being 4 mils).

[5] Referring to the use of an amulet for the acquisition of wisdom (the use of amulets was extensive in the Talmudic period): 'One should eat half of the right and left of the bird of the vineyards, and should place the rest in a brass tube and seal it with sixty seals and suspend it around the left arm.'

[6] The Gemara enumerates three similar sayings, viz. fire is a sixtieth part of Gehenna, and honey of the manna (cf. Ex. XVII, 13–31), and dreams of prophecy.

[7] R. Eleazar b Simeon was employed as an Officer of the Romans to arrest thieves, and afterwards undertook a penance, by submitting his body to pain, so making atonement for the wrong which he might have done to innocent people. The Aggadah goes on to tell how every morning they removed from him sixty basins of blood and discharge and that sixty kinds of pap made of figs were his cure.

sixty sheets for him' (B.M. 84b) and that 'sixty seamen (brought him sixty slaves bearing) sixty purses', as also the saying that Elijah was (brought and) lashed with sixty glowing rods (B.M. 85b). The same number is also found in Hag. 15a,[1] as well as in Meg. 7b, where we read that they (the household of Mari b Mar) set before (Abaye) sixty dishes of sixty different kinds of food, and he (Abaye) ate sixty pieces from off them.[2]

The Rabbis were also accustomed to use the number thirteen in a figurative not a literal sense. See Rashi (Hul. 95b, s.v. תליסר)[3] on the story that Samuel sent to him (R. Johanan) thirteen camels laden with responses on difficult ritual questions, where Rashi says that the word thirteen is only figurative. See also for the same assertion Rashi (Shab.119a, s.v. תליסר) with reference to the account in the *aggadah* of how one Joseph, who honoured the Sabbath, sold a jewel[4] for thirteen roomfuls (or vessels) of dinars. These, as well as all other references to the number thirteen, such as the load of thirteen camels mentioned above (Hul. 95b), or what is narrated earlier there (of R. Aba), how he bought meat for thirteen istra-peshitas (half-zuzim) from thirteen butchers, are only cases of the hyperbolical use of the word, as is also what is told (in Shab. 135a, of R. Ada b Ahabah, whose son was born circumcised) how he took him to thirteen circumcisers[5] until, at last, he almost mutilated him in performing the operation himself.[6] And again, what is told of Elisha Acher,[7] how he sent (the cut-up body of) a child to thirteen school-houses[8] (Hag. 15b), as similarly the narra-

---

[1] In connection with Metatron, one of the highest of the angels.

[2] The following reference may also be added: 'When Samuel Yarhinai survived Rab as head of Nehardea, seeing that R. Johanan, the Great Master of Palestine, treated him as a colleague, he sent him the intercalary calculations for sixty years (Hul. 95b). See also Ber. 58b where in the house of R. Hanna b Hanilai sixty bakers were employed during the day and sixty during the night to bake bread for the poor.

[3] In Rashi it is quoted תריסר probably by printer's error.

[4] The story told is of how Joseph, who honoured the Sabbath, was rewarded for his devoted observance of it by finding a jewel in a fish for which he received thirteen roomfuls of dinars.

[5] In order that one of them might cause a few drops of the covenant blood to flow, but since it fell on a Sabbath day none of them would perform the rite.

[6] He held the view that the Sabbath is superseded, even in the case of a child born circumcised, and only a drop of covenant blood need be shed, but his unskilful operation led to deplorable results for the boy.   [7] See p. 165, note 1.

[8] R. Meir who, with his marked tolerance, had remained associated with the apostate, went with him from one school to another, up to the number of thirteen, in all of which he (Acher) asked children to recite for him the verses which they were studying that day, hoping to take them as a prediction of his future reconciliation with Judaism. (Such verses were considered in those days as an oracle.) Of the answers given him, the last, due to mispronunciation, exasperated him and, according to one opinion, he cut the child to pieces and sent it to thirteen school-houses. According to another and more plausible view, he said that he would have liked to cut the child to pieces.

tive of the thirteen white asses (Sab. 110a).[1]

Commentators have also observed that the Rabbis employ the phrase three parasangs[2] merely as a hyperbolic expression, as is obvious from the following citations: 'He (David) went three parasangs by the light of her'[3] (Meg. 14b); 'He (Og, King of Bashan)[4] uprooted a mountain three parasangs high'[5] (Ber. 54b); 'He (Mar Ukba) ran after him (R. Hanina)[6] three parasangs along the sand[7] (but could not overtake him)' (Keth. 60b); 'He (Abaye) followed them[8] for three parasangs across the meadows' (Suk. 52a). See also Sab. 94a[9] and Yoma 20b[10] for similar references. The author of *Meor Einayim* has dealt at length with this subject. I am also aware that some contemporary students have attempted to list all numbers employed by the Rabbis in a figurative sense. Hence, I have not elaborated on the subject at greater length, since that is not my purpose in this volume, but rather to direct the attention of the serious student to the methods adopted by the Rabbis in the development of the Talmud which may give him a basis for further research.[11]

I also wish in this chapter to direct attention to the fact that numerous

---

[1] A Pumbedithan Officer was bitten by a snake, and it was suggested by way of an antidote that he should sit upon the embryo of a white ass which had not been found *trefah* (organically defective). Thirteen white asses were torn open, and all were found *trefah*.

[2] A parasang is a distance of four mils (8,000 cubits in all).

[3] Referring to Abigail, the beautiful wife of Nabal the Carmelite (1 Sam. xxv, 3). David, when he first met her, almost fell a victim to her beauty. In the *aggadic* narrative she had once unintentionally revealed her beauty, and David went three parasangs by the light (attractiveness) of it.

[4] See Num. xxi, 33.

[5] When he intended to destroy Israel. There is a fanciful *aggadah* about how the mountain which he intended to hurl upon the three parasangs long camp of Israel had been burrowed into by a swarm of locusts and fell on his neck, but did not fall to the ground, because of two of his teeth becoming embedded in it, and while he was thus burdened with it Moses had a chance to kill him.

[6] Who had issued to him a ruling which was proved to him later to be incorrect. See A.Z. 15b for a similar expression where Rabbah had sold an ass to an Israelite who was suspected of disposing of it later in a forbidden way. When Rabbah discovered that there had been an improper sale, he ran after the buyer three parasangs and some say, etc., but could not overtake him.

[7] The mention of sand is found only in reference to one parasang and not to all the three, as is erroneously quoted in the text.

[8] A man and a woman whom Abaye had suspected of going out together for an immoral purpose. Ultimately he found out that this suspicion was ill-founded.

[9] Telling how a certain officer ran three parasangs as a result of the King's anger.

[10] Telling how the voice of Geboni or Gaboni, the crier of the Temple, who summoned the priests daily to their labours, was audible for three parasangs.

[11] The subject has been admirably treated by Abraham Lebensart in a series of articles entitled 'The Numerals in the Talmud' published in the Krakau Hebrew weekly '*Ha-Mitzpah*,' 1907.

Biblical passages were quoted by the Rabbis in a form which varies from the Massoretic Text, as has already been noted by *Tosafoth* (Shab. 128, s.v. ונתן), where in reference to the sentence 'he shall give the money and it shall be assured to him',[1] they state that it is a usual feature of the Gemara to abbreviate Biblical passages. Thus, for. example, they quote the sentence 'he who is in distress shall not make legal decisions',[2] as a Biblical text (Erub. 65a). Again, 'all dreams are in accordance with their interpretation.'[3] (See also *Tosaf*. to Erub. 2a, s.v. דכתיב) in reference to the Gemara's quotation 'to the entrance of the porch of the house',[4] where they point out that there is no such verse.)[5] Yet again, you will see (Ber. 61a and Erub. 18b) the passage 'And Elkanah went after his wife'[6] quoted as though it were Scripture, and Rashi, ad loc., comments that Elkanah was one of the prophets, though in fact there is no such text anywhere in the Bible. *Maharshal* and *Maharsha*[7] have noted this passage and commented on it.[8] Another similar observation is made in *Tosafoth* (Meg. 3a)[9] on the quotation of

---

[1] In support of the ruling, loc. cit., that *Hekdesh* (hallowed things) cannot be re-redeemed by land, the Gemara quoted the passage 'He shall give the money and it shall be assured to him' as a Biblical verse, when, in fact, there is no such verse in the Bible. *Tosafoth*, pointing out the fact that the verse cannot be traced, suggests Lev. XXVII, 19, 'He shall add the fifth part of the money of the estimation unto it, and it shall be assured to him,' which implies money and not land, and so supports the above ruling. After raising some obvious difficulties regarding the proof from this Biblical verse, Tosafoth states, on the authority of *Torath Kohanim*, that the deduction is really based upon verse 25 of the same chapter, 'And all thy estimations shall be according to the shekel of the sanctuary,' the term *shekel* excluding land. It is note-worthy that *Rashi* here, as in Pes. 35b, has overlooked the fact that the verse is non-existent.

[2] In support of the statement that a person whose mind is not at ease must not pray. There is no such verse in the Bible, but R. Tam in *Tosaf*., ad loc., s.v. בער attempts to show it to be an abbreviated form of Job. XXXVI, 19.

[3] The Gemara, ad loc., asks: 'Is this a Biblical passage?' 'Yes,' is the answer, for we were taught 'whence do we deduce that every dream is realized according to its interpretation? From the text, 'And just as he interpreted it, so it was' (Gen. XLI, 13).

[4] In an attempt to prove that the words 'the entrance of the Tent of the meeting' in Lev. III, 2, refer to the entrance of both the *Hekhal* (Sanctuary) and the *ulam* (porch) and thus support the view held by R. Judah in the Mishnah.

[5] They suggest, however, that it is a combination of the verses 'to the *ulam* of the house' (Ezek. XL, 48) and to 'the door of the house' (Ezek. III, 47).

[6] In reference to the previous statement, loc. cit., that Manoah (Jud. XIII) was an *Am-ha-Aretz*, in virtue of the fact that he was walking behind his wife, since it was regarded as improper to walk behind a woman.

[7] R. Solomon Luria (1510–1563) and R. Samuel Edels (1555–1631) both famous for their Talmudical commentaries.

[8] Their observations are in reference to the statement of *Tosaf*. Ber. 61b, s.v. אלה, that the whole passage was erroneously included in the Gemara as there is no such text anywhere. But they regard such a suggestion as unacceptable, and make other suggestions which, however, cannot be harmonized with chronological facts.

[9] s.v. וילן. See also *Tosafoth* Eru. 63b, s.v. מיד and San. 44b.

the words 'And Joshua lodged that night in the midst of the vale', which
cannot be traced to the Bible.[1] See, too, Zeb. 119*b*, where they quote as
proof of their statement that the 'The rest' (Deut. XII, 9) refers to the
rest of the Ark (in Jerusalem), the words 'And it shall come to pass
when the ark shall rest', where Rashi, ad loc., says that he searched in
vain for the source of the verse.[2]

So also Rashi (Zeb. 118*b*) where he says of the quotation, ad loc.:
'And for him Taan'ath Shilo,'[3] that he searched in vain for the text.[4]
Yet another case is in *Tosafoth* (Sab. 55*b*, s.v. מעבירים),[5] where they
state that the Talmud version differs in some places from the Massoretic
text. Thus, with reference to Samson, they refer to the period of his
leadership as extending for forty years (Jer. Sot.1, 8, fol.17*b*), whereas in
our text a period of no more than twenty years is given.[6] See in this
connection *Rashba*, Responsum No. 88, on the prayer quoted in the
Gemara as offered up by Samson (Sot. 10*a*): 'Remember for my sake
the twenty-two years I judged in Israel.'[7] Another case is mentioned in
Yad Malachi,[8] para. 283, where the author deals at length with the
quotation in the *Baraitha*, beginning 'The Sages taught'[9] (para. 9),
where in the Biblical passage 'Mine is the silver and mine is the gold,

[1] Actually in Josh. VII, 9, we read 'among the people' instead of 'in the midst of the
vale', while in verse 13 of the same chapter we read: 'and Joshua went that night
into the midst of the valley.' Apparently the Rabbis combined both verses.

[2] Rashi, Tosafoth, and Berlin in his glosses, suggest several other proofs for the
assertion, e.g. 'And when the Ark rested' (Num. x, 36); 'Arise, O Lord, into thy rest,
Thou and the Ark' (Ps. cxxxii, 8); 'House of rest for the Ark' (1 Ch. xxviii, 2); 'Arise
into thy resting place' (2 Ch. vi, 42).

[3] So arguing from the word *Taanath* (which could be connected with תאניה
mourning) (Lament II, 5) that whosoever looked at Shilo (which was the first religious
centre after the settlement in Palestine) lamented the loss of joy associated with the
offerings.

[4] Rashi does quote a text with some resemblance to it from Joshua xvi, 6, 'and the
border went about eastward into Taanath Shilo.'

[5] See the Gemara, ad loc., for the statement that Phinehas (one of the sons of Eli)
did not sin (though both were accused, 1 Sam. II, 22). This is then questioned on the
ground that it is written, ibid., verse 24 מעבירים 'Ye make (the Lord's people) to
transgress', whereupon R. Huna b. R. Joshua answers that what is written is מעבירם
'He (i.e. Hophni and not Phinehas) causes them to transgress.' The Masoretic text
is מעבירים but *Tosafoth* considers this as one of the cases where the Talmud version
differs from it. The word רשי has erroneously crept into the author's text.

[6] See Judges xv, 20, and xvi, 31, where the period of twenty years is mentioned
twice. According to the notable suggestion of David Kimhi quoted by the author of
the *Yad Malachi* (see note 8), the extension of the period to forty in the Jerus. Talm. is
derived from this repetition. Kimhi's view is corroborated by other Talmudical
authorities. See *Mar'eh-ha-panim* on the Jer. (Wilno ed.), ad loc.

[7] Rashba maintains that the reading 'twenty-two' is erroneous.

[8] See p. 15, note 1.

[9] I.e. the sixth chapter of Aboth, otherwise known as Kinyan Torah (the
chapter of the possession of the Torah). This chapter is not part of the Mishna.

saith the Lord' (Hag. ii, 8), the word נְאֻם of the Masoretic text is re-placed by the word אָמַר.[1]

The same author also quotes from a manuscript of *Ritba's Novellae* on Baba Bathra, in reference to the statement (B.B. 123*b*): 'For it is written "And the sons of Manasseh were Hepher and Yishi" '; whereas in 1 Chron. v, 24, we read: 'These were the heads of their father's houses, Epher[2] and Yis'hi,' and he maintains that such varia-tions are due to the Talmudical method of altering texts or, at times, of adding to them, quoting an example from Taan. 29*b*, where the text, 'to give לכם (you) a future and hope,'[3] is quoted as 'to give להם (them), etc.' (In our editions of the Talmud this has been rectified to agree with the Massoretic text).[4] See the B.Y.,[5] Responsum 8, where this same observation is quoted on the authority of *Ramban*. In B.Y. one can find further references to incorrect Biblical quotations in the Talmud, as for example in Sheb. 35*b*, 'and Phinehas the son of Eleazar, the son of Aaron the Priest,'[6] whereas the Biblical text lacks the word 'the Priest'.[7] So, again, in M.K. 5*a*, we find the quotation: 'No alien uncircumcised in heart and uncircumcised in flesh shall enter into My Sanctuary to serve me,'[8] whereas the expression 'to serve me' does not appear in the Biblical text.

In general it may be taken that the Rabbis thought it unnecessary to cite the words precisely as they were written. They quoted as much as they thought necessary for their purpose and at times combined the earlier and the later parts of the text, so forming a single idea. Also (as can be seen in the following examples) they designated certain state-ments incorrectly as Scriptural texts. Thus, they said: 'As it is said, all dreams are in accordance with their interpretation,'[9] or again (in

---

[1] This reading is quoted by Rashi on *Aboth*, and is found in some of the present editions of the *Mishnah*.

[2] Indeed the *Maharsha*, ad loc., suggests the replacing of Hepher with Epher, and with regard to the other differences he simply attributes them to the usual Talmudic method of abbreviating Biblical texts, giving as reference Tos. Shab. 128*b*.

[3] Jer. XXIX, 11.

[4] Our author, unfortunately, omits the chief point raised by *Ritba*. It appears that in the Talmudic text used by *Ritba*, the passage given was 'to give them, etc.' בגולה (in exile). He observes that the word בגולה was added by the Rabbis in compliance with the context of the verse, whereas the Biblical text reads 'to give them, etc.' (without בגולה).

[5] I presume the initials to be the abbreviation of *Beth Yehudah*, by Judah Aryeh (Leon) of Modena, Italian Rabbi and scholar of the sixteenth century.

[6] Jud. xx, 28.

[7] In modern editions of the Talmud the word הכהן (the Priest) appears in brackets.

[8] Ezek. XXXIX, 15.

[9] Ber. 35*b*.

B.K. 81*b*): 'Regarding such a person,[1] Scripture says: 'where you can be good, beware of being called evil.' Here the *Gemara* raises the question: 'Is this found in Scripture?' 'Yes,' is the reply, 'the idea is found in the verse, "Withhold not thy hand when it is in the power of thine hand to do it." '[2] See also B.M. 10*b*: 'He (the employer) is transgressing (an injunction, viz.): "Thou shalt not delay (payment)." '[3] Even though this is not found in the Scriptural text, the Rabbis have here followed their habit of quoting the text in an abridged form, being concerned only with its meaning (so that when they were challenged for the place of this injunction in Scripture, they quoted): 'Say not unto thy neighbour "Go and come again and to-morrow I will give it to you." '[4]

---

[1] With reference to one who forbids the use of a path through a field, even though the crop has been reaped and consequently no damage ensues.

[2] Prov. III, 27.

[3] i.e. the transgression of the injunction, Lev. XIX, 13, 'the wages of him who is hired shall not abide with thee all night' is incurred only on the first morning, whilst thereafter one violates the command 'Thou shalt not delay', an injunction which is not given directly in Scripture, but indirectly in Prov. III, 28.

[4] Prov. III, 28.

CHAPTER XXXI

DEMONS, WITCHCRAFT, INCANTATIONS, DREAMS, AND PLANETARY INFLUENCES, MEDICAL PRE-SCRIPTIONS, AND CURATIVE METHODS IN THE *AGGADAH*. (INCLUDING ALSO REFERENCES TO ADDITIONS IN THE GEMARA BY THE SABORAIM)

CONCERNING the subject of demons, the evil eye, and the evil spirits referred to in the Talmud, there can be no doubt that the Rabbis believed in their existence, and consequently we should take all reference to them in their literal sense, and we should not attempt to offer other interpretations which will explain them in a sense remote from the literal.

The Rabbis talk of the existence, the natural characteristics, and the behaviour of these beings in a straightforward way. Thus, we read (Hag. 16a): 'Six things are said of the demons: in three things they are like ministering angels,[1] and in the other three they are like human beings.'[2] The Mishnah, Aboth (5, 6), says: 'The demons were created on the eve of the Sabbath at twilight'. The existence of demons was the general belief, indeed, of all the peoples of the Eastern and Western parts of the world at the time of the *Tannaim* and *Amoraim*.

They also believed in witchcraft and incantations, and although Maimonides, in his Commentary on the Mishnah, A.Z. 4, 7, with reference to the question[3] put to the elders[4] in Rome, and also in *Yad*, *Ab. Kochabim* 11, 16, is of a different opinion, yet the wording of the *Baraithoth* 1 and of the Talmud in several places must be taken literally and not in an allegorical or figurative sense. We do, however. observe a substantial difference in regard to this matter between the Babylonian and the Palestinian sages, although both believed in the existence of these beings and both tell us of conversations which they held with them, and of the marvellous things which these demons sometimes performed. Thus, for example, we read in Jer. Ter. 8, fol. 47, how, when the baths were heated by Diocletian's[5] orders, the demon Antigorus

---

[1] Viz., they have wings like the Angels, and fly from one end of the earth to the other and, like them, know the future.

[2] They eat, propagate, and die like human beings.

[3] The question was: 'Why, if God has no wish for idolatry, does He not abolish it?'

[4] i.e. Rabbis Gamliel, Eleazar b Azariah, Joshua b Hananiah, and Akiba who visited Rome in 95 C.E. See Bacher, Aggadah der Tann. 1, p. 84.

[5] Roman Emperor (A.D. 284–305) of most obscure parentage.

cooled them.¹ The story is also told in Gen. R. chap. 63. Yet these Palestinian sages did not elaborate these tales at such inordinate length as is done in the Babylonian Talmud, where they are told with great detail. For example, they tell us that the demons were members of their households, and were employed as servants. See Hul. 105*b*, where it is related of R. Papa that he had a demon as a water carrier, or Pes. 111*a*, where a warning is issued against going out into the streets on Wednesday evening.² So R. Joseph³ relates many things which he claims to have heard from the demon Joseph (see Erub. 43*a* and B.B. 73*a*).⁴ Similarly with regard to incantations: whereas nothing about them is mentioned in the Jerusalem Talmud, the Babylonian sages speak of the subject at length. They quote the words of several spells in Sab. 67*a* and *b*. Likewise in Meg. 3*a* they give the wording of an incantation,⁵ viz., 'The goat at the butcher's is fatter than I am.'⁶

Similarly in Git. 69*a* they prescribe spells for 'day blindness'⁷ and for 'night blindness'. References to such spells are also found in A.Z. 12*b*. Again in Pes. 111*b* they make several references to incantations as also to the danger of 'even numbers', but none of the cases can be admitted by common sense. Furthermore they come into conflict with the Biblical prohibition of the 'Amorite practices', but as regards this point *Rashba*, in Responsum 413, has endeavoured to meet the difficulty of such contradictions.⁸

With regard to the medical prescriptions (found in the Talmud), in many *baraithoth*⁹ we find warnings and directions how to preserve the

---

¹ The legend relates how the swine breeder, Diocletianus, despised in his youth by the Rabbis, owing to his occupation, was elevated to the imperial throne. Wishing to avenge himself on them for the humiliation he suffered at their hands, he ordered the Rabbis to appear before him as soon as the Sabbath was out, but did not serve them with the order until the Sabbath was in. In addition, he ordered the bath to be heated for seven days and nights so as to prevent them taking the necessary bath before making their appearance. Antigorus the demon, however, brought the emperor's evil plans to nought.

² And Sabbath evenings as well, when demons are abroad.

³ Similarly R. Papa, see Pes. 110*a*.

⁴ Where it is related of Rabbah that he saw the demon Hormin, the son of Lilit (a female night demon), running on the parapet of the wall of Mahuza.

⁵ To be used when one is overcome with fright though there is nothing to see.

⁶ i.e. pick on him as a victim.

⁷ The affliction caused probably by a dazzling sun was ascribed to the demons. Rashi, A.Z. 12*b*, s.v. איזדהר speaks of 'a demon appointed over the affliction of blindness.'

⁸ Our author in his glosses on B.M. 27*b* quotes *Rashba* in regard to the distinction to be drawn between a thing which has been authenticated as a cure for an ailment and another which has not been so verified. The use of the former, he says, does not involve the prohibition against 'Amorite practices'.

⁹ From what follows it would appear that our author refers here to *baraithoth* which appear in the Jerusalem Talmud.

health and how to prevent illness. They set out things which are injurious to the body and those which keep it fit. Also they gave directions how one should behave in the bath, during meal times, and during the intimacy of the sexes. Many such directions are scattered throughout most of the Treatises.[1] But it is different in the Babylonian Talmud, where we find elaborate statements on medicinal prescriptions, incantations, and a variety of curative methods. These are given in detail in Keth. 77*b*, Git. 69*a*, Sab. 66*b*, 67*a*, and in Pes. 111*b*. The student will find there a full treatment of this subject. Similarly on the subject of dreams and their interpretation and the question how far the Rabbis believed in their truth, you will find accounts in both the Babylonian and Palestinian Talmudim (Ber. ch. 9),[2] and the Midrash on Lamentations.[3]

The Rabbis also expressed the belief that 'children', (length of) 'life', and 'sustenance' do not depend on merit but on Mazal (destiny).[4] They amplify this by a lengthy description (Sab. 156*a*) of planetary influence upon man; thus, for example, they say that he who is born under the influence of a certain planet will be wealthy[5] and the like.

Rashba, in his Responsa 408 and 409, has already endeavoured to harmonize the contradictory statements in the Talmud, of which there are many,[6] and we recognize that many passages in the Talmud which were known to the early teachers (and which contradicted other passages) have been omitted from our editions of the Gemara; see Sheiltoth[7] on *Parashath Bereshit*, where reference is made to one Joseph who honoured the Sabbath[8] and where the Gaon quotes a variant

[1] i.e. of the Jerusalem Talmud, as would appear from the sentence that follows.
[2] Fol. 55 and 56 in the Babylonian Talmud.
[3] Chap. i from par. 16 onwards.
[4] The Gemara (M.K. 28*a*) puts 'life' first.
[5] Here the planet Venus wields its influence; similarly those born under the influence of Mercury will be of a retentive memory, or those born under Jupiter will be upright, and so forth.
[6] e.g. in Sab. 156*a*, that Israel is immune from planetary influence (a view held by several Talmudical teachers). See also *Tos.*, ad loc., s.v. אין and on M.K. 28*a*, s.v. אלה, where the contradiction is noted but where it is maintained that the statement in Shab. is not without exceptions.
[7] A collection of *halachic* and *aggadic* material in the form of questions based upon the weekly readings of the Torah, and compiled by Ahai Gaon, a prominent Babylonian Talmudist of the eighth century, and the first rabbinical author to write after the closing of the Talmud. He later settled in Palestine, where he wrote his Sheiltoth. Its first edition appeared at Venice in 1546. A new edition with the Commentary '*Ha'amek She'elah*' by R. Naphtali Zvi Berlin, appeared in Jerusalem 1948–50.
[8] See Shab. 119*a*, where we are told that as a reward for unwavering observance of the Sabbath he found a precious stone inside a fish which he had bought for the holy day. The stone had belonged to a Gentile, Joseph's neighbour, who, in view of a soothsayer's forecast that his possessions would ultimately pass into Joseph's hands,

reading to the effect that when the Gentile saw Joseph's turban[1] he committed suicide. This additional detail, however, is not found in the present editions of the Talmud. This point has already been observed by Rabbi Isaiah Berlin.[2] Again, Sheiltoth on the weekly portion *Ekeb*[3] quotes the story that Rabbi sent a *mezuzah* to Artaban[4] according to the version of Jer. Peah 1, 1, and ends up with the following addition: 'Soon, following this, an evil spirit entered the daughter of Artaban and, since he had only the one daughter, and the doctors were at the end of their resources, Rabbi took the *mezuzah* which, as soon as he had fixed it on the door-post, caused the evil spirit to flee'.[5] This version of the story is not found in our editions.[6]

For a further case see Meila 17*b*, in connection with the *aggadah* quoted by Rashi, ad loc., that the demon Ben Temalyon[7] had entered the king's daughter,[8] though it is not found in the Gemara as we have it.[9] Another case is in Yoma 77*a*, where a lengthy account of Dubeil,[10] the Guardian Angel of the Babylonians,[11] has been removed from the text of the Talmud though it is quoted in *Ein Yaakov*, ad loc. Again a

---

realized his property and bought a precious stone with the proceeds. It fell into a river while the owner was crossing a bridge, and was swallowed by a fish which was afterwards sold to Joseph.

[1] Which reminded him of his own in which the precious stone had been set.

[2] In his *She'ilath Shalom* on the *Sheiltoth*, ad loc.

[3] Beginning Deut. VII, 8.

[4] See J.E. 11, p. 144, to the effect that it was Rab and not Rabbi, who is here mentioned erroneously, and so also maintains Graetz, Gesch. IV, p. 257. For this there is seemingly good support from A.Z. 10*b* where it is stated that אדרכן was in Rab's company (reading אדרכן for ארטבן) and where the former is referred to as dying. See Kohut *Aruch Completum* I, 280.

[5] From this it may be seen that in Talmudic times the *mezuzah* was credited with the protective power of warding off evil spirits.

[6] This addition by the Sheiltoth is also quoted by R. Israel Eisenstein in his glosses *Amude Yerushalayim* on the Jer., ad loc.

[7] This legend of Ben Temalyon is referred to in connection with the journey undertaken to Rome by R. Simeon b Yohai and R. Eleazar b R. Yose to make representations to the authorities for the cessation of religious persecution. The source of the *aggadah* quoted by Rashi, ad loc., is not clearly given by him.

[8] And he (Ben Yohai) by pre-arrangement with Ben Temalyon exorcised it on his arrival at the Roman Court. (See J.E. I, p. 361, on such legends). Guttman, Hamashal Bitekufath Hatannaim, p. 33, identifies her with Faustina minor, the only and most beloved daughter of Antoninus Pius (A.D. 81–161), who became the wife of his nephew and successor Marcus Aurelius (A.D. 121–180).

[9] Rashi adds that, as a result of R. Simeon's anger, R. Eleazar became dangerously ill, and that it was only through R. Simeon's prayers that he regained his health. Tos., ad loc., s.v. אלו quotes the same *aggadah* as from the Jer. Talmud but no reference is given.

[10] A composition of the two Hebrew words דוב אל 'bear God'. Persia appears in Dan. VII, 5, as a bear, hence their angel is a bear-god. See Yoma, Soncino edition, p. 374, note 11.

[11] It follows from note 10 that one should read 'Persians' instead of Babylonians.

detailed account of the great city of Rome is to be found in *Ein Yaakov*, Meg. 6*b*, of which there is no trace in Talm. Meg. Another case is the reason given for the concealment of Moses' grave from the knowledge of man, which is cited by *Ein Yaakov*, Sota, but omitted in our editions of the Talmud.

Similarly in the *Halachoth Gedoloth*[1] there are many statements quoted as from the Talmud which are not found in present-day editions, as for example the following ruling contained in his halachic collection on benedictions, chap. iii: The *Mezuzah* is a positive precept the observance of which is not limited to certain specified times.[2] This may seem obvious,[3] yet it was necessary to point it out as one might think that, as the words 'when thou liest down, when thou risest'[4] are found in the chapter referring to the *Mezuzah*, they do specify certain times and so the precept may be regarded as one whose observance is dependent on certain specified times. In the Gemara (Ber. 20*b*) all this reasoning is omitted.[5] A similar case is found in *Shimusha Rabba*, a compilation of the laws of *Tefillin* by R. Shalom Gaon,[6] where many statements are quoted on the authority of *Amoraim* of which there is no trace in the Talmud. This fact had already been observed by the early codifiers, as is found noted in *Tur Orah Hayim* on the laws of *Tefillin*.[7] See further *Pachad Yizhak*,[8] s.v. גוביא[9] where several passages additional to those found in our editions are quoted from an early edition of the Talmud, published in Portugal; similarly all such stories relating to various

[1] The chief work of R. Simeon Kayyira, Babylonian *halachist* of the ninth century, in which the entire *halachic* material of the Talmud is presented in a codified form.
[2] Therefore women are not exempt from observing the precept. The initials מעשהג in our author's text are the abbreviation of מצות עשה שלא הזמן גרמא.
[3] Since it is to be fastened to the door post and to remain there always.
[4] Deut. vi, 8.
[5] The reasoning of the Gemara is as follows: The precept of the *mezuzah* is compared to that of *Talmud Torah*, the obligation of which immediately precedes it in the same chapter (Deut. xi, 19). Hence if the *Mishnah* (Ber. 20*b*) had not stated explicitly that women are not exempted from observing the precept of *mezuzah* observance, one might have deduced such an exemption by analogy with the precept of *Talmud Torah* from which they are exempt.
[6] The authority of *Shimusha Rabba* was recognized by the early Rabbis, such as Alfasi and Asheri. It is also quoted in *Tosaf.* Men. 35*a*, s.v. שי. The attribution of its authorship to Sar Shalom, Gaon of Sura, in the ninth century is questioned by critical historians. Lauterbach (*Otzar Israel* x, 95) examines the style and terminology used in the book, and he finds it difficult to believe that one of the Geonim would employ a style and vocabulary so little akin to that of the Talmud.
[7] Particularly in Siman 32 where the *Shimusha Rabba* is frequently quoted.
[8] By Isaac b. Samuel Lampronti, Italian rabbi and physician (1679–1756). The *Pachad Yizhak* (the name is derived from Gen. xxxi, 42) is a rabbinical encyclopaedia of great value and renown, arranged in strict alphabetical order, and covering the entire *halachic* and *aggadic* literature down to the latest responsa.
[9] The text erroneously reads גובא.

Talmudical sages as reflect no honour upon them, and have been removed from our editions of the Talmud, such as the incident involving Mar Samuel's father[1] and a certain Median woman[2] which is quoted in *Halachoth Gedoloth* on *Gittin*.[3] A further example is the incident in the life of Beruriah[4], the wife of R. Meir, which is barely mentioned in the Gemara (A.Z. 18*b*); and it is Rashi who gives the details of the incident which seemingly had come down orally, but are omitted in the Talmud.

So also on the contrary a considerable amount of material is to be found in the Talmud which was added to it by the Geonim of the later period, who lived a long time after the completion of the Talmud. This is attested by R. Sherira Gaon[5] in his responsa,[6] where he says that he has it on tradition that the halachic discussion from the beginning of *Kiddushin* down as far as the words בכסף מנא לן (whence with money?)[7] together with all the questions and answers in this passage was the work of the Saboraim.[8]

Similarly the *halachah* (quoted in San. 43*a*)[9] to the effect that when a criminal is led out to execution, he is to be given a goblet of wine containing a grain of myrrh,[10] as well as the added opinion quoted in the

---

[1] Abba b. Abba, generally referred to as 'the father of Samuel'.

[2] Who met Samuel's father at a distance from his home and approached him for an immoral purpose, whereupon he fled home by supernatural means.

[3] So cited in *Seder Hadoroth*. Our author, in referring to the source as '*Halachoth Gedoloth on Kidushin*' may have had in mind Asheri on Kiddushin, chap. iv, where the *Halachoth Gedoloth* is quoted. See also *Tos*., Kidd. 73*a*, s.v. מאי, where the story is partially given,

[4] Daughter of the Martyr, R. Hananiah b R.Teradyon, a great personality with a wide knowledge of the Scriptures. The Gemara relates that in the opinion of some, R. Meir ran away to Babylon because of the incident involving Beruriah. Rashi, however, tells the following story: Once Beruriah criticized the Rabbinic view (Kid. 80*b*) that women are light-minded, to which R. Meir replied that one day her own experience would testify to the truth of the Rabbis' words. The day came when she succumbed to the temptation of one of R. Meir's own disciples. Beruriah committed suicide and R. Meir fled from his home for shame.

[5] Gaon of Pumbeditha of the tenth century. In his responsa he deals with questions on religious practices, and also gives expositions and comments on certain passages of the Talmud.

[6] Actually quoted in his famous Epistle, ii, chap. 4.

[7] Ibid. 3*b*. Rashi, ad loc., s.v. בכסף, observes the repetition of the question and suggests that the first question in the Gemara is only casual, which goes to show that the Gaon's view was either unknown or unacceptable to him.

[8] From סבר 'one whose wits are keen'. Scholars of the Babylonian academies in the period immediately following that of the *Amoraim*. The *Saboraim* began their activities at the time which, in the words of the Gemara (B.M. 86*a*) was the 'end of Hora'ha' (Independent decisions from interpretations of the Mishnah). According to R. Sherira in his above-mentioned Epistle, their activities dated from the death of Rabina (500 C.E. approx.) to 589. They are regarded as the final editors of the Talmud.

[9] By R. Hiyya b Ashi in the name of R. Hisda.

[10] In order to dull his senses.

name of R. Robai as from Rab[1] (in our editions it is quoted anonymously)[2] that it is only reasonable that it (the goblet) should be provided from public funds,[3] is also an addition of the *Saboraim* and R. Robai was himself one of them. The same is true of the lesson that R. Gebhah of Argiza learned from the words 'Kinah and Demonah and Adadah',[4] or again the other lesson derived from the words 'Ziklag and Madmenah and Sansanah',[5]—all these are additions of the *Saboraim*.[6]

See *Tosafoth* Keth. 2b[7] for the statement that wherever reference is made in the Gemara to R. Ahai, it is to be understood that he belongs to the *Saboraim*. Most likely, too, wherever Rabbannai is mentioned (as in B.M. 2a)[8] he, too, is one of the *Saboraim*, as is likewise Raba Tosfai who is mentioned in Yeb. 80b.

Maimonides, in his *Commentary on the Mishna* (Zabim 4, 6), observes that the deduction made in the Gemara (Nid. 4b) from the words 'the sound of a rustling (nidaf) leaf'[9] that *Maddaf*[10] denotes a slight contact, is an addition from the *Saboraim*. See also Rashi (Yoma 62b, s.v. ומוספים) where he suggests an alternative reading on the ground

---

[1] On the identity of R. Robai see Halevi, *Doroth* III, chap. xiv, where the matter is discussed at great length and where light is thrown on many points which Graetz regards as obscure.

[2] It is, however, quoted in his name by R. Hananel (commentator on the greater part of the Talmud (990–1050), ad loc.

[3] In case the noblewomen of Jerusalem did not donate it, as recorded in the *Baraitha* (ibid.).

[4] Josh. xv, 22, viz., 'That if anyone has cause for indignation (Kinah) against his neighbour, and yet remains silent (domem) God who abides for all eternity will defend his cause.

[5] Ibid. xv, 31, expounded by R. Aha from (Be) Hozea to the effect that if a man has a just cause for complaint against his neighbour, for depriving him of his (*legima*) livelihood, and yet remains silent (*domem*) God who abides in the sneh (thorn-bush, Ex. III, 2) will defend his cause.

[6] Sherira Gaon, in his Epistle, however, quotes the latter opinion in the name of R. Haha of Hatim. This has escaped our author's observation.

[7] This reference is erroneous and should read Zeb. 102b, s.v. פריך where the *Rashbam*'s view is quoted to the effect that R. Ahai was one of the *Saboraim*. In the *Tosafot* referred to by the author, this view of the *Rashbam* is refuted and the view upheld that he was one of the *Amoraim*. Halevi, *Doroth* III, chap. xxiii, rightly suggests the deletion, after R. Ahai, of the words 'the author of the Sheiltoth quoted by the said *Tosafoth* in the name of the *Rashbam*' since the suggestion that it refers to R. Ahai the author of the *Sheiltoth* would be absolutely untenable in the light of known chronological facts, as the said R. Ahai, author of the *Sheiltoth*, lived three hundred years after the completion of the Talmud.

[8] Also ibid. 27a, v. the *Bach* (R. Joel Sirkes), so well known because of his *Bait Hadash* on *The Turim* (1561–1640) and the *Rashal* (Novellae) on the Talmud by R. Solomon Luria (1510–1563) on B.M. 2, quoting Rabina. Halpern, *Seder Hadoroth*, suggests R. Bannai as the source.

[9] Lev. xxvi, 36.

[10] Quoted in Parah 10, 1, and denoting a slight or indirect contact with the sources of defilement enumerated in Lev. xv, 2–25.

that the present version only originated with the scholars of the
tarbitza[1] (school-hall); and, according also to Tos. Men. 82*b*, s.v.
ובתרביצא he views of these scholars were added to the Gemara by
later Rabbis.

In particular I found a case in *Ritba* on B.M. where he suggests that
several of the discussions dealt with in Tractate Baba Metzia were
additions coming from R. Yehudai Gaon.[2]

A similar suggestion is advanced in *Shittah Mekubetzeth*[3] on B.M., viz.
that more than ten discussions in the tractate are additions from R.
Yehudai Gaon. See Ritba, Novellae on B.M., fol. 3*b*, where we read
that the passage beginning בין לרבן[4] down to the paragraph which
begins תניר' חייא did not originally form part of the Gemara but that
its author was R. Yehudai Gaon, and that it was interpolated into the
Talmud by later authorities, and that there are several similar additions
in that tractate.

Another similar instance is given in the same work on B.M. 15*b* where
we read that the paragraph in the *Gemara* which begins with 'But
whether we take the view of Rab or that of Samuel how does he (the
buyer) go down to the field?'[5] is an addition from Yehudai, as is also
the paragraph in B.M. 19*b* beginning 'One law refers to a gift made
by a healthy person and the other refers to a gift made by a dying
person', and there are, it is claimed again, several other similar additions.[6] See, too, *Maharsha*[7] *Hiddushe Aggadoth* on Taan. 25*a* who suggests
that the passage beginning, 'Whence did R. Hanina b Dosa get goats,
etc.'[8] down to the words 'They brought bears on their horns' is not part

[1] Derived from רבץ lie down, repose (cf. Gen. XLIX, 9; Cant. I, 7; Ps. XXIII, 2).
In Talmudical language it is also employed for 'spreading learning', in view of the
custom followed by the students of that time, of reposing on the floor while receiving
the lesson from their teacher. See Kohut, Aruch, s.v. רבץ II. It is used further for
the sprinkling of water to lay the dust (v. Mach. 3, 4; Sab. 95*a*). Hence the employ-
ment of תרביצא for (1) a garden near a house which is maintained by the sprinkling
of water; (2) a school-hall or house from which learning spreads or the places which
the students used during the heat when they could not remain indoors. See Rashi,
Taan. 6*b*, s.v. איכא דאמרי, Ber. 57*a*, s.v. אגם.

[2] Ben Mar R. Nahman 760 C.E.

[3] See p. 31, note 1.

[4] Dealing with the rival views of the Sages and R. Jose in regard to the *halachah* in
a case where two persons have deposited certain amounts with a third person, one
a smaller amount, the other a larger, and each depositor claims to have deposited the
larger amount; v. B.M. 37*a*.

[5] Referring to a dispute over a case where a man has bought a field knowing that it
did not belong to the man who sold it.

[6] These suggestions are quoted in *Shittah Mekubetzeth* on the authority of *Ritba*.

[7] The initials of *Morenu Harab R. Samuel Edels*, famous talmudist (1555–1631).

[8] In connection with the legend quoted in the Gemara of R. Hanina b Dosa's
goats which were alleged to have done damage, where R. Hanina proposed to test
the truth or otherwise of the allegation by suggesting that either the bears might

of the original Gemara text. This suggestion is also favoured by R. Isaiah Berlin in his marginal glosses ad loc.

Again I have pointed out that the text in Ber. 4*b*[1] which reads 'And why do the Rabbis mention the death penalty in this case of disobedience to their words and not elsewhere?', was not the version in the Gemara which belonged to R. Jonah Gerondi[2] since he raises this question in his commentary on Alfasi, ad loc., on his own authority (and not on the basis of the Gemara), as was early observed by the author of '*Lehem Hammudoth*'.[3]

Again it appears to me that the question, raised in Hul. 63*a*, regarding the Scriptural authority for the number of the unclean birds (unfit for food) as twenty-four in all, which runs as follows: 'If it is derived from *Vayyikra*,[4] only twenty are enumerated in that book', is a later addition, because during Talmudic times the third book of the Pentateuch was never referred to as *Vayyikra* but always as *Torath Cohanim*.[5] Scholars have also noted in Aruch[6], s.v. נִמְזוֹ[7] where an additional reason is given for the name *Gam-zu*,[8] that he fails to give the Gemara (Taanith 21*a*) as the source for this reason. It is to be presumed, therefore, that this version of the *aggadah* was not embodied in the edition of the Talmud which belonged to R. Nathan, the author of the Aruch.[9]

---

devour them or they might bring the bears home in the evening on their horns. The latter took place.

[1] With reference to the time-limit fixed by the Rabbis in the M. Ber. 1 for the reading of the *Shema* (Deut. VI, 4–9): 'The obligation for the reading should actually be extended to the dawn, but in order to prevent man from neglecting it, the Rabbis have limited it to the time before midnight'.

[2] Rabbi of Toledo (d. 1263) compiler of *Hiddushim* (Novellae) to Alfasi, which were written by several of his pupils. The commentary therefore is called either Rabbenu Jonah or Talmide R. Jonah, in abbreviation תל״ר. Originally these covered the entire work of Alfasi, but only the portion of Berachoth has been preserved.

[3] A commentary on Asheri by R. Yom Tob Lippmann Heller, the author of *Tosafoth Yom Tob* on the Mishnah.

[4] The opening Hebrew word of the Book of Leviticus. See Lev. XI, 13–23, for the laws of the clean and unclean birds.

[5] Lit. The Law of the Priests, i.e. the book which describes the function of the Priesthood.

[6] Classic Talmudic dictionary by the famous Talmudic lexicographer, R. Nathan b Jehiel of the eleventh century.

[7] Referring to Nahum Ish-Gamza (or Gimzo), a *Tanna* of the second generation (first century C.E.).

[8] Besides the explanation that גַם זוֹ is actually one word pronounced Gamzo or Gimzo, and is the name of his native place (cf. 2 Ch. XXVIII, 8), R. Nathan quotes the view, on the authority of R. Nisim Gaon, that the words גַם זוֹ (lit. this also) refer to the expression which Nahum was wont to use on all occasions, no matter how critical 'This also (*gam-zu*) will be for the best'.

[9] Kohut, *Aruch Completum*, ad loc., calls attention to the error of some copyists of the *Aruch* who have deleted this passage on the ground that this very reason is advanced in the Gemara itself. This was unnecessary since it is very likely that the

Again, I have found a use in the *aggadah* of the Talmud of the term *Machzor* (large) cycle[1] (Ber. 59b) to denote the full revolution of the sun in a circle so that it returns to its original place at a set time (after a period of twenty-eight years). This use of the word originates with the later Hillel[2] who lived after the conclusion of the Talmud[3]; see Ramban[4] in his critical glosses on Sefer Hamitzvoth[5] (Mitzvah 153). From these facts as here elucidated we may conclude that some further *aggadoth* may have been added by the later teachers probably drawn from *aggadic* books compiled by the *Saboraim* and *Geonim*. But even if that is granted, we yet regard these additions as reliable and sacred teaching, and we are solemnly bound to elucidate them in every possible way, because even the teachings of the *Geonim* carry the authority of tradition, especially as it is most natural to assume that they were added to the Talmud from *aggadic* books which were compiled much earlier than the conclusion of the Talmud, and that the redactors of the Talmud had not managed to incorporate them in it. Yet even so we have the advantage of having preserved for us the clear order of sequence in which the Talmud was originally compiled and edited.

fuller version of the *aggadah* was not embodied in the text of the Talmud of R. Nisim or R. Nathan. See also Kohut's Introduction, xxxii, on this point.

[1] With reference to the blessing of the Sun which is to be recited on the day when the sun enters upon a new cycle, i.e. every twenty-eight years.

[2] Hillel the second, son and successor of Judah III, 330–365 c.e. He was the first to publish in 359 c.e. the rules for the computation of the calendar, which had been hitherto regarded as a secret science.

[3] This statement is sweeping, and needs elucidation, as the Babylonian Talmud was concluded *ca.* 500 c.e., while the publication of the Calendar regulations by Hillel took place in 359 c.e. It is, however, probable that Hillel lived after the close of the Palestinian Talmud, and it is in view of this that Halevi, *Doroth* II, 394, maintains that his name is never mentioned in the Jerusalem Talmud. According to J.E. IV, 400, s.v. Hillel II the latter is mentioned twice in the Jerusalem Talmud in connection with *halachoth*, viz. in Jer. Ber. II, 5, and Jer. Ter. I, 4. This statement, however, has no authority, for the references may not be to Hillel II at all, since he would not naturally be called Rabbi Hillel, a designation not elsewhere used for the sage in question, and indeed there were many other Hillels (see *Seder Hadoroth*, s.v. ר' הילל). Actually the method of computing the Calendar by calculation began years before Hillel, as can be proved from Abaye's statement in Betza 4b, where he refers to a message received from Palestine saying, 'although we are well acquainted with the Calendar calculations, yet we should not depart from the ancestral custom of observing two days,' and, as is known, Abaye died 339 c.e., thirty years before Hillel's promulgation of the Calendar. However, Hillel might have been in possession of details which were not known before, and since Abaye is also quoted here (Ber. 59b) as giving the length of the period that must elapse before the blessing of the sun is to be recited as 28 years, we may assume that the other details which follow, viz. about the *Machzor* (long cycle), may be an addition of a later date, following upon Hillel's publication of the computation of the Calendar. This is the only feasible explanation.

[4] See p. 23, note 1.

[5] By Maimonides, a work which the author presented as a basis for his *halachic* work, deducing the 613 commandments from 14 roots.

We see that the subject-matter in the Talmud is well arranged and that there is a well-reasoned relationship between the various statements which are successively adduced. I have furnished examples of this in my Glosses to the Talmud. See, for instance, Ber. 9*b*, where the *aggadah* that Elijah in praying for fire from heaven, said: 'Answer me in order that they may not think that it is a work of sorcery,'[1] is quoted as a natural sequence to the *aggadah* immediately preceding it, viz. 'that the righteous one (Abraham) may not think that', etc.[2] And see Rashi, Ber. 10*a*, s.v. מאי דכתיב (where he says of the whole *aggadah* on Hezekiah and Isaiah there quoted, that it is inserted only because of its concluding part which refers to Hezekiah's diligence in reciting the *tefillah*—eighteen benedictions—immediately following the *Ge'ulah*).[3] Another example is in Ber. 14*a* where one of the school of R. Ami put a question to R. Ami whether a man who is in duty bound to fast (is permitted to take a mere taste). This subject has no connection with the subject under discussion except for the fact that it is preceded by another question put to R. Hiyya by a member of his school.[4] Similarly the *aggadoth* in Git. 6*b* and 7*a* were so arranged merely by reason of some such similarity between them.[5] Even where the similarity is only in the meaning of a word they arranged the passages together, as in the following instance: A question is raised in Git. 36*b*, as to the meaning of the word '*ulbanah*'[6] (insult or inconvenience), and this is followed by the *aggadic baraithah*, 'They who suffer insults[7] (ne'elabin), but do not offer insults, etc.'

On the other hand several *aggadoth*, such as those which serve as the opening words to the Midrash on Esther, or the *aggadah* of Git. 68*b* which begins with the words 'For a rush of blood to the head the

[1] Although at the outset this *aggadah* is seemingly out of context.
[2] Moses was instructed (Ex. XI, 2) to acquire silver and golden vessels from the Egyptians, so that Abraham should not think that one half of the decree (Gen. xv, 14) 'They will make them serve', was fulfilled, and the second half 'They will go out with a great substance', was unfulfilled. The connecting link between the two *aggadoth* is the use of the phrase 'shall not think'.
[3] A prayer for redemption which precedes the *amidah* (eighteen benedictions).
[4] i.e. they found it natural to refer *en passant* to a different question put by a member of another school to his master.
[5] As, for example, Rab Hisda's warning against the terrorizing of one's household is followed by R. Judah's threats regarding the consequences of such terrorizing, and this by Rabba b bar Hannah's saying that the three things which are to be said to a household before the Sabbath commences should be said gently in order not to terrorize them; and this again is followed by the words of R. Abahu who gives a further warning against the terrorizing of one's household.
[6] Used with reference to the institution of Prosbol (see p. 89, note 1), which the rabbis call an ulbanah of the judges.
[7] Viz. an assumption of power or a submission, i.e. submission to a law of which at heart they disapprove (Jast. s.v. עולבנא).

remedy is', etc., have not the slightest connection with the subject
which precedes them. Indeed the style and the general run of the
passage indicates that it has been interpolated from some other context,
yet in every case where the passage is associated with an *Amora*, it is
clear that it was incorporated in the Talmud before the close of its
redaction. Thus, for example, in Git. 55*b*, R. Johanan says 'What does
the verse "Happy is the man that feareth continually"[1] denote?"[2] etc.,
which saying has a close association with (R. Assi's reference) made
previously to three successive decrees issued by the Roman Government.[3] Indeed, very much can be written on this subject but this is not
the place to do so.

[1] Prov. xxviii, 14.
[2] The passage goes on to relate elaborately and in detail several tragic incidents in
connection with the Judeo-Roman war (70 c.e.).
[3]   (i) Whosoever spares the life of a Jew, shall himself be killed.
      (ii) Whosoever kills a Jew shall pay a fine.
      (iii) Whosoever kills a Jew shall himself be put to death.

CHAPTER XXXII

THE CONTRADICTORY VIEWS REGARDING THE *AGGADAH* AND ITS PLACE IN TALMUDIC TEACHING

Before concluding the study of this subject I think it opportune to attempt to offer a number of observations which may serve to straighten out some views advanced by the Rabbis on the *aggadah* which appear at first sight to be contradictory of one another, since in some instances they express themselves in favour of *aggadah*, in others most unfavourably. Take, as examples, the following illustrations: In *Sifre*, Section Ekev,[1] they say in its favour, 'If you wish to know Him by Whose word the world came into being, study *aggadah*, through which you will come to know Him'; whereas in Hag. 14*a* we read on the contrary (a retort like the following made by R. Eleazar to R. Akiba): 'Akiba, what have you to do with *aggadah*? Confine yourself to (the exegesis of the laws concerning defilement contained in) *Nega'im* and *Oholoth*'.[2] See also Jer. Maas. III, where R. Zera is quoted as sharply criticizing the Aggadists and as comparing their books to those of the sorcerers.[3] In particular we find R. Joshua b Levi's[4] views of the *aggadah* and its usefulness most contradictory. On the one hand we find him expressing the highest opinion of the *aggadoth* and explaining, for instance, the words 'Because they regard not the works of the Lord'[5] as referring to the *aggadoth* (Mid. *Tehilim* 28, 5).[6] And indeed he himself

[1] Deut. VII, 8. See *Yalkut Shimoni* on Deut. VIII. This saying is quoted in the *Sifre* anonymously, as coming from the *Doreshei Reshumoth*, those who interpret the law metaphorically.

[2] These two tractates dealing with the laws of defilement are regarded as the most intricate in the section *Taharoth* of the Mishnah. This retort indicates that the *aggadah* was regarded as intellectually inferior to the *halachah*; and that R. Akiba, an intellectual giant in *halachah*, should not, in R. Eleazar's opinion, spend his time upon a subject of less importance.

[3] Heb. קוסמין. There are variants of this word. Some read קיסמין (chips, fragments), others קיטמא (ashes). The first, however, is the more likely, in view of the fact that the *aggadoth* included charms, incantations, etc., which were an alien growth in *aggadic* literature.

[4] Palestinian *Amora* of the early part of the third century. A contemporary of R. Johanan and Resh Lakish.

[5] Ps. XXVIII, 5.

[6] See also B.B. 10*a* where he interprets the term 'glory' in the passage 'The wise shall inherit glory' (Prov. III, 35) as referring to the *aggadists*.

was eulogized by the rabbis as an *aggadist* (B.K. 55*a*,[1] Ber. 10*a*).[2] But this seems irreconcilable with the passage in Jer. Shab. 16, 1, where he pronounces severe strictures on the man who writes down *aggadah*, saying that 'he has no share in the world to come' and again, 'He who expounds *aggadah* ought to be banned[3] and he who listens to *aggadah* will receive no reward'; and there he continues as follows: 'I have never in my life looked into the *aggadic* books, save once, and I am still troubled by nervousness at night about this misdeed.' Eminent authors had already noted these contradictions, such as the author of *Mateh Mosheh*[4] in his Introduction to the work, and the author of *Me'or Enaim*, chap. xv, section *Imre Binah*, and still earlier Radbaz[5] in his Responsa. In my own Novellae on B.K. 52*b*, published in the Vienna edition of the Talmud, I referred briefly to this problem and said that although R. Joshua had indeed praised the study of the *aggadoth*, i.e. their contents and subject-matter, he was against committing the *aggadoth* to writing, in view of the law laid down (Tem. 14*b*; Git. 60*b*) that words transmitted orally may not be recited from writing; consequently, he said, whoever commits the *aggadah* to writing has no share in the world to come. Similarly, whosoever expounds written *aggadah*[6] or listens to others so expounding it is, as pointed out by the Commentator *Yefeh Mar'eh*, ad loc.,[7] indicated thereby as one who will receive no reward because to record them in writing was forbidden, according to the above principle that oral teachings must not be written down. On the other hand the *aggadoth* which had been transmitted orally were not only not disparaged in themselves by R. Joshua b Levi, but, on the contrary, were held by him in high regard for their importance as inculcating lofty ideals, since they deal not only with the legal obligation of observing and practising the commandments of the Torah, but with the acquisition by man of ethical ideas and laudable virtues; yet notwithstanding

[1] Where R. Hiyya b Aba referred R. Hanina b Agil for information in *aggadah* to R. Tanhum as an intimate of R. Joshua b Levi, who was an expert in *aggadah*.

[2] Where it is stated that R. Shimi b Ukbah had edited the *aggadoth* before R. Joshua b Levi.

[3] The Talmudic text reads: מתחרך (gets charred thereby). It has, however, been suggested that we should adopt the more likely reading: מתברך, a euphemism for 'to be blamed', i.e. banned. Cf. Job. II, 3.

[4] A liturgical work by R. Moses b. Abraham, Rabbi of Premisla (Poland), of the sixteenth century and disciple of R. Solomon Luria, the most renowned Talmudist of the age.

[5] The abbreviation of R. David ben Zimra or Zamiro, Spanish Talmudist and Cabbalist (1479–1559).

[6] In fact, referring to the same text in Soferim 16, 2, he reads אגדתא כתובה (written *aggadah*).

[7] Novellae on the Jer. Aggadoth by R. Samuel Jaffa Ashkenazi (Constantinople), a contemporary of R. Yom Tob Zahalon (Safed), 1557–1638, with whom he corresponded on a most difficult halachic problem (Zahalon Responsa, N. 40).

all this importance attaching to them, R. Joshua b Levi did not approve of giving them precedence over the *halachah* by committing them to writing, since the prohibition against committing to writing orally transmitted laws still prevailed. Indeed, that prohibition against recording the fixed *halachoth* and the well-established principles of *halachic* decisions was not relaxed even during the Amoraic period, as will be explained later. Therefore, according to the view of R. Joshua b Levi, the *aggadoth* also must remain restricted to oral transmission, and must not be recorded in books.[1]

It appears, however, that this warning was not heeded by the people, since *aggadoth* were found recorded in books in the early days. See Git. 60a where we read that R. Johanan and Resh Lakish were studying books of the *aggadah* on the Sabbath Day because of (the Scriptural words) 'when it is a time to work for the Lord they break Thy Law'.[2] Now the discussion there is only over the permissibility or otherwise of studying them on the Sabbath[3] on the ground that it might have the appearance of reading secular documents[4] on the Sabbath, whereas the question of the writing down of *aggadoth* in itself does not form any part of the discussion, since scholars were already accustomed to record them, even prior to the days of R. Johanan and Resh Lakish, as we find

[1] See Sab. 156a where an *aggadah* is quoted from a notebook of R. Joshua b Levi. This appears to clash with his own attitude and strong views regarding the commitment of the *aggadoth* to writing. Weiss, *Dor* III, 59, suggests that the derogatory remarks about the writers of the *aggadah* must be ascribed to another *Amora* of the same name. He finds support for this assumption in a reference to R. Jose Patiras, in Jer. M.K. 3, 5, as the father-in-law of R. Joshua b. Levi קדמייא (lit. first). This word קדמייא is commonly explained as indicating that he married twice and that Ben Patiras was his first father-in-law; but why not say, argues Weiss, that the word is used to distinguish this R. Joshua as the first of the name from the one who lived at a later period? There is also another view that, since in the time of R. Joshua b Levi sectarians had increased in number, and so many *aggadic* interpretations alien to the spirit of Israel had crept into the *aggadoth*, it was only against the perpetuation of this particular sort of *aggadoth* that R. Joshua b Levi had warned his contemporaries (see *Otzar Israel* I, p. 108, and v, p. 88). Our author enlarges on this point further on in this chapter.

[2] Ps. cxix, 126, their interpretation of the verse being 'It is a time to work for the Lord, for they have broken Thy Commandments', i.e. they took it to mean that although writing was not permissible, they could not dispense with committing it to writing since the *Aggadah* might otherwise be forgotten.

[3] Since the contention of the Gemara that the *aggadah* was not meant to be written down, is put forward not in virtue of a prohibition to do so, for the actual prohibition refers to *halachoth* only (see Git. 60b), but in virtue of another ruling, that they belong to the category of books which may not be saved on the Sabbath day (see Sab. 115a) and consequently may not be read or carried on that day, according to the principle that an article which may not be used may not be carried. Later, however, when the *aggadah* was threatened with oblivion, its writing could no longer be dispensed with (see the Novellae of our author on Git. 60b).

[4] See Sab. 116b. This, however, is the author's own view, and I can find no direct support for it in the Gemara text.

it recorded, for example, in the Jer. Kil. 9, 3, and Jer. Keth. 12, 3, and in Gen. R., chap. 33, that R. Hiyya[1] did not rise in the presence of Rabbi the Holy,[2] because his mind was at the time occupied with the study of the book of *aggadoth* on Psalms. We note, therefore, that at the time of Rabbi and R. Hiyya, the *aggadoth* were already recorded in book form. Similarly we read in San. 57*b*, and in Genesis R., Section Bereshit[3] that Jacob (b Aha) found written in the book of the *aggadah* of the school of Rab that a Noahite (heathen) may be executed on the decision of a single judge[4] and on the testimony of a single witness.[5] We thus see that the *aggadoth* of the School of Rab had been recorded in a book, and since Noahite precepts are not adduced for the purpose of arriving at judicial decisions, they were regarded as of the *aggadic* class, and therefore included in the *aggadoth* of the School of the Rab.[6]

I can also produce some novel material from the Talmud and Midrash, showing how the Rabbis made use of the *aggadic* books to interpret the meaning of certain words in their vocabulary (giving the impression that those books were already well known), as, for example, the statement in Shab. 80*b* 'Or if you like I may say that *andifa* means the forehead, as in the passage where we read of a certain Galilean that, when he was lecturing (on the passage relating to the Chariot)[7] a wasp came off the wall and stung him on the *andifa* (forehead).'[8] Obviously

---

[1] The reference is to R. Hiyya Bar Abba surnamed Rabbah (the Great or the Elder), a Palestinian *Tanna* of the second century, not to be confused with the Palestinian *Amora* of the same name, who lived at the end of the third century.

[2] This is an unfortunate error, for it should be R. Ishmael b R. Jose (Rabbi's contemporary). The incident is as follows: Rabbi the master praised his pupil R. Ishmael as a great and pious man. Once the latter entered the bath-house where he met R. Hiyya who treated him so indifferently that he was prompted to mention the fact to Rabbi. The latter inquired for the reason of R. Hiyya, who ascribed his indifference to R. Ishmael's presence to the fact of his being, at that moment, deeply occupied with the study of the *aggadah* on Psalms.

[3] The fact is not to be found in Gen. R.

[4] As opposed to the general law that a charge involving the extreme penalty must be tried by a court of twenty-three judges (M. San. 4, 1).

[5] See Deut. XVII, 6, for the Scriptural law requiring not less than two witnesses in civil and criminal cases. Our author has inadvertently reversed the order of judge and witnesses.

[6] Weiss, *Dor*, III, p. 158, suggests that all laws relating to the Noahites had been collected, and to distinguish them from the specifically Jewish laws, the Rabbis named the collection the '*Book of Aggadah*'.

[7] The first chapter of Ezekiel which deals with the heavenly chariot.

[8] The details of this incident are as follows: The Galilean was a chance visitor in Babylon, who having been requested to lecture on the chapter relating to the Chariot, said to his audience: 'I will lecture to you as R. Nehemiah lectured to his companions.' But since such a subject was not allowed to be lectured on publicly, but restricted to those who had been initiated and were therefore fit for it, he was the victim of a sting which had fatal results.

the proof advanced by the Gemara has no validity[1] unless we assume that the lecture given by the Galilean was upon a well-known *aggadah* recorded in writing, for the Gemara produces its proof for the translation of *andifa* as forehead from the fact that in the *aggadah* book *andifa* was so translated. (I believe that this argument was made known to me some time ago by a certain scholar.)[2]

Another scholar has called my attention to the Midrash, Ex. R., chap. iii, where a written *aggadah* is quoted as follows: 'Not the serpent kills, but the sin kills, as is recorded in the story of R. Hanina b Dosa'.[3] One could dispute the adequacy of this proof, since the passage might refer to a similar *aggadah* which had been transmitted orally and was familiar to everyone, like the story of R. Hanina b Dosa and the wild ass quoted with commentary in Jer. Ber. 5,[4] and quoted more briefly in the Babylonian Talmud (Ber. 33*a*), particularly as we know Exodus R. to be one of the later, not one of the earlier, Midrashim.[5] I shall, therefore, offer a clearer and more adequate proof from the Midrash Gen. Rabba, chap. lxxiii, on the verse 'And Jacob fed the rest of Laban's flock'.[6] Resh Lakish says this means the defective amongst them, the sickly amongst them, the word הנותרות[7] being interpreted like the word ונתור found as part of an *aggadah* in Hul. 59*b*[8] in the phrase ונתור שינא (meaning 'fell out'). Hence we see that the Midrash

[1] For there is nothing to prove that the term *andifa* referred to in the story signifies 'forehead', unless the incident was recorded in writing and such was the interpretation attached to the word in the record.

[2] Assumed to be Nachman Krochmal with whom Chajes had scholarly exchanges of view. See p. 85, note 1.

[3] In a remarkable way he killed a dangerous wild ass which had injured several people and carried its carcass on his shoulders into the school-house saying 'it is not the wild ass that kills, but it is the sin that kills' (Ber. 33*b*). This proves that the *aggadah* had been committed to writing and was known to the Midrashic teachers.

[4] The story in the Palestinian Talmud is slightly different, to the effect that the wild ass had attacked R. Hanina b Dosa whilst he stood in prayer, and he did not move, in accordance with the ruling of *Mishnah* (Ber. v, 11) that 'even though a snake twist round his heel, he must not interrupt his prayer'. After he had finished his prayer, he found the wild ass dead at the entrance of its hiding place, whereupon he exclaimed, etc.

[5] The earliest one is *Bereshith Rabbah*; according to Zunz, *Gottesdienstliche Vorträge des Judentums*, the Midrash to Exodus is separated from it by five hundred years (see also J.E. viii, p. 562).

[6] Gen. xxx, 36.

[7] Which is derived from יתר left over.

[8] When the Roman Emperor asked R. Joshua b Hananiah to explain what sort of greatness was ascribed to Israel by its being compared to a lion, and insisted upon his showing him the special lion to which they were compared, the lion in question gave a roar which caused the teeth of everyone present to fall out. It may be noted that, whilst in the Midrash Caesar is mentioned as having been thus affected, in the Gemara it is stated that Caesar himself fell off his throne and the teeth of everyone else fell out.

brings proof of its interpretation of the Biblical word from another word which the Rabbis used in an *aggadah* elsewhere. That *aggadah* was so familiar that it served as a source for both the Babylonian Talmudical teachers and the Palestinian compilers of the Midrash.[1] At all events one should note the expression 'as thou sayest' employed by the Midrash in reference to this *aggadah*, an expression used only when they are about to quote a Scriptural passage in support. In many cases we can see that the *aggadah* had already been committed to writing in the days of the early teachers.

If this conclusion is correct one might wonder why the Gemara (Tem. 14*a*) should raise an objection against R. Dimi[2] for having indited a letter on an *halachic* subject—an objection based on the dictum that those who write down *halachoth* may be compared to those who burn the Torah,[3] and on the further dictum 'These[4] thou mayest write, but thou mayest not write words transmitted orally'. But surely the interdiction to record subjects orally transmitted[5] had been relaxed for generations before this time. It is clear, however, that only *aggadic* subjects were so committed to writing lest they might be forgotten, according to the statement of the Jer. Ber. 37*b*, 'A covenant[6] has been concluded that he who studies *aggadah* by means of the written book is not likely to forget it so quickly.' The writing down of *halachoth*, however, was still prohibited in his time as before. These were studied only by word of mouth; and it was only at a later period[7] that *halachoth* were normally reduced to writing. Thus the objection raised in the Tract.

---

[1] The generally accepted opinion is that R. Hoshaia, the Palestinian Amora of the first generation, was the author of *Bereshit R.* See the Novellae of the author on Tos. Git. 60*a*, s.v. אתמוהי where he states that the Midrash Ex. R. had not as yet been compiled at the time of the Tosafists (the twelfth and thirteenth centuries).

[2] And not R. Zerah, as erroneously given in the text. R. Dimi was an *Amora* of the fourth century who was wont to carry *halachic* messages between Palestine and Babylon. In the case in question he had found an *halachah* in support of a view different to one held by R. Joseph, and looked for someone to carry the information by letter to R. Joseph.

[3] Rashi advances two reasons for this analogy. (1) These 'writings' would not be allowed to be saved from burning on the Sabbath day by removing them from one domain to another (see Shab. 16, 1); (2) they may not be preserved, but must be destroyed by burning.

[4] i.e. the words of the written Torah.

[5] As, for example, the *Megillath Taanith* (record of the days of the year on which fasting and mourning were forbidden) was in a written form. See Erub. 62*b*, 'The Scroll of Fast Days which is written,' and also Sab. 13*b*. Its authorship goes back to the first century.

[6] This is an idiomatic expression to describe an established belief.

[7] Scholars are at variance over the actual date when the *halachic* material of the oral laws was committed to writing. Cf. in this connection Melziner, *Introduction to the Talmud*, pp. 5 et seq., for the origin of the objection to writing down the material of the oral laws and interpretations. See also J.E. ix, p. 426.

Temurah (against R. Dimi for writing down an *halachah* in a letter) was quite justified in view of the fact that the interdiction against committing *halachoth* to writing was still in force at the time. And as regards the *baraitha* attributed to R. Jose the Galilean and quoted in *Halachoth Gedoloth*[1] on the laws of *Hesped*[2] to the effect that the words 'Where is the receiver, where is the Scribe'[3] refer to the scribes of the Midrash and *halachoth* who are due to receive their reward, this would show that as far back as the days of R. Jose the Galilean who preceded by a whole generation the close of the Mishnah by R. Judah ha-Nasi[4] *halachoth* had already been committed to writing. It should be explained that the phrase *scribe of halachoth* refers to those *halachoth* which are contained in the *Megillath Setarim* (concealed scrolls). On this collection, see Rashi on Sab. 6*b*, and B.M. 92*a*,[5] according to whom the *Tannaim* were accustomed to write *halachoth* in scrolls and hide them. Similarly we find that several scholars, such as Levi, Zeiri, and Ilfa, made brief *halachic* notes in their diaries among their business records (see Shab. 156*a* and Men. 70*a*).[6] Furthermore it appears that a copyist's error has crept into the text of the *Baraitha* in question as quoted by *Halachoth Gedoloth*. The *Baraitha* comes originally from the Midrash on Prov. XVI, and there the reading is 'students of the Midrash and *aggadoth*', and not 'scribes of *halachoth*' as quoted above. At all events we have shown that, in the days of Rabbi and R. Hiyya, the scholars had already begun to commit the *aggadoth* to writing, whilst R. Johanan and R. Simon b Lakish went further by reading them even on the Sabbath day, and in so doing making clear that they regarded them as holy writings, and not on the level of secular documents which are forbidden to be studied on the Sabbath Day.

With regard to the objection raised by the Talmud (Git. 60*a*) that they were not intended to be written, at first sight this seems irreconcilable with our definite conclusion that *aggadoth* were committed to writing in earlier times. But this objection was not raised on the ground of the prohibition that things which were orally transmitted must not be written down since, in fact, from this standpoint, *aggadah* would not be included in that category at all, as *aggadoth* are not reckoned as material

---

[1] Written by R. Simon of Cairo who settled in Babylonia during the second half of the eighth century. Others believe the author to have been R. Yehudai Gaon, who wrote the *Halachoth Pesukoth*, but most historians incline to the former opinion.

[2] Orations for the dead.

[3] Is. XXXIII, 18. The word *sofer* in Aramaic has the connotation of 'teacher'. See Targum O. to Gen. XLIX, 10.

[4] R. Judah ha-Nasi lived from 135–200 C.E.

[5] Also Rashi Shab. 96*b*, s.v. מגילת.

[6] These two sources mention only Levi and Ilfa. I have not been able to trace the source for Zeiri.

orally transmitted; and besides, the Gemara (ibid.)[1] expressly states 'These thou mayest write, but thou mayest not write *halachoth*', thus making it clear that it is only to *halachoth* that the interdiction applies and not to *aggadoth*. But the above objection was raised on the basis of another prohibition which rests on the ruling that they (*the aggadoth*) do not belong to those writings which would be permitted to be saved on the Sabbath from burning,[2] and one who writes them down is consequently compared to those who burn the Torah.[3] It was for this reason that the prohibition of writing applied also to the *aggadoth*. And since they are subject to this prohibition their reading is also forbidden on the Sabbath, because they had been written without permission, and being such they are regarded as though they had never been written at all. See Tos. Sab. 115a. s.v. לא where corroboration is given by R. Porath.[4] So also we find that R. Hiyya studied the *aggadah* on the Psalms[5] at the bath-house because he did not regard it as invested with special holiness, since it had been committed to writing without permission, on the ground mentioned above that they did not belong to those writings which may be saved (on the Sabbath) from a fire and that, therefore, whoever writes them down is compared to those who burn the Torah.

Again, the reason why R. Johanan and Resh Lakish read them even on the Sabbath was on the ground of the Scriptural passage 'When it is a time to work for the Lord, they break (Thy Torah)',[6] for there was already a binding covenant[7] that an *aggadah* recorded in writing would not easily be forgotten, whereas the writing of *halachic* material remained prohibited, and the halachah was studied only orally. In this way the apparent contradiction in R. Joshua b. Levi's views on the *aggadah* is cleared up. That is, although he expressed words of praise for the *aggadoth*, saying that through them one came to know Him by Whose word the world had come into being, yet it was not right, in his view, to reduce them to writing; and of those who wrote them down, he said 'he who commits the *aggadah* to writing has no share in the world to

---

[1] On the authority of the *Tanna* of the School of R. Ishmael.

[2] See Sab. 115a.

[3] See Tem. 14b and Rashi, s.v. כשורפי.

[4] Who says that in view of the fact that the writing down of such matter was not permissible, its reading on the Sabbath was also not permitted, because the writing is as though it was non-existent and the reading of the matter consequently is done orally, a view which involves the principle that written material ought not to be quoted orally. The logic of this theory is rather strained.

[5] Cf. Sab. 10a for the rule that, in the inner chamber of the bath-house where people stand undressed, the reciting of the *Shema* and *Amidah* is not permitted.

[6] Ps. cxix, 126.

[7] See p. 4, note 3.

come and that he who expounds the *aggadah* will be charred (or banned)'. It was against those who wrote them down that he was angry and he was not satisfied with the action of R. Johanan and Resh Lakish in removing that interdiction. However, he highly esteemed and treasured the *aggadoth* in themselves. As regards the quoting of *aggadoth* from his notebook (mentioned in Sab. 156a and referred to above),[1] the material quoted was not actually of the *aggadah* category, but dealt only with the recording of births, and such material could legitimately be exposed to burning by fire, without rendering the writer liable for such transgression, as in the case of those who burn the Torah.

[1] The fact appeared to clash with his own attitude and strong views against the committing *aggadoth* to writing.

CHAPTER XXXIII

THE DATES OF COMPLETION OF THE MISHNAH AND TALMUD

IT now remains to us to deal with the dates when redactions of the Mishnah and the Talmud were completed.

We all know that a collection of Mishnah was in existence before the time of Rabbi (Judah ha-Nasi).[1] The Rabbis say (Shab. 123b) that the Mishnah there discussed[2] was taught in the days of Nehemiah b Hachaliah. Consequently all the *halachoth* in the *Mishnayoth* of Betza, chap. i, there referred to come from the days of Nehemiah b Hachaliah, early in the era of the Second Temple, when he had been forbidding the removal of utensils on the Sabbath Day. Again (in San. 40a), the *Mishnah* refers to Ben Zakkai examining witnesses as to the stalks of the figs,[3] and the *Gemara* (ibid. 41b)[4] establishes that the said *Mishnah* had been taught at the time when R. Johanan b Zakkai was still a disciple sitting at the feet of his Master,[5] and its position (as recorded before) was not changed (by the editor, R. Judah ha-Nasi). And R. Sherira Gaon in his Epistle[6] already refers to this evidence. Similarly the *halachoth* in the first chapter of Tract. Sab. were compiled at the time when the Rabbis went to visit Hananiah b Hezekiah b Garon (in the upper chamber)[7] as mentioned by me earlier. Another fact quoted as proof by *Hacham Zebi*,[8] Responsum 10, and in the *Sefer Kerithoth*[9] which is re-quoted by R. Jacob Hagiz[10] in his *Etz ha-Hayim* on the Methodology of the Talmud,[11] is the reference made in the last *Mishnah* of Kelim to the

---

[1] *c.* the end of the second century c.e.

[2] Permitting a small number of utensils to be moved on the Sabbath Day, but forbidding all others, see p. 45, note 2.

[3] Of a tree under which the murder was alleged to have been committed.

[4] Where the identification of Ben Zakkai is discussed.

[5] i.e. prior to his ordination. That is why he is referred to as Ben Zakkai, without the title given at ordination.

[6] Part I, chap. iii.

[7] See Sab. 1, 4. See also Frankel, *Darkhei ha-Mishnah* (p. 51) and Halevi, *Doroth* 1, p. 187, with regard to the actual date when this took place.

[8] R. Zebi Hirsch Ashkenazi, Talmudic scholar of the seventeenth century, Rabbi of Amsterdam and Lemberg. The Collection of his responsa is considered very valuable for *halachic* practice.

[9] A methodology of the Talmud by R. Samson of Kinon, French Talmudist of the thirteenth century, one of the greatest Rabbinic authorities of his time.

[10] Palestinian Talmudist who was born at Fez, 1620, and died at Constantinople, 1674; chief opponent of Sabbatai Zebi.

[11] His book on Talmudic Methodology is the *Tehillath Hochmah* mentioned later, whereas the *Etz ha-Hayim* is a treatise on the Mishnah.

words of R. Jose, 'Blessed are thou, O Kelim, for thou didst enter in uncleanness, but hast gone out in cleanness!' This proves that, as far back as the days of R. Jose,[1] the collection of the *Mishnayoth* of *Kelim* was already in existence in the same form as that in which we have them to-day. See also Pes. 57*b* for the statement that Issachar of the village of Barkai had never learned our *Mishnah*[2]; which proves that, although the *Mishnah* in question actually quotes the *halachah* on the authority of R. Simeon,[3] yet it must undoubtedly have been the *Mishnah* of a much earlier age which should have been known even to Issachar of the village of Barkai, who lived during the time of the (Second) Temple.

Another proof can also be furnished from the statement (Yoma 53*b*) that they (his fellow priests) said to the High Priest that he should not make a habit of doing so, that is, reciting lengthy prayers (in the Holy of Holies), for we have learned that he 'should not prolong his prayers'.[4] We see thus that this *Mishnah* was already in its place in the collection as early as the time of the High Priest (in question).

Proof has also been produced from the first *Mishnah* in Pesachim[5] where the question is raised 'why have they said that two rows in a wine vault must be searched?'[6] i.e. the later *Mishnah* as given here only elucidates an earlier one.

In several cases again references are made to an earlier *Mishnah* as opposed to the ruling of the later *Mishnah*.[7] Again the Rabbis (in Yoma 16*a*) say that the authority for (the anonymous *Mishnayoth* in) Middoth[8] is R. Eleazar b Jacob; while in Yoma 14*b* R. Simeon of Mizpah[9]

[1] R. Jose b Halafta, a Palestinian Tanna of the 4th generation, whereas R. Judah ha-Nasi lived a generation later.

[2] He is referred to in connection with the following incident: Once the King Jannæus (Alexander) and his Queen had a dispute as to which meat was better, that of the lamb or that of the kid. The opinion of Issachar, who was then High Priest, was sought; and his view was that if the kid were the better, it and not the lamb would be used for the daily sacrifices. When reference was made to this view, R. Ashi said that Issachar had never learned our Mishnah (i.e. Kerith. 6, 9) where R. Simeon infers from Scriptural verses that the one is as tasty as the other.

[3] R. Simeon bar Yohai, disciple of R. Akiba, in the period following the revolt of Bar Kochba (A.D. 131–135).

[4] Lest he should alarm Israel by his delay in coming out, which might be attributed to a mishap.

[5] Where it is taught that a place to which *hametz* is never brought needs no searching.

[6] Their explanation is that these two rows are a place into which *hametz* might be brought.

[7] See Sanh. 3, 4; Eduy. 7, 2; Git. 5, 6; Naz. 6, 1, for references to *Mishnah Rishonah* (Earlier *Mishnah*). For a full treatment of the subject, see J.E. VIII, p. 610.

[8] Lit. 'measurements', viz. the measurements of the Temple. A treatise in *Kodashim* (hallowed things), the fifth division of the Talmud.

[9] Called thus either because he was a native of Mizpah (town of Benjamin) (Josh. XVIII, 26) or because he was in charge of the watchtower of the Temple (see Jastrow).

is said to be the authority for Tamid.[1] So also we have the statement (Ber. 29a) that on the day of the appointment of R. Eleazar b Azariah as Nasi the tractate Eduyoth[2] was studied. Again we find that the tractate Ukzin[3] had already been compiled by the time of 'R. Simeon b Gamaliel[4] the father of Rabbi (Hor. 13b). See also Tosaf. B.K. 94b, s.v. בימי where it is definitely stated that a written collection of *halachoth* was in existence before the time of Rabbi, and that he only arranged them in order. As support for this statement they quoted the above-mentioned fact that as far back as the days of R. Simeon b Gamaliel the Mishnas of Ukzin were already in existence in various forms. The wording of the following *Baraitha* (Pes. 107b) also proves our contention. 'Even King Agrippa,[5] who normally had a meal every day at the ninth hour of the day, on that day (the eve of Pesach) did not eat (until nightfall).'[6] From the course of the story it appears that this *halachah* was taught during Agrippa's lifetime and the *Tanna* has used his practice as an example. Again, one detects the style of the *Mishnah* of the first chapter in B.K. as being somewhat different from the style in the other chapters, both in the choice of language and the arrangement of the material. The Rabbis have, in the most precise way, called attention to this fact in their observation (B.K. 6b) that 'this *Tanna* of the Mishnah text was a Jerusalemite who preferred a condensed form of expression'. This means to say that the *Mishnah* (in question) was one

He was a contemporary of R. Gamaliel II (cf. Peah 2, 6). This statement denotes that the Tractate Tamid was not edited by Rabbi, the redactor of the *Mishnah*, but had come down from R. Simeon of Mizpah as its compiler.

[1] Lit. continuous. The treatise which deals with the continual or daily offerings, brought morning and evening (Ex. xix, 33-42. Num. xxviii, 1-8).

[2] Lit. 'testimonies' (or 'the choicest', from the Talmudic *Ediyoth*) a tractate (containing selected *halachoth* which usually begin with the words 'So and so testifieth') in *Nezikin*, the fourth of the Orders of the Mishnah.

[3] Lit. 'Stalks'. The tractate deals with the *halachoth* relating to the various parts of the plants, defining which of them are susceptible to uncleanness.

[4] A serious controversy arose between R. Simeon b Gamaliel, who was the Nasi, on the one hand, and R. Meir and R. Nathan, who were the occupants of important offices in the College, the one as *Hakham* (sage), and the other as the *Ab beth-din* (head of the Court), these two offices ranking next to that of the *Nasi*. This controversy led to R. Meir and R. Nathan challenging the *Nasi's* competence in the subject-matter of tractate *Ukzin*. In order to save the Nasi from serious embarrassment, R. Jacob b Karshi, an Amora, went and sat behind the Nasi and repeatedly expounded the Tractate to him, thus acquainting him with its complex contents. The story thus proves that a collection of these *halachoth* had been made a generation before Rabbi.

[5] It is not clear whether this refers to Agrippa I (10 B.C.-44 C.E.) or to Agrippa II (28-100 C.E.). Both were of Edomite descent.

[6] See Pes. 10, 1, where it is taught that on the eve of Passover it is not permissible to eat between the time of the evening offering and nightfall so as not to interfere with the bringing of the Paschal Sacrifice and also in order that the *matza* (unleavened bread) might be eaten with a good appetite.

of the earlier *Mishnahs* which were collected by a Jerusalemite scholar whose style was peculiarly his own, and which Rabbi incorporated in his compilation without alteration.

Authors have also dealt at length with various pieces of evidence to prove that Rabbi only drew up the six orders of the Mishnah, but did not commit it to writing during his lifetime. The text was simply preserved orally by repetition in conformity with the arrangement made by Rabbi. I have dealt with this subject at considerable length[1] in my book *Torath Nebiyim*. I have also found that R. Jacob Hagiz[2] in his book *Tehillath Hochmah* which is an introduction to the Methodology of the *Mishnah*, arrived at a similar conclusion. The proof he gives is from the passage in Erub. 62*b* which I have already mentioned, viz. 'like (the halachoth contained in) *Megillath Taanith*[3] which is a written and resting (i.e. generally accepted) document', upon which Rashi observes that *Megillath Taanith* is purposely mentioned because no other *halachic* material, not even the smallest amount, had been committed to writing during the lifetime of the *Talmudic* teachers, except that contained in the said scroll. One can, therefore, see that even at the time of the *Amoraim*, Abaye and R. Jacob b Abba,[4] the Mishnah was not yet in the form of a written book. This fact may also be inferred from the wording usually employed in the text, since if it were otherwise, they would naturally have referred to the Mishnah as proof, and would have said, for example, 'like (the *halachoth* contained in) the Mishnah which is a written and resting document'. See also Rashi B.M. 33*a* for the statement that both the Mishnah and the Gemara were committed to writing during later generations, that prior to the redaction of the Mishnah by Rabbi only a few of the tractates had been compiled, such as *Kelim*,[5] *Middoth*,[6] *Eduyoth*,[7] *Tamid*,[8] and a few chapters on different topics, and that it was Rabbi who collected the Mishnayoth and brought them into a unified order. In them he normally sets out the views of R. Akiba and R. Meir, but anonymously, and if it happened that the *halachah* which he favoured had emanated from an individual, he recorded it none the less as if it had come down from the sages

---

[1] See first note on chapter *Torah sheb'al-peh*, p. 16*b*.
[2] See p. 254, note 10.
[3] See p. 88, note 6. The Scroll is the subject of a query put by R. Jacob b Aba to Abaye, viz. whether a disciple would be permitted to decide on *halachoth* of the scroll in a locality that is under his teacher's jurisdiction.
[4] Who lived a short time after the redaction of the Mishnah by Rabbi.
[5] Lit. 'vessels', but covers all articles in common use, such as clothing, implements, and utensils of all kinds, which are susceptible to uncleanness.
[6] Lit. 'measurements', i.e. of the Temple.
[7] Lit. 'testimonies' or 'choicest', see note 2 on p. 256.
[8] See p. 256, note 1.

generally. The following facts have also been used in support of the above contention. For instance, we find Rab and Samuel at variance as to whether we should read in the Mishnah[1] (Erub. 53a) מְעַבְּרִין[2] or מְאַבְּרִין.[3] The sages also were in doubt whether the word 'festivities' (in Mishna A.Z. 1, 1)[4] should be written אֵידֵיהֶן[5]; or עֲידֵיהֶן[6] and there are many other similar cases. If, however, the *Mishnah* had been committed to writing in their lifetime, they could have tested their views by the text, as we see in a similar case of a dispute with regard to the number of verses in the Torah, that the Gemara retorts: 'Let us bring the Book of the Law and verify the facts' (Kid. 30a).

Evidence is also furnished by Rashi's comment on the Gemara's statement (B.M. 33b): 'They subsequently taught men to run after the *Mishnah*.'[7] 'This,' he says, 'was lest they should, as a result of forgetfulness, confuse the names of the Sages and so set aside their rulings by permitting things which are otherwise forbidden.' But had the *Mishnah* been committed to writing, it could not have led to such errors.

There are also some variant readings in the text of the *Mishnah*, found in the Babylonian Talmud as compared with that of the Jerusalem Talmud, as may be seen in the *Mishnayoth* of *Shebiith*, chap. ix, or of *Terumoth*, chap. v (I have not been able to square the statements of R. Jacob Hagiz with the facts since I find no reference made by him to these variations).[8] I have also found another such variant in Sotah, chap. vii, 1, where the Babylonian text reads 'These things may be said "*bekhol lashon*" ("in any language"), while the Jerusalem text reads "*bileshonam*" ("in their own tongue").' Had Rabbi actually written down the Mishnah text by that time, this passage could have been verified in the written text; but as the Amoraim then studied these *Mishnayoth* orally, such variants could easily occur.

Again I have found some other differences between the Jerusalem and Babylonian Talmuds in the order of the chapters; so, for example, in the Tractate Megillah, it is found in the Babylonian text that the

---

[1] With reference to the extension of the 'Erub' ('the Sabbath boundaries') for a further 2,000 cubits.

[2] From the root עבר, in *Pi'el*, to be pregnant, to extend. See Job xxi, 10.

[3] From the root אבר wing, in *Pi'el*, to make a wing. In the Bible it is found in the *Hif'il* only, Job xxxix, 26.

[4] Which prohibits the transaction of business with idolators for the three days preceding their 'festivities'.

[5] Which would actually mean calamity (cf. Ps. xviii, 19; Job xxxi, 23) but used here figuratively for festivities.

[6] Lit. 'testimony', i.e. festivals which testify to their idolatry.

[7] i.e. to prefer the Mishnah to the Gemara.

[8] The present writer has, unfortunately, not been in a position to verify the author's statement here, by reference to *Tehillath Hochmah*.

chapter beginning *Benai Ha'ir* (the people of a town) forms the fourth and last chapter,[1] whereas in the Jerusalem Talmud it is the third chapter.

There is also a difference with regard to the chapter *Helek* of Sanhedrin. In the Babylonian Talmud it is placed last (and eleventh) in the order, whereas in the Jerusalem Talmud, it is changed to stand as the tenth chapter, and the chapter beginning *Elu hanechnakin* (these are to be strangled) is placed last.[2] We must, therefore, conclude that the reversal of the order was the result of oral study, and that the texts had not yet been written down.

There is also a further point in favour of our view; we know that, as a rule, authors who commit their works to writing make reference in one passage to another, using such words as 'As I have written above', or 'As I shall mention below', whereas in the whole of the Talmud we cannot find such expressions used by the sages, e.g. 'We are taught in such and such a Tractate', but instead we find simply 'We are taught'. Similarly they do not say 'We have dealt with the matter at great length in such and such a tractate', except for one such reference in the Tractate *Tamid*[3] to the Tractate *Yoma*. But it has been long known to us that the Tractate *Tamid* was compiled during the Geonic period[4] when the Talmud had already been committed to writing.

Again the objection raised in the Gemara (Tem. 14*b*)[5] against R. Dimi, who sought to convey a *halachic* decision by letter, an objection made on the ground that those who record *halachoth* are like those who burn[6] the Torah, also proves that had the Mishnah been committed to writing already during the time of the *Amoraim*, there could have been no objection to writing down decisions or *halachoth* in a letter. The

[1] In all our present editions this chapter is placed as the third chapter in both the Babylonian and the Jerusalem Talmuds.

[2] See *Tos. Yom-tob* on the first *Mishnah* of chap. Helek, where he defends the order of the Jerusalem Talmud, which has been followed in the printed editions of the Mishnah. He quotes Maimonides and Asheri in support of this view, whilst Rashi advocates the Babylonian order as correct. A similar variation in the order is found in the Tractate *Menachoth* as between the standard *Mishnah* edition and that of the Babylonian Talmud, viz. chap. vi in the Talmud edition is arranged as chap. x in the *Mishnah* edition.

[3] See Tamid 27*b*.

[4] Seemingly it is for this reason that it is not included in the number of the thirty-six tractates of the Talmud and the Gemara does not deal with chapters iii, v, vi, and vii.

[5] See p. 250, note 2.

[6] Tchernowitz, *Toledoth ha-Halachah* 1, 2, offers a plausible interpretation of this Talmudic term. Since, says he, the superiority of the written Torah consisted in its being written and in each of its letters and dots being carefully interpreted, as soon as *halachoth* are also committed to writing, the Torah's supremacy and integrity will be undermined, hence 'burned', because of the *halachists*' daring handling of the text.

following point also may be advanced as evidence for the view in question, viz. that the Gemara always employs the phrase 'We were there taught' and never uses the phrase 'For it is there written'. This proves that it did not then exist in writing. It is true that the phrase 'it is written' is found in citations from the *Megillath Taanith*, but Rashi (Taan. 12*a*), explaining the reason, says that that was because it was a scroll written to record miraculous happenings (for this, see Shab. 13*b*). If therefore the whole Mishnah had been committed to writing by Rabbi during the time of the *Amoraim*, the wording 'as it is there written' would have been used in citations as in the case of the *Megillath Taanith*. The fact that the expressions used throughout are 'We were taught' or 'as we were taught' proves that the *Mishnah* then was taught only orally.[1]

I may advance one other proof from the statement made on the authority of R. Hiyya (B.M. 85*b*) regarding the efforts he made to spread the Torah. He trapped deer (made scrolls from their skins) and wrote out the five books (of Moses) for five children, and taught the six Orders of the *Mishnah* to six children. The latter, according to Rashi, he taught orally. Why did R. Hiyya not tell us that he wrote down the six Orders of the *Mishnah* also if, as Maimonides holds,[2] the Mishnah had already been committed to writing by Rabbi before that time? We must, consequently, conclude that Rabbi had not actually written down the *Mishnah* but had only collected the *halachoth* and arranged them in their proper order (for oral teaching). In this connection, see also Keth. 69*a* where it is stated that Rab wrote to Rabbi between the lines of a letter, seeking his opinion on a case where brothers had pledged away their father's property.[3] On this passage Rashi comments that in sending him the letter of greeting, he inserted the said query 'between the lines',[4] because it was forbidden to reduce to writing *halachic* material which was normally transmitted orally. He thus worded the question by placing dots over letters of certain words in the space between the lines, thereby indicating his actual purpose in writing. V. Git. 60*a* for the statement that writing in an irregular manner was not forbidden. At any rate the passage proves that, at the time of Rabbi, *halachoth* had not as yet been committed to writing. But, besides all this, if Rabbi had already committed the *Mishnah* as a whole to

---

[1] i.e. even after it had been arranged in order by Rabbi.

[2] V. Introduction to his Commentary on the Mishnah.

[3] By selling or mortgaging it. The question arose as to how far their sisters, the daughters of the deceased, had a right to claim their share of this property.

[4] R. Hananel in Tos. s.v. תלה says that this was one of several *halachic* questions put to Rabbi by Rab; hence, in R. Hananel's view, *halachoth* were already committed to writing at that time.

writing, how could R. Johanan, who was his disciple's disciple,[1] have conceived the idea that those who write *halachoth* are to be likened to those who burn the Torah (Tem. 14*b*)? On the basis, therefore, of all the above facts adduced by Rabbi Jacob Hagiz, and those humbly added to them by myself, we may regard the view of Maimonides as advanced in the Introduction to his Commentary on the *Mishnah*, to the effect that Rabbi had committed the Mishnah to writing, to be unfounded, and as one to be definitely set aside.[2]

It is stated (Sab. 138*b*) that a time may come when the Torah will be forgotten by Israel, according to the words of Scripture, 'and the Lord will make thy plagues heavy'.[3] Again, a time will come when a woman will take a loaf of the *Terumah*[4] (and go round the Synagogues and Academies to get a ruling whether it is unclean or clean, and none will know how to answer her),[5] but the *Gemara* goes on to ask, 'Is not such a thing made explicit in the written Law?' (No; the purpose of the question is rather) to find out (the degree of uncleanness to which it belongs), whether to the first or second degree. But that question, too, could be answered from a Mishnah, for we learn[6] that if a *sheretz*[7] is found in an oven, the bread within it is of the second degree of uncleanness, but men will still be in doubt over the question which R. Ada b Ahabah asked Raba.[8] And Rashi on the retort given above 'Is this not made explicit', remarks 'Surely the written Law was at their disposal, and they could read it and discover the answer'. Consequently the question which follows, 'But is there not a *Mishnah* on the point?' can similarly be understood as implying a similar retort, viz. 'Surely the Mishnah was available to them in writing,' for had the Mishnah not existed in writing at that time, there could be no ground for such a retort since, even in a case where a law was explicitly stated in a Mishnah, it could be that since the Mishnah was being studied orally, the law was liable to be forgotten. One may, therefore, take the other view that the Mishnah had indeed been committed to writing. In fact this point

---

[1] Cf. A.Z. 36*b*, with reference to the *Gezerah* upon a heathen infant to contract and cause uncleanness by flux.

[2] This criticism on the part of our author of Maimonides' view is all the more surprising if we bear in mind his general tendency to defend the Rambam. Cf. his works '*Darkhei Moshe*' and '*Tifereth l'Moshe*'.

[3] Deut. xxxviii, 59.

[4] The heave offering from the yield of the yearly harvest which is to be given to the priest (v. Num. xxviii, 8 ff.).

[5] Thus showing how little of the Torah will be known.

[6] Kelim 8, 5.

[7] A dead reptile which causes defilement to utensils and food.

[8] Why, if the oven is to be regarded as replete with uncleanness, the bread, in this case, should not be of the first degree of uncleanness?

caught the attention of R. Jacob Hagiz, but since Rabbi subsequently[1]
urges upon everyone to 'run to the *Mishnah* rather than to the Gemara',
in order that the Mishnah might not be forgotten, it is to be understood
as implying that although the *Mishnayoth* were studied orally, they were
nevertheless familiar to all. Thus Tos. on Hul. 110*b*, s.v. דחנן quotes
the above-mentioned retort 'But is there not a Mishnah on the point' as
proving that the *Mishnayoth*[2] were familiar to all. It is indeed surprising
that this proof put forward by the Tosafists should have escaped the
notice of Rabbi Hagiz. We see thus that Rashi's view that the Mishnah
was committed to writing at a later date is well founded and corroborated by many passages in the Talmud. And this is even more applicable
to the case of the Gemara. Hence the view of Maimonides remains
incomprehensible.

I set myself to read carefully the Epistle of Sherira Gaon[3] and I have
noticed several contradictory statements in it. Thus, in one place, he
states that Rabbi wrote the Mishnah, whilst in another place he states
that Rabbi made the arrangement of the *Mishnayoth*. Apparently he
holds the view that Rabbi had committed the Mishnah to writing, but
only secretly for his own use, and not for his disciples whom he taught
the *Mishnah* orally. This is what he says: 'It is certain that it was Rabbi
who compiled the six Orders of the *Mishnah* so that students might
learn the *halachoth* in their proper order. And so it is stated (Yeb. 64*b*):
When was the Mishnah compiled? During the days of Rabbi.' (In our
editions the text reads: 'Who compiled the Mishnah? Rabbi.') Further,
the Gaon says[4]: 'And Providence sent Rabbi down from Heaven, and
he was the possessor of both Torah and wealth, etc., and he decided to
bring order into the *halachoth* so that all the Rabbis might be able to
study them in a standard form, and not as in earlier days when everyone
studied them in his own version.' Still later he says[5] 'And it was in the
days of Rabbi, the son of R. Simeon b Gamliel, that conditions so
favoured him that he compiled and *wrote* down (the *halachoth*)'.

On the whole there are several contradictions in the Epistle of R.
Sherira Gaon[6] on this question and, to reconcile them, one may simply

---

[1] On seeing that everyone was abandoning the Mishnah and going to the Gemara
(v. B.M. 33*b*).
[2] Though they were studied orally.
[3] With reference to this question.
[4] Ibid., concluding paragraph of chap. ii.
[5] At the beginning of chap. iii.
[6] Apart from this one particular case of contradiction, the author does not point out
any of the others. Weiss, *Dor*, IV, p. 164, regards Sherira as sharing the view that
Rabbi himself had written out the *Mishnah* in full, whilst Meilziner, *Introduction to the
Talmud*, p. 6, includes him amongst those holding an opposite opinion, but adds that
this is only according to one version of his Epistle. In fact, two versions have come

assume that the *Mishnayoth* were recorded in writing by Rabbi, in the same way as (the *halachoth* of) the *Megillath Setarim*, but were not made available to the students for public study.[1] I shall deal with the whole question of this Epistle at greater length elsewhere.

Again there are several subjects treated twice in the *Gemara* where the treatment in one passage is unlike that of the other. Take the subject of the prohibitions laid upon the Nazirite.[2] It is discussed twice, once in Pes. 44*a* and again in Nazir 36*a*, and if you will read it through attentively you will find changes in the wording, omissions or additions in one passage which make it different from the other. A similar case you will find in the treatment of the problem 'Whether one refers in a vow to a thing in its earlier (forbidden) state or in its present permissible condition.'[3] This subject is treated in Ned. 11*b* and in Naz. 22*a*; see *Tosafoth*, s.v. *Mar Zutra*, where it says that the teachers who treat the subject in one place are in disagreement with those who deal with it in the other place. See again Pes. 114*b* for the discussion of whether religious precepts need be performed with deliberate intention or not, where objections are raised against the former view from various *baraithoth*. The same discussion is repeated in R.H. 28*b*, but there the objections are supported by different evidence. This has been also noted by the *Tosafists* (see Tos. Pes. 115*a*, s.v. מתקיף).

Another case is found in Pes. 12*a* with reference to a stringent preventive measure enacted by R. Judah 'lest one should eat it'[4], where

down (Waxman, *History of Jewish Literature*, i, p. 429), one emanating from the Spanish School, the other from the French School, the chief differences between them lying in the passages referring to this question. The passage referring to the writing down of the Mishnah by Rabbi emanates from the version of the Spanish school; the French version makes no reference whatever to this subject. The contradictory statements in the Epistle may therefore be due to a combination of the two versions.

[1] This subject is widely discussed by the historians of Talmud. See Frankel, *Darkhe ha-Mishnah*, p. 217; S. P. Rabinovitz on Graetz, ii, p. 298, and *Dor*, i, p. 94. The latter rejects the conclusions of our author.

[2] See Num. vi, 3.

[3] There lay before the man in question flesh of a peace offering and ordinary permissible food beside it, and he uttered a vow that the permitted food should be treated like the other. The question arises whether he intended his vow to relate to the thing in its original state, i.e. before the sprinkling of the blood when it may not be eaten, or meant to relate it to its present permissible state, after the sprinkling of the blood. This is the subject as set forth in *Nedarim*. In the version in *Nazir* a word is used, denoting the 'final' instead of 'present' state from the root צנן cold, i.e. when the article has already cooled down and is fit for use.

[4] The actual passage deals with the time-limit for the eating of *hametz* on the eve of the Passover, where R. Meir and R. Judah are at variance. According to R. Meir the preventive measure should apply only to one hour, but according to R. Judah, it should apply to two hours. The wording used by our author is not found in the text of Pesachim, but R. Judah's more stringent ruling has the same basis 'lest he may eat', though it is not explicitly mentioned.

objections are raised against his ruling from various *Baraithoth*, whereas in Yoma 14*a*, where an objection of a similar kind is raised, viz. 'Did R. Judah indeed enact such a preventive measure, lest one should eat it?',[1] it is raised from yet another *Baraitha*.[2] See also Tos. Zeb. 91*a*, s.v. מוספי, for a reference to the question raised about a case where there is one thing the observance of which is a constant duty, and another the sacredness of which is of a higher degree,[3] as to which has precedence over the other.[4] This question is discussed in Zeb. 91*a* and in Men. 49*a* but the *Baraithoth* quoted in the two tractates to settle the problem are different. The reason for this is that each tractate was redacted separately and each of the sages arranged his *halachoth* in accordance with the particular tractates which were available to him, so that each sage treated the subject differently on the basis of different sources and in a different form, and the *halachoth* in each case were edited and completed by different sages. In this fact may lie a justifiable reason why we do not find in the Gemara even the slightest reference to any support from another tractate. This is because the similar *halachoth* in different tractates were edited by different sages and the sage who edited one *halachah* might not have seen how another similar *halachah* had been edited by another sage.

Yet, in other cases, we have proof that in one tractate the sages omitted points on a particular subject, because they were relying on their treatment of it in another tractate. See *Ran* on Ned. 12*a*, s.v. והוא where he observes that the text, as found there in the Gemara, has a lacuna, since the retort ought to have been made here also, as it is in *Shebuoth*, 'Is this not self-evident?'[5] Apparently then the passage relies on the text dealing with the same subject in the tractate Sheb. 20*a*, and

[1] Here the question is raised in connection with R. Judah's ruling that the High Priest as a mourner may not officiate at all during the day of his becoming a mourner, as a preventive measure lest he should eat of the hallowed things which were prohibited to him on that day.

[2] It should read 'Mishnah'.

[3] Such as the blood of the daily offerings or that of the sin offerings which is of a higher degree of sanctity than the burnt offering.

[4] When both are of the same degree of holiness, but one is a constant duty and the other only a periodic duty as, for example, the daily whole burnt offerings and the additional offerings, the question would not arise since it is clear that the former would have precedence over the latter (see Zeb. 10, 1; Hor. 12*b*). The question arises in the case where one is only a periodic duty but of a higher degree of holiness. (See Rashi, Zeb. 90*b*, s.v. תדיר.)

[5] The following *Baraitha* is quoted in both tractates, Ned. 12*a* and Sheb.20*a*: 'If one says "Behold, I shall not eat meat and drink wine on the day that my father or teacher died", this has the binding force of the vow mentioned in the Torah' (Num. xxx, 3). Samuel said this is so provided that he was under a vow uninterruptedly from that day; and the retort which follows, 'Is this not self evident?' is made in the tractate *Shebuoth*, but not in the tractate *Nedarim*.

the omission here is presumably made, in virtue of the fact that both tractates Shebuoth and Nedarim were edited by one and the same sage. We find a similar view held by the Tosafists (see Tos. Git. 72a, s.v. ומשום) to the effect that where a subject was dwelt upon at length in one place, the editor did not feel it necessary to repeat the discussion in another place. This shows that the chapter of Gittin, beginning מי שאחזו was edited later than chapter beginning התקבל.[1] All the more can we arrive at a similar conclusion in the case of tractates where there is an omission in the one of matter dealt with in another in connection with the same subject, the sages having relied on their fuller treatment of the subject in one place. Through this fact we can ascertain which tractate was edited first. On the other hand, where subjects are repeated in different places with variations in the wording, it goes to prove that they were edited by two separate sages. This is not, however, true in the case of the discussions in the Jerusalem Talmud, where, although many passages, both *halachic* and *aggadic*, are found repeated, such as the stories of the death of Rabbi, related in Kil. 9, 3, and repeated in Keth. 12, 3, or the *aggadoth* recorded in Peah 1,[2] and given again at the end of Kid. 1, and similarly the report of the departure of R. Hananiah, the nephew[3] of R. Joshua,[4] from Palestine for Babylon, mentioned in San. 1, and repeated in Ned. 6, 8, yet the subject-matter as given in one tractate is very similar to that of the other, without additions or omissions, and the story in the one is very similar to the story in the other, which proves that because the Jerushalmi was edited solely by R. Johanan,[5] consequently all the material, *halachic* or

[1] The subject referred to in Tos. Git. 72a, and already discussed earlier in the Gemara 66b, is the view held by R. Jose that verbal instructions in legal matters cannot be passed on to another agent, but still where the husband asks two men to tell the Scribe to write, the Bill of divorcement is valid. On this a retort was made that a calamity might result from such a ruling as, for example, where he says to two persons 'tell the Scribe to write and so and so to sign', they may, out of fear of offending the Scribe, agree that only one of them should sign and the Scribe with him. Earlier in 67a the answer to this point was made that, although a divorce-bill of this kind, signed by the Scribe as a witness, is valid, this should not be done, and therefore R. Jose made no provision against such a probability. This was, however, omitted in the later chapter 72a, because its repetition was no longer found necessary.

[2] Interpretations of the first *Mishnah* of the tractate which gives a list of the *mitzvoth* that have no limit and those that bring a reward both in this life and in that to come.

[3] The text erroneously reads 'Haninah' and 'brother'.

[4] *Tanna* of the second century. The name of his father is unknown. When he saw many of his contemporaries being killed as a result of the Bar Kochba rebellion he decided to secede from the Palestinian authorities and create a new centre in Nehar Pekodin, Babylonia, where he made arrangements for the fixing of the Calendar, a right which had always been exercised by the Palestinians. He was, however, urged through special messengers to desist from thus disrupting the religious unity of Israel.

[5] Bar Nappacha, died 279 C.E.

aggadic, which is found more than once, is given in the same style. Not so, however, in the case of the Babylonian Talmud, the editing of which was shared by a number of scholars, each of whom was charged with the compilation of one, two or at most, three tractates. It is true that Tos. on Hul. 2*b,* s.v. אנא is definitely of opinion that R. Ashi alone was the editor of the *Gemara,* but this probably means that he had arranged the chief subjects only, and that he further scrutinized the contents of the tractates in detail, and whatsoever appeared satisfactory to him as it stood, he left unaltered.[1]

With regard to the completion of the Jerushalmi at an earlier date than that of the Babylonian Talmud[2] we have already referred to the view of Alfasi found (in his digest) at the end of the last chapter of Erubin, that, for this reason, the *halachah* rests with the Babylonian Talmud where it differs from the Jerusalem Talmud, i.e. because it was completed at a later date.[3] We have also touched upon the views collected by the author of *Yad Malachi* in his 'Rules of the two Talmudim' on the authority of R. Jonathan, as quoted in *Shittah Mekubezeth* on *Kethuboth,* to the effect that the *halachoth* over which R. Johanan and Resh Lakish are represented in the Babylonian Talmud as differing all originated from the Jerusalem Talmud and were transferred from it to the Babylonian, and that only those *halachoth* which were regarded as inconclusive were left in the Jerusalem version, and not incorporated in the Babylonian compilation. See also, on this point, Asheri at the end of the last chapter of Erubin[4] and *Sefer Mizvoth Gadol,* on the laws relating to Erubin.

The later authorities, indeed, quote Alfasi's ruling as definite and final. A certain scholar,[5] however, has drawn my attention to the observation made by the *Tosafists* on Yeb. 21*a,* s.v. וימותר[6] that the decision of the Jerusalem Talmud to the effect that the father-in-law's wife is included amongst the forbidden degrees, for appearance's sake, must have been issued later than that of the Babylonian Talmud which declared such marriage permissible, which indicates that, in their view, the Jerusalem Talmud was edited at a later date than the Babylonian. But this raises no real difficulty, because the *halachah* in question is

---

[1] Cf. on this subject Kaplan, *The Redaction of the Babylonian Talmud.*
[2] It is generally accepted that the Palestinian Talmud was finished *ca.* 425, and the Babylonian provisionally *ca.* 500, while its definite completion was in the middle of the sixth century. See Waxman's *History of Jewish Literature,* i, pp. 125 and 130.
[3] The Babylonian sages were more conversant with the views held by the Palestinians than the reverse. Frankel in his *Mebo ha-Jerushalmi* disputes these arguments, but his facts are questioned by Halevi in *Doroth* II, pp. 102–136.
[4] Where he arrives at conclusions similar to those of Alfasi.
[5] Presumably N. Krochmal, see p. 85, note 1.
[6] In this case Rabbenu Tam.

actually quoted from a *Baraitha* which preceded the Jerusalem Talmud, and in a case where we have an anonymous *Baraitha* in the Babylonian Talmud, and an *halachah* on the same point laid down in the Jerusalem version, the decision should rest with the latter.[1] See Responsa *Noda b'Yehudah*, ii,[2] on *Eben ha-Ezer*[3] for a treatment at length of the said observation of *Tosafoth*.

I have already furnished proof elsewhere that the Babylonian Talmud was completed at a later date than the Jerusalem Talmud, as we see in Rashi Nid. 8*a*, s.v. וא"ר. R. Eleazar is quoted in Jer. Ber.[4] We see thus that the Babylonians relied on what was more fully stated in the Jerus. Talm., and for this reason they, in their Talmud, stated it more briefly.

More definite evidence is found in Ta'an. 16*a*, where the question is raised as to why men are to go to the cemetery,[5] whilst in the Mishnah as in the *Baraitha*, there is no reference made to the duty of going to the cemetery on a fast day. This point is noticed by Rashi,[6] who explains it by quoting from the Jerus. Talm., ad loc., which makes it clear that the Rabbis hold it to be a duty to go out to the cemetery on a fast day. But I have produced a still more convincing proof that the Jerusalem Talmud was already known to the Babylonians in my glosses on Nazir, from an explicit comment in the Gemara 20*b*, which runs 'seeing that Rab ruled in a more stringent case (that the evidence is not conflicting) would he not rule likewise in a less stringent one?'[7] This

[1] See Halevi, *Doroth* III, p. 67, where the argument of the author is strongly opposed on the ground that the wording in *Tosafoth*, that the 'prohibition' (of marrying one's father-in-law's wife) is of later date, is not necessarily meant to refer to the Jerushalmi, but to the Geonim. A similar suggestion is advanced by Eisenstein in his *Amudei Yerushalaim* on the Jerushalmi, ad loc. Indeed it may be inferred from the word שמא used by *Tosafoth* ('perhaps it was prohibited later') that it need not necessarily refer to the Jerushalmi.

[2] By R. Ezekiel Landau, the distinguished Rabbi of Prague (1713-1793), one of the greatest Talmudists of his time whose responsa are regarded as authoritative. Our author probably refers to the first part of Responsum No. 26.

[3] The third section of the *Shulchan Aruch* of Karo.

[4] A more correct version in accordance with the original text is as follows (see M. Ber. v, 2): 'We make mention of the *Habdalah* (the section in the *Amida* referring to the distinction between the Sabbath and week days) in the fourth benediction.' R. Akiba says *Habdalah* should be said as a fourth benediction by itself, while R. Eliezer holds that it should be said together with the thanksgiving, which is the eighteenth benediction. R. Eleazar is then quoted in the Gemara as saying that the *halachah* rests with R. Eliezer.

[5] On a fast day.

[6] s.v. ולמה.

[7] This refers to a dispute between the Shammaites and the Hillelites recorded in the *Mishnah*, Naz. III, 7, where two groups of witnesses bring conflicting evidence concerning avowal of naziriteship. In the Gemara a distinction is suggested between two groups and one group; the former is regarded as the stringent case and the latter as the less stringent.

fact that Rab ruled so in a more stringent case is not mentioned in our (the Babylonian) Talmud but such a reference is found in the Jerusalem version (San. 5, 1), as is observed by Rashi, ad loc.

We see, therefore, that our Talmud relied on that fact that Rab's ruling, as stated in the Jer. Talm., was already known to everybody and that, therefore, it was not necessary to quote it again. We have thus a clear and explicit proof that the Jerusalem Talmud was methodically arranged before the Babylonian. See also on this point Ned. 3b which reads 'In the West[1] it was said that one *Tanna* deduced (the validity of substitutes)[2] from the words 'to vow a vow'[3] whilst another deduced it from the verse, 'he shall do according to all that goes forth from his mouth'.[4] This, as stated by *Ran*, is based on the Jerus. Talm., viz. that from the phrase 'he shall do according, etc.', both (vows and their substitutes) are deduced. We can, therefore, see that the dispute (over this question) mentioned in the Jerus. Talm. was a fact known to the scholars of the Babylonian Talmud.

Again, at times, we find in the Jerus. Talm. a reversal of the opinions held by R. Johanan and Resh Lakish, as they are given in the Babylonian Talmud; for example in connection with the *halachah* relating to the *get*[5] (Git. 17b), where the Babylonian Talmud states (on the authority of Resh Lakish) that R. Simeon declared the *get* valid only if it were signed immediately, i.e. in the night (following) but not if it were signed ten days afterwards,[6] in the Jer. Talmud this view is attributed to his interlocuter, R. Johanan, while R. Johanan's view is ascribed to R. Lakish. In this matter I have already laid down as an essential rule that, in cases where disputes of Palestinian scholars are involved, since the Jerusalem Talmud was compiled by Palestinian scholars, its view is to be adhered to, because they, having been conversant with the views of the scholars of the same country, studied them with greater care and accuracy than did others. On the other hand, where the views of Babylonian scholars in dispute, as given in the Bab. Talm., are reversed in the Jer. Talm., the Babylonian version is the more correct. Again, where the reversal of the Babylonian in the order

[1] Referring, according to the view held by the *Ran*, to the Jerushalmi.
[2] Words which are used by way of abbreviation in place of those which are normally used to express a vow; see *Mishnah*, i, of Ned.
[3] Num. VI, 2.
[4] Num. XXX, 3, the word 'all' embracing here every form in which a vow can be made.
[5] Bill of divorcement which had been written out and signed on different dates; see Git. 2b.
[6] Because there is the possibility that he had become reconciled to her in the interval.

given in the Jerushalmi concerns views held by Tannaim, in that case, too, the Jerusalem version enjoys preference; for example, the *halachah* which is quoted in Sab. 12, on the authority of R. Hananiah b Akabiah to the effect that scribes of *tefillin* and *mezuzoth*, just as they are to stop their work for the purpose of reading the *Shema*, are to do so also for their prayers, and for the putting on of the *tefillin*, and for the observance of all the other Commandments of the Law, is also quoted in the Babylonian Talmud (Suk. 26*a*) also on his authority, but there it is given in the opposite form, viz. that the scribes of, etc., are free from the obligation of the *Shema* and the *tefillin* while engaged in their work.

See, too, *Yad Malachi*, ii, 'Rules of both Talmudim' par. 7, who supports the above view on the authority of *Tosafoth* (Bech. 22*b*, s.v. תירום) that in a case where the version of a *Baraitha* in the Jer. Talm. is different from that in the Babylonian Talmud we should rely more on the text of the Jerus. version, because they (the Palestinian scholars) were better versed in Palestinian *Baraithoth* than were the Babylonians.[1]

With regard to the Jerusalemite *aggadoth*, their style is mostly similar to that of the *Midrashim* and invariably unlike that of the Babylonian Talmud, as I hope to show in dealing with the subject elsewhere. Even incidents from actual life are quite differently related in the Jer. Talm. from the accounts in the Babylonian. See, for example, Jer. Sab. 6, 9, where it is related that R. Johanan and Resh Lakish were very eager to meet Samuel in Babylon[2] but decided to wait for a heavenly voice, and that the voice, when it came, pronounced the Scriptural verse 'And Samuel is dead',[3] so they noted the date, and later found that he had actually died on that very date. In the Babylonian Talmud (Hul. 95*b*), however, where the story is also told, it is stated that he had not died at that time.

The Jerusalemite *aggadoth* were collected at a later date (than the rest of that Talmud) since we find the name of the Roman Emperor Diocletian mentioned in Jer. Ter. 8, and that of Lulian,[4] the emperor, mentioned in Jer. Ned. 4, in the following form: 'When Julian, the emperor, went from there, 1,200,000 men went with him' (in the Jer. Shebiith 3, hal. 8, this refers to Diocletian). Now the Emperor Diocletian lived after the Jerusalem Talmud had been completed, and the

---

[1] There is no such statement in *Tosafoth*. The author of the *Yad Malachi* is actually quoting the view of another authority, R. Hayyim b Attar, in his *Peri To'ar*, whilst the *Tosafoth* come to no conclusion in the matter.

[2] But were not certain if he was still alive.

[3] 1 Sam. XXVIII, 3.

[4] Corruption for Julian.

Emperor Julian who fought against the Persians and was defeated by them reigned still later than Diocletian.[1] These facts have been a subject for discussion by critical scholars. Thus, although R. Johanan (Nappacha) edited the Jerusalem Talmud, the *aggadoth* were nevertheless collected at a still later date. Thus, for example, in the *aggadah* in Yoma 1, 1 (which tells us how the High Priests of the Second Temple were guilty of accepting bribes) we shall not understand the illustration 'the young ass has bent down the Menorah', unless we remember the similar passage in the *aggadah* in Bab. Shab. 116b 'an ass came up and trampled upon the lamp'[2] which the Jerusalemite teachers probably had in mind. Similarly the *aggadoth* on the words 'He that formeth the mountains and createth the winds,'[3] which states that this was one of the six Scriptural passages which caused Rabbi to weep when he read them, refers probably to a similar *aggadah* in Bab. Hag. 4b.[4] And so also no doubt in the case of several *aggadoth* from earlier times, such as those of R. Hiyya and R. Johanan and Resh Lakish, they were collected and arranged as we have them at a much later date as has been mentioned above. This is all I wish to say in my treatment of this subject.

---

[1] Diocletian was born in 245 and died in 313 c.e., and Julian, nephew of Constantine the Great, was born in 351, and died in 363. The statement, therefore, that both lived after the conclusion of the Talmud is chronologically incorrect, for it is generally held that the Jerusalem Talmud was finished *c.* 425 (see p. 266, note 2) unless indeed the reference is to others of the same name who lived at a later date.

[2] Both *aggadoth* refer to judges who, open to bribery, accepted gifts from both parties.

[3] Amos iv, 13, from which they deduced the mysteries of creation, one of which is said to be how the mountains were suspended in the wind. This is quoted in the Babylonian Talmud, Hag. 12b.

[4] Where a number of instances are quoted of the Rabbi weeping on reading certain verses in Scripture.

INDICES

GENERAL INDEX

Aaron: 231

Abaye, amora: 121, 130, 132, 146, 173, 186, 227, 228, 242, 257

Abba b Abba: 211, 238

Abba Hilkiah: 147

Abba b. Kahana: 163

Abba Meromania: 146

Abbahu, of Caesarea: 116, 144, 171, 215, 217, 243

Abigail: 168, 228

Abin Halevi: 145

Aboth di R. Nathan: 18, 37, 53, 181

Abraham, the Patriarch: 148, 156, 163, 170, 177, 211 f., 222, 243

Abraham Arya de Boton: 37

Abraham b David (of Posquieres), 67, 96

Abraham ibn Daud (of Toledo): 96

Absalom b David: 173, 180

Abudraham, D.: 82, 97

Achan b Carmi: 164

Adam: 148, 186

Adda b Ahaba: 227, 261

Adler, N.: xiii

Aesop: 215, 217, 218

Aggadah: 22; treatment by Chajes of, xviii; purpose of, 139 ff.; Halachah and, 140, 141 f., 143 ff., 148, 154, 195, 198 f., 247, 250 ff.; authority of, 141 ff.; traditionally received, 148 f.; hermeneutical rules and, 154 ff.; exaggeration in, 154 ff.; why based on Scriptural text, 159 ff.; heightened praise and condemnation, 162 ff.; obscenity in, 170 f. ; identification of names in, 172 ff.; expounding of names in, 176, 179; Book of Chronicles and, 176, 178 f.; Canticles and, 179; literal meaning of Scriptural text and, 176 f.; interpretation of *vayehi* and *vehayah*, 180 ff.; Divine Providence and, 174 ff.; *Al Tikre*, 189 ff.; intended to arouse interest, 195 ff.; anthropomorphism in, 201, 203 ff.; attitudes to, 201 ff.; on world-to-come, 206 f.; miracles in, 208 ff.; parables in, 214 ff.; hyperbolic numbers in, 224 ff.; added by Saboraim and Geonim, 240 ff.; contradictory views regarding, 245 ff.; prohibition of writing of, 246 ff.; *see* Law, Oral; Talmud

Agrippa, king: 256

Aha of Be Hozea, amora: 239

Aha of Lydda, amora: 222

Ahab b Omri: 165 f.

Ahai Gaon: 235

Ahai b. Huna: 239

Ahasueras: 23, 173, 219, 223

Ahaz: 42, 164

Ahimelech b Ahitub: 225

Akabia b Mahalalel: 52–3

Akiba b Joseph: ix, xix, 11, 21, 54, 75, 95, 113, 142 f., 147, 158, 173, 196 f., 209, 215, 216, 233, 245, 255, 257, 267

Albo, Joseph: 220

Alexander the Great: xiii, 147

Algazi, Solomon Nisim: x, xi

Amaziah, king: 149

Ammi, amora: 143, 243

Amnon: 40

Amon b Manasseh: 164

Amoraim: viii, x, xvii, xviii, xix, 78 f., 95, 111 f., 134, 143, 144, 199, 208, 218, 233, 237, 244, 258, 259, 260

Amoz, king: 149

Amram b Kehath: 1, 149

Amraphel, king: 173

Anah b Seir: 168, 172

Antigonus of Soko: 47, 181

Antiochus IV, Epiphanes: 181

Antoninus Pius, Emperor: 216, 236

Apocrypha: 153

Arad: 172

Aristobulus: 48, 181

Artaban, Parthian king: 236

Artaxerxes: 172

Asher b Yechiel: 18, 96, 119, 123, 125, 143, 182, 237, 238, 241, 259, 266

Ashi, amora: 79, 143, 182, 255, 266

Ashkenazi, Z. H.: 254

Asi, amora: 66, 116, 143, 244

Awira, amora: 197

Azulai, H. J. D.: x, 182

Baba b Buti, 52, 152

Balaam: 40, 164, 165 f., 168, 173, 174

Bacher, W.: x, 21, 233

Bachrach, *see* Jair Hayyim b. Moses Samson

Banaah, tanna: 211 f.

Banett, Mordecai: xiii

Baraitha: 35, 79, 95, 96, 111, 139, 140, 142, 148, 192, 208, 218, 219, 220, 233, 234, 239, 251, 263, 269

Bar Kappara, Eleazar: 141, 224

Bar Kochba: 93, 95, 148, 181, 216, 255

Bath-Sheba: 162, 167

Benjamin: 149

Ben Rehumi: 146

Benvenisti, H.: xi

Beor, father of Balaam: 173

Berachiah, amora: 145, 163

Berlin, I.: 225, 226, 230, 236, 241

Berlin, N. Z.: 235

Bertinoro, Obadiah: 119

Beruriah, wife of Meir: 238

Bezalel Ashkenazi: x, 31

INDEX OF BIBLICAL AND OTHER PASSAGES

	PAGE
XI, 26	114
XII	173
XII, 31	32
XV, 30	165
XVII, 18	168
XVIII, 36	146
XVIII, 37	204
XXI, 21	165
XXII, 20, 25	166

2 KINGS

II, 23	157
II, 24	164
XVI	164
XVIII ff.	149
XVIII	42, 82
XVIII, 11	149
XXI	165
XXII, 1 ff.	162
XXIII, 25	162
XXV, 8	149

ISAIAH

I, 18	210
I, 28	34
VII, 20	205
XIX, 6	176
XXIV, 21	185
XXIV, 23	190
XXVII, 1	206
XXVII, 3	193
XXX, 22	42
XXXIII, 18	251
XLIX, 3	141
XLIX, 6	193
XLIX, 15	203
LV, 8	139
LVI, 1	154
LVI, 7	203
LVIII, 13	44
LIX, 21	156
LX, 21	193
LXII, 8	203
LXIII	185
LXIV, 3	206

JEREMIAH

IV, 3	157
XI, 10	184
XIII, 17	206
XXIII, 29	160
XXIX, 11	231
XXX, 10	160
XXXI, 19	206
XXXI, 20	160
XXXII, 44	33
XXXIV, 5	33

EZEKIEL

III, 47	229
VII, 11	190

	PAGE
XXXII, 18	190
XXXIX, 15	231
XL, 48	229
XLIV, 9	33

HOSEA

VIII, 12	24

AMOS

III, 2	215
IV, 3	270

MICAH

IV, 6	204
VI, 8	32

HAGGAI

II, 8	231
II, 12	45

ZECHARIAH

III, 7	192
VIII, 19	42, 132

MALACHI

II, 2	172
III, 6	186
III, 10	43

PSALMS

XVIII, 19	258
XIX, 23	189
XXIII, 2	240
XXIII, 18	205
XXVIII, 5	245
XXIX, 2	190
XXXVII, 22	20
XLIV, 23	88
XLIV, 24	107
XLV, 4	177
XLVI, 9	189
L, 23	189
LV, 18	82
LV, 22	58
LXII, 12	160
LXVI, 3	144
LXXII, 19	96
LXXV, 7	146
LXXVIII, 45 ff.	185
LXXIX, 8	176
CIV, 21	186
CVI, 43	176
CXI, 8	32
CXIX, 63	122
CXIX, 126	108, 139, 247, 252
CXXXII, 8	230

PROVERBS

	PAGE
III, 6	141
III, 17	101, 132
III, 27	82, 232
III, 28	232
III, 35	245
IX, 5	206
XVI, 5	156, 157
XX, 27	198
XXI, 14	154
XXII, 29	214
XXIII, 6	157
XXVIII, 14	244

JOB

I, 14 f.	185
II, 3	246
XV, 7	2
XXI, 10	258
XXXI, 23	258
XXXII, 2 ff.	173
XXXVI, 19	229
XXXIX, 26	258
XL	206

CANTICLES

I, 7	240
I, 12	179
II, 4	179
V, 13	145
VII, 3	32

RUTH

I, 1 ff.	175
I, 2	179
II 4	81
IV, 1	175
IV, 7	81
IV, 20	175

LAMENTATIONS

II, 5	230
II, 8, 18	36
III, 17	96

ECCLESIASTES

I, 9	22
II, 17	179
IV, 12	156
IV, 22	179
VIII, 8	179
XI, 6	175
XII, 9	161

ESTHER

I, 4	173
IV, 5	172
IX, 19, 27	83